The

GALBRAITH

READER

From the works of John Kenneth Galbraith

The
GALBRAITH
READER

*Selected and arranged
with narrative comment
by the editors of Gambit*

ANDRE DEUTSCH

First published 1979 by
André Deutsch Limited
105 Great Russell Street London WC1

Printed in Great Britain by
Lowe & Brydone Printers Ltd
Thetford Norfolk

ISBN 0 233 97006 1

To

C O N N I E

from the author and the editors

Foreword

ON LOVELL THOMPSON

That authors should, on occasion, express affection for their editors is not remarkable. Some make their living by fiction, by nourishing illusion. Others have not yet discovered how editors behave when they turn in a bad manuscript or the readers finally become aware and disappear. Lovell Thompson is the exception in this tenuous relationship. By all writers who have come his way over a lifetime, without exception, he has been both admired and loved. He has been admired as one of the talented writers of our time; he has been loved as a friend whose friendship regularly went beyond strict financial calculation, a rare thing in the publishing world.

A few years ago, when he formed his own publishing company, Lovell proposed a book—a reader—that would be selected from my writing. Wisely or otherwise, it would include the resurrection of some pieces long lost to view. I promptly agreed and interposed only two conditions, both easily met. The selection would be entirely Lovell Thompson's. So would any interstitial comments or interpretation. I would then have the pleasure of learning what my old friend thought worthwhile and thought about it. But of more practical consequence I would be protected from a temptation that I know to be overwhelming: that is to intervene helpfully where judgment of my writing or interpretation of my ideas is involved and to press my own revisionist preferences with much vigor. Remarkably the bargain held. This is Lovell's book, his view, his selection. I would only add one protective word. As much or more than most writers I have changed my mind—and, unlike Churchill, I have not, when eating my words, always found them a wholesome diet. But it was Lovell's prerogative, if he wished, to prefer the original to the correction. And anyone who pays an author the compliment of going over all his past writing for a selection such as this has surely earned the right not only to his own judgment of the writer but his own preference as to what he wrote.

JOHN KENNETH GALBRAITH

Cambridge
Spring, 1977

Publishers' Note

*P*erhaps the greatest strength of the editors of this volume is the degree of their ignorance of its subject matter. We knew we didn't know anything about economics but we thought we knew what we liked and that that would be sufficient. We did not know what we were in for. Had we known we might never have begun.

What we were in for was like being a gang of unlettered thieves loose in the Louvre after hours, with a failing flashlight, a dull knife, and a deadline at dawn. How can you even begin to organize your larceny until you have learned the secret of the labyrinth and fondled the treasures of its innermost sanctums one by one. We should have made a hostage of a guide. Moreover, simple merit could not be our only standard. We had difficulties the great art dealers never faced. Portability was our first consideration. You can't go hocking the Nike of Samothrace on Fifty-seventh Street without getting into trouble. You would need a crane in the first place, and she would dangle from it like a wrecker's ball amid the walls of glass. A small painting on the other hand . . . or even a detail from a large one . . . ? We ended in broad daylight frantically hacking canvasses from their stretchers with a blade now dulled beyond recognition by haste and greed, then back to our basement tunnel, as the guards took up their daily positions in the long galleries far above our heads.

We are triumphant and fearful, wearied, worried, and waiting the judgment of the fence. And we are above all grateful to the master who turned off the alarm system for a night. While grabbing what we liked—and could cram in one satchel volume—we learned a hell of a lot about "art."

We owe much to numerous accessories before and after the fact: Eileen Grieve of the Gambit staff has been a graceful and infallible center of operations throughout the whole publishing process from primary selection to final setting. Barbara Curran, also of Gambit, has unobtrusively substituted felicity when copying our incoherence. Alice Chludzinski and Laurie Brown have edited, copy-edited, advised and supervised, and protected us from the Freudian inanities of composing machines. Andrea Williams of the Galbraith office voluntarily became that all-knowing and essential hostage guide. She read much of the work in its early stages, and helped to give whatever form it may have. It was our policy to go back to first editions of Mr. Galbraith's work whenever they were available. That would hardly have been possible without the friendly patience of Mrs. Robertson of the Boston Athenaeum, with our incessant renewals of out-of-print material. Albert Bachand of Haddon Craftsmen, where this volume was set, rescued us at one point when layout problems seemed just too much to cope with. We are grateful to Austin Olney of Houghton Mifflin Company's trade division for support in moments of depression, to Marcia Legru for ingenious and humane assistance in the disentangling of certain complex contractual matters, and to Barbara Amidon for defining for us the necessary copyright protocol, both also of that company's trade division. Permission to reprint was kindly granted by Time Inc., David McKay Co., Inc., and Harvard University Press, and most kindly of all, by Houghton Mifflin Company itself, for permission to draw at will on the whole volume of Galbraith's writing. Finally we, the editors, owe something to each other for sticking together so as not to get stuck separately. Beyond everything, we owe all to John Kenneth Galbraith, without whom it's only fair to say, this book could not have been written, but more than that, he has hardly seemed to notice our stoppings and startings, perversities and insistences, our indecisions and decisions. He has given it all, throughout our long frenzied night of robbery, a most kind and impersonal interest, asked no questions, and always listened. To him for the great privilege of working on this book, we offer our deeply affectionate thanks.

Now as to our guilt for our barbarous maraudings, and senseless defacements, we bear it lightly. As we made our escape in the morning light, we saw behind us bare canvasses cleanly stretched on frames, brilliant paints, and brushes newly washed. We have but made space for new insights and greater understandings. That is the privilege of thieves.

LOVELL THOMPSON
for the editors

Ipswich
June, 1977

Contents

[xiii]

Contents

The

GALBRAITH

READER

BOOK
I

The Clansman

as

Candide

PART ONE

Introductory

The Scheme of Things

Given the opportunity, most men construct their lives as one would construct any work of art, whether it be an epic, a painting, a symphony, a wheelbarrow or a bicycle — and each according to his inclination, his ability and the tools and materials at hand. Perhaps no one has much choice, and perhaps the perception of deliberate composition is illusory; almost everything has to have a beginning, a middle and an end.

Whether the impression is illusory or not, the writings of John Kenneth Galbraith provide a picture of a life deliberately planned from the beginning, after a careful consultation with the laws of improbability. Reading the books in the order of their publication, and in all their variety of form and theme, is a serpentine pursuit, through the landscape of our recent history, of the inception, growth and acceptance of a new view of economic life and its workings. It leaves the reader with a sense of having not only an understanding of the practical stresses that shape an industrial society but also with an eerie impression of having inspected the engines of fate and even for an instant of having touched the controls.

This anthology is an attempt through selection to compress that experience between the covers of a single volume. The work fits itself snugly into the all but inevitable pattern — first the shaping of a practical skeptic, then the sense of something missing in the accepted economic view, next the search for the missing element and last the reexamination of the old system in the light of the new understanding and the long joyful task of application as of the man who invented the wheel and then settled down to work out all its possibilities and uses.

There is of course a laurel still awaiting those who are both fortunate and deserving — the "seventh" day when man may rest and happily regard what he has made.

Although this book is divided into those standard periods, its subject matter goes beyond the presentation of a revised system of economics. Unlike many academic economists, the author's career has included a considerable variety of professions: writer and journalist, bureaucrat, diplomat, economist and teacher. Galbraith's writings have provided our highly industrialized and capitalistic world with a new understanding of its ailments and inconsistencies and in so doing pointed to a cure; but they are interspersed with reports and accounts derived from his varied experience, all of which has enlarged and supplemented his economic view. It is the interplay between the wayward incidents of life and the unbending structure of economic theory that provides that eerie second image that lies at the heart of understanding. Not only the thought but the thinker, not only the what but the why — these are essential ingredients, not often available for the making of that second guess on which the best judgment usually hangs.

Galbraith argues his case and, in an unusual variety of forms, tells of the experience and scholarship that led him to his thesis — exposition, history, fiction, reportage, criticism and reminiscence. Without regard for literary form, we have here seen these writings as of three different kinds.

The first of these is of course those books that set forth the broad sweep of a unified and coherent critique of twentieth-century society as seen through the medium, not of "economics" but of a term more commonly and more accurately used when Galbraith was a student — "political economy." To this group we have assigned American Capitalism, The Affluent Society, The New Industrial State and Economics and the Public Purpose, along with certain secondary pieces that demonstrate the consistency of Galbraith's thinking over a period approaching four decades.

The whole thesis is clearly foreseen in the first of these, American Capitalism. Each of the next three books, while presenting a whole picture, gives major attention to a particular part of the structure, and whether by the intention of the author, the nature of the thesis or the self-deception of the editors, the parts seem to follow each other chronologically. The Affluent Society devotes a considerable section to the birth and early development of economic theory as the necessary source of understanding in its time and of our misinterpretation of today's phenomena. The next, The New Industrial State, turns its fullest attention to the workings of those phenomena as nourished by that misunderstanding. The last of the series, Economics and the Public Purpose, closes with a series of chapters devoted to the desirable remedies if ultimate catastrophe is to be avoided.

Though these books are lavishly annotated, their force depends largely on the manifest and incontrovertible logic of what is said. To the lay reader, Galbraith's logic seems Newtonian. No open-minded man with a lump on his head will deny that he has been fallen upon, and come to think of it, he cannot say why he should not have been spared and why the apple should not have fallen up, unless of course, a force of gravity or its equivalent exists.

The author is surely aware of this reliance on the strength of inevitable logic. As a scholar he may even think he has chosen the easy way out. That, as we see it, has given rise to the books in the second category, to which we assign two titles — The Great Crash (1929), and Money. To us it seems as if the author himself like Antaeus felt the need, after dealing so much in large principles and the entirety of the socioeconomic structure, to touch base — to fortify both himself and his readers with a much more detailed and intimate analysis of the workings of the more central organs of his body of thought. The result is certainly two of his best books.

The final grouping is the necessary evidence for the second guess and is much more personal. These selections provide us — and no doubt the author himself — with a view of the extraordinarily varied experience from which he has drawn the primary insights that must always direct the scholar and the theorist in his studies. They also reveal the frustrations and delights of a teacher, economist, writer, politician and diplomat, confronted by a world of students and others — stupid, frivolous, self-seeking, malevolent, brilliant, visionary, angelic, perceptive, prodigious — inferior and superior.

The editors have no authority for this grouping and this analysis.

Though the author has suffered it, he has most certainly not en-dorsed it. If it has no other virtue, it has at least the virtue of having provided us with a seemingly unified structure on which to arrange a most various diversity of writings. At the opening of each selection the reader will find a brief paragraph which will attempt to place the succeeding passage in this scheme of things. The first two groups are arranged pretty much in the order of their publication. The third group is placed so as to provide an indirect comment on the back-grounds of the other two. Remarks by the editors will always be shown in this modified italic face as are these introductory comments.

—The Editors

PART TWO

THE HARDSHIPS OF SPRING

SELECTION 1

*T*he Canadian Scotch have much in common with the Yankees. This is not surprising. They share an instinctive Calvinism, a low-average to poor soil and a moderate to harsh and consistently treacherous climate. There is, however, a yet more conclusive relationship — a good many Yankees are, or are descended from, the Canadian Scotch.

The Puritan ethic is generally credited with being the single progenitor of the New England Conscience, which by a formidable power of parthenogenesis has taken root in acid soil wherever it may be found throughout the continent. However, the indigenous stock has improved with the centuries. Though still a poor-soil plant, its late blossom fills the air with a spiced sweetness unlike the ranker perfume of earlier times. Formerly "conscience" led to the hanging of witches; now it may lead to the verbal persecution of witch hangers.

Whence came this fresher invigorating strain? Is its source central heating, better times, or immigration and different blood? It is all of these of course, but among them all one thing has gone unnoticed. Canadians like the rest of us have been subject to the magnetic pull of the great cities. Migration from Eastern Canada into the New England states throughout the late nineteenth and early twentieth centuries has been continuous and considerable. For a full century the well-to-do New England household was apt to be entrusted to the care of a Scotch Canadian from Nova Scotia, Prince Edward Island or New Brunswick. For many a child, home was a hard-minded and mysteriously loving Canadian woman of extraordinary competence and devotion to her trust. The New England conscience had fallen into good hands.

Times have changed, but New England and the nation still have that hard-minded, wry, and tolerant voice to listen to in John Kenneth Galbraith. There follows here Galbraith's memory of his people who had settled not in the Maritime Provinces but in Ontario.

The Scotch[1]

AN UNINTERESTING COUNTRY

THE UPPER SHORE of Lake Erie extends east and a little to the north from the mouth of the Detroit River in a very flat arch. The arch has a little of the shape of an overpass spanning a very wide road. The actual shoreline is not much to see; for great distances it consists of a nearly vertical bank of clay a couple of hundred feet or so in height, at the base of which is a narrow sand and gravel beach. Streams and inlets are few, for, as the result of an illogical arrangement of the local terrain, the principal drainage for much of the land north of the lake is provided by a stream that runs parallel to the shore before it turns off north to flow into Lake St. Clair. The lake itself is not wonderful; on the horizon it is gray and blue but inshore the water is often rather muddy.

The land that lies back of the lake struck me even as a boy as being rather uninteresting. Other children of which one reads had

[1] Chapters 1–5 from *Made to Last* (London: Hamish Hamilton, 1964), pp. 9–61.

streams to patrol and mountains to climb and some natural curiosities such as caves or springs. We had none of these. A spring was only a muddy hole where the cattle watered. One brook ran in a dull way from the end of a tile drain just beyond our farm to the lake five or six miles to the south. It had water in it only for a few weeks in the spring and after especially heavy rains. After 1920, when we rebuilt our house, we were warned that it carried the overflow from the septic tank. The only available hill could be climbed in a matter of four or five minutes.

This peninsula which juts down between Lake Erie on the south and Lake St. Clair, Lake Huron and Georgian Bay on the north is very flat. Our part, indeed, was once a lake bed and the waters as they receded took with them all topographical interest. Nor did they leave it uniformly productive. The two buttresses of the Lake Erie arch, Essex and Kent counties across the Detroit River from Detroit and Lincoln and Welland counties across the Niagara from Buffalo, are very fertile. Fruit, vegetables, beans and tobacco flourish. But at the apex of the arch where I was born the soil is sometimes rather sandy, gravelly or poorly drained or otherwise inhospitable. However, there are superb stretches of deep black earth and these are mixed up more or less at random with the poorer land. And soil quality does not lend itself to dogmatic categories. The desolate sandy stretches which once went unwanted and almost unfarmed have been found in the last forty years to grow very good tobacco. It is a great mistake, incidentally, to imagine that tobacco is a heat-loving plant which matures only under a subtropical sun. This is a myth perpetuated by the tobacco ads. It is not believed by men who know tobacco best.

II

In the year 1803 a young Irish nobleman, Colonel Thomas Talbot, arrived at the apex of the arch at the precise point where the stream that originates in the aforementioned tile drain runs into Lake Erie. Here there is a miniscule break in the clay bank where a very small boat could be moored. This smallest of harbors was given the name Port Talbot and has ever since remained innocent of commerce. But for fifty years a rude manor house on top of the promontory was the headquarters of the Colonel. It was called Malahide Castle after his ancestral home and was the capital of a vast fief which had been awarded by the English crown to the Irish aristocrat for no discernible reason.

The land in this seignory was densely covered with hardwoods— maple, beech, ash, oak, hickory, elm and ironwood. It was also the hunting ground of a few Indian tribes of negligible interest and distinction. About a hundred and thirty years ago, this land was settled and cleared. The settlement was strongly encouraged by Colonel Talbot who believed that he had a bargain which entitled him to two hundred acres for each settler established on the land, fifty of which was to go to the settler and a hundred and fifty of which was to reward the Colonel. The claim was doubtful but never effectively disputed, and it increased his original stake of some five thousand acres approximately twelvefold.

Colonel Talbot preferred Englishmen as settlers: "My advice," he wrote a friend, "is that you should, as much as possible, avoid placing Highland Scotch settlers . . . as of all descriptions they make the worst settlers on new roads — English are the best."[2] Highlanders, however, were the ones available; they were being driven from their crofts by sheep farming and the pressure of poverty, reasons which were later improved to include the search for liberty, opportunity and political independence. And while the Colonel thought ill of the Scotch, this was apparently in a competition that excluded the Irish and all other races except the English. None of the others did Colonel Talbot want at all. He settled the Highlanders in dense communities where they could communicate with each other in Gaelic, and hoped for the best.

This, for him, was not altogether good. The Colonel was Irish, aristocratic, eccentric, irreligious and often drunk, and he was in possession of land that the Scotch believed they should own. The first five of his sins his settlers were willing to leave to the later judgment of a righteous God. The ownership of the land was a more urgent matter. They bought it, and though the price was modest, they never ceased to protest.

The Talbots have long since disappeared. The Colonel was a bachelor and his estate passed to his nephew, Colonel Richard Airey. Colonel Airey was recalled to England and to the colors in 1852, and sent on to the Crimea where he was the subject of one of history's most awesome military misfortunes. His and no other was the name

2 C. O. Ermatinger, *The Talbot Regime* (St. Thomas, Ontario: The Municipal World Limited, 1904), p. 106.

on the order that launched the Light Brigade. In comparison with such towering incompetents as Lord Raglan when he served as aide or Lord Cardigan who led the charge, it is doubtful if the Colonel was much to blame. But he was never seen again at Port Talbot. Nor were others of his family.

III

By the time Colonel Talbot was answering to his Maker and Colonel Airey to his board of inquiry, the forests had been cleared away and burned or used to build frame houses with steeply pitched roofs, sometimes with wood fretwork under the gables, which were painted white with green trim. Often they were painted only once. Sometimes, in spite of the abundant wood, the settlers built square plain houses of white brick. Barns and outbuildings stood back of the house and, except in the rarest instances, were never painted at all. The forests did not quite disappear. Some swamps and gravelly tracts were not worth clearing. And at the back of each farm it was customary to continue a woodlot from which fuel and a little timber and in some cases maple syrup could be obtained. With the passage of years, these little forests have become thin and attenuated, often only a little more than a dense fringe between the fields. In the autumn when the leaves are gone, the countryside has a stubbly appearance rather like that of a man who has shaved in poor light with a very bad razor.

Yet it would be wrong to think of this as a land without beauty. On the contrary, I remember it, and quite accurately, as having a breathtaking loveliness. The difference is that this country does not flaunt its beauty everywhere and always. It is condensed both as to time and place. On a dozen winter mornings, the snow was deep over the fields and fences and sat in great patches on the evergreens in the yard. The purity of color was matched by equal purity of line. Even the steep roofs of the houses disappeared under a white mantle, with somewhat of the architecture of an English thatch curving gently out from the eave and up to the ridgepole. Sun was not good for this landscape; it brought back a certain hardness of line, and even on the coldest days it destroyed the snow on the surfaces that were protected from the wind. But a full moon turned everything into a shimmering fairyland. On such nights we went skating at Gow's gravel pit and came home in subdued wonder at what we saw.

Then the snow became old and used, and the mud and steaming manure piles and derelict machinery showed through. But there were other moments — one of them when the apple trees blossomed and the grass was rich and green against the newly seeded land and another when the oats and mixed grain stood in shocks and the green had given way to bleached gold. The maples provided their special moment of grandeur in the fall.

In what remained of the woods, the spring brought thick patches of violets and forget-me-nots and a little later of wild phlox. A hilly stretch of land a half mile or so from our house was covered with sumacs. Every three or four years, circumstances favored blackberries and one picked them for hours under a bright green and red canopy of sumac encountering at intervals one's neighbors similarly engaged. I cultivated a reputation as an attentive and diligent picker, for it provided me with a passport to this paradise. Near the lake is a little church and churchyard, and down a draw a few hundred yards distant one has a view out on the water. Here Colonel Talbot and his retainers are buried. We were taught, as a matter of tradition, to regard their resting place with detached repugnance. They had not yet been forgiven for owning the land. This is also a small but beautiful place.

IV

As the country was settled, small hamlets appeared. The English guided the larger political life of the community so the larger political subdivisions had English names or commemorated Scottish aristocrats. Elgin County was for James Bruce, 8th Earl of Elgin and 12th Earl of Kincardine, Governor-General of Canada 1846–1854; Aldborough, Dunwich, Southwold and Yarmouth townships were after their English namesakes. But the Scotch had their way with the microeconomic places — Iona, Wallacetown, Cambellton, Fingal, Crinan, Glencoe, Port Bruce, Cowal. Most of these were merely a corner where some individual, more enterprising or more adverse to manual labor than the rest, had started a store which had then been followed by a blacksmith and, less frequently, a tavern.

In the early eighteen-seventies, the railroads arrived. The short way between Buffalo and Detroit lay across the Ontario peninsula; problems of international transit of goods and people which would have caused endless difficulty in the twentieth century were worked out more or less automatically. The trains simply ran out of the United

States, through Canada and back in again. The Canada Southern Railway, later the Michigan Central and later still the New York Central, was laid out a few miles north of the lake. For a few brief years the shoreline of the lake had been an axis in the simple geography of the land. One went down to the shore and took ship to the outer world. But always the lake front was rivaled by the roads, execrable though these were. And with the arrival of the railroad, the lake became part of the back country. One went to it once or twice a year for picnics. Occasionally a hot summer evening was relieved by a rush of fresh cool air and people spoke of the lake breeze. But many who lived not three miles away never saw the lake at all.

Every six or eight miles along the railroad, where it crossed a road, the railway company built a station. For a while, at least, no village on the railroad failed to flourish. And no trading center off the railroad ever did again. In time, the railroads went into decline and the highways came, but by then the pattern was set.

v

By the latter decades of the last century, this countryside was curiously complete. The towns have not changed much since, the farms only a little more. One of the better traveled of the old roads, known as Back Street in other days, has become Queen's Highway No. 3. At the apex of the arch, it lies midway between the lake and the railroad. It has its own hideous roadside commerce but it has never attracted the solid traders away from the older municipalities on the railroad. Population has not exploded; nor have people been extruded. But it is not my purpose to write of this community as it is today but as it was fifty years ago when I knew about it as a boy. I mean to give a true picture of life in the Scotch-Canadian community in the early decades of the century.

I am engaging in this exercise in social anthropology principally for my own benefit. Others may wonder why they should concern themselves with the manners, customs and behavior of the Canadian Scotch, commonplace or curious, in this particular region at this particular point in history. I confess that this question has also crossed my mind. I can only issue a reasonable warning. If anyone is in search of serious economics or grave politics or if he is short of either time or money he should leave this book in the bookstore or lending library or, having bought it, petition at this point for the return of the purchase price. For others the financial risk can presumably be absorbed. And it is my experience, at least, that few things require so little time as to close a book and put it permanently away.

THE SCOTCH

AN EFFORT was once made to have the road on which we lived called Argyll Street, as an attempt was also made to have the second road to the north called Silver Street. But the community had a strong preference for blunt nomenclature. The road to the north ran through light, sandy soil. It continued to be called Starvation Street even though it was said by some that the name had an adverse effect on land values. Our road was once also an unfavored stretch. The adjacent concessions had been settled first and the sows of the early settlers had taken their litters back to our neighborhood in search of mast. It came as a result to be called Hog Street. In an effort to retrieve something from total inelegance, the Dutton *Advance* had added an extra "g" but Hogg Street was the best that was ever done with it.

Hogg Street is in Dunwich Township some five or six miles from the lake, and it runs parallel to the shore for some six miles from the Currie Road to the Southwold Township town line. Not even in the Western Isles are the Scotch to be found in more concentrated solution. Beginning at the Currie Road were first the McPhails and Grahams, then more Grahams, the McFarlanes, the McKeller property, Camerons, Morrisons, Gows, Galbraiths, McCallums, more McPhails, more Morrisons, Pattersons and among others the Mc-Leods. Along the way were the Gilroys who may not have been Scotch and a man by the name of Malone. He had moved out from town in very recent times, it was said for his health. But Hogg Street was not exceptional in its commitment to the Highlands, and many parts of the township were much more specialized as to clan. To the north, around a hamlet called Cowal, nearly everyone was named McCallum. The Campbells were similarly grouped around another minute village bearing the not inappropriate name of Campbellton. One or two roads were occupied more or less exclusively by Grahams. In the larger towns, those of four or five hundred people and upward, one encountered a measure of racial diversity. Along the lake, a few families of Irish extraction fished and supported a small Catholic church. And a few prosperous farmers on the immediate shore traced their ancestry to the disgruntled Tories who came to Canada after the American Revolution. In Canada the Tory émigrés are called United Empire Loyalists, and it is known that they migrated out of affection for the King and a deep commitment to personal liberty. Elsewhere there was a scattering of English and Irish names. But nearly everyone was Scotch. Certainly it never occurred to us that a well-regulated community could be populated by any other kind of people. We referred to ourselves as Scotch and not Scots. When, years later, I learned that the usage in Scotland was different it seemed to me rather an affectation.

II

Gogol once observed that there are "many faces in the world over the finish of which nature has taken no great pains, has used no fine tools, such as files, gimlets, and the like, having simply gone about it in a rough and ready way: One stroke of the axe and there's a nose, another and there are the lips, the eyes gouged out with a great drill, and without smoothing it, nature thrust it into the world saying: 'It will do.' "[3] A stranger, on encountering one of our neighbors, would have rightly concluded that he had been fashioned in the manner described by Gogol, although with some additional attention to the durability of materials.

Our Scotch neighbors might be tall or short, stocky or lean, although most of them were unremarkably in between. But it was evident at a glance that they were made to last. Their faces and hands were covered not with a pink or white film but a heavy red parchment designed to give protection in extremes of climate for a lifetime. It had the appearance of leather, and appearances were not deceptive.

This excellent material was stretched over a firm bony structure on which the nose, often retaining its axemarks, was by all odds the most prominent feature. Additional protection, though it may not have been absolutely essential, was provided for most of the week by a stiff-bristled beard. The story was told in my youth of a stranger who, in a moment of aberration, poked one of the McKillop boys on the jaw. He would not have been more damaged, it was said, if he had driven his fist into a roll of barbed wire. In any case, he was badly wounded. Our older neighbors wore a moustache. This was no clipped nailbrush but a full-flowering piece of foliage which grew and straggled and sagged at the ends as nature had obviously intended. In

[3] In *Dead Souls*, ch. 5.

natural shades it might be black, red or gray. However on many of our neighbors, as the result of an informal rinse, it came out a rich tobacco brown.

On Sundays and at funerals, a Scotchman presented himself in a pepper-and-salt suit or sometimes a solid black, high-laced shoes with broad toes, a stiff collar and a four-in-hand tie with the knot falling some distance away from the collar button. The man always looked smaller and more shrunken than his clothes, perhaps partly because it was considered sound economy to buy things a little on the large size. During the rest of the week he seemed a good deal more at home in his attire.

On superficial view, a man's working garments changed little from season to season. The basic components were high-bibbed overalls of blue denim, a blue work shirt and a blue denim smock with steel buttons. These faded steadily and rather agreeably with wear and eventually stabilized at a light sky blue, at least when clean. In the winter more garments — a waistcoat, sweaters, woolen trousers, fleece-lined underwear — were added underneath. (Heavy outer clothes, while they were put on for such sedentary tasks as driving to town, lent themselves poorly to active toil.) As spring turned to summer, the nether garments were shed while the external covering and appearance remained the same. However, a few clans continued to believe that the Canadian climate was not to be trifled with. Although sweaters, vests and the second pair of pants were discarded, it was considered safer to wear the heavy underwear right through. All of us had heard the story of two elderly and childless neighbors of ours who had the affectionate custom of going each year to the lake for a picnic. While the roast chicken, pickles, pie and cold tea were being put out on the cloth, the husband always went up the bank to bathe. One year he returned downcast; he had lost his vest. A joint search failed. But the following year he returned rejoicing.

"I hae found it, Jean!"

"Found what, John?"

"My waistcoat, Jean. 'Twa under my undershirt."

III

An enduring problem among the Scotch was that of personal nomenclature. As I have noted, a certain number of the clans transported themselves to Canada in bulk, or, in any case, re-formed their ranks quickly on arrival. McCallums, Campbells, Grahams and Mc-Killops were· exceptionally numerous. That so many had the same surname would not have been serious had they not so often had the same Christian names as well. To call a son something other than John was to combine mild eccentricity with unusual imagination. And even an unusual imagination did not normally extend beyond Dan, Jim, Angus, Duncan or Malcolm. A fair proportion of the people we knew were called John McCallum. The John Grahams and the John Campbells were almost equally numerous.

The Scotch eliminated the danger of confusion by giving everyone a nickname. The parents having failed, the neighbors stepped in. The nickname might turn on some feature of a man's farm or location; most often it was inspired by some prominent personal trait. Since an unpleasant trait invariably makes a stronger impression than an agreeable one, the nicknames were usually unflattering and often offensive.

There were Big Johns and Little Johns and once there had been Wee Johns, but this form had gone out of use. There was also Black John and Johnny Rua, the latter being Gaelic for red and referring not to politics but to beard and complexion. More regrettably there was (or within recent memory had been) a Lame John, a Dirty John, a Lazy John, numerous Old Johns, a Bald John, a Nosey John and a Piggy John who was named for the number of, and his own re-semblance to, his livestock. Most of the McCallums were Presby-terians; one who was not bore the proud name of John the Baptist.

The Scotch often tagged people with offensive nicknames even when they were not needed for identification. In later years I knew a boy whose parents had named him R. (for Robert) S. McTavish. The McTavish were a small clan; no further identification was neces-sary. But it pleased everyone to take advantage of the initials and call my friend Arss. The Scotch often commented on this practice of giving people disagreeable names. Those who had somehow escaped had no objection. Those who hadn't were very glad to see others suffer.

IV

In all sophisticated societies, nothing is so nearly a social absolute as cleanliness. And nothing serves so universally as an index of character and worth. In a rich country, poverty, when combined with cleanliness, becomes respectable. "They are poor but very clean." In an underdeveloped country, regular bathing serves as an offset to an inadequate Gross National Product. "They haven't much money but they are clean and tidy." In the United States even few intellectuals are socially so secure that they can afford a gamey smell. For Madison Avenue, this has been a rich source of reward.

In 1837 one Mrs. Jameson, the wife of a judge of the province and a Frances Trollope of her time and place, visited Port Talbot and the Scotch settlements and reported on the state of the inhabitants. She was especially impressed by "Their clannish attachments and their thrifty, dirty habits — and also their pride and honesty." They had not changed appreciably by my time.

Our neighbors lived close to the soil and close to their livestock. Inevitably traces of both clung to them. Nor could everything be attributed to external influences. Men worked and perspired, and a nightly bath was highly impractical. Water would have had to be hauled and heated; anyone taking a bath pre-empted the kitchen, the one warm room in the house, which was needed by other people for other purposes. And a bath didn't do much for personal daintiness without a change of underwear. A daily change would have required a much larger investment than most of our neighbors would have thought reasonable, and the laundry involved would have been an intolerable burden. Better a mildly malodorous husband than a dead wife. The sensible compromise adopted by our neighbors was to clean up once a week. This was accomplished on Saturday night before going to town and it meant that a man remained in fairly good condition for church the following day. This modest and practical standard was, however, rigorously enforced. Failure to conform subjected a man to adverse comment. Two men are talking in the town of Dutton as a third approaches.

"Watch it, Mac, here comes Andy Leitch!"

"Yeh, I see. The air is a mite blue behind."

"Wish there was a breeze. They say Andy's had no bath since he fell in the sheep dip."

"You're right, lad. Scratch the 'Le' of a Leitch and you have it."

v

But overgeneralization is the enemy of science. If the Scotch had certain resemblances in texture, attire and aroma, they otherwise displayed a pleasing diversity of personal traits. A sense of humor was not their most prominent feature but some, like our next-door neighbor Bert McCallum, were very amusing. They were not, as a rule, easily aroused to anger but occasionally one encountered a man, or a woman, who had the reputation of a hot temper. Few were belligerent and most were pacifist. During the First World War, when young Canadians were volunteering enthusiastically for euthanasia on the Western Front, the Scotch regarded the whole enterprise with reserve. They did not think the slaughter ennobling or especially necessary; more surprising, perhaps, they had instinctive misgivings about the men who were in charge. On both points they anticipated by some decades the judgment of historians. Yet, when inspired by alcohol, a Scotchman became very combative. In our community, a man did not get dead drunk but fighting drunk. The resulting battles were part of our folk history.

Some characteristics were specialized as to family or clan. Thus, the Camerons were very prolific. Sons and daughters married young and had children with celerity. This was also true of many of the McCallums. The McKellers, by constrast, had ceased to marry, and the local clan had only a few more years to survive. The Galbraiths a generation earlier had shown the same tendency. My paternal grandfather was a member of a family of seven. Only three married and these three couples, six in all, produced a total of only five children. The literature of celibacy is silent on the position of those who do not get born. To anyone who has only narrowly made it, the point is not without interest.

Differences in the size of family were related in considerable part to a sharp difference of opinion on the economic role of offspring. The Camerons in my time regarded children as a valuable earning asset. Only the minimum amount of money need be spent on their improvement. The marginal cost of getting and preparing an additional pair of hands thus being small, the more the better. This doctrine required that girls work as well as boys, and the Cameron girls worked with a will. In our case, as with quite a few other clans, education was deemed necessary. This cost money and, much more important, it greatly delayed entry into productive employment. (Proponents of the other system also felt that the individual so educated too often left the farm or that he returned with an exaggerated view of the possibilities of substituting mental for manual labor.) Whatever the merits of the two systems, where education was favored, the number of children had to be curtailed, and that was the accepted practice.

The total avoidance of marriage was not so explicitly defended by an economic rationale. There is no doubt, however, that it reflected the prudent tendencies of the community which extended not infrequently to the question of whether a wife was really economically essential. The families of bachelors and spinsters, which were a commonplace in our neighborhood, had presumably decided in the negative.

This calculation is not yet obsolete. Within the recent past a Hollywood press agent was looking for a family of bachelors to publicize a film called *Seven Brides for Seven Brothers*. After an international search, he found seven unmarried brothers a few miles from Hogg Street toward the lake. It would have been a logical place to look first.

OF LOVE AND MONEY

THE VIRTUE and marital fidelity of our neighbors, from all outward appearances, were impressive. And more penetrating study would not have altered the impression. No one had ever received a divorce or asked for one. No one knew anyone who had been divorced. This was partly because until after World War I there was no divorce law. What God had wrought in Canada, man could put asunder only by a special Act of the Canadian Parliament. Each year a certain number of Canadian couples did petition for such special legislation but they were much richer and far more willing to spend money for their personal peace than any of the rural Scotch.

In most countries where it is difficult to dissolve a marriage the community comes to take a rather tolerant view of informal recombinations where these obviously add to happiness or even pleasure. Thus, the Italians, who have no divorce law, have gone far to perfect arrangements which make one unnecessary. The Scotch resorted to no such expedients. A tall and stalwart Highlander who lived very near our place had once been unfaithful to his wife, an almost incredibly unattractive woman, to the eventual impregnation of a maiden who lived a mile away. The baby, so it was said, was brought home in a red bandanna handkerchief and in any case was tolerantly reared by the wronged wife. By rough calculation from the age of the issue of this unblessed union, it all must have happened about 1890. It was still a lively subject for conversation when I was in primary school in 1919. No other instances of infidelity were immutably a part of the local lore.

Among the unmarried, the standards of deportment, by what were unquestionably the standards of the community, were equally high. To father an illegitimate child was to sacrifice one's citizenship for some years. The effect on the mother was more disastrous; if, thereafter, she married at all it would be to someone who was permanently devoid of position — a hired man, a man who drank, or at best someone with fifty acres and no alternative. We did not speak of shotgun marriages for firearms were not much known in the community; a boy who was compelled into marriage as the result of pregnancy was described as having put his partner "up a stump." This was also a serious social setback and though it would eventually be forgiven or forgotten it would be a rewarding topic of conversation for many months. Years before, one of the notably energetic McCallum boys was courting one of two sisters of the same name. (No suggestion of incest or inbreeding can be implied. The McCallums were so vast and dense a clan that, in the absence of an exceptional willingness to travel, marriage within the clan was inevitable.) An adventuresome type, he sometimes visited his beloved by climbing up on the summer kitchen and into the bedroom that she shared with her sister. When danger in the shape of the senior McCallum threatened, he would crawl into bed between the girls. By the worst of luck he got the wrong girl pregnant. Though he promptly married her and the McCallums were good farmers and intelligent and public-spirited people, he was celebrated unfavorably by the local historians for a long time and only gradually did the adventure come to redound to his advantage.

II

In many cultures obloquy attaches to unlicensed intercourse, especially if it becomes, in one way or another, a matter of record. This is rarely sufficient to prevent it. Thus the continence and fidelity of the Scotch call for additional analysis.

More must be attributed to the absence of opportunity than would first be imagined. There was no place, literally none, where a questing husband could take someone else's interested wife and go to bed. He couldn't visit her house when her husband was away for the reason that husbands were rarely if ever away for as much as overnight. In any case, a man's horse and buggy were as firmly identified with his personality as his nose, hair or gait and they would be seen passing down or up the road or tied in the yard. In the center of Khatmandu, the capital of Nepal, is a temple and around all four sides of it couples engage imaginatively in copulation for all eternity. (One talented woman rewards two well-endowed and highly aroused lovers simultaneously.) A visit by a couple to the McIntyre House in Dutton would have been almost equally unreticent.

Unmarried affection encountered similar barriers. The girl's dwelling was filled with parents and siblings and thus unavailable to anyone less adept at second-story operations than the aforementioned McCallum. Resort to the barn, the classical arena of bucolic love, was an outright admission of intent. Also it would have been regarded by the better or even the average class of girl as rather vulgar. The couple could go riding together; chaperones were unknown and boys and girls, engaged or otherwise, went anywhere together. This, however, was allowed not out of liberalism but from a knowledge of the Canadian climate. In winter a cutter lent itself to lovemaking only at the cost of extreme contortion and an occasional chilling exposure. The alternative was a snowbank. Things were not appreciably more agreeable in the autumn on the frozen ground, in the spring in the mud or in summer under the onslaught of the mosquitoes. Chastity was everywhere protected by a vigilant nature. With closed and heated automobiles, things have doubtless changed but that is only conjecture based on a general view of human nature.

III

Something had also to be attributed to the uncompromising Calvinism of our upbringing. We were taught that sexual intercourse was, under all circumstances, a sin. Marriage was not a mitigation so much as a kind of license for misbehavior and we were free from the countervailing influence of movies, television and John O'Hara. Among the rougher element of the community, after the weather, the wisdom of selling cattle and the personality of the schoolteacher had been touched upon, conversation would often be taken over by one or another of the acknowledged masters of salacious detail. However, in contrast with other cultures, no one ever boasted of his own exploits, presumably because there was no chance he would be believed. More often a shy or especially puritanical participant would be accused of fornication with some highly improbable lass. Interest would center on the way he denied it. The charge would then be repeated, and coupled with more graphic, though even more imaginary detail, and a pleasant hour or two would thus be whiled away. Members of the more prestigious clans never participated in such pastime. In our family we would have been visited by a Jovian wrath had it been known that we even listened. The mere appearance of my father at a neighborhood gathering would turn the conversation back to crops.

An important feature of an austere education in such matters is that it need influence only one of the two people involved to be fully effective. And uncertainty as to the state of conviction of the other person, plus the moral consequences of miscalculation, can be a powerful deterrent. One such experience had a durable effect on me.

At some time during adolescence, I encountered a novel by Anatole France which made unlicensed sexual transactions, especially if blessed by deep affection and profound mutual understanding, seem much more defensible than I had previously been allowed to suppose. It was summer and I was deeply in love. One day the object of my love, a compact, golden-haired girl who lived on Willey's Sideroad, a half mile away, came over to visit my sisters. They were away and we walked together through the orchard and climbed onto a rail fence which overlooked a small field between our place and Bert McCallum's. Our cows were pasturing on the second-growth clover in front of us. The hot summer afternoon lay quiet all around.

With the cows was a white bull named O. A. C. Pride, for the Ontario Agricultural College where my father had bid him in at an auction. As we perched there the bull served his purpose by serving a heifer which was in season.

Noticing that my companion was watching with evident interest, and with some sense of my own courage, I said: "I think it would be fun to do that."

She replied: "Well, it's your cow."

IV

But I think most of the virtue of the Scotch was to be attributed to the fact that love for a good woman (or bad) was not the only ruling passion. There was also love for money.

One indication was the respect which was accorded to money in everyday conversation. People do not speak lightly about the things they hold dear. On occasion, at a threshing or of an evening at Bert

McCallum's, the same rough-spoken clansmen to whom I have referred would consider the ability of a well-to-do, middle-aged neighbor to satisfy the demands of his young, vigorous and healthy wife. There might be jovial suggestions of the need to lend him, figuratively, a hand. But no one would ever dream of bringing up the man's bank balance or of voicing a wish that he might enjoy that. Such things were sacred.

The ordinary farmer referred to his wife, whatever her age, as "My auld woman" or "My auld lady." These terms did not necessarily imply dislike or disrespect; like the terms "dear" and "darling" in more refined communication they were neutral. But no such casual reference was ever made to money. No one spoke of "jack" or "dough" or "lettuce" or "long green." When it came into the conversation, as it often did, it was referred to respectfully as money or dollars.

This was, I think, pure love. Some have always wanted money for what it would buy. Some have wanted it for the power it conferred. Some have sought it for the prestige it provided. The Scotch wanted it for its own sake. Money in this community conferred no power. And while a good bank balance unquestionably enhanced a man's self-respect, he certainly did not think enough of the prestige it provided ever to dream of admitting to its amount. Two techniques for accumulating assets have always been in some measure in competition. One is to earn money; the other is to avoid spending it. Our neighbors enthusiastically employed both. When he visited Scotland with Boswell, at the time the migration to America was getting under way, Dr. Johnson observed, "A man, who keeps his money, has in reality more use from it, than he can have by spending it."[4] With this the Scotch continued to agree.

v

The passion for money as money reinforced continence and fidelity in several ways. For one thing, faithful and chaste behavior was the least expensive. Within the family, children were comparatively costless but an illegitimate child could call for cash. A boy married when, with his auld man's help, he could make a down payment on a farm and manage the rest under mortgage. The compulsions of an unpremeditated pregnancy would badly upset this timetable. Many might

[4] James Boswell, *Journal of a Tour to the Hebrides*. Thursday, 26th August (1773).

think that it made better financial sense to leave the community for a year or so and the girls, knowing this, had an inducement to chastity. Sex education among the Scotch depended largely on experience, instruction by the learned of one's own age and informal deduction based on the behavior of breeding stock. But most parents took occasion to tell their young of the serious financial risks which were inherent in yielding to what they unhesitantly called the baser instincts.

More important, the love of money meant that as other passion receded, a man's life did not become less meaningful. Marriage for life, especially if decided on by the principals, is an exceedingly hazardous arrangement, as all experience shows. The line between love and lust is one that participants can neither draw for themselves nor on which they can accept counsel. And love is less than durable. If it is deemed central to life, its disappearance means either that life is totally barren or that a remedy must be sought in adultery, divorce and replacement or, should the culture allow, bigamy, polygamy or polyandry, all of which are in the area of the original disaster where, to some extent at least, one failure presages another. The love of money meant that a man's emotions were reliably engaged until the day he died.

VI

Yet the Scotch were also notably wary of any person who allowed his emotions to rule him. As many people expect a woman to love men without being a nymphomaniac, so the Scotch expected a man to love money without being a miser. Excessive preoccupation with economy would not cost a man his membership in the society but it could be the cause of considerable adverse comment. One of the great McKillop clan was always known as Codfish John. (Dried codfish was the cheapest form of protein available in the winter months. It was universally detested and a man who fed it to his family, hired hand or the neighbor who, in accordance with the custom of the community, might drop in unannounced for a meal, was suspected of stinginess.) Many stories were told of Codfish John's economies. His wife did not average one new dress a decade. Her only recreation, and similarly that of the family, was a weekly trip to church in a democrat behind a plow horse. All community festivals — the Wallacetown Fair, the Caledonian games, the Christmas concert — were denied to his family; they were believed to implant ideas of extravagance even in the not excessively impressionable mind of a McKillop. On Christmas Eve, so it was said, John lit the lamp and entertained his bairns by making rabbits on the wall. The entertainment did not continue long because of the expense of the oil and the possible wear on the wallpaper. When he was finally being lowered into his grave at Black's Cemetery west of Wallacetown, it was said that he lifted the cover of the coffin and handed out his coat, waistcoat, pants and undershirt. That was not widely believed. But he did warn his wife to take up the parlor carpet before the funeral.

Interestingly, it was always said of Codfish John, as of anyone else who was excessively frugal, that he was "very Scotch."

HUSBANDRY

LIVES ARE measured off and the passage of time given meaning either by the rotation of the earth on its axis or by its more gradual but much grander movement in orbit around the sun. For urban dwellers, the teeming hordes of Southern California and those who live in the tropics, it is the succession of day and night that is important. But the fortunate people of the planet, although the blessing is not universally recognized, are those who live by the seasons. The seasons have an unpredictability and an individuality which appeal both to the sporting instinct and the very great need for simple topics of conversation:

"It looks like a late spring."

"Early winter this year."

"Nice autumn."

The seasons also work a great and magical change in the landscape — there is far more difference between a Vermont farm in the summer and the same farm in the winter than there is between San Diego and São Paulo. This means that people who live where the seasons are good and strong have no need to travel; they can stay home and let change come to them. This simple truth will one day be recognized and then we will see a great reverse migration from Florida to Maine, New Hampshire and on into Quebec.

Although the climate of southern Ontario is not especially severe, the seasons have a very satisfactory accent, and this is sharpened by the cycle of agricultural operations. Here I must digress to another poorly understood point.

In modern times, especially in the United States, notions of natural beauty have been extensively compromised by the Cult of the Wilderness. The justification for this cult is plausible enough. Men have seen the squalor of the places where people live or travel — the slums, the suburbs that were blighted at birth, the formless sprawl beyond, the highways made hideous by billboards and the evidently insatiable appetite of the American motorist for fried food and the excessively enterprising notion that all abutting acreage should be devoted to satisfying it. They have assumed the corollary which is that beauty is only to be found where people are not. A number of articulate and extremely self-assured prophets — the late Theodore Roosevelt, the late Gifford Pinchot, the late Harold Ickes, the late Richard Neuberger, the late Bernard DeVoto and the happily highly extant Stewart Udall — have driven home the point in speech and print. The result has been the preservation of a great deal of wilderness that would otherwise have been lost to desecration, and everyone should be grateful.

But in fact, man at his best has done far more for landscape than this implies. The surviving English countryside, hedged, cultivated, trimmed and green, is lovely; a couple of thousand years ago the unkempt fens and forests and occasional patch of poor tillage could not have been very attractive. Similarly with France. The Rhine and Moselle would not be interesting without the vineyards, and Iowa with the red barns and green corn must be more agreeable than when it was a monotonous waste of high grass. Northern Vermont with its pastureland, barns and rich smell of cow manure is much more attractive than southern Vermont which is much closer to wilderness. Farmers, unlike outdoor advertisers and those who serve the motorist, have no apologies to make to nature.

II

The agriculture of the Scotch did less for the landscape than most. The architecture, as I have observed, was intrinsically an eyesore. So in general, were the Scotch. The forest had been left in very untidy form. Yet, in conjunction with the seasons, there was a sufficient and changing loveliness. The fields of ten or twelve acres were a mosaic of endlessly varied design. In the spring, some showed the deep green of the winter wheat. In others, the black wet earth dried gradually to a light brown and the teams plodded over it to prepare for the spring grain and corn. Summer came with the fruit blossoms, the pastel shades of the oats and, a little later, the strong green of the corn. Then the hayfields were stripped to a greenish brown and the wheat and corn to a yellow and amber. In the autumn, the wheat fields turned green again and furrows of the fall plowing showed startlingly black against the first snow. Then the snow covered the whole land. On some days there was no color at all; only the dead gray of the driving storm.

In the common theory of farm management, farmers seek to maximize their net income. The Scotch were certainly not averse to net income but their equal concern was with minimizing gross outlay. They did not care to spend money for personal consumption if it could be avoided. And they did not care to spend it for productive purposes either if that could be prevented. To spend either their own or borrowed money meant some risk of loss. The goal of their agriculture was a safe, one-way flow of income, the flow being in their direction.

The basic farm was a hundred acres. This included cropland, rough pasture and a woodlot. The basic labor force was the farmer, his wife and his sons. The first problem in eliminating outlay was to eliminate the need for hired labor.

Most of the work on a hundred-acre farm could, in fact, be performed by one man and a team of horses. A few tasks — haying, harvesting, cutting wood, breaking a colt — required two people, and a very small number of tasks, such as threshing, required a crew. Beyond a certain time the Scotch were reluctant to work their wives in the fields. But a young wife could, it was felt, give a hand on those tasks where two people were required. And as she grew older, sons became available to take her place. If a crew was required, the Scotch "changed work." The neighbors came over and helped, and this labor was repaid in kind. The annual payroll thus remained at nil.

But implicit in this economy was an arrangement of tasks which, while avoiding peaks and valleys in the need for labor, kept the one man reasonably employed the year around. This was accomplished by a combination of livestock and field husbandry which spread the demand for labor very adequately over the year. The animals required a good deal of attention through the Canadian winter but could do very well by themselves on the summer pasture. The field crops confined their demands to the summer and these, in turn, had their own well-considered sequence. Oats, the basic cereal for livestock and on which the Scotch themselves started the day, were in the ground and growing before the corn land needed to be prepared. Beans came just before or just after the corn. Then came haying and then, in measured succession, the wheat, oat and bean harvest. Equally important were the tasks such as cutting wood, taking grain to the gristmill, putting the manure on the land (hauling shit in the brief language of the average clansman) which were undemanding as to time. These filled up the space between the jobs that could not be postponed.

A good farm manager was, perhaps most of all, a man who combined the tasks compelled by season with the more permissive operations in an intelligent order of priority. Every once in a while there would be someone for whom the intellectual problem would be simply too great. He would do the wrong things first, the right things last or, in the more common case, would always be hopelessly behind on everything. His neighbors regarded him with pity and sorrow but, perhaps most of all, with secret satisfaction as a visible proof of their own personal superiority.

This timetable was, of course, terribly vulnerable to bad weather. A cold wet spring would delay spring seeding and put this into the time reserved for preparing corn or bean land. A wet June could shove haying into the wheat harvest. And so forth. The community set considerable store by equanimity in these matters, but for a certain number this was not possible. This minority watched the weather nervously and impatiently and complained bitterly when it did not accord with their needs. They invited adverse comment.

"Johnny Morrison git on the ground this morning?"

"Yeh, I saw him. Over by the culvert he could've used the *Lusitania*."

"It's a late spring."

"You got to take it as it comes."

III

The same intricate combination of crops with animal husbandry that minimized the need to pay for outside labor minimized also the need to pay for anything else. In our neighborhood, wheat and beans were sold for cash. Everything else — oats, oat straw, hay, corn and more occasionally roots and barley — was fed to beef cattle, hogs, sheep and chickens. The animals turned the feed into salable products or into manure which largely eliminated the need for commercial fertilizer. The combination of crops, including the generous supplies of legumes for feed, also sustained the soil. The horses also turned their feed into energy which eliminated the need to purchase gasoline. (The Scotch came eventually to tractors but with considerable reluctance.) From the red and white grade Shorthorns (which, though kept for beef, were expected to produce milk for the household as well), the white Yorkshire or red Tamworth hogs, from the chickens of uncertain ancestry and from the orchards and gardens came the principal components of the family ration. However, the Scotch made no fetish of self-sufficiency in personal consumption. Once they had made their own cloth and ground their own wheat. But they had sensibly come to agree that factories and mills could do some things much more efficiently than they. Too much town-bought food remained a mark of profligacy. No one would think of buying canned fruit, jam or marmalade at the store. But only the most backward clans considered it a mark of merit to live completely from their land. Adam Smith was a Scot and while none of our neighbors had heard of him, his enunciation of the principle of the division of labor was respected within reason.

IV

On our farm the new year began not on January 1, which was a date of purely formal significance with the deepest and deadest part of the winter still to come, but in March with the arrival, as to timing, of the least permissive of all farm tasks, namely the tapping of the maples. The sun, when it shone, would now have traces of warmth. But the gray snowbanks would still be in the woods and the nights were still cold, for a run of sap must be refreshed by a nightly frost. No agricultural operation has ever been invested with so much glamour as the making of maple syrup and the reason is simple: none ever had such magic.

We tapped about two hundred trees, few enough so that we knew the personality of each. In a hollow on the southeast corner of the woods was a vast gnarled specimen which always had its three buckets full and often running over. I still think of that tree with affection, admiration and gratitude. On the more exposed westerly side of the woods were almost equally sizable specimens which scarcely produced a drop. We regarded them with dislike and resentment. Like Massachusetts Democrats they had successfully divorced promise from performance.

Sap in those days was collected in a wooden tub mounted on a sleigh or stoneboat. A circular track wound through the black, silent woods. The horses pulled the tub from point to point along this track. At each stop we fanned out with pails to collect the sap from the red buckets. If the run was good there might be a pleasant air of urgency about this task for numerous buckets would be spilling over. The sap was then boiled in a flat rectangular pan, about three feet by six or seven, which sat on a cement arch over a vigorous log fire. Immediately back of the arch, from which the operation could be watched, and with the whole front open to the fire, was the small, shed-roofed sugar shanty. As everyone has heard but only the fortunate know at first hand, there is no aroma on earth like that of boiling sap. In good years it was necessary to boil all night to keep abreast of the run. Then hour after hour the white steam billowed off into the black night or, on occasion, rolled into the shanty as a special reward. Neighbors who did not make syrup came across the fields and through the woods to sit and watch the fire and the steam and enjoy the smell. One could take a dipper, dip out a pint or two of the thickening sap, cool it in a snowbank and drink it all. It combined a heavenly flavor with a remarkable laxative effect.

The flavor of the syrup then produced was far better than what a less fortunate generation now gets from Vermont or Quebec. I learned the reason in what I believe was my first introduction to scientific method. Two brothers named John and Angus McNabb, who lived over near the Thames River, went into production of maple syrup on a commercial basis: they bought covered buckets and an evaporator and a galvanized tank for the sap and set out to make a quality product. It was bland and tasteless and Jim McKillop showed them why.

As the sap dripped into the open buckets, quite a few dried leaves fell in too. A large number of brown moths were also attracted by the moisture, sugar or both. So were the field mice. Jim rightly suspected that these had something to do with the flavor and on the night of the experiment, he put a quart or so of water into a sap bucket and added a handful of moths, two dead mice and several milligrams of mouse droppings which he had got from a mouse's nest. He boiled all of this into a good thick stock and added it to a gallon of the insipid McNabb syrup. There was no question; the flavor was miraculously improved.

For years in the United States the colleges of agriculture, state experiment stations, Beltsville, food processing companies, canners, container manufacturers, Birdseye people and advertising agencies have been proceeding on the assumption that nothing counts so much in food as purity. Purity, quite possibly, has its place. But there is considerable need for a research project along the lines of Jim McKillop's experiment to ascertain how much of the flavor once associated with our staple foods was the result of soundly conceived contamination.

v

The maple season or, at the latest, the time for seeding spring grains, was greatly welcomed by the farmers for another reason. It was the beginning of escape from the thralldom of chores. Livestock were out of doors and eventually on their own pasture. The whole day was free for the tight succession of tasks — preparing, seeding, planting, harvesting — which were considered the serious business of the farm. For while this system of agriculture was designed to keep a man occupied during the winter the winter work was considered tedious and a trifle degrading. As cattle, horses, poultry and to a lesser extent the sheep came into winter quarters, they required the same increase in personal services as a tourist coming from a camping trip to a hotel. These were the chores. To confess that one was "only doing chores" was to imply that one had not been really employed.

At first glance, it was rather pleasant work. One went into the half-dark barn at half past six or seven to hear the cows protesting comfortably at the ending of their night of rest and contemplation. The milking of the one cow, the release of the suckling calves to the rest, and the feeding of cattle and horses took an hour. After breakfast, another three hours were needed to throw down and prepare feed, turn the stock out for water, groom the horses, clean the stables and nail up the astonishing number of things which, in any twenty-four hour period, could come loose.

Partly this work was disliked as all personal service is disliked. While animals are less officious than people, they are, in their own way, as quietly demanding and many can convey the same impression that the world was made for them. This naturally breeds resentment. But the more important problem lay in the brevity of the work cycle. Clearly the most unfortunate people are those who must do the same thing over and over again, every minute, or perhaps twenty to the minute. They deserve the shortest hours and the highest pay. The Scotch had no experience of this industrial drudgery but they did compare those tasks that had to be done every day with those that were related to the more spacious cycle of the seasons and thus had to be performed but once a year. They much preferred the latter.

One learned of all this from cleaning out the cow stables. It was a far from unpleasant task. One shoveled the accumulation in an unfastidious way; metal rang against concrete with brisk clang. Presently one could look with satisfaction at a stretch of clean and glistening floor. But even before the fresh bedding was brought in, the enviable persistalsis of the bovine would begin to work its havoc. First from one direction, then from another would come the rhythmic, plopping sounds. In an hour or two one's handiwork would be in an advanced state of destruction. In contrast, one could look down a row of beans from which the grass and Canada thistle had been hoed away, and know it would remain fairly clean for the rest of the summer.

In World War I, as I have elsewhere noted, passion for the Allied cause burned very low among the Scotch. But here and there a lad joined up in advance of conscription. He then went off to serve in the armies of Field Marshal Sir Douglas Haig where, in all but the most exceptional instances, he was promptly killed. It was invariably said that he went because he was tired of doing chores.

THE MEN OF STANDING

AT FIRST GLANCE, the Scotch would seem to have made up one of the world's more egalitarian communities. While some were poor, none was rich. All worked with their hands and went as equals to the polls. No man's income was reflected in his dress or reliably in his house. The conventions of the community required that income and liquid assets be a secret between a man and his wife. In any case, farm income, unlike salary income, yields no exact figure by which people can be known and graded with precision. (Given the respect accorded to money by this culture, accurate information on the income and assets of the members would have been of considerable interest.) The common social distinction of all industrial communities, capitalist and communist alike, is between those who give (or transmit) orders and those who take them. But in this community, a few hired hands apart, everyone worked for himself. The Scotch set much store by this. In brief moments of philosophical reflection, the point was often made about farming. "It's hard work but a man's his own boss." It did not occur to my neighbors that this might signify a hard taskmaster or, on occasion, one of questionable competence.

Yet, in fact, this was a highly stratified society. The community gave a good deal of attention to the question of precedence. There was also an agreeable certainty as to where a man stood. This last is important. If one must have a hierarchy it adds greatly to peace and security of mind if it is made clear to everyone just where he belongs.

II

There were three social classes. At the bottom were those who, although by all outward signs they were treated like everyone else, did not enjoy full citizenship. Their views did not command respect; no one would think of quoting them except possibly as an example of error. They also knew they did not belong and were reconciled to the fact in varying degree.

At the top, in turn, were the Men of Standing. They were so described and, except in rare instances, were also aware of their position. Others sought their views and in some measure accepted them, especially on matters removed from the common knowledge of the community. A measure of guidance might be needed on who had burned down the Canadian Parliament buildings; it was believed that some drunken Tory had tossed his cigar into a pile of paper but the opposing theory that it was done by the Germans needed expert rebuttal. On the causes of the burning of the McWilliam house everyone naturally had an opinion of his own.

Between the disenfranchised and the Men of Standing were the much larger group whose views determined the position of the others. The number of contented outsiders in any society is always small. The lecturer who never got to be professor, the newspaperman who has descended into public relations and the politician who, however righteously, is out of office, all nurture a deep if secret sorrow. But we also, all too often, underestimate the capacity of men for contentment. One can be a professor without being an Oppenheimer, a pundit without being a Reston, or a politician without being a Kennedy. Most of the Scotch were content to be considered ordinary citizens so long as they could determine who, because of being better or worse, were not. This they addressed themselves to assiduously.

More than politics, the weather, crop prospects, prices or any other topic, the Scotch discussed one another. The ideas, behavior and misdeeds of third persons are alluring topics in all societies; they undoubtedly owe some of their fascination to the omnipresent sense of indecency in talking about someone who isn't around to defend himself. Be this as it may, the Scotch talked constantly, clinically and unabashedly about each other. A man's farming methods, marketing decisions, livestock purchases, machinery acquisitions, wife, family, relatives, temperament, drinking, stomach complaints, tumors, personal expenditures, physical appearance and his political, social and economic views were dwelt on in detail by his neighbors. Out of this discussion came the consensus as to his place. All distinctions are, in some degree, vicarious and thus invidious. But few could claim to be founded on so intimate an examination of person and personality. And while the Scotch did not quickly change their minds about those to whom they had accorded positions of honor or had excluded from membership, they kept their people subject to constant scrutiny. If there must be an aristocracy, it is well no doubt that it be kept under continuous surveillance.

III

Some of the excluded, to begin with the lowest class, suffered their segregation for purely objective reasons. No hired man had full citizenship. A good worker might be much praised but he was still a hired man. To belong, a man had to own land and this requirement also excluded the comparatively rare family which rented land. We heard — and the *Farmer's Advocate* and other farm journals were at pains to point out — that in England and in Iowa a tenant farmer was often just as respectable as a man who owned land. The Englishmen and the Iowans were entitled to their tolerance but it was not so with us. Our neighbors made no fetish of land; none was ever seen holding the good earth in his cupped hands and gazing soulfully at the sky, and any such behavior would have been taken as indication of an incipient mental disorder. But it was cheap land that had brought our ancestors from Scotland in the 1830's and 40's and anyone who didn't own some by (say) 1925 was pretty obviously a failure.

As a souvenir of Colonel Talbot's design for an unearned increment, a certain number of families still farmed fifty-acre tracts — the original inheritance. This did not qualify a man either — a man who farmed a fifty was not taken seriously on any important subject and would not ordinarily be elected to public office. Since it was perfectly possible for a hired man, tenant or a fifty-acre farmer, by combining diligence and rigid economy with a large mortgage, to own a hundred acres, these barriers to acceptance were not as harsh as they sounded. No agitator ever arose to denounce them. The people so excluded were not very competent. If it hadn't been land they would probably have lost out for some other reason.

A man was also excluded from society if he were either unneighborly or dishonest. But these faults were so rare that almost no one was ever disqualified. No one ever locked his house or feared that his livestock might be stolen. Men stuck to their bargains and negotiated their disputes. One drinking man apart, none of our neighbors had ever been inside a courtroom. The nearest police officer with jurisdiction was twenty miles away; during the twenty years that I knew the community, I never heard that he had occasion to visit it.

Men were honest because public opinion would have ruthlessly excluded from the society a man who, in the local language, "was not quite straight." The judgment would have been certain and final and the punishment would have extended to his wife and children. Only a hardened criminal who was also a case-hardened hermit could have survived such public obloquy. A man would have been excluded with almost equal severity if he had shown himself to be unneighborly. Every farm was subject to sudden emergencies. Wives or livestock had difficult births; death struck; a barn had to be raised or a horse removed from a well. There were also the regular jobs, notably threshing, which required a crew. The common law on these matters was also clear and well enforced.. A man was obliged to put his neighbor's need ahead of his own and everyone did. Occasionally there were complaints that a man called for help too readily. But no one ever declined. Again the social penalty would have been too severe. It is a great mistake to imagine that prisons and fines are the only means that a community has of enforcing its laws. Nor are they necessarily the most drastic.

IV

Three other things could lead to loss of full citizenship but with somewhat less certainty than, say, the ownership of insufficient land. These were alcohol, laziness and ignorance.

The Scotch were divided into two groups, those who drank and those who didn't. If a man drank like a gentleman, it would not hurt his position in the community. Unfortunately it was not on record that anyone ever had. Men drank for only one reason, namely to get drunk. No one imagined that alcohol had any other purpose. In consequence, a drinking man regularly ended up bruised, battered and, in the absence of an especially talented horse, in the ditch. If this happened only on rare and festive occasions, it did not hurt too much. But if it occurred with any frequency — if neighbors had regularly to come in and do a man's chores while he was being restored after a tear — it cost him his membership. He lost it immediately if he got put on the Indian List.

This curiosity of sumptuary legislation enabled the wife of a habitual drinker to have her husband proclaimed an honorary aborigine. In Ontario, as in other North American jurisdictions, the sale of alcohol to the surviving tribesmen was subject to heavy penalties. These penalties applied to all on the list. Although to be on the Indian List involved total disgrace, it was not supposed that it ever stopped a determined drinker from getting liquor. There were many tales of how wives whose proscribed husbands had succeeded in getting drunk had had the hell beat out of them.

The traditions of the community required everyone to like work or say that he did. A good man did not shrink from the tasks of pure drudgery — pitching hay, pulling a crosscut saw, forking manure. But not everyone could sustain the required reputation. A few got started later in the morning than others, were tolerant of thistle and fallen fences, had to go more often to town or yielded more readily to unpleasant weather or the notion that wives were expendable. They often compounded their felony with excuses — unshod horses, lumbago, broken tools — which everyone knew to be bogus.

This did not lead to automatic exclusion. As noted, our next-door neighbor was Bert McCallum. His house, unpainted and surrounded by tall, spare spruce, was on the west of his farm; ours, sheltered by friendlier maples, was on the east side of ours so that we were only a couple of minutes apart. Bert was unquestionably lazy. His barns were in disrepair; something of importance fell off his buildings each year and was never nailed back. His agriculture involved the minimum expenditure of energy; the result in everything from weeds to drainage was deplorable. But Bert was almost everyone's best friend. He was a small man with merry eyes and a quick laugh. Though bald in principle, wispy locks of undernourished hair strayed over his head at random. His mind was well-stored with information on a large number of practical matters — how to handle an unruly horse, give it emergency aid, shingle a shed, or prescribe for piles. He always handled the stacking of the straw which was the one skilled job at a threshing. His instinct indeed was to be helpful on everyone's problems except his own. He was an authority on all of the things, interesting, amusing, ridiculous and mildly obscene, that had happened in the township in the previous twenty years. His house, such of it as remained, was a kind of informal neighborhood club, a place where on a winter evening anyone might drop in. Bert sat in his sock feet by the stove and made everyone welcome. Unlike many good conversationalists he seemed on occasion to enjoy listening.

Yet Bert only narrowly escaped the consequences of his indolence. It was discussed and in degree condemned. But there were always people — my father was one — who turned the conversation to Bert's virtues which everyone had to concede. So he was allowed to escape with the reputation of being a little too easy-going. But a lesser man would have been convicted and lesser men were. About a mile from our place on Willey's Sideroad near the school was an exceptionally devout citizen who prayed and read the Scriptures every morning. His piety, which was very rare among the Scotch, was supposed to be what kept him from getting onto his fields at a decent hour. It did not earn him forgiveness, at least among the mortal. He was considered to be of no account; the bolder children, sensing that they had a duty to perform, shouted "Lazy Jim" at him on their way home from school.

The most interesting ground for exclusion was ignorance. Most societies are reluctant so to label a man; they would more readily call him a sex fiend or a crook. This is because people are wary of the reputation of intellectual arrogance. The Scotch were subject to no such fears. If a man lacked information or the ability to put knowledge to useful purpose, this deficiency was part of the community consensus. In consequence, it paid him no attention and denied him respect. He might talk but no one listened. From an early age we knew that certain people were simply dismissed from consideration as ignorant.

If a man didn't make sense, the Scotch felt it was misplaced politeness to try to keep him from knowing it. Better that he be aware of his reputation for this would encourage reticence which goes well with stupidity. And there is advantage in having the unwary and undiscriminating on notice. The Scotch were strikingly immune to demagogy. One reason was the total lack of hesitation in ascribing ignorance to demagogues. Potential followers were warned from the outset.

As a small personal footnote, I have never thought the practice of the Scotch in this respect entirely wrong. As a result I have rarely managed to avoid telling the intellectually obtuse what I feel they ought to know. Even when I have remained silent, I have usually succeeded in conveying an impression. It shows the influence of upbringing. It is not a formula for personal popularity or political success and, for a diplomat, it can complicate relations with the State Department.

I turn now to the characteristics which distinguished the highest class, the Men of Standing.

v

To achieve distinction in this community, one needed to have all of the normal requirements of membership in something more than merely adequate amount. A Man of Standing was likely to have more than a hundred acres, although land in large amounts did a man no good. The McMillan boys who farmed, rather badly, a large, flat and poorish area near Dutton got no extra credit for their acres. A Man of Standing had, as a matter of course, to be strictly sober, a diligent worker and a competent farmer. Beyond these necessary but by no means sufficient conditions were the special factors which, depending on circumstance, assisted a man up this ladder.

Regrettably perhaps, family was one. No one would have dreamed of suggesting that one clan was inferior to another, and certainly none would have conceded it. Yet it was tacitly agreed that some were better. The McDiarmids, Fergusons, Blacks, McAlpines, McCrimmons, Elliotts and a goodly number of McKillops were of this elite. So, I am obliged to say, were the Galbraiths. We were strongly cautioned against suggesting our superiority and, as a youngster, I found this a baffling restraint. For a long while, I swung between disavowing it and apologizing for it. Neither seemed a wholly satisfactory solution.

Size was also an important crutch. The Men of Standing were usually, although not invariably, very large. In this, the Scotch were not alone; most societies favor tall men and discriminate against the short and, since this seems manifestly unfair, a conspiracy of silence covers the whole thing. The short man does show that he is aware of his disadvantage for he rarely encounters a tall man without inquiring how he finds beds that fit, what he does in a railway birth or a modern automobile, or how is the weather up there. These are passive admissions of inferiority. The tall man never dreams of replying in kind — of asking the small man how he reaches up to tie his shoelaces — for he senses that his friend is struggling under a handicap and is too decent to mention it. In 1944 in commenting on his forthcoming contest with Thomas E. Dewey, Franklin Roosevelt said that people would always vote for the big man with the little dog in preference to the little man with the big dog. So, of course, they did.

The superior confidence which people repose in the tall man is well merited. Being tall, he is more visible than other men and being more visible, he is much more closely watched. In consequence, his behavior is far better than that of smaller men. Along with the Galbraiths, many of the Blacks, McDiarmids and McKillops were very tall.

Animals were also used by the Scotch as a social lever and more intelligently than in most societies.

Almost instinctively people turn to animals, alive or dead, to advance their position but the strategy in doing so is poorly understood. Men and women who sense their inferiority seek to compensate by getting the support of superior horses, dogs or dead mink. They often succeed only in suggesting the contrast. Nothing so accentuates a used skin, desiccated hair, fibrous breasts, angular knees and gnarled legs as a rich and glossy fur coat. At horse shows, the crowd subconsciously compares the slope-browed and slack-chinned men who ride horses with the magnificent beasts that carry them.

However, distinguished animals add to the distinction of distinguished people. This the Scotch understood. The average clansman had average livestock and avoided subjecting himself to unfavorable comparisons. Those who felt able to run the risk had good livestock and were admired for their judgment. The Scotch were not especially fond of horses and they detested dairy cattle. A good herd of beef cattle — Shorthorns, Aberdeen Angus or Herefords — was the mark of a distinguished family. Good sheep and good collie dogs also added to a man's position.

VI

The decisive source of esteem, the obverse of that which led to exclusion for ignorance, was information and the ability and willingness to put it to sensible use. This was, by all odds, the most admired trait. It was partly a matter of education and even those clansmen who considered education unnecessary for their own families and likely to inculcate an aversion to manual labor deferred to it in others. But education was only important if combined with good sense. It was, if anything, a handicap if combined with a tendency to suggest silly or extravagant courses of action. The community did not suffer fools gladly. It liked educated fools least of all.

But neither was it sufficient merely to make good sense. There were quite a few men who were well informed and wise but who never got beyond a statement of their views. Only a thin line divides the articulate man of wisdom from the windbag. The Scotch expected a man to prove his wisdom by putting it to useful purpose.

And his useful wisdom could not be confined to such areas of immediate or ultimate self-interest as his own farm or church. A man needed to act on improvement of the roads, the promotion of telephone service, the cooperative purchases of binder twine, or the management of the Wallacetown Fair. He should certainly serve on the Township Council. It was also important that in all his actions he bear in mind his neighbors' concern for saving money.

The Men of Standing had, in short, to earn their esteem. This had a highly practical aspect. Every community needs a great many communal services. To pay for them is expensive; and only a poor class of talent is available for money. By rewarding such work with honor and esteem, the very best men can be had for nothing. Only a minority of the Scotch were susceptible to such blandishment. But those who were not sensed the importance of according it to those who were. Thus, it was a very good thing to be a Man of Standing and a very good thing to have them in sufficient supply.

*A*fter reading these chapters from The Scotch, it is impossible not to wonder how the narrow dirt road out of Iona Station could lead to Washington, war-prostrated Germany, New Delhi, Peking and the eight-lane highways of the world.

In a piece written for a volume entitled Let There Be Light and created for an anniversary of the University of California, where he took his graduate degree, Galbraith tells of his graduate years and by inference begins the story of the road from Iona Station. Here are some passages from that short essay.

Berkeley in the Thirties[1]

ONE DAY in the autumn of 1930 I was gazing at the notice board in the post office of the main men's residence at the Ontario Agricultural College at Guelph in Canada, where I was then a

[1] "Berkeley in the Thirties," from *Economics, Peace and Laughter* (London: André Deutsch, 1971), pp. 336–352. Previously appeared in *The Atlantic Monthly* (June, 1969).

[46]

senior. It was usually an unrewarding vision but on this day it advertised a number of research assistantships at the Giannini Foundation of Agricultural Economics at the University of California. The annual stipend was $720 for unmarried scholars. I copied down the details and applied. Sometime later I received a letter from George Peterson, Associate Professor of Agricultural Economics, saying that I had been selected. I was surprised and so were my professors, who detested me and thought the people at Berkeley were crazy. I quickly accepted; in that second year of the Great Depression the monthly salary of sixty dollars, if not princely, was by far the best offer of any kind I had. In fact it was the only offer of any kind I had. From that day on the University of California has engaged my affection as no other institution — educational, public or pecuniary — with which I have ever been associated.

One Sunday afternoon in the summer of 1968, with my wife and oldest son (who followed me to be an assistant at the University of California Law School) I strolled across the California campus — over Strawberry Creek, by the Campanile, down by the Library, out Sather Gate. I was taught, as were most of my generation, that no one should allow himself the weak luxury of sentiment or even emotion. To this day when I write "Love" at the end of a letter I always remind myself that it is only modern affectation, in all respects a matter of form. I was suddenly overwhelmed by the thought that I loved this place — the paths, trees, flowers, buildings, even the new ones. I was deeply embarrassed.

In the thirties, for some reason related either to the eccentricities of the California crop year or climate, the university opened in August. Accordingly in July of 1931 I borrowed $500 from an aunt, one of the few members of our rural family still to command such capital, and, almost literally, set sail for California. I boarded the steamer which plied between Port Stanley on the north shore of Lake Erie and Cleveland, where, by prearrangement with our local jeweler and oculist, I met his nephew who had a graduate fellowship at California in astronomy. At five o'clock the following morning we set out in the 1926 Oakland automobile my companion had acquired for this trip. The car was in terrible condition and almost immediately got worse. To save money he had bought a five-gallon gasoline tin and a one-gallon container for oil so that we could stock up on these products whenever, as happened in those days, our path led us through a region being ravaged by a price war. Such at least was the theory.

About thirty miles out of Cleveland my friend stopped to check the gas (the gauge was broken) and look at the oil. The car absorbed the whole five gallons of gasoline and the whole gallon of oil. For the rest of the trip we averaged around a quarter gallon of gas and a half pint of oil to the mile. To this day I shudder at the cost.

The journey took ten days not counting twenty-four hours at Casey, Iowa, where we were laid up with a broken connecting rod. That, too, had a lasting effect. It was raining hard, and as we waited for the repairs, we listened to the local farmers, who used the garage as a club, discuss Hoover. I became a life-long Democrat. It was about six o'clock on a bright summer evening when we got to Berkeley and drove up Bancroft Way to the International House. The hills behind were very bleached and sere but the low sun glistened on the live oaks and the green lawns and the masses of pink geraniums, which elsewhere are only geraniums but in Berkeley are the glory of the whole city. The sun also lit up the vast yellow-buff facade of the International House with the large Spanish arches of the portico below. We passed into the great hall, then gleaming new, and combining the best mission style with the finest in Moorish revival. I thought it a place of unimaginable splendor.

Eventually the International House was to prove a bit too expensive even for one who earned sixty dollars a month and was, as a result, one of the more affluent members of the community. My capital had been depleted by that terrible car. But for the first few months at Berkeley this nice Rockefeller benefaction — it had counterparts in New York, Chicago, Paris and Tokyo — housing several hundred students of both sexes from the United States and many foreign lands, was to be my window on the Berkeley world. Never before had I been so happy.

The world on which I looked down could not be recognized in important respects by Mario Savio[2] or his successors. I must stress that I had just emerged from the Ontario Agricultural College and this could have distorted my vision. Once I was asked by *Time* magazine about this academy; I replied, thoughtlessly, that in my day it was certainly the cheapest and possibly the worst in the English-speaking world. This was tactless and wrong and caused dissatisfaction even after many years. (No one questioned my statement that the college was inexpensive.) At OAC students were expected to keep and also to know and cherish their place. Leadership in the student

2 Mario Savio was a student radical leader at the University of California at Berkeley during the disturbances of 1964.

body was solidly in the hands of those who combined an outgoing anti-intellectualism with a sound interest in livestock. This the faculty thought right. Anyone who questioned the established agricultural truths, many of which were wildly wrong, was sharply rebuked, and if he offended too often he was marked down as a troublemaker. A fair number of faculty members had effectively substituted the affable and well-clipped manner and moustache of the professional country-man for the admitted tedium of science. But unquestionably the place did build health.

At Berkeley I suddenly encountered professors who knew their subject and, paradoxically, invited debate on what they knew. They also had time to talk at length with graduate students and even to come up to International House to continue the conversation. I first discovered at Berkeley from Henry Erdman, who had until recently been the head of the Agricultural Economics Department, and How-ard Tolley, who had just succeeded him as the Director of the Gian-nini Foundation, that a professor might like to be informed on some subject by a graduate student — might not just be polite but pleased. So profound was that impression that I never stopped informing people thereafter. The pleasure I have thus given has been very great. (Howard Tolley, after a year or two, went on to Washington to be-come head of the Agricultural Adjustment Administration under FDR. I shall mention him again in a moment. In 1968, after the elapse of a third of a century, I was back in Berkeley one Sunday to urge the case and, more important, since everyone was persuaded, to raise money for Eugene McCarthy. I was not at all surprised to see Henry Erdman in the front row. He believed strongly in keeping informed.)

Although we had stipends, we agricultural economists were second-class citizens. Our concern was with the prices of cling peaches, which were then appalling; the financial condition of the Merced irrigation district, which was equally bad; the prune industry, which was chronically indigent; and other such useful subjects. I earned my research stipend by tramping the streets of Los Angeles and also Oakland and San Jose to ascertain the differing preferences as to pack-age and flavor — sage, orange blossom, clover — of Mexican, Jewish, Negro and (as we then thought of them) ordinary white Americans, for honey. No differences emerged. This kind of work was not well regarded by the nonagricultural, or pure, economists. Thorstein Veblen was still being read with attention in Berkeley in the thirties. He distinguishes between esoteric and exoteric knowledge, the first having the commanding advantage of being without "economic or industrial effect." It is this advantage, he argues, which distinguishes the higher learning from the lower. Ours, obviously, was the lower.

We suffered from another handicap. Agriculturalists, in an indistinct way, were considered to be subject to the influence of the California Farm Bureau Federation and, much worse, of the opulent and perpetually choleric baronage which comprised the Associated Farmers of California. Actually our subordination was not all that indistinct. Both organizations told the Dean of the College of Agriculture and the Director of Extension what they needed in the way of research and also conclusions. They were heard with attention, even respect. No one was ever told to shape his scholarly work accordingly; men were available who did it as a matter of course.

The nonagricultural economists, whatever their differences in other matters of doctrine, were united in regarding the farmers, even more than the bankers or oilmen, as an all-purpose class enemy. In time I acquired a certain reputation in economic theory and other branches of impractical knowledge and also as a rather circumspect critic of the agricultural establishment. So I was accorded an honorary status as a scholar, my agricultural handicaps notwithstanding. I was then even more happy.

The Department of Economics at Berkeley has never been considered quite as eminent as that at Harvard. The reason is that the best Californians have always come to Harvard. As this is written of the twenty-three full professors of economics at Harvard no fewer than seven, nearly one-third, were recruited at one stage or another in their careers from the University of California at Berkeley. And economics at Berkeley has long had a marked personality. In the early thirties, years before the Keynesian revolution, Leo Rogin was discussing Keynes with a sense of urgency that made his seminars seem to graduate students the most important things then happening in the world. I learned Alfred Marshall from Ewald Grether, who taught with a drillmaster's precision for which I have ever since been grateful. Marshall is the quintessence of classical economics and much of what he says is wrong. But no one can know what is wrong if he does not understand it first. My memory also goes back to M. M. Knight's seminar in economic history, a gifted exercise in irrelevancy. Once Robert Gordon Sproul, then the president of the university, had said in one of his booming speeches that, after all, a university was run for the students. Knight, a brother of the even more noted Frank H. Knight of the University of Chicago, attacked this doctrine for two full sessions. A university, he argued with indignation, was run for the faculty and, to affirm the point, he announced his intention of introducing a resolution at some early faculty meeting to exclude the students from the library. They got in the way.

We graduate students were also fond of Paul Taylor, who spoke out unfailingly for the small farmer in California; Charles Gulick, who spoke out for the farm workers, who then as now aroused great animosity and a measure of righteous anger for wanting a union and a living wage; and Robert Brady, who was the friend of the consumer and other lost causes. Brady taught courses in the business cycle and set great store by exhaustive bibliographic research. One of my friends met this requirement by going to the card catalogue in the library and copying into the appendix of his thesis everything that appeared there under the headings Cycle, Business, and Cycle, Trade. Brady sent over for some of the latter items which were new to him and they turned out to be works on bicycles, tricycles and motorcycles published by the Cycle Trades of America. We always heard there was quite a scene.

A few years after I left Berkeley I became deputy head of the Office of Price Administration in charge of the World War II price controls. This was a post with unlimited patronage — eventually, as I recall, I had some seventeen thousand assistants. In addition to Mr. and Mrs. Richard Nixon and many other promising people, numerous of my former professors, including Howard Tolley, Harry Wellman (later the acting president of the university) and Robert Brady turned up on our staff. Brady had scarcely arrived before he was assaulted hip and thigh by the Dies Committee — later better known as HUAC and now as HSC — for saying in a book on German fascism that American capitalism was only technically better. To complicate matters further, Dies had got hold of the edition published by the Left Book Club in England. It had something on the cover about not being for public sale. I handled the defense on the Hill with the handicap of knowing that everything I said in favor of Bob would immediately be used against me. Brady later attributed his troubles to the oil companies and said I was their tool. He had proposed that people conserve oil by not draining the crankcase for the duration of the war or ten thousand miles, whichever was less. I did not endorse the idea. This was mostly because with everything else it never got to my attention. But if it had, I might have remembered that Oakland car and the way it changed itself and wondered if it would have made much difference.

The graduate students with whom I associated in the thirties were uniformly radical and the most distinguished were Communists. I listened to them eagerly and would have liked to join both the conversation and the Party but here my agricultural background was a real handicap. It meant that, as a matter of formal Marxian doctrine, I was politically immature. Among the merits of capitalism to Marx was the fact that it rescued men from the idiocy of rural life. I had only very recently been retrieved. I sensed this bar and I knew also that my pride would be deeply hurt by rejection. So I kept outside. There was possibly one other factor. Although I recognized that the system could not and should not survive, I was enjoying it so much that, secretly, I was a little sorry.

In the ensuing twenty years many of those I most envied were accorded an auto-da-fé by HUAC, James Eastland or the late Joseph R. McCarthy. Their lives were ruined. Phrases about the unpredictable graces of God kept constantly crossing my mind.

One man who did not get called by Joe McCarthy was Robert Merriman, a vital and popular graduate student and teaching assistant who came down to Berkeley from Nevada in the early thirties. As an undergraduate he had been wholesome and satisfactory and even took an interest in ROTC. But Berkeley had its effect and so (as he told friends) did the great waterfront strike of 1934, where he saw soldiers deployed against the strikers. Hugh Thomas' brilliant book, *The Spanish Civil War*, tells the rest of his story. Interrupting a traveling fellowship in Europe in 1936, Merriman went to Spain, where (one assumes as an uncalculated consequence of ROTC) he commanded the Abraham Lincoln Battalion on the Jarama and then went on through many battles to be chief of staff of the XV International Brigade. A major and by now long a veteran, he was killed (possibly executed after capture by the Nationalists) on the Aragon front in 1938. He must have been the bravest of our contemporaries; he so impressed Ernest Hemingway that he became in part the model for Robert Jordan (the professor from Montana in *For Whom the Bell Tolls*). The California campus has ornaments for lesser heroes who died nearer home for more fashionable beliefs. There are some naïve, haunting lines written by John Depper, a British volunteer, of the Battle of Jarama that might serve:

> *Death stalked in the olive trees*
> *Picking his men*
> *His leaden finger beckoned*
> *Again and again.*

A year ago in Chicago I was on a television discussion program with Robert Merriam, a White House aide to President Eisenhower and once Republican candidate for mayor of Chicago against Richard Daley. He said that for many years he had been investigated assiduously by the FBI because of his name. Merriman was not completely forgotten.

I would not wish it thought that our life in the thirties was limited to politics and great matters of the mind. One roamed through San Francisco, climbed Mt. Diablo, went up to the Sierras, where someone was always imagining that the Depression might make panning gold profitable again, and consumed (I most diffidently) alcohol stolen from the chemistry laboratories and mixed with grapefruit juice and, after repeal, a blended whiskey of negligible cost called, to the best of my memory, Crab Orchard. I have difficulty in believing that the latter-day intoxicants and suffocants do worse. In any case, we were all greatly impressed one night when a girl who had been over-stimulated by these products ceremoniously removed her clothes in the patio of the International House and spent the late hours of the evening doing orgiastic obeisance to the heavens above and, more than incidentally, to the windows of the men's rooms around.

In those days people came to Berkeley from all over the world and, naturally enough, no one ever left. The reasons were social and economic as well as cultural. As a student, teaching fellow, or even a nonstudent, one could be a respected member of the *community* and it counted against a person not at all to have no income. But the moment one left Berkeley he became a member of the great army of the unemployed. As such, he was an object of sympathy and lost his self-respect. In general, graduate students avoided taking their final degrees lest they be under temptation, however slight, to depart. When, in 1933 and 1934, jobs suddenly and unexpectedly became available in Washington — NRA, PWA, AAA[3] — almost everyone got busy and finished up his thesis. Even my Communist friends reacted favorably to the exorbitant salaries which economists commanded in the New Deal.

Among the people who appeared in Berkeley, my mind returns to a slim, boyish-looking girl who, improbably in light of her build, claimed to have been in Texas Guinan's[4] chorus before turning to

[3] Spelled out, these New Deal agencies were the National Recovery Administration, Public Works Administration, and Agricultural Adjustment Administration.
[4] A famous figure in the Prohibition years, Texas Guinan welcomed customers to her gaudy nightclubs with the greeting, "Hello, sucker."

higher learning. More recently she had been in Tahiti and then in Bora Bora, where she had gone native and had as proof a comprehensive suntan. Now she was doing graduate work in anthropology on the basis of credentials, partly forged and partly imaginary, from a nonexistent undergraduate institution in the city of New York. I fell deeply in love with her; on our second or third date, as we were walking up Strawberry Canyon back of the stadium, she asked me if I thought it right, as an economist, to be wasting both her time and mine. Nothing in my Canadian and Calvinist background had prepared me for such a personal concept of efficiency. A little later, after an all-night party in San Francisco, she insisted on being taken to the Santa Fe Station. She had just remembered that, on the day following, she was scheduled to marry a banker in New Mexico. Much later I met her in New York. She was just back from Haiti (not Tahiti) and was preparing to marry a Pan Am pilot. She told me she was working on her memoirs and was being encouraged to the task by Westbrook Pegler.[5] I was by then a promising young member of the Harvard faculty. I first worried that she would publish her recollections and then, after a time, that she would not.

Though we graduate students expected the revolution very soon and planned to encourage it, we did not expect any help from the Berkeley undergraduates. Not that they would oppose — they would simply, as usual, be unaware that anything was happening. A singular accomplishment of American higher education, as one reflects on it, was the creation of a vast network of universities, public and private, which for a century, until the sixties, caused no one any political embarrassment of any kind. In other countries they created trouble from time to time, but not here. A control system which subtly suggested that whatever the students most wanted to do — i.e., devote themselves to football, basketball, fraternities, college tradition, rallies, hell-raising, a sentimental concern for the old alma mater and imaginative inebriation — was what they should do, was basic to this peace. The alumni rightly applauded this control system and so, to an alarming extent, did the faculty. An occasional nonpolitical riot was condoned and even admired; some deeper adult instinct suggested that it was a surrogate for something worse. At Berkeley in the thirties this system was still working perfectly. Com-

---

[5] A popular and controversial syndicated columnist, Westbrook Pegler became increasingly reactionary, and finally almost paranoid, in his views after the mid-1930s.

ing up Bancroft Way to the International House of an evening one saw the fraternity men policing up the lawns of their houses or sitting contentedly in front. Walking along Piedmont at night one heard the shouts of laughter from within, or occasional bits of song or what Evelyn Waugh correctly described as the most evocative and nostalgic of all the sounds of an aristocracy at play, the crash of breaking glass. Here were men with a secure position in society and who knew it and who were content. On a Friday night they would do their duty at the pep rally shaming the apathetic; on Saturday they would be at the stadium and on Saturday night, win or lose, they joined with the kindred souls of earlier generations, men they did not hesitate to call brother, to whoop it up as a college man was meant to do. The *Daily Californian* was the approving chronicle of this world — of the Big Game, the Axe, the cards turned in unison in the cheering section to depict an Indian or a bear, the campaign to send the band to Oregon to support the team. In 1932 Norman Thomas came to the campus and spoke to a small assembly in a classroom. Neither Hoover nor Roosevelt dreamed of favoring us. Hoover did speak to a vast audience of indigent citizens from the local Hooverville down on the Oakland flats and was cheered uproariously when he told them that, at long last, the Depression was over. They had not heard. Only once was there a suggestion of student involvement. The financial condition of the state of California in those days was appalling. State workers were being paid with tax-anticipation certificates. Even the governor, James (Sunny Jim) Rolph, sensed that something was wrong. In 1932 and 1933 there were threats to cut the university budget. When it seemed that these were serious, the students were encouraged to assemble and ask their relatives and friends to petition their legislators to relent. Perhaps that was the camel's nose, the seed of the Frankenstein. As to persuading the legislature, however, it was considered less important than a promise by the university to retrench voluntarily and to begin with the Agricultural Extension (Farm Adviser) Service. No one said so but we agriculturalists certainly felt that our pragmatic approach to scholarship had paid off for everybody.

In the 1960s Dean Rusk, Lyndon Johnson, General Westmoreland, Lewis Hershey and Ronald Reagan accomplished what not even the most talented of our teachers had ever hoped to achieve. The undergraduates became politically concerned. When the time comes to award honors to those who made our universities the center of our political life, it will be a great injustice if the men of affirmative, as distinct from the negative, influence are featured. Now, I would suppose, Berkeley is the most intense intellectual and political community in the world; perhaps, indeed, it is the nearest thing to a total university community in modern times. As such it would be silly to suppose that it could be altogether tranquil. Often in these past years, following some exceptionally imaginative outbreak on Telegraph Avenue, I've heard a colleague say: "You know that sort of thing could never happen here." I've always been too polite to say why I agreed. And the statement could be wrong. As other university communities succumb to the concerns so long a commonplace at Berkeley, they, too, cease to be tranquil.

Not everyone is as restrained as I am about Berkeley. A few weeks ago I shared a seat on an airplane with a young colleague newly recruited, like so many before him, from the University of California. I asked him if he missed it. He replied, "Christ, yes! At Berkeley you worked all morning in the library and then at noon you went out into the sun and there was always a demonstration going on or something. Man, that was living!"

The days passed. During my second year my stipend was raised to seventy dollars a month, allowing me to save a little money and also to have a larger social life. Then in my third year I was sent to Davis, which, for the benefit of non-Californians, is in the Sacramento Valley not far from Sacramento. It is now a full-fledged university but in those days it was the center of agricultural research and instruction too closely associated with orchards, insects and the soil to be carried on at Berkeley. It cultivated, in other words, the lowest of the lower learning. At Davis I was the head of the Departments of Economics, of Agricultural Economics, of Accounting and of Farm Management. I also gave instruction in all of these subjects and, with the exception of one elderly dean who gave lectures to nondegree students, I was also the total teaching staff in these disciplines. During the year I also had time to write my Ph.D. thesis and I do not recall that I was especially rushed. Certainly such was my love for Berkeley that I went there every weekend. At Davis my pay was $1,800 and I was able (by way of repayment of my own college debts to my family) to send my younger sister to college.

The Davis students were also highly stable. My course in beginning economics was required for some majors. The scholars so compelled shuffled in at the beginning of the hour, squeezed their yellow corduroy-clad bottoms into the classroom chairs, listened with indifference for an hour and then, by now conveying an impression of manfully suppressed indignation, shuffled out. Only once in the entire year did I arouse their interest. I gave some support to the textbook case for lower tariffs. Coming as they did from the sugar beet fields, olive orchards, cattle ranches and other monuments to the protective tariff, they knew that was wrong and told me so. My best remembered student that year was a boy who had an old Ford runabout who spent his weekends putting up signs on the highways which warned motorists to repent and prepare at a fairly early date to meet their God. In response on an examination to a question about the nature of money, he stuck resolutely to the proposition that it (not the love of money but money itself) was the root of all evil. I tried to reason with him, but in vain. So I flunked him, for his contention seemed to me palpably untrue. That was my only personal encounter in those years with any form of student dissent.

One day in the spring of 1934 I was in Berkeley putting the finishing touches on my thesis. A Western Union boy came into the room with a telegram offering me an instructorship at Harvard for the following year at $2,400. I had not the slightest idea of accepting, for I was totally happy at California. But my rapid advance in economic well-being, plus no doubt the defense of my faith against that student, had made me avaricious and I had heard that one won advances in academic life by flashing offers from other universities. I let it be known over the weekend that "Harvard was after me," and, on the following Monday, went by appointment to see the Dean of the College of Agriculture to bargain. I carried the telegram in my hand. The Dean, a large, handsome and highly self-confident man named Claude B. Hutchison, who later became the Mayor of Berkeley, was excellently informed on all matters in the college and his intelligence system had not failed him on this occasion. He congratulated me warmly on my offer, gave me the impression that he thought Harvard was being reckless with its money and said that, of course, I should go. In a moment I realized to my horror I had no choice. I couldn't now plead to stay at two-thirds the price. The great love of my life was over. I remember wondering, as I went out, if I had been right to flunk that nut.

BOOK

II

*The Road
from
Iona Station*

PART ONE

DIRT ROAD TO BLACKTOP

SELECTION *3*

---

*W*hat follows does indeed take us far from Iona
Station and far from student days whether at the Ontario College
of Agriculture or the University of California at Berkeley, and in the
last selection of this Book II, far also from Candide, that troublesome
young skeptic who was awkward with young women, irritating to his
professors and perhaps even a bit naive in his attack upon the citadels
of established economic theory.

Via Harvard and more briefly Princeton, the road leads out to
Washington, D.C., New York, war-torn Germany and back once more
to New York and, after a decade's absence, to Harvard. The traveler
who returned was not quite he who departed. Along the way, no doubt
as the product of an unusual experience in the practical application
of economic theory, he had perceived a line of reasoning that could
resolve the unsightly contradiction that separated visible fact from
the accepted economic view.

One thing, however, one suspects that Candide did not yet understand: that he who finds a simple road to peace is seldom thanked by
the generals of the opposing armies.

During the World War II years, Galbraith served as economic
adviser to the National Defense Advisory Committee and later as

[61]

deputy head of the Office of Price Administration. Immediately thereafter he became a member of the board of editors of Fortune magazine. In 1945 on leave of absence from Fortune and with the War Department he spent five months overseas studying the effects of Allied bombing, seeing the war criminals and interrogating Albert Speer at length. Soon after his return he wrote for Fortune a series of articles on what he had seen and heard. Here is one of those articles chosen as the most general of the group for its picture of the economist as military industrial strategist and also for its study of technique for the administering of a highly complex industrial machine in an intricately advanced society under conditions imposed by a continuously compounded crisis.

While still at Berkeley Galbraith had broadened his base in agricultural economics to include the whole field of general economics, both applied and theoretical. He was then admirably qualified to perform the duties assigned to him by our war-time government. The Fortune series was his first venture into writing for the general public on economic affairs both national and international.

Germany Was Badly Run [1]

During the war citizens of Allied countries and their governments alike shared the conviction that Germany was applying every ounce of its resources to victory and doing it with ruthless efficiency. Since V-E Day, when Germany's wartime records and officials became available, some surprising discoveries have been made. German industrial mobilization, especially in the early years of the war, was by no means complete, and German war management was no model of efficiency. The following article on Germany's war management was written by Fortune Editor John Kenneth Galbraith, who recently returned from Germany after serving as a director of the U.S. Strategic

[1] "Germany Was Badly Run," *Fortune* (December, 1945), pp. 173–178, 196–200.

Bombing Survey; while there he supervised the collection of Germany's war-production records and the examination of production officials to assess the effect of the Allied air war on the German economy.[2]

THE VICTORY over German fascism won't be complete until the notion that the Nazis fought a model war has been liquidated. They did not. The Germans were no better organizers than their democratic opposition. They were no more efficient. They may not have been so good.

Germany was the first western power to start preparing for war but it was among the last to see the importance of full mobilization. The preparations themselves were less formidable than was supposed at the time. In 1938, before the Munich agreement, a group of high generals made plans to arrest Hitler to prevent a war with the Czech Army because they didn't believe they were strong enough to win. According to Colonel General Halder, then Chief of Staff, the *Putsch* was called off because the day before it was scheduled to occur news came that Chamberlain was flying to Berchtesgaden and the danger of war was thus averted.

When Hitler announced at the beginning of the Polish campaign that he had spent 90 billion marks for armaments he was, for once, widely believed. The records show, however, that his reputation for mendacity is intact; he inflated the figure on expenditures by between a third and a half. At the time of the attack on Poland, Germany had but three armored (panzer) divisions with a total of about 600 tanks; army transport, communications, and the supply organization all had to be improvised. The German government statistician who had charge of armament statistics in the closing years of the war wrote in a private history of the preparations: "Public views of the scale of armaments in the last prewar years . . . were very much exaggerated. The German Government of the time did nothing to contradict these exaggerated ideas, on the contrary they probably seemed to it desirable propaganda, for they produced an illusion of warlike strength that in reality was not available." In comparison with what the opposition had done, however, Germany's preparations *were* formidable. What it had was on hand, not on order.

After war broke out in 1939 German war production increased but slightly. In the last half of 1939 Germany was making about sixty

[2] Original article headnote.

tanks a month. In 1940 production averaged 136 a month; 1,643 tanks were made in the whole year and 3,801 in 1941. England, popularly believed to be far behind in production, made 1,397 tanks in 1940 and 4,844 in 1941. The U.S. made about 5,000 in 1941. The story of aircraft is much the same: Germany produced only 8,000 combat planes in 1940, the year the Luftwaffe was defeated over southern England, and only 9,500 the following year. England produced more aircraft in both years than Germany did, and in 1941 U.S. output passed Germany's. For most other types of arms the comparisons are similar. Except for the manpower drafts of the Wehrmacht, German civilians through 1941 were little affected by the war. Civilian consumption, at record levels just prior to the war, fell by less than 10 percent in 1940 and 1941.

The principal explanation is that the Nazi leaders were supremely confident of their superiority when the war broke out and the early campaigns confirmed their optimism. The Polish and French campaigns were cheap and easy and did not seriously deplete the sizable stocks of finished munitions that had been built up. After France was defeated, even though the war with England was still on, the Germans cut back production. The state of mind of the German leaders at the time may, perhaps, be compared with that in the U.S. after V-E Day. The French Army, which they considered the major enemy, had been eliminated. Although a secondary enemy was still to be polished off, victory seemed in hand. The Germans actually viewed the further campaign against England and even the later attack on Russia as exploitation of a victory that had already been achieved.

This overconfidence may well have cost the Germans the Battle of Britain. It is now clear that the battle was called off because the Luftwaffe was losing more planes and pilots than it could afford. The R.A.F., meanwhile, was badly exhausted; only a few planes and battle-weary pilots were left. If the Germans had been liberally supplied with reserves they might have finished off the remaining British flyers.

THE LESSON IN TOTAL WAR

After Germany turned east it was to pay the full price for overconfidence. The decision to attack Russia was made in November, 1940, seven months before the German armies marched, yet as the official statistician subsequently commented, "No preparations had been made to obtain a genuinely large-scale increase of armament production." Plans called for defeating Russia in four months, another cheap and easy blitzkrieg that required only limited effort. The first three months of the Russian campaign went entirely according to plan. In the early autumn of 1941, after sweeping victories at both ends of the long front, Hitler concluded that this war too was over. He again ordered a cutback in production and authorized reconversion. Even demobilization of some troops was ordered. Field commanders were slow to release men, and before any were returned Germany was caught in the catastrophe at Moscow.

Moscow was a more decisive turning point in the war than Stalingrad. Whole German divisions lost their entire equipment. An enormous amount of transport was lost in the snow and cold and casualties were severe. Several hundred locomotives were ruined in what must have been the most spectacular freeze-up in all history. And this time Germany's stockpiles of weapons and ammunition were heavily depleted. Most important, there was no large current production out of which the losses could be quickly replaced.

Indeed, as a result of the cutbacks in the previous months production was still falling — the output of all weapons in December, 1941, was nearly 30 percent less than it had been the previous July. The U.S., in January, 1942, its first full month of war, had scarcely begun to arm; yet in that month German and U.S. production of armaments were in the aggregate about equal and Germany had been at war for more than two years. Germany was caught napping at Moscow at almost the same time as the U.S. was caught napping at Pearl Harbor.

The increases in German production that occurred after the defeat at Moscow are the best proof of the undermobilization in those early years. When the full extent of the defeat became apparent in Berlin the cutbacks of the previous autumn were rescinded and the German leaders called for strenuous efforts to repair the losses. German war production was never cut back again; it increased and continued to increase, in spite of bombing and the manpower drafts of the Wehrmacht, until mid-1944. In July, 1944, deliveries of all kinds of munitions, including aircraft and submarines, were more than three times as large as in January, 1942. Tank production had increased sixfold, airplane production more than threefold. Output of antiaircraft guns and ammunition and many other critical items had increased ten to twentyfold. These increases did not, however, occur all at once; expansion was at times slow and erratic and at no time was it enough. Civilian consumption in 1942 and 1943 remained about 80 percent of the prewar level, high enough to support an exceedingly comfortable standard of living. Even at the peak in 1944 German industry had reserves of plant, labor, and materials that were not being used for the war.

TEUTONIC INEFFICIENCY

Overconfidence was not the only trouble in the early years. When the war broke out German supply service was poorly organized; procurement was handled independently by each of the three branches of the Wehrmacht — the Army, Navy, and Air Force. In each service it was mainly in the hands of elderly or incompetent soldiers who, as in all peacetime armies, had been relegated to these tasks. Each service competed with the others in placing contracts; the industrialists played one against another on prices and deliveries. The services quarreled among themselves over allotments of raw materials and each one specified small differences in the gauge and caliber of its weapons and ammunition so that its stocks could not be appropriated by a sister service. Moreover, the administration of priorities and control over the civilian economy and basic industries such as steel were in yet another department, the Economics Ministry. This was an overstaffed and slow-moving bureaucracy headed by the somnambulant and bibulous Walther Funk.

In 1941, after nearly two years of war, Hitler made Fritz Todt, the efficient builder of the *Autobahnen* and the Westwall, a kind of coordinator of supply. This was a hlafway effort at reform: separate procurement and divided responsibility continued. In February, 1942, Todt was killed in an airplane crash and his successor was the now famous Albert Speer, Hitler's personal architect and redesigner of Berlin. He was thoroughly accomplished in jurisdictional warfare and eventually he succeeded in establishing a single supply ministry. It was the experience of every belligerent that without central control of procurement no effective scheduling of armament production to available plant and materials — in short no systematic planning of production — was possible. The U.S. learned this lesson slowly but Germany was just as slow. Not until 1943 did Speer finally maneuver Funk out of control of civilian production. And not until the winter of 1944 did he get control of Luftwaffe procurement; in Germany (as in Britain) expenditures for the Air Force and anti-aircraft defenses accounted for about half of all arms expenditure.

The Germans had the same division of authority between war production and manpower controls that caused trouble in Washington and they had no more success in working it out. The German manpower chief was Sauckel, Gauleiter of Thuringia and a particularly horrible specimen. Sauckel became a bitter enemy of Speer, and even in Berlin, where official bickering was a commonplace, their quarrels were notable. One feud, for example, was over the use of foreign labor. Sauckel had an unrestrained enthusiasm for bringing foreign workers to Germany; the vigor with which he chased down Frenchmen had won him the title in Berlin, of all places, of the "Father of the Maquis." Speer, on the other hand, believed it more efficient (the question of humanity did not enter) to use French workers in French factories, Belgian workers in Belgium, and so forth. For a time he promised workers in designated French factories that they would be immune from conscription if they labored faithfully for the Reich. Sauckel fixed that. In furtherance of his war with Speer he instructed his agents to make a special draft of workers so exempted.

In the U.S., official rows are usually settled when they get into the papers. Germany had no press to dramatize rows such as the one between Speer and Sauckel and bring them to a crisis. They continued their feud to the end — they were still denouncing each other when taken into custody. The only solution that would have satisfied either would have been to get the other into a concentration camp. Even Jesse Jones and Henry Wallace had more limited objectives.[3]

Germany suffered also from incompetent officials. As the experience of the U.S. and the United Kingdom showed, only the hard tasks of war show up the drones. In the U.S. and Great Britain the combing out of incompetents went on fairly continuously throughout the war. No similar weeding-out occurred in Germany. With such exceptions as Darré, the mad Minister of Agriculture, and Hess, the mad peacemaker, virtually all of Germany's prewar politicians were still in office in 1945. Most of them had been in office since 1933. The list includes Dr. Robert Ley, housing chief and head of the Labor Front, who, until his capture by the Allies, had been drunk for years. There was also Ribbentrop, in late years another notable drunk. He had been largely discredited by his behavior and by his assurance that the democracies would not go to war over Poland and would

[3] In Franklin Roosevelt's first administration, Henry A. Wallace was Vice President and head of the Economic Defense Board. Jesse H. Jones was U.S. Secretary of Commerce.

remain neutral in Germany's holy war against Russia. But he was still in office.

The list of incompetents includes Göring. During the last two years of the war his mismanagement of the Luftwaffe came as near as anything in Germany could come to an open scandal. He interfered erratically in procurement and tactics. Few if any of his subordinates seem to have had any faith in his leadership. Hitler was fully aware of the complaints against Göring and became mightily displeased with his Air Force. But Göring remained. German officials and generals agree that Hitler kept Göring because of personal loyalty, although Göring's prestige, the product of years of propaganda, probably made him difficult to fire. No military organization since Coxey's Army has been in such disesteem as the Luftwaffe in Germany in the closing months of the war. "We were like telephone poles," one German air general complained after his capture, "even the little dogs didn't respect us."

An old guard also continued to monopolize regional and local administration. During the war the power of the gauleiters increased greatly as they were assigned a wide variety of wartime tasks. Nearly all of the gauleiters were old party men — crude, ill-educated, political thugs. Many of them resisted efforts to close down nonessential industries in their gau or even efforts to move important and vulnerable industries to less dangerous locations. A number of them were among the most sybaritic rulers of modern times. Taking Göring and the other Berlin chiefs as their model, they lived lives of astonishing luxury and they had unlimited graft with which to pay the bill.

In the last two or three years of the war engineers and technicians were drawn from industry for wartime administration, especially for organizing war production. However, the Wilhelmstrasse was never engulfed by energetic volunteers as was Washington in 1941 and 1942. To intelligent men the Nazi Government was neither an attractive nor even a safe employer.

THE SOFT WAR

Speer, the arms minister, was a clear exception to the common run of German politicians, although Backe, the food minister, and Doenitz, the master of the submarines, seem also to have been efficient. Speer was a comparative newcomer in the Nazi high command; a tall, black-haired, and young-looking man of forty, he became with Hitler and Martin Bormann, Hess's successor as head of the party organization, one of the three most important civilians in Germany during the war. The threefold increase in war production between 1942 and 1944 added enormously to Speer's stature — and he took personal credit for the entire achievement.

This increase was impressive but Speer never succeeded in getting all Germany's manpower and resources into the war. The single most mystifying fact about German industry during the war is that most plants continued throughout to work one shift; in 1944 between 80 and 90 percent of all workers were on the first shift. Only a few high-priority industries worked multiple shifts. The airplane plants worked one shift until early 1944. The submarine yards were on one shift throughout. To black out the yards would have presented difficult but not insuperable problems. Each evening the great Blohm & Voss shipyards in Hamburg and the other submarine makers in Kiel and Wilhelmshaven closed down for the night. So far as one can determine, simple inertia was the most important reason for continuing single-shift operation. German industry was accustomed to one-shift operation and Germany's leaders didn't force the change. Long hours were not used as a substitute for two-shift operation, except in comparatively few industries. The average work week, popular myths in the U.S. to the contrary, was around fifty hours in 1944.

Germany was exceedingly well supplied with plant and machinery. If labor had been scarce, one-shift operations would be understandable. But there was no severe labor shortage. Though in the late years Germany was always shy of able-bodied Germans for the Wehrmacht, all Europe supplied manpower for industry and German employers agree that most of the foreign workers turned in a good day's work. There was also a large reserve of womanpower that was not mobilized. Germany had no women's military services comparable to the WAC or the WAVES or the women's auxiliaries in Britain. Except in agriculture, few women worked during the war; fewer women were employed in German industry in this war than in the last. "I was always disturbed," Munitions Minister Speer told Allied officials, "when I saw your magazines and their pictures of factories full of women." Germany had the rare distinction of being the one major belligerent that went through the war without a servant problem; it had 1,500,000 domestic servants in 1939 and 1,300,000 in 1944. In 1943 (over the protest of production officials) some 50,000

Ukrainian women were imported to make life easier for the German *Hausfrau*.

The failure to recruit women is attributable partly to the old Nazi doctrine that their place was in the home and the delivery room, but more to inertia and official laxity. The Berlin chiefs and the gauleiters weren't inclined to set an example by surrendering their own servants or mistresses or even their wives; the wives of the workers, allowed to decide for themselves, found it more comfortable to remain at home.

In July, 1944, after the Normandy breakthrough, Goebbels was named Plenipotentiary for Total War — for the total war that Germany's leaders and Germany's enemies had both supposed it had been fighting for nearly five years. The decree stated: "The *present* war situation makes incumbent the exhaustive use of all resources for the armed forces and armament." A noisy but apparently determined effort was made to get women, children, and also bank clerks, shop-keepers, and postmen into the war industries. It was too late. By the autumn of 1944 the German economy was disintegrating and, because of destruction of transport and factories, unemployment was actually appearing. A country that waited for the St. Lô breakthrough had waited too long.[4]

Germany did a better job of organizing its raw-materials supply than it did in utilizing its labor and plant. Prewar Germany had to import iron ore, copper, nickel, chrome, tungsten, manganese, oil, rubber, and almost everything else except coal. Stockpiles when the war began were surprisingly small; of only a few imported materials did Germany have as much as a year's supply. But what the Germans had they conserved skillfully. Then the victories in 1940 and 1941 supplied them with just about everything they lacked except oil and rubber, both of which could be synthesized.

At the beginning of the war Germany had 23 million metric tons of steel capacity and the conquests provided another 17 million tons, principally in Lorraine, Belgium, and Luxembourg, or a total theoretical capacity of 40 million tons. Though actual production never reached capacity, in 1943 it was nearly 35 million tons. By anything except U.S. standards, that is a liberal supply of steel. In wartime Germany, nonetheless, as in the U.S., steel always looked

[4] At St. Lô on July 25, 1944, American troops broke out of the Cotentin peninsula, launching the great Allied encirclement of German forces west of the Seine.

scarce; German officials considered it the limiting factor on their arms production. The shortage was always more apparent than real, for the Germans never devised a wholly successful control over their steel supply. Like Americans, they were slow to learn that there couldn't be enough steel both for armaments and for civilian products and nonessential construction. They also discovered that to devise a workable system of allocating steel was a tough job. While Washington and Pittsburgh went through the birth pangs of priorities, there were similar labor pains in Berlin and Essen. A simple priorities system had been established in the late thirties, and when war broke out it promptly broke down. For the next four years continuous efforts were made to devise a method of supplying essential manufacturers with the quantity — but only the quantity — of steel they needed. Many manufacturers continued to receive, as the Germans themselves put it, about half what they asked for and about twice what they could use. And until well along in 1943 civilian manufacture, nonessential construction (usually of a political character), and manufacturers' inventories got a share of the steel supply while directly or indirectly the production of armaments suffered.

Though by 1944 the allocation system had been substantially improved, German industrialists finished the war with a hoard of finished and semifinished steel amounting by some German estimates to 15 million tons or nearly a half year's peak production. A good deal of this hoard had been accumulated after 1943, when a substantial minority of German industrialists began to believe that the war was lost. A tangible asset like steel, they concluded, would be more likely to survive unconditional surrender than reichsmarks in the bank or in government loans.

However, sabotage by cynical industrialists was not so damaging as poor management. The German leaders did not foresee the need of clamping down on nonessential uses of steel and rigorous planning of the supply. Speer and his production chief, an engineer named Saur, considered themselves men of action; they had little time for the painstaking plans that careful control of basic materials requires. Final responsibility for allocating steel supplies — and also for all long-range planning — was given to a broken-down textile manufacturer from Cottbus named Kehrl. This hollow-eyed and emaciated hack seems to have worked hard at his job but was largely ignored. It is surprising that he got by as well as he did.

DOES A DICTATOR HELP?

The most interesting question about German war management is the extent to which it suffered from Hitler — or from the circumstance that Germany was a dictatorship. That it did suffer is certain but the story isn't simple. Hitler has been widely pictured as an inveterate and uninformed meddler and in a sense he was. But more accurately Hitler was a dictator who set no limits to the range of his authority. He controlled not only those decisions that are the normal business of the chief of state but also an enormous number of decisions that in any ordinary government would be delegated to subordinates or to specialists.

The German armies were run from Hitler's headquarters; Hitler took full personal command after the reverses in 1942. Once a day (in emergencies sometimes twice) Keitel and Jodl of the General Staff, the Supreme Commanders of the Army, Air Force, and Navy and their Chiefs of Staff met with Hitler for a briefing on the day's operations of the Wehrmacht. Until mid-1944 the meetings lasted from twelve-thirty to three or four o'clock in the afternoon, but thereafter they were held later and later at night; in the climactic months after the Ardennes counteroffensive they were held in the early hours of the morning in the bunker below the Chancellery garden in Berlin.

The orders issued after these briefings were not confined to broad strategy; they specified minute details of tactics — the deployment of an infantry division in the east and the relief of another in Normandy. No experienced field commander nor even any faithful reader of Tolstoy needs to be told that these orders were not always carried out. Often they bore little relation to conditions on the battlefield. When the U.S. Third Army moved on Koblenz, General Model got orders from the bunker to throw in two divisions to stem the attack. There was a vast difference between divisions on the battle map in the bunker and divisions in the field. According to Speer, who was on the front at the time, the divisions in question consisted of only a few hundred men, twenty-odd tanks, and no gasoline whatever.

Hitler also masterminded the home-front decisions. He met with the production officials at least once a week and would express a judgment on five to twenty questions presented to him and would issue a half dozen to a dozen orders of his own. Again these were not just policy decisions. When a new series of tanks was under consideration, Hitler gave the final word not only on the number to be produced but also on the kind of engine, the position of the armor, and the type of armament the tank should mount. At a typical meeting in the fall of 1944 he ordered: (1) that an air-cooled Diesel engine be designed and produced; (2) that surplus shell cases be used for smoke ammunition; (3) that some railroad construction in Norway be continued; (4) that Jodl and Guderian be notified when important plants were endangered by retreats; (5) that special efforts be made to repair air-raid damage in the Ruhr and restore traffic; (6) that production of anti-aircraft guns and glass land mines be increased. He also agreed to a proposal that railway trains be armed and issued some instructions about a new airplane.

Field commanders visited Hitler regularly at his headquarters in Berlin or elsewhere and, except on ordnance, Hitler seems to have been considerably influenced by the complaints of the general who saw him last.

A number of German generals have sharply criticized Hitler's judgment on military matters — Colonel General Franz Halder, until October, 1942, Chief of the General Staff, characterized him in a well-publicized interview as having "the military capabilities of a mediocre corporal." However, the generals who are most critical are not impartial witnesses. During the war the high officers divided into two exceedingly well-defined parties. The first party never cared much for Hitler and, as he began to lose the war, came to like him less and less. In the second group were the party-line generals — Keitel, Jodl, Kesselring, Rommel, Dietrich, Model, and probably Rundstedt — all of whom were loyal to Hitler or at least professed their loyalty. By the end of the war the second group held virtually all of the important commands. Those of the first group that survived had been pushed aside.

It is the old generals of the first group that criticize Hitler's military sense, and their attacks are more bitter than convincing. All believe it was an error to have risked a war in 1939 — the General Staff plans named 1944 or 1945 as the year when Germany would be completely ready. But by 1944 Russia and even the western allies might have been relatively much better prepared than they were in 1940. Certainly the early campaigns went well enough. Similarly, some of the old generals criticize a change that Hitler made in their plan for the attack on France. The General Staff plan called for wide flanking movement through the Low Countries. Shortly before the attack Hitler ordered a breakthrough at Sedan; this, the generals argue, enabled the British to escape at Dunkirk, whereas otherwise they would have been isolated by the drive down to the coast. It is equally possible, however, that the startling success of the campaign resulted from the drive through Sedan. Certainly the German High Command was as surprised as the opposition at the Wehrmacht's speedy success in France. One can dismiss most of this criticism as merely an exercise in hindsight.

But whether Hitler's judgment was good or bad it is clear that he made too many decisions, too many of which inevitably were snap decisions. And all of his decisions were made with the egoist's certainty that they were infallible, so that right or wrong they could not be seriously debated, much less reversed.

The most important decision Germany took during the war — the decision to declare war on the U.S. — partly illustrates the point. The German Government, according to its surviving members, did not know beforehand that Pearl Harbor would be attacked. Most high Nazis, like most Americans, got the news over the radio. Hitler summoned a meeting, which apparently lasted but an hour or two. After some preliminary inquiries about German obligations under the Three-Power Pact, he made two points. First: the U.S. had already gone to war with Germany, was already sinking German submarines and supporting Britain and Russia. Second: a declaration of war would be a formidable show of solidarity between the Axis allies while otherwise the Three-Point Pact would be dead. Open war would come soon anyway, so Germany would assume the initiative. There seems to have been little or no discussion of the political crisis that might develop in the U.S. if Germany did not declare war. That Roosevelt might be forced to concentrate U.S. resources in the Pacific and abandon his policy of viewing Germany as the major enemy seems not to have been considered.

A less dramatic example of capricious decision was the case of the Me-262; it can be considered the archetype of scores or even hundreds of Hitler's decisions during the war. The Messerschmitt 262 was a twin-engined jet fighter, with a top speed of 500 to 550 miles an hour or more. It was easily the most modern fighter in actual use during the war; the P-51 (Mustang), the plane that more than any other defeated the German Air Force, was a good 100 to 150 miles an hour slower. In force the Me-262, as limited experience showed, could have inflicted serious losses on the bomber formations of the A.A.F.

The Me-262, in development since the early years of the war, was flight-tested in 1943. In spite of urging from the manufacturers the Luftwaffe did not show great interest in the plane until the spring or summer of 1944. Then it was ordered into full production and about the same time or a little later Hitler intervened with an order that the plane be converted into a fighter-bomber. He deplored the use of so valuable a weapon in a purely defensive role; it should be used, he told the Luftwaffe generals, to carry the war to the enemy.

Apparently almost every competent airman in Germany was shocked by the decision. Even Göring was dismayed. But the Führer had spoken and there was no recourse. Several months were wasted in an effort to redesign the plane to carry a bomb load. When the effort was finally abandoned in the autumn of 1944, time was running out. The best that the new plane could become was a dangerous nuisance.

It is worth speculating for a moment on what would have happened in Washington had the President, by some chance, intervened with a similar decision. First Generals Marshall and Arnod would have gone to him and tried to get the decision reversed. Unless the President really had his Dutch up, they would most likely have succeeded. Had they failed, then it is fair to assume that General Somervell would have gone to see Hopkins, another general would have had a word with Admiral Leahy, and someone else would have enlisted the help of Senator Barkley. Hopkins, Leahy, and Barkley would have had a word with the Old Man and meanwhile news of the controversy would have leaked out to the Washington *Post* and Drew Pearson. A number of maneuvers for circumventing the decision would have been devised further down the line. Before they could have been put in effect, the President would most likely have surrendered — and probably denied there was ever any difference of opinion whatever. All of this would have taken a couple of weeks; someone perhaps would have complained of the slow and circuitous ways of democracy. Germany got quick decisions but speed is not an advantage if the decisions must later be reversed. A process of decision making that devotes more time to preliminary dispute but yields decisions that stick can be more economical. Perhaps that is one of the advantages the democracies enjoyed in the war.

''IF YOU TELL A BIG ENOUGH LIE''

Hitler, in his decision to use the Me-262 as an attack bomber, ignored the hard fact that Germany was desperately on the defensive and hence needed defensive weapons. He was moved instead by the doctrine that there are inherent as well as heroic values in the offensive. Hitler's alert but undisciplined mind was peculiarly susceptible to doctrine. Since the Nazis invented most of ·their own doctrine, decisions were often based not on fact but on the official propaganda line.

Only a part of Germany's fantastic propaganda was a deliberate effort to mislead the German people, a point that must be emphasized. Part and perhaps most of it was what Germany's leaders wanted to believe. The very theme of German wartime propaganda is an example. In contrast with the British theme of "Blood, sweat, and tears" or the American theme of "Avoid overconfidence," the German slogan was "Victory is certain." Some such slogan may have been necessary to keep up the spirits of the long-suffering *Herrenvolk* but it was also highly agreeable to Germany's leaders. Complete confidence in victory, in turn, was an important cause of Germany's delayed and partial mobilization. Germany's leaders, and a whole army of subordinate officials, failed to recognize the need for all-out effort because they believed their own newspapers.

Distortions of the truth affected decisions even when the distortions were deliberate. Hitler in the last two years of the war became increasingly annoyed by American production figures as quite accurately reported by German intelligence. Finally he ordered that no American production figures were to be quoted to him — nor were they to be believed by German officials or even discussed in private conversations. (The order seems to have been widely violated.) The enemy's production is an important datum for a country fighting a war. The German leaders preferred the comfortable fiction that the figures lied.

At the end even the Propaganda Ministry had to be curbed for telling unpleasant truths. Through a special section of the ministry a careful check was kept on the morale of the German people. This office, headed by one Schaffer, received and tabulated for the top officials reports from all parts of the Reich and it had access as well to the reports of the Gestapo. In the summer and autumn of 1944 the reports became more and more disturbing: they told of growing war weariness among the people, declining confidence in the leaders, and a popular conviction that the war was lost. In November the Nazis took decisive action. They fired Herr Schaffer.

If German war management was poor how did the German armies manage to fight so well and so long? The Wehrmacht, in the days of its great successes, occupied all Europe except for a few odd corners. It reached the Volga and almost reached the Nile. When it was finally thrown on the defensive it stood off the armed millions of Russia, the U.S., and the British Empire for two and a half years.

The simple fact is that Germany should never have lost the war it started; the undermobilization and overconfidence of the early years help solve the very real mystery of why it did. In the early years Germany's advantages were enormous: it had a large margin over its enemies in preparation, it held the initiative, and it had the moral advantage of being the only country that wanted to fight. Had the Nazi leaders applied their own formula of total war from the beginning they could hardly have avoided overwhelming the opposition they met before 1942.

Even after the tide turned at Moscow and Stalingrad, Germany's position was strong. There was the well-publicized advantage of internal lines of communication that grew shorter and thicker as the communications of all Germany's enemies became longer and more tenuous. German weapons were of good quality, German scientists and technologists were ingenious, and because of the short pipelines new weapons could be quickly put into use. Most important of all, there is little doubt that Germans are durable and skillful fighters with a well-disciplined acceptance of the idea of getting killed. Except in the east they were well moated by the ocean and the Mediterranean. They should have been hard to defeat. That they were defeated is conclusive testimony to the inherent inefficiencies of dictatorship, the inherent efficiencies of freedom.

SELECTION *4*

*I*n 1948 Galbraith returned to Harvard as Professor of Economics. His serious writing as an economist then began and, in 1949, Longmans Green published a compendium, Years of the Modern: An American Appraisal, containing an article by Galbraith entitled "The American Economy, Its Substance and Myth."

Along with ghostly echoes of phrases since become well known — "conventional doctrine," "countervailing power" — one sees in it the not-so-shadowy outline of the controlling themes in the author's later work. In paragraph after paragraph, and section after section, the reader can retrospectively foresee, book by book, almost the totality of Galbraith's economic writing over the next twenty-five years.

The refusal to believe the given ideas of his teachers, simply because they appeared manifestly untrue, must go back to convictions acquired at Berkeley or long before, but that skeptic's view had surely been given a new authority by the years in the Office of Price Administration. As a laboratory that office must have seemed to the young economist the realization of the impossible dream.

The American Economy:

ITS SUBSTANCE AND MYTH[1]

APART FROM Switzerland and one or two of the adult offspring of socialist England, the United States is the last of the developed countries that finds it politic, or even possible, to call itself a capitalist country. In this sense — and it is to be recalled that in different countries the same institutions are called by different names — the United States is the last of the capitalist countries. This essay is an enquiry into the attitude toward capitalism of the last refuge of avowed capitalism. It is an important subject.

Since the end of World War II, one segment of American comment had depicted this attitude in exceptionally brilliant colors. We are presented to ourselves and to strangers as a lone island of youthful confidence and self-assurance in a world that is either searching for a debilitating security or has taken refuge in an all-embracing authoritarianism. Uniquely, we are sure of the quality and durability of our economic institutions.

Unhappily there is much that belies this heroic image. In a week of strictly random selection early this year, the newspapers reported that the retail businessmen of the United States were launching "the largest combined promotional effort in the history of retailing" because in the words of one of the architects of this somewhat breathtaking enterprise, "We have fallen short of selling our American system along with our products." The President of Columbia Uni-

---

[1] "The American Economy: Its Substance and Myth," in *Years of the Modern: An American Appraisal*, ed. John W. Chase (New York: Longman, Green & Co., 1949), pp. 151–174.

versity — by tradition a source of grave advice as to our fate — warned the American people that they were threatened by expanding bureaucracy, the disappearance of private ownership, and, more remotely, by dictatorship. The radio sought nightly to rally the citizen's interest in what it termed "your economic system," and it added a plea that he struggle to make it work better. The sickly behavior of the stock market could be explained only by a general foreboding of disaster.

All this, it must be stressed, was in a time of exceptional well-being. Viewed merely as a technical device for providing individuals with the things they want, or are persuaded they should have, American capitalism had been demonstrating remarkable vigor. The resulting rewards, if less widely distributed than the most ardent defenders of the system might imagine, were almost certainly leaving more people more nearly satisfied with their livelihood than ever previously in modern history. Anyone who seeks to understand American capitalism must, if he seeks honestly, find an explanation for a pervasive insecurity amid actual or realizable well-being.

II

The explanation begins with the absence of an accepted or acceptable *rationale* of what we still choose, with such semantical variations as "free enterprise," "private enterprise," and the "price system," to call capitalism in the United States. The words accepted and acceptable must be emphasized. The problem begins with the existence of an interpretation of contemporary economic life, which I shall outline in a moment, that is neither accepted by a great majority of Americans nor wholly acceptable as a characterization of things as they are. Broadly, very broadly, speaking, the line of belief and disbelief separates those who have, or are associated with, the responsibility for the direction of business enterprises — a responsibility of undoubted importance in the American community — from those who are not. On the one hand are the businessmen who actively accept the interpretation; on the other, the workers, farmers, and influential and unclassifiable millions of teachers, preachers, civil servants and wage-earning journalists who passively reject it. The consequences are serious for both but especially for those who are adherents. Their interpretation of modern capitalism serves them as a faith; it does not provide them with any usable explanation of the economy of which they are a part. Their eyes tell them that their faith is not shared by what is clearly a majority of their fellow-citizens. Their common sense not infrequently tells them that their faith is not one by which a nation can live. It is scarcely to be wondered that they are troubled men.

What may, for the convenience of a title, be called *the conventional doctrine of American capitalism* now belongs not with those ideas that are communicated through books, lectures, or sermons, but with those that result from simple acceptance of normal and commonplace attitudes. Nevertheless, its antecedents in the realm of ideas are identifiable — and the pedigree is important. The core of what is believed to be true of American capitalism was taught by Adam Smith and, through the nineteenth century, by the succeeding generations of the great English classicists. The United States itself produced many exponents of these ideas but comparatively few innovators. (To some extent the final word as to what is true or not true in economics must still be given by an Englishman.)

In barest essential, the classical *rationale* of capitalism was a theory, first, of how the individual was motivated, and second, of how he was limited in the exercise of power to what was good for the community. Man exerted himself because of the prospect of participating in some practical way in the fruits of his own efforts. This share was assured, yet the possibility of profiting excessively was precluded, by the fact of competition. The individual could not misuse power, for he was assumed to have none. If he sought to exploit either those from whom he bought or those to whom he sold, both suppliers (including his workers) and his customers would abandon him in favor of a competitor. Man was made into a social animal by self-interest, and kept so by the man across the street.

The system of economics that was erected on these ideas was a structure of many embellishments and some grandeur. Neither the embellishments nor the grandeur survive, but the doctrine of motivation and limitation of power remain intact in the conventional doctrine of American capitalism. They lie at the root of the most profound source of uneasiness of the American conservative, the fear of the state.

The state, which the Marxians presented as the handmaiden of the businessman, designed to serve his merest whim, has emerged in the United States as the specter that haunts his dreams. Once the basic tenets of the conventional doctrine are recognized and its hold over men's minds conceded, the reasons for the fear become plain.

There is little that the state can do that is necessary and much that is damaging. If an individual in pursuit of his own interest can do no wrong, it follows that he need not be guided, directed or coerced by authority. If competition denies power to the individual — if his prices, wages, production and profits are controlled by his competitors — then there is no reason for the state to restrain misuse of private power. Why intervene to control that which does not exist?

Until the nineteenth century, the recurrent experience of man was with the privileged, corrupt, ill-conceived or intellectually presumptuous acts of his sovereign. This was an added reason for decrying intervention. The presumption of an intrinsically evil sovereign also survives in the conventional doctrine of American captalism.

While little has happened to divorce the businessman in America from the conventional doctrine, much has happened to make it irrelevant for other groups. Most important has been the changing motives of the state. In the United States in the post-revolutionary years, as in England at the same time, the state was either the enemy of the burgeoning business classes or, at best, the capricious friend of those who enjoyed special favors. It was the friend of no other considerable group except its own employees. In nearly all Western countries during the nineteenth century and in the United States more recently, it has appeared as the friend of the many. So far as the New Deal had revolutionary significance, this was it. Although Americans at large may still consider the Federal government awkward, indecisive, and even unreliable, they consider it benign. Yet in the conventional doctrine it remains malignant; such articulators of the doctrine as the spokesmen of the National Association of Manufacturers faithfully so picture it. It is hardly surprising that, to the recipient of social-security benefits, guaranteed farm prices, good roads or R.E.A.[2] power, this aspect of conventional doctrine makes no sense. Within a matter of a century, Western governments have changed from being mainly malevolent to mainly benevolent. The change remains unrecognized in traditional doctrine but not at the polls.

At the same time, there has been a change in the character of capitalism, that has struck at the underpinnings of the conventional doctrine. It can no longer be denied that the modern corporation (and likewise the modern trade-union) has power. Corporations have power not because they have escaped from all competition —

[2] Rural Electrification Administration.

the hold of the conventional doctrine is greatly strengthened by the continuance of intense commercial rivalry — but because they have largely escaped the kind of competition that precludes power. The prices and the costs of the individual wheat grower and even the individual small soft-coal operator are given by the market; the amounts they produce and, in the last analysis, the profits they make or the losses they take are beyond their control. Should any one choose to exercise his ultimate sanction against society and go out of business entirely, he would not be missed. Competition in their case — the competition of many small individuals — is still an effective solvent of private power.

But neither the wheat grower nor the bituminous-coal operator is the archetype of capitalist enterprise in America. In the thirties the figure of "200" became a magic symbol in describing the American economy; it was used to denote the number of firms that roughly but unmistakably produced on the order of half of the physical product of the economy. Each of these corporations does exercise power. The United States Steel Corporation exercises unmistakable though not unlimited control over the prices which people pay for steel. It has power to alter these prices in accordance with its assessment of the interests of its owners, management, workers and the public. Such power as the government exercised over these prices in wartime differed in degree but not in kind. One of the most hotly debated questions of the last three years has been whether the steel industry's decisions on prices and on construction of new capacity have been in the public interest. It need hardly be suggested that this debate presupposes that the steel industry has power to govern in, or against, the public interest. As with steel, so with the remainder of the great core of American business enterprise. The presence of such power in private hands is obviously inconsistent with a doctrine that defends capitalism on the ground that it denies power to anyone.

No such ostentatious conflict between doctrine and fact could have gone unnoticed. It has not. And the manner of its recognition has deeply aggravated the insecurity of the businessman. If he denies that he has power — power not accorded him by the conventional doctrine — he stands refuted by the very decisions he must make, for this is not power that can be assumed or divested at will. If he defends his exercise of power as judicious and in the public interest, he admits to having plenary powers to govern the economy. He risks conceding that the state should hold him to account for his stewardship.

The businessman's discomfiture is enhanced by the reaction of liberals to his exercise of power. In a tradition that survives almost alone in the United States, one powerful wing of American liberalism accepts the conventional doctrine as a norm. But, unlike the businessman, it does not assume that the *status quo* approaches the norm. Its all but invariable conviction is that the existing organization of business is sharply inconsistent with the basic requirements of the conventional doctrine. It therefore insists, primarily through vigorous enforcement of the antitrust laws, that the exercise of private power be reduced. Those business practices, most notably collusion between firms, that facilitate the exercise of power must be proscribed. An unremitting, though generally unsuccessful, agitation for the dissolution of existing aggregations of corporate power is maintained. The goal is a business structure that, by dispersing power between many units, denies effective power to anyone. Thus an underlying structure of business, conforming to the logic of the conventional doctrine, would be achieved.

It is possible to argue that the antitrust laws have, over time, been an important source of security for capitalism in the United States. The notion that legislative power resides in private hands — more simply, that one individual exercises authority over the wealth, income or well-being of another — is deeply repugnant to the juridical sense of the American people. To admit of the fact, even though the fact be anything but new, is to demand that something be done. But for a good half-century the counterpart demand for action has been uniformly channeled into an insistence that the antitrust laws be enforced. The latter have thus become a universal lightning rod for liberal emotions. The antitrust laws have not been ineffective. On the contrary, they have probably been a valuable restraint on antisocial exercise of power. And they are a reasonably accurate reflection of what is deemed fair in business relations. But they have not altered the structure of the economy in the direction of the liberal's dream, though oddly enough, they continue to enjoy an all but unique position in the affections of American liberals. The latter concede in effect that past results have been unsatisfactory; they remain fully persuaded that some day enforcement will achieve their goals. Meantime, American capitalism has avoided what, had this dissent taken other forms, might have been a formidable challenge.

Few businessmen have been able to view the antitrust laws with the philosophical calm that they may well merit. On the contrary, in the individual case they pose a peculiarly difficult problem. No business-man can deny their utter consistency with the conventional doctrine; none can enjoy the opprobrium of being charged with violating the law. And as the antitrust laws are now financed and enforced, the responsible heads of every large business in the United States must expect, at least once in their lifetimes, to be haled into court to answer for behavior deemed at variance with the very doctrine by which they defend their existence. The shafts of the businessman's friends, in the United States, are no less painful than those of his foes.

III

— There is a further way, less by content than by omission, in which the conventional doctrine contributes to insecurity. There is no place in the doctrine for the experienced fact of the devastating de-pression. Apart from some rhythmic cycles of good business and bad — or less unemployment and more — its norm is full employ-ment. Deviations from this norm are assumed to be self-correcting.

Against this stands experience. The Great Depression without doubt was the most penetrating psychological experience of modern America. World War II involved death or deep sorrow for a few; fear and discomfort for a few more; employment, improved living, escape from dull routine, and unaccustomed and not unpleasant re-sponsibility for others. By contrast the Great Depression was a nearly universal experience in fear and hardship, as well as in the unbearable loss of self-esteem that goes with sudden descent into poverty.

Adherents of the conventional doctrine were no less shaken by this experience than others. It is a measure of the power of the doctrine that a limited number of its adherents were able, by the end of the thirties, to argue that the depression, so far from being an organic breakdown, had really been precipitated and prolonged by unwise government intervention. A considerably larger number, by the end of the war, were willing simply to stand on the flat assurance that any repetition of the earlier disaster was improbable.

A majority undoubtedly thought otherwise, and governed their personal affairs on the assumption of a recurrence of depression. This particular source of uneasiness was reinforced by the sweeping capture of American economics in the late thirties by John Maynard (later Lord) Keynes. Scholars whose tendency to exaggeraton is not seriously suspect, have unblushingly called it the "Keynesian Revolution."

The achievement of this ivy-covered uprising was the destruction of a proposition that, tacitly and with many dissenters, had ruled American thinking on economics for more than a century, a proposition known to economists as *Say's Law of Markets*. Say's Law held, simply, that the production of goods provided in the aggregate the demand that would seek them out and buy them. Hence, given a little time, a market was assured for all that was produced. It was a comforting theorem: there might be temporary overproduction of individual commodities but not of all products. If a capitalist society always provided a market for all it produced, it obviously was immune to serious or long-continued depression.

It would be hard, though not yet impossible, to find an American economist who still subscribes to the historic dictum of Jean Baptiste Say. Keynes's conquest of Say was less a triumph of primacy than of authority and orderly logic. Generations of greenbackers, populists, and proponents of the free coinage of silver had, in effect, rejected Say's Law by citing the advantages of supplying more money — of having the government directly or indirectly supplement the private demand for goods — in times of economic distress. When the ingenious Peter Cooper ran for President in 1876 on the Greenback ticket, he argued the case for his party on grounds that Keynesians would now consider commonplace. Keynes, however, had the advantage of the American habit of accepting British tutelage in economics, coupled with unparalleled intellectual and expository talents. His conquest was all but complete.

The effect of the intellectual repeal of Say's Law was to undermine the assumption that the economy found its equilibrium when it was producing all it could. Very specifically, in their search for personal security, men might seek to save more than would be spent by those who, in response to unrelated stimuli, were investing for future production. The economy could find its equilibrium with men and resources unemployed.

To American intellectuals with few exceptions, Keynes was a hopeful figure. He provided a rational explanation of the Great Depression and its persistence. It was an explanation that proved capable of withstanding, though not without amendment, the most searching attack directed against any writer since Marx. He also offered a formula for securing capitalism against disaster which, although it accorded a prime role to the state, involved no all-embracing intervention. Taxes and public expenditures had always affected the volume

[86]

of private saving and of total investment; it remained to use these instruments in time of depression to discourage excessive savings and to supplement investment. The scope for independent business decision would remain substantially unimpaired. The person who found the prospect of mass unemployment intolerable no longer had to consider alternatives to capitalism — including the plunge into the cold sea of comprehensive central planning. The exponent of the unorthodoxy of Keynes found, to his comfort, that he could claim to be saving capitalism.

The effect of Keynes on adherents of the formal doctrine was complex. One influential group of businessmen embraced a broad Keynesian view of the American economy. A new business organization, the Committee for Economic Development, made its appearance with a firm though unproclaimed commitment to his views. Others stood firm — but with an added source of disquiet. A depression is a misfortune; to have it proclaimed as in the nature of things is worse. Still more devastating was the emergence of the state, the natural enemy of capitalism, as the instrumentality of its survival.

Keynes had one other unsettling consequence. Capitalism was returned suddenly to the defensive in the ancient argument over profits. The old attack on profits, never quite as acute in the United States as in Europe, was based on issues of social justice and equity. How defend income which made some men rich beyond measure and left others poor; how devise a rationalization that would cover the fortuitous gains of adventurers and heirs, the rewards of pirates as well as the compensation of sober, God-fearing producers?

The concern over the righteousness of profits had been disappearing. The rich speculative returns of the frontier were gone; the progressive income and capital-gains tax were taking a share; the more uninhibited forms of fiscal adventure had been outlawed. In addition, the trade unions had demonstrated their capacity to appropriate some of the share of good earnings, and corporations seemed more disposed to reserve earnings for their own use. Competitive ostentation in private expenditure with its associated irritations largely disappeared as a social pastime in the late twenties. As a result, business profits came to be justified, even among professional dissidents, by a doctrine of expediency. It might not be possible to say that profits bore any close proportion to social contribution. But they obviously energized those who sought them. So be it.

So it might have remained except that profits are intimately associated with the Keynesian problem of saving. Profits provide the major opportunity for that particular saving that might outrun investment and bring a downward adjustment in total expenditure and production. And the worst offender is not the corporation that is open-handedly distributing dividends to playboy heirs, but the one that is austerely acquiring cash reserves to protect itself against some future disaster. The most virtuous businessman by the old standards was in danger of becoming the worst sinner by the new.

The influence of ideas on events was never better illustrated than by the effect of these views on the great postwar debate on profits. Only to a negligible extent was it argued that businessmen were getting more than they earned or deserved. There were no expressions of envy. The issue was strictly whether these profits were the precursor and progenitor of depression. This was Keynes's handiwork.

IV

Clearly the conventional doctrine as a faith has had a severe buffeting both from ideas and from events. Until the outbreak of the war one might have concluded that, under the strain, it was losing its hold on its former adherents. The term laissez-faire had become, among conservatives themselves, one of opprobrium. Even the term capitalism had acquired overtones which careful semanticists sought to avoid. In the war years, however, the American economy recovered its strength. The prestige of wartime achievements accrued on the whole to business. Much flexibility in relating cause to effect is permissible in American economic and political discussion; accordingly, it was possible to point to the achievements of the economy, under what amounted to comprehensive planning, as general proof of the efficacy of free enterprise. This was accompanied by a resurgent energy in the enunciation of the formal doctrine.

At the same time a new tenet was added: the proposition that nonintervention by the state in the economy is a necessary condition for the preservation of freedom. From today's newspaper, one cites what amounts to a standard formulation: "The free exchange of goods has been the forerunner and prerequisite of all freedom among peoples and nations. Slavery and serfdom are the inevitable results of a controlled economy." The stakes in the war on state power, by this extension of the doctrine, became not alone material values. There was now a threat not only to the body but also to the soul.

The notion of a unique association of freedom with free enterprise was taken up by a hardy band of advocates including some former socialists who brought to their new cause the single-minded ardor of the convert. Like devout Marxians, they reserved their strongest condemnation not for their extreme opponents, the Communists, but for such deviationists as British Socialists abroad and New Dealers at home.

It was the good fortune of this group of revivalists to find a prophet of skill and influence in the scholarly Professor Friedrich Hayek whose *Road to Serfdom,* published in 1944, must be counted one of the influential books of the period. Professor Hayek, arguing with skill and a certain unconscious selectivity in evidence, held that once a country began to assume collective responsibility for any of its economic problems, it presently assumed responsibility for all life. The irresistible character of this trend he verified mostly by reference to Germany, a country which some might be disposed to consider a special case, and where still others have attributed the rise of fascism to the incapacity or unwillingness of doctrinaire government to rise to the problems of popular welfare. He passed over the apparent survival of individual freedom, as it is conventionally understood, in face of the collective experiments of Scandinavia, England — and the United States. Nevertheless, Professor Hayek did much to rehabilitate the conventional doctrine. Its reverses at the hands of inhospitable ideas and even more inhospitable circumstances during the years of the Great Depression had vastly weakened its promise of material welfare. Professor Hayek added an impressive moral justification for the exclusion of the state. Few authors have ever attracted a more approving audience. Once again, it is interesting to note, the United States had looked abroad for authority in political economy.

The process of complementing and enlarging on Professor Hayek's ideas in the latter years of the war and in the early postwar years has resulted in one of the most fascinating literary eruptions in the entire history of capitalism. In form, it has ranged from vast and nearly unreadable volumes sponsored by the National Association of Manufacturers to succinct treatises designed to instruct in one lesson. Rigorously devoid of either humor or doubt, it is dogmatic rather than persuasive, and based firmly on the view that unbelievers are fools, knaves, or weaklings. Given the basic tenet, namely, that government is the implacable enemy of freedom, it obviously must follow that Communists, Socialists, New Dealers, reformers of every variety, should all be marshaled into one great legion of the damned.

The effect of this literature has, no doubt, been to affirm the beliefs of some whose adherence to the official doctrine was largely subjective. As such, it has helped deepen the rift that divides those who hold to the conventional doctrine from those who do not, for it is certain that there have been few converts among the latter. Education, to succeed, must be reasonably compatible with the experience of the individual toward whom it is directed. A resident of a public-housing project is not easily persuaded that he has less liberty than an inhabitant of an adjacent slum; the farmers of the Tennessee Valley are not easily convinced that the T.V.A. has enslaved them; cotton growers have learned that they can remain at war with Washington while accepting government loans.

Freedom, if it is defined to include the privilege of unbridled expression, is never really complete: it is imperfect for everyone. A government employee thinks twice before condemning the actions of his superior, and so does a vice-president of the Chase Manhattan Bank. In recent times, residents of public-housing projects may have been uniquely privileged in their opportunity to speak plainly about their landlord. If the will to freedom in the United States is so enfeebled that subservience to authority can be purchased by the benevolences of the Federal government, the prospect for freedom is probably hopeless in any case. Fortunately, there is little evidence of the danger. Even those who are most alarmed are inclined to argue that the danger is the result of aggregating individually harmless or even benign actions. The mathematics involved are reassuring. And they do not assert that the present state of freedom is seriously impaired. The danger has shown a persistent tendency to be always in the future. As we have moved into the future, the danger has remained one year, one bill, or one session of Congress ahead.

Accordingly, the substance of these fears can be discounted; so also can its unflattering reflection on the character of the American people. But the fact of this fear remains important, especially for its contribution to insecurity. It was remarked, once before, that Americans need to take account of fear itself.

v

It would be idle to suppose that the uneasiness about American economic institutions will be resolved at any time in the foreseeable future. The ideas that underlie it are not lightly held. Nor are they, more than any other faith, subject to revision because of evidence, experience or persuasion. One system of the political economy will continue to rule at the business conventions and another at the polls. Washington will continue to be the arena of conflict between the two. Everyone will expect the worst.

Happily, the prospect is far less horrible than the protagonists can allow themselves to suppose. For one thing, the conflict takes place in a context in which the most difficult of all problems have been solved. There is no physical barrier to producing a tolerable and even comfortable living for all Americans with, in addition, a considerable margin for serving the whims, social compulsions and neuroses of the well-to-do and something additional for waste. Such a situation is almost, if not quite, a matter of experience. We are the first nation to find ourselves in this happy technological position. No one should underestimate its importance as a solvent of social strains. In other countries the unprivileged must still be helped at the expense of the privileged. In the United States, there is something for both.

We are also aided by the happy circumstance that most of our concerns are in the area of prognosis rather than of experience. The difference is that prognosis can be wrong, and in this instance it probably is. The businessman's insecurity in regard to the state concerns what might happen, not what has — and this attitude needs to be set against the fact that, in the two decades of depression, New Deal, and war, a great deal has happened. The liberal's alarm over the possession by the modern corporation of legislative power that is inconsistent with any available doctrine of government is something he has experienced and survived. If we have begun the descent into serfdom — and no on can deny that government in America is far more comprehensive than it was fifteen years ago — it has not yet inhibited the speech or action of those who voice the fear. One would assume that they would be the first victims.

Only depression is in the realm of experience. And here there has been further experience of escape to new levels of employment, production and welfare which reduced radical dissent in the United States to defending the proposition that prosperity could not last.

None of this should lead the reader to suppose that this is an exercise in optimism and reassurance. In the United States no economic commentator is taken seriously unless he is a prophet of doom. This essay is meant to be taken seriously. Yet when we turn to the rules by which we live *in fact* rather than in ideas, there is some comfort to be gained. Seven propositions concerning the American economy would seem to be valid. If they do not assure its survival in the future, they appear at least to explain its survival to date.

1. In economic affairs there is far more latitude for variation and even for error than is commonly supposed. A generous endowment in physical resources and a high development of intellectual resources increase this latitude. In both respects the United States is fortunate. We should not flatter ourselves that we would have been wise enough to have survived had this not been the case. In few matters are Americans so dogmatic as in their insistence that there is only one path to economic salvation. "Do as I recommend — or face ruin" is our stock argument for a policy. In fact in the usual (though certainly not in every) public decision on economic policy, the choice is between courses that are almost equally good or equally bad. It is the narrowest decisions that are most ardently debated. If the world is lucky enough to enjoy peace, it may even one day make the discovery, to the horror of doctrinaire free-enterprisers and doctrinaire planners alike, that what is called capitalism and what is called socialism are both capable of working quite well.

2. In an industrial community which entrusts half of its production to a mere handful of concerns, competition no longer closely circumscribes private power. The pleasant nineteenth-century image of the manufacturer whose prices, wages, even his investment in new machinery, are controlled by the actions of others unknown to him, can hardly be taken seriously except by those who are determined to do so. So we must concede that the individual businessman is the possessor of power of wide social consequence. The liberal had best begin to reconcile himself to a plain fact of life. The businessman, likewise, must come to expect social judgments on the social responsibility he has assumed. The trade union must expect to be similarly judged — although the fact will not come to most union leaders as a surprise.

3. The liberal may also take comfort from the fact that a much neglected but surprisingly effective process acts to curb power in the modern economy. One of the unfortunate consequences of the old orthodoxy was a myopic concentration on competition as the restraint on private power. As competition atrophied, it was easy to assume that private power was becoming increasingly absolute. The facts have probably been to the contrary. Competition — restraint from the same side of the market — has been replaced by restraint from the opposite side of the market. The spectacular case has been the labor market.

No buyer of labor in the United States has power equivalent to that exercised by large corporations a half-century ago. The reason is that the power of the corporation nourished the countervailing power of the trade union. Moreover, this process of checkmate is pervasive. The power of the steel industry as a seller required that the automobile companies be powerful as buyers and accorded advantages to those that were. The power of the canning industry as a buyer is matched by the farm cooperative on the one hand and by the chain stores on the other. There is nothing fortuitous about the tendency for power to beget countervailing power; it is organic. However, it does not work evenly. The buttressing of weak bargaining positions has become, as a result, one of the most important of the functions of government.

4. In this system, the autonomous powers of those who guide the modern American corporation acquire their justification not in principle but in practice. They are defended by the theory of administration, not by the theory of economics. Some way must be found, in an economy that produces as many things for as many tastes as that of the United States, to effect a wide decentralization of the power of *final* decision. Nothing else is so important, and a goodly number of disadvantageous decisions is a modest price to pay for this decentralization. No one can say much in defense of the design (or price) of American automobiles but no one can view with equanimity the problems which would arise were there an appeal from General Motors to higher authority. On decentralization of final decision depends much of the capacity of the economy for accommodation and for change. This is one of the important recent discoveries of the left. Even in avowedly socialist countries, capitalism, though defeated as an idea, survives because of the absence of administratively acceptable alternatives.

5. It would be hard to prove that the American economy selects its business decision makers by merit, and rewards them in strict accordance with their contribution to the social welfare. But clearly it does recruit diligent men who are rarely accused of failing to take either themselves or their tasks seriously. Many die young. Management in the United States regularly accuses workers of low productivity; American labor, which is not restrained in its criticisms, rarely returns the charge. By contrast, most British and continental trade-unionists have long since ceased to suppose that the boss is useful. The personal earnings of management in the United States,

even when adventitiously out of line with accomplishment, are not a subject of much concern mostly because envy, in this land, is almost exclusively confined to the contemplation of others of nearly equal income.

6. Just as the exercise of private economic power is justified on purely pragmatic grounds, so with public authority. There is no controlling principle governing the relation of American government either to the economy or to freedom. Each act of the government can safely be judged on its merits provided only that these are viewed comprehensively. Americans, as each election in recent times has made increasingly clear, do in fact, take a largely pragmatic view of the role of the state. Were others similarly persuaded that the role of government is a practical not a moral issue, they might be happier men.

7. On economic matters there are, in harmony with American capitalism as it is, three ways in which state power must be exercised. There are, first, the task for which the state has superior competence. The provision of education, economic security, a substantial amount of housing, indispensable medical services and, no doubt in the near future, a minimum standard of nutrition are all of this sort.

Second, the state must intervene to align the exercise of private power with the public welfare. This is an exceedingly complex affair and the ancient instinct of liberals, which is that the intervention should be such as to establish a predisposition toward the right decisions rather than to make the decisions, accords with the broad aim of decentralization of authority. The intervention is, however, far less narrowly confined to reducing the exercise of private power by developing competition than American liberals continue to suppose. It may consist in large measure in helping to establish countervailing power. By far the most durable accomplishments of the government in the last two decades have not been in regulation or in the reestablishment of competition. They have been in supporting trade unions to a point of bargaining equality with employers, in arming farmers with the bargaining alternative of being able to sell to the government, of placing the force of law behind the minimum-wage demands for unorganized workers. These are the measures, not the antitrust laws, which have most effectively regulated the exercise of private power. It is also clear that they fit a good deal more logically into capitalism as it is.

Finally, and most important of all, it would appear certain that private decision will have to be supplemented by action that will ensure tolerably full use of the resources of the economy.

No one should suppose that this is an easy task — the day when New Dealers could pin their hopes on public works and public spending is past. The income which is subject to control by the government is small compared with the possible changes resulting from an exercise of private decision. There are still only the most imperfect and limited designs for expressing the government's effect on income — for supporting consumption, expanding public investment and diminishing the appropriate taxes in the event of a slump. The problem may not be safely solved until some effective way is found of expressing the profound social interest in a high and stable level of private business expenditure, including, in particular, private investment.

The chances are favorable, nonetheless, that we shall find means of keeping the economy functioning at tolerably high levels. There are no physical barriers. We are greatly helped by the fact that there is no single path to salvation that must be found to the exclusion of all others. Nothing in the theory or practice of American government would justify complacency in our ability to select a single right course from among many plausible wrong ones were that the problem. Happily it is not.

The barriers to a solution of the central problem of the American economy are far more in the area of beliefs than in the area of fact. As this essay has sufficiently emphasized, the triumph of practical action over confining doctrine has, in modern America, been a substantial one. It is reasonable to suppose that it will rule in the future. This may not be a solvent for the present uneasiness but it is still a reassuring thought.

PART TWO

BLACKTOP TO THRUWAY

SELECTION *5*

---

*I*n 1952 two books by Galbraith were published: A
Theory of Price Control *from Harvard University Press and* American
Capitalism *from Houghton Mifflin Company. The background experience can be seen clearly in both books, and selections from both
follow.*

*Though the two books were published in the same year, the bulk of
the* Theory of Price Control *was written some seven years earlier. In
1946 and 1947 Galbraith wrote two articles: one, "Reflections on Price
Control" for the* Quarterly Journal of Economics, *the other, "The
Disequilibrium System" for* The American Economic Review. *Both
were used substantially as written in the* Theory of Price Control.
*That book clearly comes straight out of the Washington wartime
"laboratory";* American Capitalism *on the other hand seems to have
been derived from earlier and more general thinking via the article in*
Years of the Modern. *The nub of the first comes in a chapter entitled
"The Disequilibrium System" — a phrase the author uses to denote a
form of organization intended to maintain economic balance under
wartime conditions. In the second selection the author renews his
quarrel with his admired disciplinarian professor, Ewald Grether, and
the conventional doctrine of Alfred Marshall.*

It is hard to place the selection from The Theory of Price Control in any of the three classifications earlier proposed. It is certainly not a book in the mainstream of the author's socioeconomic thesis, of which the last selection can be seen as the beginning. Even more certainly it cannot be seen as written to escape the incessant pressure of that prime assignment — as were the first two selections. If anywhere it belongs in the nuts-and-bolts category to which were assigned two of the author's best: The Great Crash (1929) and Money.

Almost all good writing begins with a need in the author to explain something to himself — a strong emotion, a childhood terror, a line of reasoning that needs testing on paper or the reexamination of circumstance to be sure that it justifies a general statement. This last kind of need produces the nuts and bolts group and here The Theory of Price Control seems to belong.

However, the book is distinctly technical. It is written for other economists, practical and otherwise. It employs familiar words to symbolize quite elaborate systems, as "birdie," "three-bagger," "shrink" or "internal combustion" are used by most of us. There is a certain Humpty-Dumptyism about it all — "When I use a word, it means just what I choose it to mean." On the other hand the woeful alternative is gobbledygook. Galbraith chose the former, but clearly the lot of him who writes on technical matters is not a happy one.

One might think that technical discussion could be omitted from this book of Galbraith readings, the purpose of which is to display the origin and growth of a particular view of economic life in the mind of its author. It is, however, essential to that purpose. Economic behavior was first seen as largely beyond man's control, somewhat as the weather is today. Over two centuries it has come to be viewed as a force of nature which can be harnessed. The pages used here map the meeting ground of theory and practice and the interaction between the two. They also exhibit the great all-embracing purpose of economic thought, and most particularly of Galbraith's: to find a way to prevent human nature from turning against itself.

A Theory of Price Control

THE DISEQUILIBRIUM SYSTEM [1]

WITHIN THE last ten years, price control as an instrument of economic policy has been used in two substantially different contexts. During World War II it was used in conjunction with an extensive mobilization of economic resources for military use. The ostensible and, in large measure, the actual objective to which all others were subordinate was the task of mobilization. More recently, price control has been employed with the primary objective of stabilizing prices. This has been done at a time when the economy was under inflationary pressure as the result of arms expenditure. However, only a comparatively small fraction of the total current resources of the economy has been going into defense use; it has not been seriously claimed that these were making preclusive claims on the economy or that price control was motivated for reasons other than the protection of the civilian economy. It is appropriate, and even necessary, therefore, to examine price control separately in each of these two contexts. It by no means follows that the policy appropriate in the one case is appropriate in the other. Price control and the companion controls over wage and other incomes will later be examined in the context of full or relatively full mobilization. First, however, it is necessary to have a full view of the structure of the mobilized economy in which such controls are employed.

II

During World War II the United States, partly by improvisation, partly by plan, developed a system of mobilizing economic resources that, by the commonly accepted standard of results, proved highly satisfactory. The American system was not unique; in its major contours it resembled that of the other belligerents which were forced to

[1] Chapter 4, "The Disequilibrium System," from A Theory of Price Control (London: Oxford University Press, 1952), pp. 28–40.

make an abrupt conversion from a largely unplanned to a largely planned utilization of resources. It is my purpose, somewhat in the tradition of market theory, to idealize the system that was so devised and to examine its central features.

The form of wartime organization employed by the United States, and with variations by the other major belligerents with the exceptions of Russia and China, I have termed the "Disequilibrium System." Under this system the incentives and compulsions of an unplanned economy were supplemented or supplanted by three new forces for determining economic behavior. These were (1) a more or less comprehensive system of direct control over the employment of economic resources, (2) a nearly universal control over prices, and (3) an aggregate of money demand substantially in excess of the available supply of goods and services. Because it was a distinctive and pervasive feature of the system, I have used this disequilibrium of demand and supply to name the system as a whole. To these three determinants might be added a fourth which, although supplementary, represented the area of the greatest wartime failure in the United States. That is the use of an effective system of rationing to reinforce price control in those markets that approximate conditions of pure competition.

I am assuming throughout this chapter that the mobilization objective is to attain maximum resource employment of the greatest possible efficiency, to get a militarily optimal allocation of resources between military and civilian use, and to distribute the former between different kinds of production, and present and future output, in accordance with a given but not static plan. These ends should, if possible, be so served that the way is open for eventual restoration of prewar property rights and status and the normal functional mechanics of the economy. This conservative objective is presumably secondary, if as during the last war, the doctrine of total war is avowed. This doctrine — the doctrine that the *only* objective is victory — was asserted by all the leading belligerents in the last war although it is doubtful if any, with the possible exception of Russia, could be said to have followed it in economic practice.

III

The role of direct controls over resource use in the system can be quickly indicated. For regulating the use of resources, the available choice is between the incentives and compulsions of the market, and authority. Market incentives are incapable of producing the comprehensive transfers in resource employment that any considerable mobilization requires. An effort by the government to monopolize steel supply by offering high prices would necessarily be defeated by the inelasticity of demand for steel by some private buyers. So with other resources. The response to such market incentives would also be highly uncertain. Sellers in imperfect markets who take a comprehensive view of their position do not seek to maximize profits at any given point of time. For this reason they will not willingly accept a government order, even though it is immediately more profitable than any alternative, if it promises to impair their long-run position in the market. The automobile industry, in late 1941 and early 1942, was displaying normal market behavior in preferring manufacture of automobiles to tanks or aircraft, even assuming the latter netted higher immediate returns.

All this holds whether or not there is price control. Although for purely administrative reasons the introduction of a comprehensive system of price control probably precludes the use of market incentives on a large scale, it actually makes possible their use within limits. With price control it becomes possible to create *and maintain* a differential return for favored industries. However, this is a detail. For a full-scale mobilization, the government must specify by order where and how plant, materials, and, if the mobilization is complete, labor resources are to be used.

With this very brief comment, I take leave of the subject of direct control over resource use — of the vast subject of materials allocation, control of the use of manpower, procurement, and so forth. This summary dismissal does not mean that I consider this part of the control structure either unimportant or easy to employ. It is neither. But my concern here is with other aspects of the system.

IV

The comprehensive control of prices and the general excess of demand, the two other determinants of economic behavior that are vital to the disequilibrium system, were both the objects of an important miscalculation before the war. Price control, as I have noted, was widely regarded as unwise and technically unworkable. Since a general excess of demand was what made price control unworkable, such an excess would be eliminated by the movement of prices to a new and higher position of equilibrium. Further increments of demand with given supply would be eliminated by a further succession of such movements, that is, by inflation. Since the technical feasibility of holding prices in face of an excess of demand was not recognized, it was not supposed that the latter could exist. It is not surprising, therefore, that the role of an excess of demand in relation to the functioning of a mobilized economy remained unexamined. In World War II such a surplus of demand played an important role, the significance of which we have only gradually perceived.

The aims of wartime industrial mobilization I have defined as the bringing of all possible resources into efficient use and their planned allotment to military and civilian use and between present and future production. The allocation and reallocation of resources by authority present no problem in principle, and the practical problem, as the wartime experience showed, though difficult is not insuperable. It is not clear, however, that direct controls are similarly effective for ordering normally unused resources, especially labor, into the market. Yet the mobilization of unused labor power is, perhaps, the most important single requirement for a general increase in national output. Such a mobilization was accomplished in the United States with apparent success and with but limited resort to authority. While one needs to be wary of such comparisons, the experience of the United States seems to have compared not too unfavorably with that of England, which used a combination of authority and incentives, and very favorably with Germany, which relied heavily on authority.[2]

The first contribution of excess demand was to provide a taker for anyone who offered his or her services. Frictional unemployment was eliminated, in effect, by providing a market adjacent to every worker.[3]

[2] The increase in male (native) German workers between 1939 and 1943 did not exceed the natural rate of increase. The number of women gainfully employed actually declined in the early years of the war, and although it was higher by a few hundred thousand at the end of the war, the proportion of all women in gainful employment did not increase. In the early part of the war, there was still some (Nazi) doctrinal objection to use of women in factory work, but it had been subordinated to expediency by 1943 or 1944, and by then the government was actively trying to get women into industry. Cf. *Effects of Strategic Bombing on the German War Economy* (Washington: U.S. Strategic Bombing Survey, 1945), pp. 29 *et seq.*

[3] This consideration led the CED economists to urge the maintenance of an excess of demand (and price control) in the early reconversion period. Cf. *Jobs and Markets*, Research Study for the Committee for Economic Development (New York: McGraw-Hill, 1946).

Excess demand, in other words, established and sustained a nearly universal labor shortage. No one who wanted to work could complain of his or her inability to find a job, and no one who did not want to work could plead inability to find employment as an excuse. Once in the labor market, such labor power, even with the slight controls over manpower that were invoked in the United States, became subject to a measure of direction as to use.

However, what may perhaps be called the passive contribution of excess demand was at least as important. I have reference here to the kind of wage and income policy which is permissible when such an excess of demand is being allowed to develop. Its effect is best seen by contrasting what was possible under the disequilibrium system with what could have been done had it been necessary to keep aggregate demand equal to supply at a given level of prices.

To maintain equilibrium would have required energetic measures to restrain the expansion of incomes. Since *ex hypothesi* prices would be stable, hourly rates would not have been under undue pressure. But other contributions to income would have had to be watched with care. Overtime and doubletime would be dangerous, as would payments (usually at inflated productivity rates) to new arrivals in the labor market, and as would payments under incentive schemes. Yet these inducements to labor power at the margin were of the utmost importance for the expansion of output that occurred during World War II; approximately half of the real increase in gross national product between 1940 and 1944 has been attributed to individuals not normally in the labor market and to the increase in the average work week.[4] It seems reasonable to argue that much of this increase occurred because the disequilibrium system made it possible to advance the price of marginal labor power with almost complete disregard for fiscal consequences.

It was likewise possible to reward the marginal entrepreneur, the inefficient old one or the inexperienced newcomer, with a similar neglect of fiscal effects. The relation of taxes to incentives could

[4] *America's Needs and Resources* (New York: Twentieth Century Fund, 1947), p. 13. The estimates, admittedly crude, attribute 48 percent of the real increase from 1940 to 1944 to increased hours and "emergency" workers, 26 percent to absorption of unemployed, 13 percent to normal increase in the working force, and the rest to increased productivity. Some of the latter can be attributed to the shift from low- to high-efficiency employment encouraged by high take-home pay.

also be largely elided. Had taxes during World War II approached the rates necessary for equilibrium at prewar prices, their relation to incentives would certainly have become a matter of substantive, as distinct from verbal, concern.

To refocus the discussion somewhat, excess demand during the war was the counterpart of a buffer of unemployed resources, especially unemployed workers — the buffer that is necessary for price stability in the absence of price control. If markets are uncontrolled, any near approach to full employment of normally employed workers will lead, in a strong market, to price increases followed by wage increases or to wage increases followed by price increases.[5] In the imperfect market where labor costs are established by collective bargaining, there is no basis either in theory or experience for assuming stability in price and factor costs at full employment. On the contrary, as I shall argue in more detail later, there is every reason to expect a continuing interaction of wages and prices. Under the disequilibrium system by contrast, it was possible to dispense with the buffer of unemployed resources which would have been necessary for equilibrium stability and to substitute, through surplus demand, a positive pressure on resource use. It was a practical way of adapting modern capitalism — a capitalism characterized by oligopoly in product markets and strong unions in factor markets — to the wartime imperative that all possible resources be employed and if possible under approximately stable conditions of prices and costs.

During World War II, and in considerable measure afterward, the fact that an excess of demand was allowed to accumulate behind the control structure was viewed as a weakness in fiscal management. Given better management, it would have been appropriated by taxation or, perhaps, stabilized in the hands of its possessors by forced saving. The present argument runs sharply to the contrary. Viewed in relation to the objective of developing maximum military potential, the accumulation of some volume of excess demand was not undesirable. On the contrary, it contributed to, or made possible, a more effective organization of resources than the apparent alternative. However, it also seems certain that few policies need to be administered with closer attention to the limits and to the context within which they are appropriate. I now turn to the limits within which an excess of demand is desirable.

[5] Cf. Paul A. Samuelson, *Econometrica*, July 1946, p. 191.

v

The indulgent Providence that (so far) has protected the United States was especially kind in bringing it to the disequilibrium system with a prior faith in the idea of maintaining equilibrium of aggregate demand and supply at a ruling price. For, to the extent that there was a sense of guilt in allowing demand to exceed supply, there was a motive for keeping the excess of demand as small as possible. That was fortunate, for an excess of demand is advantageous and even tolerable only to a point. The volume of demand in excess of current supply that adds to, or is consistent with, additions to aggregate output, I propose to call the "margin of tolerance." It is of the utmost importance for understanding the disequilibrium system to know what determines this margin of tolerance.

The counterpart of the current excess of aggregate demand is, of course, an equivalent volume of current saving. The explanation of the high actual volume of current savings during the war is complex and in considerable measure conjectural. Without doubt, patriotic compulsions, reinforced by Treasury appeals and community pressure, affected the average propensity to save by individuals whose income was not changed. For those whose income was increasing, a low (marginal) propensity to consume may be assumed. But it would seem clear that the proximate cause of much, if not most, of the increased saving was price control. At a minimum, price control associated a variety of inconveniences with spending money; at a maximum, through shortages, it removed a large number of the accustomed objects of consumption. The normal choice between specific objects of consumption and saving could not be exercised. Individuals and firms who had no intention of saving became involuntary holders of cash or its equivalent. The disequilibrium follows from the circumstance that in the absence of price control and attendant shortages, they would have spent their income for the given supply of goods and in so doing would have established equilibrium at a higher price level.[6]

[6] It was once suggested to me that since this group did hold cash balances, the term "forced equilibrium" would be preferable to "disequilibrium." This I judge to be a matter of taste; I opted for the shorter term and for the notion that "equilibrium" is more meaningful, in this context, as a description of the market relationships that would have obtained in the absence of price control.

For individuals who are exercising a normal choice between saving and consumption, who are equating the marginal utility of money to spend with that of money to save, there is no new problem of incentives. For those who may loosely be termed "involuntary savers," incentives become a matter of first-rate importance. It may be assumed that the marginal utility of money for this group will show a tendency to fall as the proportion of savings to total income increases or, secularly, if a given (high) proportion of saving is continued over a long period. When for either or a combination of these reasons it falls to the point where there is a general withdrawal of marginal labor effort, it may be said that the margin of tolerance in the disequilibrium system has been exhausted.

It seems unlikely that in the United States during World War II any such point was reached or even approached. There was the happy circumstance that within the memory of the present generation, the dollar had not gone through hyperinflation. There was no general expectation of a collapse of values as a result of military defeat. Moreover, throughout the war there was a strong conviction that the current high employment and income was merely an interlude between depressions. This elasticity of expectations, to use Professor Lange's term,[7] was reinforced by manufacturers who promised a flood of inexpensive and elegantly streamlined goods after the war and by the Treasury with its rediscovery of the sovereign virtues of thrift. Perhaps most important of all, consumption after savings was high — for most workers higher than before the war. Had there been a sharp reduction in opportunities for current expenditure, workers might well have revised their attitude toward acquiring and holding dollars, the redundancy of which would be a matter of day-to-day observation.

In any case had the ratio of savings to income become too high at some point, or had a less high ratio continued too long, incentives would have been weakened. An admirable arrangement for, in effect, getting current work in return for a promise of future consumption or security would have disintegrated. Workers, equating the marginal disutility of labor effort with diminishing marginal utility of income for saving, would, in the absence of strong patriotic compulsions, have abandoned overtime and Sunday work, and marginal workers would have withdrawn from the market rather than add to their stock of savings. A good thing would have been overdone.

[7] *Price Flexibility and Employment* (Bloomington: Principia Press, 1944).

Its large margin of tolerance must be counted one of the major sinews of American strength in World War II, in interesting contrast with Germany where the margin would appear to have been decidedly thin. Because of the inflation of the mark in the twenties, the accumulation of cash balances was clearly a less attractive alternative to spending for Germans than for Americans. It may be doubted if many Germans supposed, even if they won the war, that Hitler would permit them to enjoy a lush, secure peace. Especially from 1943 on, there was a strong undercurrent of feeling that Germany would, in fact, lose the war. In the United States the principal (although it will be apparent that I now believe mistaken) reason for restraining the expansion of demand was to protect the price controls. In Germany price and rationing controls were perfectly secure — they even survived combat and the fantastic disorganization that followed — and there was no serious wartime black market. Partly for this reason and partly, perhaps, because they were callous practitioners of financial heterodoxy, the German leaders during the war period seem not to have been greatly worried over the expansion of demand.[8]

As a result, Germany far exceeded its margin of tolerance. Women, as I have noted, were not attracted by the opportunity of earning money in industry; indeed, during the war some employed women apparently withdrew from the labor force as they became beneficiaries of substitute cash income in the form of servicemen's allowances. There was a recognizable tendency for entrepreneurs. especially from 1943 on, to hold materials or inventory, or to acquire equipment, rather than to produce end products for sale, the result of which would be an increase in cash balances.

In the years between 1945 and 1948, Germany presented a sharply etched picture of a country that had completely exhausted its margin of tolerance and where, as a result, the disequilibrium system had entered the final stages of disintegration. Price control was still fairly effective in face of an approximately sevenfold expansion in the means of payment as compared with prewar years and a fall in output to between a third and a half of prewar volume. This control was supplemented by a reasonably efficient rationing system, and even through much of this period the black market was still fairly limited. A large part of the middle class and many workers had all the money they could spend without working or they could acquire it by a

[8] Earlier, as Burton H. Klein has pointed out, orthodox influences were a good deal stronger. "Germany's Preparation for War: A Re-examination," *American Economic Review*, March 1948.

few days' work each week. It was all but inconceivable that anyone would work to acquire marks to save. The unwisdom of exchanging scarce energy for redundant marks, in those years of hunger, involved no subjective balance of psychic gain and disutility at the margin. It presented a simple problem of physiology which most Germans readily solved.

VI

It follows from the foregoing that one of the critical tasks of wartime economic management, perhaps the most critical task, is to exploit but not exhaust the margin of tolerance. In order to maximize the output of nonconsumable military end products and investment, the government must use its opportunity to get these in return for currently unspendable money. It must not go so far with this involuntary saving that it weakens incentives.

Over a longer period, the state faces an equally important task of fiscal craftsmanship in so handling matters that the margin of tolerance, to be exploited in emergency, is kept as great as possible. This consists, above all, in maintaining public confidence that savings in any period will have high future value, either for the purchase of goods or for their contingency value for personal security. As I have suggested, the margin of tolerance during World War II was wide. There was the general expectation of a postwar depression when the purchasing power of such savings would increase, as would also the need for them for personal security. Also, the experience with the savings of World War I was favorable — they were subsequently spendable at prices considerably below wartime levels, and the 1921 depression emphasized their importance for personal security.

As a result of developments following World War II, we shall not be so fortunate again. The inflationary increase in prices during these years will be the basis of expectations for the years following any future crisis, if such a crisis is our misfortune. The war bonds that the Treasury merchandised during the war years as the world's soundest investment — and which were sufficiently so regarded that people worked for them instead of for goods — turned out, in fact, to be inferior both as to capital protection and yield to a middle-grade oil stick. It would be nonsense to suppose that the American people missed the lesson that was involved. Nor, in my judgment, was this misfortune inevitable; things were managed badly in these years. The impatient men who refused to work gradually away from wartime controls and taxes, who insisted on precipitately junking both at the price of inflation, are responsible for dissipating a vital source of national strength. This might be forgiveable, did the condemnation rest only on the subtleties of economic theory. But the lessons of economic theory here coincide, as indeed they usually do, with the copybook maxims which stress the importance of good faith and integrity.

PRICE CONTROL AND THE DISEQUILIBRIUM SYSTEM[9]

IV

THERE REMAINS one further problem, not of policy, but of technique, in the administration of price control under the disequilibrium system. That consists in making an appropriate distinction between imperfect and more or less purely competitive markets and in providing, by way of formal rationing, the necessary reinforcement to price control in the latter markets. This is not a general necessity for all competitive markets, but it is indispensable, particular situations of equilibrium aside, for markets for wage goods. Rationing acquires added significance because two important classes of wage goods, food and clothing, are sold on proximately competitive markets.

In spite of important initial successes, the greatest failure in the operation of the disequilibrium system during World War II was in the association of rationing with price control.

From the earliest days of OPA, or rather of its predecessor agencies, the indispensability of rationing as a supplement to price control was fully recognized by the economists associated with the enterprise — a fact that is hardly surprising in view of the generally unsanguine attitude toward price control as such. The efforts to have administration of price control and rationing associated in the same agency were justified and pressed on economic grounds. For these reasons, a clause was inserted in the original charter of the Office of Price Administration and Civilian Supply (OPACS), giving it

[9] Part IV, Chapter 5, "Price Control and the Disequilibrium System," A *Theory of Price Control*.

authority to make "consumer allocations."[10] When this authority was later lost to the Supply Priorities and Allocations Board (SPAB), responsibility for rationing rubber tires was obtained from the dying Office of Production Management, because it seemed certain that whatever agency rationed tires would eventually have responsibility for rationing other commodities.

The early rationing programs were ably conceived and executed — a case could be made that the rationing of meats, canned goods, and fuel were among the outstanding administrative achievements of the war. Meat rationing, as I have observed, showed particularly the indispensability of rationing for price control, for it quickly brought order to markets that price control, ex-rationing, had reduced to near chaos. The lesson was fully observed in the OPA.[11] The markets in which rationing programs were being developed were generally those in which price control required such reinforcement.[12] This was at least distantly related to a growing appreciation of the different requirements for effective control in different classes of markets.

Yet, as the result of an unhappy combination of bad politics and malignant stupidity, this fine beginning was partially abandoned in favor of helter-skelter distribution at fixed prices. The result was a breakdown of price controls in a number of these markets — the classic breakdown that undergraduates were expected to foretell. The Office of Price Administration was not entirely blameless in this debacle. For a period in 1943 there was a disposition by policy-makers to look upon rationing not as essential for price control but as an unhappy byproduct of price regulation. However, the major responsibility for this piece of destruction belonged to the commodity

[10] A euphemism invented at the time because it was feared that the word "rationing" had an unacceptable connotation of scarcity and distress.

[11] In December of 1942, for example, I suggested to the "Price School" of OPA that we had come to the point where, in some measure, price control "passes out of the hands of the price department and into the hands of the rationing department."

[12] Perhaps I should make it clear that I do not suggest that support to price control is the only criterion in deciding whether a product should be subject to formal rationing. The product may be of sufficient importance for public health, morale, or efficiency so that the less precise or less equitable controls that would be exercised by sellers in the absence of formal rationing cannot be trusted. The formal rationing of fuel oil during the war had some such rationale. See my paper before the American Economics Association, January 1943, "Price Control: Some Lessons from the First Phase " (*American Economic Review Supplement*, March 1943).

czars who shared responsibility with the OPA for the rationing programs and to the Department of Agriculture. The latter agency in particular was responsible for the doctrine that increased rations would be popular with the American people even though supplies were not available to meet them. The "honoring of ration tickets" had been regarded, by those who designed the system, as the *sine qua non* of successful administration. When this principle was breached, the popular basis for rationing disappeared. The consumer was no longer assured of her aliquot share in what was available. The admittedly cumbersome machinery required for effective rationing, when it no longer guaranteed this, became not only burdensome but superfluous. The integrity and even the usefulness of the rationing system having been destroyed, the easy next step was to urge or order the abandonment of all rationing controls. This sealed the fate of price control in the competitive markets and, in some measure, the fate of price control as a whole.

SELECTION 6

---

*S*een in the laser beam of hindsight, American Capitalism is a less complete book than it appeared at the time of its publication. The centerpiece — the idea of "countervailing power" — does
not not quite tell us whose will be the last three fingers on the baseball
bat. Moreover, many other issues are raised and, no doubt deliberately,
never sufficiently expanded. They are, for example, some comparative
comments on socialist economics, further investigations of the phenomena of inflation and depression, and an enlarged examination of
the history of classical economic theory. Such questions lie beyond
the apparent scope of the book, but it could hardly have been written
without their being raised. American Capitalism answers many questions for its readers. It must surely have asked many more of its author.
The answers became the central arch of Galbraith's economic theory,
their implementation the secret of a good economy for the industrial
world.

One cannot but wonder when precisely the economist perceived the
full outline of the complete economic thesis that later became the
substance of those three central books: The Affluent Society, The New
Industrial State, and Economics and the Public Purpose. It must have
been a moment of delighted wonder and it seems reasonable to sup-

pose that it may well have happened before, or perhaps even during, the writing of the article in Years of the Modern. At any rate American Capitalism is an examination and a considerable enlargement of what was put forth in the earlier short essay. Phrases suggested in that essay are refined and institutionalized in the later work. The divided nature of the American economy is defined and more clearly seen. For the author the work and thought of the next two decades are outlined. There remained only the labor of construction and the need for time and peace. As it turned out, these last two commodities were all too seldom available. As many a writer has, the author must have felt like Jefferson longing to return to the gardens of Monticello.

Charles Hession in his book Galbraith and his Critics calls attention to a paragraph by V.S. Navasky in the New York Times. Here it is:

> In 1951 Galbraith rewrote and included two of his price-fixing articles with much new material in a book entitled The Theory of Price Control. The general lack of attention this book received seems to have disappointed him very much. His reaction has been reported subsequently as follows:
>
> > I think most people who have read it would say that it is the best book I have ever written. The only difficulty is that five people read it. Maybe ten. I made up my mind that I would never again place myself at the mercy of the technical economists who had the enormous power to ignore what I had written. I set out to involve a larger community. I would involve economists by having the larger public say to them, "Where do you stand on Galbraith's idea of price control?" They would have to confront what I said.*

Somehow Galbraith's voice doesn't echo clearly in the quotation but, in the light of later events, it does have the ring of general likelihood.

Galbraith had now tried two roads to the expression of his thought. With the two articles in economic journals and with their publication in book form, he had tried to reach directly the minds of his professional colleagues. The second made their notice only an incidental dividend. He would speak directly to their troops. This he did

* Charles H. Hession, John Kenneth Galbraith and His Critics, (New York: New American Library, 1972), p. 25.

with American Capitalism. *That was, by far, the more successful book of the two. The choice meant giving a course in economics to his interested subjects along the way — teaching them what his colleagues would have already known. It was a long task but Galbraith had no choice for now at last the theory had captured the theorist.*

In the introduction to later books, the author often suggests that there is no mystery in the science of economics that cannot be phrased in good English prose that any intelligent and persevering reader can understand. It is clear that we shall see no more of "Candide."

American Capitalism

THE THEORY OF
COUNTERVAILING POWER[1]

ON THE NIGHT of November 2, 1907, the elder Morgan played solitaire in his library while the panic gripped Wall Street. Then, when the other bankers had divided up the cost of saving the tottering Trust Company of America, he presided at the signing of the agreement, authorized the purchase of the Tennessee Coal & Iron Company by the Steel Corporation to encourage the market, cleared the transaction with President Roosevelt and the panic was over. There, as legend has preserved and doubtless improved the story, was a man with power a self-respecting man could fear.

A mere two decades later, in the crash of 1929, it was evident that the Wall Street bankers were as helpless as everyone else. Their effort in the autumn of that year to check the collapse in the market is now recalled as an amusing anecdote; the heads of the New

[1] Chapter IX, "The Theory of Countervailing Power," *American Capitalism* (London: Hamish Hamilton, rev. ed., 1957).

[114]

York Stock Exchange and the National City Bank fell into the toils of the law and the first went to prison; the son of the Great Morgan went to a Congressional hearing in Washington and acquired fame, not for his authority, but for his embarrassment when a circus midget was placed on his knee.

As the banker, as a symbol of economic power, passed into the shadows his place was taken by the giant industrial corporation. The substitute was much more plausible. The association of power with the banker had always depended on the somewhat tenuous belief in a "money trust" — on the notion that the means for financing the initiation and expansion of business enterprises was concentrated in the hands of a few men. The ancestry of this idea was in Marx's doctrine of finance capital; it was not susceptible to statistical or other empirical verification at least in the United States.

By contrast, the fact that a substantial proportion of all production was concentrated in the hands of a relatively small number of huge firms was readily verified. That three or four giant firms in an industry might exercise power analogous to that of a monopoly, and not different in consequences, was an idea that had come to have the most respectable of ancestry in classical economics. So as the J. P. Morgan Company left the stage, it was replaced by the two hundred largest corporations — giant devils in company strength. Here was economic power identified by the greatest and most conservative tradition in economic theory. Here was power to control the prices the citizen paid, the wages he received, and which interposed the most formidable of obstacles of size and experience to the aspiring new firm. What more might it accomplish were it to turn its vast resources to corrupting politics and controlling access to public opinion?

Yet, as was so dramatically revealed to be the case with the omnipotence of the banker in 1929, there are considerable gaps between the myth and the fact. The comparative importance of a small number of great corporations in the American economy cannot be denied except by those who have a singular immunity to statistical exidence or a striking capacity to manipulate it. In principle the American is controlled, livelihood and soul, by the large corporation; in practice he seems not to be completely enslaved. Once again the danger is in the future; the present seems still tolerable. Once again there may be lessons from the present which, if learned, will save us in the future.

II

As with social efficiency, and its neglect of technical dynamics, the paradox of the unexercised power of the large corporation begins with an important oversight in the underlying economic theory. In the competitive model — the economy of many sellers each with a small share of the total market — the restraint on the private exercise of economic power was provided by other firms on the same side of the market. It was the eagerness of competitors to sell, not the complaints of buyers, that saved the latter from spoliation. It was assumed, no doubt accurately, that the nineteenth-century textile manufacturer who overcharged for his product would promptly lose his market to another manufacturer who did not. If all manufacturers found themselves in a position where they could exploit a strong demand, and mark up their prices accordingly, there would soon be an inflow of new competitors. The resulting increase in supply would bring prices and profits back to normal.

As with the seller who was tempted to use his economic power against the customer, so with the buyer who was tempted to use it against his labor or suppliers. The man who paid less than the prevailing wage would lose his labor force to those who paid the worker his full (marginal) contribution to the earnings of the firm. In all cases the incentive to socially desirable behavior was provided by the competitor. It was to the same side of the market — the restraint of sellers by other sellers and of buyers by other buyers, in other words to competition — that economists came to look for the self-regulatory mechanisms of the economy.

They also came to look to competition exclusively and in formal theory still do. The notion that there might be another regulatory mechanism in the economy has been almost completely excluded from economic thought. Thus, with the widespread disappearance of competition in its classical form and its replacement by the small group of firms if not in overt, at least in conventional or tacit collusion, it was easy to suppose that since competition had disappeared, all effective restraint on private power had disappeared. Indeed this conclusion was all but inevitable if no search was made for other restraints, and so complete was the preoccupation with competition that none was made.

In fact, new restraints on private power did appear to replace competition. They were nurtured by the same process of concentration which impaired or destroyed competition. But they appeared not on the same side of the market but on the opposite side, not with competitors but with customers or suppliers. It will be convenient to have a name for this counterpart of competition and I shall call it *countervailing power*.[2]

To begin with a broad and somewhat too dogmatically stated proposition, private economic power is held in check by the countervailing power of those who are subject to it. The first begets the second. The long trend toward concentration of industrial enterprise in the hands of a relatively few firms has brought into existence not only strong sellers, as economists have supposed, but also strong buyers, a fact they have failed to see. The two develop together, not in precise step, but in such manner that there can be no doubt that the one is in response to the other.

The fact that a seller enjoys a measure of monopoly power, and is reaping a measure of monopoly return as a result, means that there is an inducement to those firms from whom he buys or those to whom he sells to develop the power with which they can defend themselves against exploitation. It means also that there is a reward to them, in the form of a share of the gains of their opponents' market power, if they are able to do so. In this way the existence of market power creates an incentive to the organization of another position of power that neutralizes it.

The contention I am here making is a formidable one. It comes to this: Competition which, at least since the time of Adam Smith, has been viewed as the autonomous regulator of economic activity and as the only available regulatory mechanism apart from the state, has, in fact, been superseded. Not entirely, to be sure. I should like to be explicit on this point. Competition still plays a role. There are still important markets where the power of the firm as (say) a seller is checked or circumscribed by those who provide a similar or a substitute product or service. This, in the broadest sense that can be meaningful, is the meaning of competition. The role of the buyer on the other side of such markets is essentially a passive one. It consists in looking for, perhaps asking for, and responding to the best bargain.

[2] I have been tempted to coin a new word for this which would have the same convenience as the term competition and had I done so my choice would have been "countervailence." However, the phrase "countervailing power" is more descriptive and does not have the raw sound of any newly fabricated word.

The active restraint is provided by the competitor who offers, or threatens to offer, a better bargain. However, this is not the only or even the typical restraint on the exercise of economic power. In the typical modern market of few sellers, the active restraint is provided not by competitors but from the other side of the market by strong buyers. Given the convention against price competition, it is the role of the competitor that becomes passive in these markets.

It was always one of the basic presuppositions of competition that market power exercised in its absence would invite the competitors who would eliminate such exercise of power. The profits of a monopoly position inspired competitors to try for a share. In other words competition was regarded as a *self-generating* regulatory force. The doubt whether this was in fact so after a market had been pre-empted by a few large sellers, after entry of new firms had become difficult and after existing firms had accepted a convention against price competition, was what destroyed the faith in competition as a regulatory mechanism. Countervailing power is also a self-generating force and this is a matter of great importance. Something, although not very much, could be claimed for the regulatory role of the strong buyer in relation to the market power of sellers, did it happen that, as an accident of economic development, such strong buyers were frequently juxtaposed to strong sellers. However, the tendency of power to be organized in response to a given position of power is the vital characteristic of the phenomenon I am here identifying. As noted, power on one side of a market creates both the need for, and the prospect of reward to, the exercise of countervailing power from the other side.[3] This means that, as a common rule, we can rely on countervailing power to appear as a curb on economic power. There are also, it should be added, circumstances in which it does not appear

[3] This has been one of the reasons I have rejected the terminology of bilateral monopoly in characterizing this phenomenon. As bilateral monopoly is treated in economic literature, it is an adventitious occurrence. This, obviously, misses the point and it is one of the reasons that the investigations of bilateral monopoly, which one would have thought might have been an avenue to the regulatory mechanisms here isolated, have in fact been a blind alley. However, this line of investigation has also been sterilized by the confining formality of the assumptions of monopolistic and (more rarely) oligopolistic motivation and behavior with which it has been approached. (Cf. for example, William H. Nicholls, *Imperfect Competition within Agricultural Industries*, Ames, Iowa: 1941, pp. 58 ff.) As noted later, oligopoly facilitates the exercise of countervailing market power by enabling the strong buyer to play one seller off against another.

or is effectively prevented from appearing. To these I shall return. For some reason, critics of the theory have seized with particular avidity on these exceptions to deny the existence of the phenomenon itself. It is plain that by a similar line of argument one could deny the existence of competition by finding one monopoly.

In the market of small numbers or oligopoly, the practical barriers to entry and the convention against price competition have eliminated the self-generating capacity of competition. The self-generating tendency of countervailing power, by contrast, is readily assimilated to the common sense of the situation and its existence, once we have learned to look for it, is readily subject to empirical observation.

Market power can be exercised by strong buyers against weak sellers as well as by strong sellers against weak buyers. In the competitive model, competition acted as a restraint on both kinds of exercise of power. This is also the case with countervailing power. In turning to its practical manifestations, it will be convenient, in fact, to begin with a case where it is exercised by weak sellers against strong buyers.

III

The operation of countervailing power is to be seen with the greatest clarity in the labor market where it is also most fully developed. Because of his comparative immobility, the individual worker has long been highly vulnerable to private economic power. The customer of any particular steel mill, as the turn of the century, could always take himself elsewhere if he felt he was being overcharged. Or he could exercise his sovereign privilege of not buying steel at all. The worker had no comparable freedom if he felt he was being underpaid. Normally he could not move and he had to have work. Not often has the power of one man over another been used more callously than in the American labor market after the rise of the large corporation. As late as the early twenties, the steel industry worked a twelve-hour day and seventy-two-hour week with an incredible twenty-four-hour stint every fortnight when the shift changed.

No such power is exercised today and for the reason that its earlier exercise stimulated the counteraction that brought it to an end. In the ultimate sense it was the power of the steel industry, not the organizing abilities of John L. Lewis and Philip Murray, that brought the United Steel Workers into being. The economic power that the worker faced in the sale of his labor — the competition of many sellers dealing with few buyers — made it necessary that he organize for his own protection. There were rewards to the power of the steel companies in which, when he had successfully developed counter-vailing power, he could share.

As a general though not invariable rule one finds the strongest unions in the United States where markets are served by strong corporations. And it is not an accident that the large automobile, steel, electrical, rubber, farm-machinery and non-ferrous metal-mining and smelting companies all bargain with powerful unions. Not only has the strength of the corporations in these industries made it neces-sary for workers to develop the protection of countervailing power; it has provided unions with the opportunity for getting something more as well. If successful they could share in the fruits of the cor-poration's market power. By contrast there is not a single union of any consequence in American agriculture, the country's closest approach to the competitive model. The reason lies not in the difficulties in organization; these are considerable, but greater difficulties in or-ganization have been overcome. The reason is that the farmer has not possessed any power over his labor force, and at least until recent times has not had any rewards from market power which it was worth the while of a union to seek. As an interesting verification of the point, in the Great Valley of California, the large farmers of that area have had considerable power vis-à-vis their labor force. Almost uniquely in the United States, that region has been marked by persistent attempts at organization by farm workers.

Elsewhere in industries which approach the competition of the model one typically finds weaker or less comprehensive unions. The textile industry,[4] boot and shoe manufacture, lumbering and other forests industries in most parts of the country, and smaller wholesale and retail enterprises, are all cases in point. I do not, of course, ad-vance the theory of countervailing power as a monolithic explanation of trade-union organization. No such complex social phenomenon is likely to have any single, simple explanation. American trade unions

[4] It is important, as I have been reminded by the objections of English friends, to bear in mind that market power must always be viewed in relative terms. In the last century unions developed in the British textile industry and this industry in turn conformed broadly to the competition of the model. However, as buyers of labor the mill proprietors enjoyed a far stronger market position, the result of their greater resources and respect for their group interest, than did the indi-vidual workers.

developed in the face of the implacable hostility, not alone of employers, but often of the community as well. In this environment organization of the skilled crafts was much easier than the average, which undoubtedly explains the earlier appearance of durable unions here. In the modern bituminous coal-mining and more clearly in the clothing industry, unions have another explanation. They have emerged as a supplement to the weak market position of the operators and manufacturers. They have assumed price- and market-regulating functions that are the normal functions of managements, and on which the latter, because of the competitive character of the industry, have been forced to default. Nevertheless, as an explanation of the incidence of trade-union strength in the American economy, the theory of countervailing power clearly fits the broad contours of experience. There is, I venture, no other so satisfactory explanation of the great dynamic of labor organization in the modern capitalist community and none which so sensibly integrates the union into the theory of that society.

IV

The labor market serves admirably to illustrate the incentives to the development of countervailing power and it is of great importance in this market. However, its development, in response to positions of market power, is pervasive in the economy. As a regulatory device one of its most important manifestations is in the relation of the large retailer to the firms from which it buys. The way in which countervailing power operates in these markets is worth examining in some detail.

One of the seemingly harmless simplifications of formal economic theory has been the assumption that producers of consumers' goods sell their products directly to consumers. All business units are held, for this reason, to have broadly parallel interests. Each buys labor and materials, combines them and passes them along to the public at prices that, over some period of time, maximize returns. It is recognized that this is, indeed, a simplification; courses in marketing in the universities deal with what is excluded by this assumption. Yet it has long been supposed that the assumption does no appreciable violence to reality.

Did the real world correspond to the assumed one, the lot of the consumer would be an unhappy one. In fact goods pass to consumers by way of retailers and other intermediaries and this is a circumstance of first importance. Retailers are required by their situation to develop countervailing power on the consumer's behalf.

As I have previously observed, retailing remains one of the industries to which entry is characteristically free. It takes small capital and no very rare talent to set up as a seller of goods. Through history there have always been an ample supply of men with both and with access to something to sell. The small man can provide convenience and intimacy of service and can give an attention to detail, all of which allow him to co-exist with larger competitors.

The advantage of the larger competitor ordinarily lies in its lower prices. It lives constantly under the threat of an erosion of its business by the more rapid growth of rivals and by the appearance of new firms. This loss of volume, in turn, destroys the chance for the lower costs and lower prices on which the firm depends. This means that the larger retailer is extraordinarily sensitive to higher prices by its suppliers. It means also that it is strongly rewarded if it can develop the market power which permits it to force lower prices.

The opportunity to exercise such power exists only when the suppliers are enjoying something that can be taken away; i.e., when they are enjoying the fruits of market power from which they can be separated. Thus, as in the labor market, we find the mass retailer, from a position across the market, with both a protective and a profit incentive to develop countervailing power when the firm with which it is doing business is in possession of market power. Critics have suggested that these are possibly important but certainly disparate phenomena. This may be so, but only if all similarity between social phenomena be denied. In the present instance the market context is the same. The motivating incentives are identical. The fact that it has characteristics in common has been what has caused people to call competition competition when they encountered it, say, in agriculture and then again in the laundry business.

Countervailing power in the retail business is identified with the large and powerful retail enterprises. Its practical manifestation, over the last half-century, has been the rise of the food chains, the variety chains, the mail-order houses (now graduated into chain stores), the department-store chains, and the co-operative buying organizations of the surviving independent department and food stores.

This development was the countervailing response to previously established positions of power. The gains from invading these positions have been considerable and in some instances even spectacular.

The rubber tire industry is a fairly commonplace example of oligopoly. Four large firms are dominant in the market. In the thirties, Sears, Roebuck & Co. was able, by exploiting its role as a large and indispensable customer, to procure tires from Goodyear Tire & Rubber Company at a price from 29 to 40 percent lower than the going market. These it resold to thrifty motorists for from a fifth to a quarter less than the same tires carrying the regular Goodyear brand.

As a partial consequence of the failure of the government to recognize the role of countervailing power, many hundreds of pages of court records have detailed the exercise of this power by the Great Atlantic & Pacific Tea Company. There is little doubt that this firm, at least in its uninhibited days, used the countervailing power it had developed with considerable artistry. In 1937, a survey by the company indicated that, for an investment of $175,000, it could supply itself with corn flakes. Assuming that it charged itself the price it was then paying to one of the three companies manufacturing this delicacy, it could earn a modest 68 percent on the outlay. Armed with this information, and the threat to go into the business which its power could readily make effective, it had no difficulty in bringing down the price by approximately 10 percent.[5] Such gains from the exercise of countervailing power, it will be clear, could only occur where there is an exercise of original market power with which to contend. The A & P could have reaped no comparable gains in buying staple products from the farmer. Committed as he is to the competition of the competitive model, the farmer has no gains to surrender. Provided, as he is, with the opportunity of selling all he produces at the impersonally determined market price, he has not the slightest incentive to make a special price to A & P at least beyond that which might in some circumstances be associated with the simple economies of bulk sale.

The examples of the exercise of countervailing power by Sears, Roebuck and A & P just cited show how this power is deployed in its most dramatic form. The day-to-day exercise of the buyer's power is a good deal less spectacular but also a good deal more significant. At the end of virtually every channel by which consumers' goods reach the public there is, in practice, a layer of powerful buyers. In the food market there are the great food chains; in clothing there are the department stores, the chain department stores and the department store buying organizations; in appliances there are Sears,

<hr />

[5] I am indebted to my friend Professor M. A. Adelman of the Massachusetts Institute of Technology for these details.

Roebuck and Montgomery Ward and the department stores; these latter firms are also important outlets for furniture and other house furnishings; the drug and cosmetic manufacturer has to seek part of his market through the large drug chains and the department stores; a vast miscellany of consumers' goods pass to the public through Woolworth's, Kresge's and other variety chains.

The buyers of all these firms deal directly with the manufacturer and there are few of the latter who, in setting prices, do not have to reckon with the attitude and reaction of their powerful customers. The retail buyers have a variety of weapons at their disposal to use against the market power of their suppliers. Their ultimate sanction is to develop their own source of supply as the food chains, Sears, Roebuck and Montgomery Ward have extensively done. They can also concentrate their entire patronage on a single supplier and, in return for a lower price, give him security in his volume and relieve him of selling and advertising costs. This policy has been widely followed and there have also been numerous complaints of the leverage it gives the retailer on his source of supply.

The more commonplace but more important tactic in the exercise of countervailing power consists, merely, in keeping the seller in a state of uncertainty as to the intentions of a buyer who is indispensable to him. The larger of the retail buying organizations place orders around which the production schedules and occasionally the investment of even the largest manufacturers become organized. A shift in this custom imposes prompt and heavy loss. The threat or even the fear of this sanction is enough to cause the supplier to surrender some or all of the rewards of his market power. He must frequently, in addition, make a partial surrender to less potent buyers if he is not to be more than ever in the power of his large customers. It will be clear that in this operation there are rare opportunities for playing one supplier off against another.

A measure of the importance which large retailing organizations attach to the deployment of their countervailing power is the prestige they accord to their buyers. These men (and women) are the key employees of the modern large retail organization; they are highly paid and they are among the most intelligent and resourceful people to be found anywhere in business. In the everyday course of business, they may be considerably better known and command rather more respect than the salesmen from whom they buy. This is a not unimportant index of the power they wield.

There are producers of consumers' goods who have protected themselves from the exercise of countervailing power. Some, like the automobile and the oil industry, have done so by integrating their distribution through to the consumer — a strategy which attests the importance of the use of countervailing power by retailers. Others have found it possible to maintain dominance over an organization of small and dependent and therefore fairly powerless dealers. It seems probable that in a few industries, tobacco manufacture for example, the members are ordinarily strong enough and have sufficient solidarity to withstand any pressure applied to them by the most powerful buyer. However, even the tobacco manufacturers, under conditions that were especially favorable to the exercise of counter-vailing power in the thirties, were forced to make liberal price concessions, in the form of advertising allowances, to the A & P[6] and possibly also to other large customers. When the comprehensive representation of large retailers in the various fields of consumers' goods distribution is considered, it is reasonable to conclude — the reader is warned that this is an important generalization — that most positions of market power in the production of consumers' goods are covered by positions of countervailing power. As noted, there are exceptions and, as between markets, countervailing power is exercised with varying strength and effectiveness. The existence of exceptions does not impair the significance of the regulatory phenomenon here described. To its devotees the virtues of competition were great but few if any ever held its reign to be universal.

Countervailing power also manifests itself, although less visibly, in producers' goods markets. For many years the power of the automobile companies, as purchasers of steel, has sharply curbed the power of the steel mills as sellers. Detroit is the only city where the historic basing-point system was not used to price steel. Under the basing-point system, all producers regardless of location quoted the same price at any particular point of delivery. This obviously minimized the opportunity of a strong buyer to play one seller off against the other. The large firms in the automobile industry had developed the countervailing power which enabled them to do precisely this. They were not disposed to tolerate any limitations on their exercise of such power. In explaining the quotation of "arbitrary prices" on Detroit steel, a leading student of the basing-point system some years ago recognized, implicitly but accurately, the role of countervailing power by observing that "it is difficult to apply high cartel prices to

[6] Richard B. Tennant, *The American Cigarette Industry* (New Haven: Yale University Press, 1950), p. 312.

particularly large and strong customers such as the automobile manufacturers in Detroit."[7]

The more normal operation of countervailing power in producers' goods markets has, as its point of departure, the relatively small number of customers which firms in these industries typically have. Where the cigarette or soap manufacturer numbers his retail outlets by the hundreds of thousands and his final consumers by the millions, the machinery or equipment manufacturer counts his customers by the hundreds or thousands and, very often, his important ones by the dozen. But here, as elsewhere, the market pays a premium to those who develop power as buyers that is equivalent to the market power of those from whom they buy. The reverse is true where weak sellers do business with strong buyers.

v

There is an old saying, or should be, that it is a wise economist who recognizes the scope of his own generalizations. It is now time to consider the limits in place and time on the operations of countervailing power. A study of the instances where countervailing power fails to function is not without advantage in showing its achievements in the decisively important areas where it does operate. As noted, some industries, because they are integrated through to the consumer or because their product passes through a dependent dealer organization, have not been faced with countervailing power. There are a few cases where a very strong market position has proven impregnable even against the attacks of strong buyers. And there are cases where the dangers from countervailing power have, apparently, been recognized and where it has been successfully resisted.

An example of successful resistance to countervailing power is the residential-building industry. No segment of American capitalism evokes less pride. Yet anyone approaching the industry with the preconceptions of competition in mind is unlikely to see, very accurately, the reasons for its shortcomings. There are many thousands of individual firms in the business of building houses. Nearly all are small; the capital of the typical housebuilder runs from a few hundred to a few thousand dollars. The members of the industry oppose little market power to the would-be house owner. Except in times of ex-

[7] Fritz Machlup, *The Basing Point System* (Philadelphia: Blakiston Co., 1949), p. 115.

tremely high building activity there is aggressive competition for business.

The industry does show many detailed manifestations of guild restraint. Builders are frequently in alliance with each other, unions, and local politicians to protect prices and wages and to maintain established building techniques. These derelictions have been seized upon avidly by the critics of the industry. Since they represent its major departure from the competitive model, they have been assumed to be the cause of the poor performance of the housing industry. It has long been an article of faith with liberals that if competition could be brought to the housing business all would be well.

In fact were all restraint and collusion swept away — were there full and free competition in bidding, no restrictive building codes, no collusion with union leaders or local politicians to enhance prices — it seems improbable that the price of new houses would be much changed and the satisfaction of customers with what they get for what they pay much enhanced. The reason is that the typical builder would still be a small and powerless figure buying his building materials in small quantities at high cost from suppliers with effective market power and facing in this case essentially the same problem vis-à-vis the unions as sellers of labor. It is these factors which, very largely, determine the cost of the house.

The builder is more or less deliberately kept without power. With few exceptions, the manufacturers of building supplies decline to sell to him direct. This prevents any builder from bringing pressure to bear on his source of supply; at the same time it helps keep all builders relatively small and powerless by uniformly denying them the economies of direct purchase. All must pay jobbers' and retailers' margins. A few builders — a spectacular case is Levitt & Sons of Long Island — have managed to circumvent this ban.[8] As the result of more effective buying, a much stronger position in dealing with labor, and the savings from large-scale production of houses, they have notably increased the satisfaction of customers with what they receive for their money. Few can doubt that the future of the industry, if its future is to improve on its past, lies with such firms.

Thus it is the notion of countervailing power, not of competition, which points the way to progress in the housing industry.

[8] Levitt has established a wholly owned building-supply company to buy materials for its projects. (*Fortune*, August 1947, p. 168.) He also, most significantly, grew to importance as a non-union employer.

What is needed is fewer firms of far greater scale with resulting capacity to bring power to bear upon unions and suppliers. It is the absence of such firms, and of the resulting economies, which helps explain why one sector of this industry — low-cost housing where cost is especially important in relation to ability-to-pay — has passed under government management. In the absence of an effective regulating mechanism within the industry in the form of counter-vailing power, private entrepreneurship has been superseded. In accordance with classical expectations the state has had to intervene. Only the failure was not of competition but of countervailing power.

VI

The development of countervailing power requires a certain minimum opportunity and capacity for organization, corporate or otherwise. If the large retail buying organizations had not developed the countervailing power which they have used, by proxy, on behalf of the individual consumer, consumers would have been faced with the need to organize the equivalent of the retailer's power. This would have been a formidable task but it has been accomplished in Scandinavia where the consumer's cooperative, instead of the chain store, is the dominant instrument of countervailing power in con-sumers' goods markets. There has been a similar though less comprehensive development in England and Scotland. In the Scandinavian countries the cooperatives have long been regarded explicitly as instruments for bringing power to bear on the cartels; i.e., for the exercise of countervailing power. This is readily conceded by many who have the greatest difficulty in seeing private mass buyers in the same role. But the fact that consumer cooperatives are not of any great importance in the United States is to be explained, not by any inherent incapacity of the American for such organization, but because the chain stores pre-empted the gains of countervailing power first. The counterpart of the Swedish Kooperative Forbundet or the British Co-operative Wholesale Societies has not appeared in the United States simply because it could not compete with the A & P and other large food chains. The meaning of this, which incidentally has been lost on devotees of the theology of cooperation, is that the chain stores are approximately as efficient in the exercise of countervailing power as a cooperative would be. In parts of the American economy where proprietary mass buyers have not made their appearance, notably in the purchase of farm supplies, individuals (who are also individualists) have shown as much capacity to organize as the Scandinavians and the British and have similarly obtained the protection and rewards of countervailing power. The Grange League Federation, the Eastern States Farmers' Exchange and the Illinois Farm Supply Company, cooperatives with annual sales running to multi-million-dollar figures, are among the illustrations of the point.

However, it must not be assumed that it is easy for great numbers of individuals to coalesce and organize countervailing power. In less developed communities, Puerto Rico for example, one finds people fully exposed to the exactions of strategically situated importers, merchants and wholesalers and without the apparent capacity to develop countervailing power in their own behalf. Anyone, incidentally, who doubts the force of the countervailing power exercised by large retailer-buying organizations would do well to consider the revolution which the entry of the large chain stores would work in an economy like that of Puerto Rico and also how such an intrusion would be resented and perhaps resisted by importers and merchants now able to exercise their market power with impunity against the thousands of small, independent and inefficient retailers who are their present outlets.[9]

In the light of the difficulty in organizing countervailing power, it is not surprising that the assistance of government has repeatedly been sought in this task. Without the phenomenon itself being fully recognized, the provision of state assistance to the development of countervailing power has become a major function of government — perhaps *the* major domestic function of government. Much of the domestic legislation of the last twenty years, that of the New Deal episode in particular, only becomes fully comprehensible when it is viewed in this light. To this I shall return in the next chapter.

VII

I come now to the major limitation on the operation of countervailing power — a matter of much importance in our time. Countervailing power is not exercised uniformly under all conditions of

[9] This is the subject of a detailed study published by the Harvard University Press. (*Marketing Efficiency in Puerto Rico* by John Kenneth Galbraith, Richard H. Holton and colleagues, 1955.)

demand. It does not function at all as a restraint on market power when there is inflation or inflationary pressure on markets.

Because the competitive model, in association with Say's Law, was assumed to find its equilibrium at or near full employment levels, economists for a long time were little inclined to inquire whether markets in general, or competition in particular, might behave differently at different levels of economic activity, i.e., whether they might behave differently in prosperity and depression. In any case the conventional division of labor in economics has assigned to one group of scholars the task of examining markets and competitive behavior, to another a consideration of the causes of fluctuations in the economy. The two fields of exploration are even today separated by watertight bulkheads, or less metaphorically, by a professorial division of labor and course requirements. Those who have taught and written on market behavior have assumed a condition of general stability in the economy in which sellers were eager for buyers. To the extent, as on occasion in recent years, that they have had to do their teaching or thinking in a time of inflation — in a time when, as the result of strong demand, eager buyers were besieging reluctant sellers — they have dismissed the circumstance as abnormal. They have drawn their classroom and textbook illustrations from the last period of deflation, severe or mild.

So long as competition was assumed to be the basic regulatory force in the economy these simplifications, although they led to some error, were not too serious. There is a broad continuity in competitive behavior from conditions of weak to conditions of strong demand. At any given moment there is a going price in competitive markets that reflects the current equilibrium of supply-and-demand relationships. Even though demand is strong and prices are high and rising, the seller who prices above the going or equilibrium level is punished by the loss of his customers. The buyer still has an incentive to look for the lowest price he can find. Thus market behavior is not fundamentally different from what it is when demand is low and prices are falling.

There are, by contrast, differences of considerable importance in market behavior between conditions of insufficient and excessive demand when there is oligopoly, i.e., when the market has only a small number of sellers. The convention against price competition, when small numbers of sellers share a market, is obviously not very difficult to maintain if all can sell all they produce and none is subject to the temptation to cut prices. Devices like price leadership, open book pricing and the basing-point system which facilitate observance of the convention all work well because they are under little strain. Thus the basing-point system by making known, or easily calculable, the approved prices at every possible point of delivery in the country provided protection against accidental or surreptitious price-cutting. Such protection is not necessary when there is no temptation to cut prices. By an interesting paradox when the basing-point system was attacked by the government in the late depression years it was of great consequence to the steel, cement and other industries that employed it. When, after the deliberate processes of the law, the system was finally abolished by the courts in April 1948, the consequences for the industries in question were rather slight. The steel and cement companies were then straining to meet demand that was in excess of their capacity. They were under no temptation to cut prices and thus had no current reason to regret the passing of the basing-point system.

These differences in market behavior under conditions of strong and of weak demand are important and there are serious grounds for criticizing their neglect — or rather the assumption that there is normally a shortage of buyers — in the conventional market analysis. However, the effect of changes in demand on market behavior becomes of really profound significance only when the role of countervailing power is recognized.

Countervailing power, as fully noted in the earlier parts of this chapter, is organized either by buyers or by sellers in response to a stronger position across the market. But strength, i.e., relative strength, obviously depends on the state of aggregate demand. When demand is strong, especially when it is at inflationary levels, the bargaining position of poorly organized or even of unorganized workers is favorable. When demand is weak the bargaining position of the strongest union deteriorates to some extent. The situation is similar where countervailing power is exercised by a buyer. A scarcity of demand is a prerequisite to his bringing power to bear on suppliers. If buyers are plentiful — if supply is small in relation to current demand — sellers are under no compulsion to surrender to the bargaining power of any particular customer. They have alternatives.[10]

[10] The everyday business distinction between a "buyers" and a "sellers" market and the frequency of its use reflect the importance which participants in actual markets attach to the ebb and flow of countervailing power. That this distinction

Broadly speaking, positions of countervailing power have been developed in a context of limited — or, more accurately, of not unlimited demand. This is partly because such periods have had a much higher incidence in history than the episodes of unlimited or inflationary demand. It is partly because periods of drastically restricted demand, by providing exceptional opportunity for aggression by the strong against the weak, have also provided an exceptional incentive to building countervailing power. Much of the structure of organization on which countervailing power depends traces its origins to such periods.

The depression years of the thirties, needless to say, were a particularly fruitful period in this respect. Accordingly, and in sharp contrast with most other types of business, these years were very favorable to the development of the chain stores and also of various group buying enterprises. The intensity of the trade agitation against the mass retailers, culminating in 1936 in the passage of the Robinson-Patman Act (designed as we shall see presently to limit their exercise of this power), was itself a measure of the chain's advantage in this period. By contrast, during the years of strong demand and short supply of World War II, the chain stores lost ground, relatively, to independents. As this strong demand in relation to supply destroyed their capacity to exercise countervailing power, their advantage disappeared. It is likewise interesting to note that the trade agitation and resentment against the chains almost completely disappeared during the war and postwar years.

The depression years also provided a notable inducement to the trade-union movement. With prosperity in the forties and fifties labor organization too lost its momentum. Finally, to the depression years we owe nearly all of the modern arrangements for exercise of countervailing power by and on behalf of the farmers.

Given this structural accommodation by the economy to limited demand, the appearance of unlimited demand is somewhat devastating. There is everywhere a shift of bargaining power to sellers. The balance of force appropriate to limited demand is everywhere upset.

---

has no standing in formal economics follows from the fact that countervailing power has not been recognized by economists. As frequently happens, practical men have devised a terminology to denote a phenomenon of great significance to themselves but which, since it has not been assimilated to economic theory, has never appeared in the textbooks. The concept of the "break-even point," generally employed by businessmen but largely ignored in economic theory, is another case in point.

The market power of strong sellers, until now offset by that of strong buyers, is enhanced. The countervailing power of weak sellers is suddenly and adventitiously reinforced.

These effects can again be seen with greatest clarity in the labor market. Here they also have their most portentous consequences. In industries where strong firms bargain with strong unions, the management of the former has what has come to be considered a normal resistance to wage increases when demand is not pressing upon capacity. To yield is to increase unit costs. The firm cannot with impunity pass along these higher costs to its customers. There may be a question as to whether other firms in the industry will follow suit; there will always be a question of the effect of the higher prices on sales. If the demand for the products is in any measure elastic the consequence of the higher prices will be a loss of volume. This, with its effect on employment in the industry, is something of which modern union leadership, as well as management, is usually conscious. Thus the trial of strength between union and management associated with collective bargaining is, essentially although not exclusively, over the division of profits. When demand is limited, we have, in other words, an essentially healthy manifestation of countervailing power. The union opposes its power as a seller of labor to that of management as a buyer: principally at stake is the division of the returns. An occasional strike is an indication that countervailing power is being employed in a sound context where the costs of any wage increase cannot readily be passed along to someone else. It should be an occasion for mild rejoicing in the conservative press. The *Daily Worker*, eagerly contemplating the downfall of capitalism, should regret this manifestation of the continued health of the system.

Under conditions of strong demand, however, collective bargaining takes on a radically different form. Then management is no longer constrained to resist union demands on the grounds that higher prices will be reflected in shrinking volume. There is now an adequate supply of eager buyers. The firm that first surrenders to the union need not worry lest it be either the first or the only one to increase prices. There are buyers for all. No one has occasion, as the result of price increases, to worry about a general shrinkage in volume. A strong demand means an inelastic demand. On the other hand, there are grave disadvantages for management in resisting the union. Since profits are not at stake, any time lost as the result of a strike is a dead loss. Worker morale and the actual loss of part of the working force to employers who offer better wages must be reckoned with. Thus when demand is sufficiently strong to press upon the capacity of industry generally to supply it, there is no real conflict of interest between union and employer. Or to put it differently, all bargaining strength shifts to the side of the union. The latter becomes simply an engine for increasing prices, for it is to the mutual advantage of union and employer to effect a coalition and to pass the costs of their agreement on in higher prices. Other buyers along the line, who under other circumstances might have exercised their countervailing power against the price increases, are similarly inhibited. Thus under inflationary pressure of demand, the whole structure of countervailing power in the economy is dissolved.

We were able to witness one fairly good example of this dissolution of countervailing power in the continuing rounds of wage and price increases following World War II. The full coalition between management and labor, under the conditions of inflationary demand of these years, was partly disguised by the conventional expressions of animosity and by the uncertainty of management as to how long the inflation would last. However, by 1950–51 the "Fifth Round" was negotiated with scarcely an important strike. The President of the United States Steel Corporation, in yielding to the union in November 1950, indicated a *de facto* coalition when he pointed out that the "half-cent" inflation in steel prices, which would be passed along to customers, was a small price to pay for "uninterrupted and expanded" production. The consequences of this failure of countervailing power in times of inflation are considerable. They take on added importance with the easing of the depression psychosis with the passage of years. I shall now examine the role of the state in the development of countervailing power.

COUNTERVAILING POWER
AND THE STATE[11]

IN THEIR RELATIONS with government, the American people have long shown a considerable ability to temper doctrine by pragmatism. The ruggedly conservative businessman who excoriates Statism, the Welfare State and the State Department, has never allowed his convictions to interfere with an approach to the govern-

[11] Chapter X, "Countervailing Power and the State," *American Capitalism.*

ment for a tariff if he really needs it. The impeccably conservative business journal which editorially condemns Keynesians and deficit spending as heralds of disaster does not fail to point out on the financial page that the effect of the deficit in the new budget, which it so deplores, will be favorable to business volume and earnings. The up-country cotton or tobacco planter whose belief in States' rights is unequaled except by his mistrust of civil rights votes, nonetheless, for federally administered marketing quotas, a remarkably comprehensive form of agricultural regimentation.

Since the phenomenon of countervailing power is of much practical importance, even though it for long went unrecognized in economic and political theory, we should expect, in line with our highly pragmatic approach to government, that it would have been the object of a good deal of legislation and the subject of a good deal of government policy. As the last chapter has made clear, there are strong incentives in the modern economy for developing countervailing power. Moreover, the group that seeks countervailing power is, initially, a numerous and disadvantaged group which seeks organization because it faces, in its market, a much smaller and much more advantaged group. This situation is well calculated to excite public sympathy and, because there are numerous votes involved, to recruit political support.

In fact, the support of countervailing power has become in modern times perhaps the major domestic peacetime function of the federal government. Labor sought and received it in the protection and assistance which the Wagner Act provided to union organization. Farmers sought and received it in the form of federal price supports to their markets — a direct subsidy of market power. Unorganized workers have sought and received it in the form of minimum wage legislation. The bituminous-coal mines sought and received it in the Bituminous Coal Conservation Act of 1935 and the National Bituminous Coal Act of 1937.[12] These measures, all designed to give a group a market power it did not have before, comprised the most important legislative acts of the New Deal. They fueled the sharpest domestic controversies of the New and Fair Deals.

There should be no problem as to why this legislation, and the administrations that sponsored it, were keenly controversial. The groups that sought the assistance of government in building counter-

12 The first Act was declared unconstitutional in 1936; the second was allowed to expire during the war when an excess of demand had more than adequately reinforced the bargaining power of the mine operators.

vailing power sought that power in order to use it against market authority to which they had previously been subordinate. Those whose power was thereby inhibited could hardly be expected to welcome this development or the intervention of the government to abet it.

Because the nature of countervailing power has not been firmly grasped, the government's role in relation to it has not only been imperfectly understood but also imperfectly played. One is permitted to hope that a better understanding of countervailing power will contribute to better administration in the future.

II

The role of countervailing power in the economy marks out two broad problems in policy for the government. In all but conditions of inflationary demand, countervailing power performs a valuable — indeed an indispensable — regulatory function in the modern economy. Accordingly it is incumbent upon government to give it freedom to develop and to determine how it may best do so. The government also faces the question of where and how it will affirmatively support the development of countervailing power. It will be convenient to look first at the negative role of the government in allowing the development of countervailing power and then to consider its affirmative role in promoting it.

At the outset a somewhat general distinction — one that is implicit in the discussion of the last chapter — must be made between countervailing and original power.[13] When, anywhere in the course of producing, processing or distributing a particular product, one or a few firms first succeed in establishing a strong market position they may be considered to be the possessors of original market power. They are able, as the result of their power over the prices they pay or charge, to obtain more than normal margins and profits.[14] These are at the expense of the weaker suppliers or customers. This is the monopoly position anciently feared by liberals and as anciently condemned by economists, and their instincts were sound. Countervail-

[13] William J. Fellner in his book, *Competition among the Few: Oligopoly and Similar Market Structures* (New York: Alfred A. Knopf Co., 1949), observes that the market power of unions, in relation to that of corporations, is of a neutralizing not an additive character. It will be evident, I think, that this involves a distinction to the one I am making.

[14] Technically prices or margins in excess of marginal costs.

ing power invades such positions of strength, whether they be held by suppliers or customers, and redresses the position of the weaker group.

The rule to be followed by government is, in principle, a clear one. There can be very good reason for attacking positions of original market power in the economy if these are not effectively offset by countervailing power. There is at least a theoretical justification for opposing all positions of market power. There is no justification for attacking positions of countervailing power which leaves positions of original market power untouched. On the contrary, damage both in equity and to the most efficient operation of the economy will be the normal consequence of doing so.

The problems of practical application of such a rule are mostly in the field of the antitrust laws and they are a good deal more difficult than the simple articulation of the rule implies. However, a general distinction between original and countervailing power is, in fact, now made in the antitrust laws — it has been forced, against the accepted current of ideas concerning competition, by the practical reality of the phenomenon itself.

In the first development of positions of market power, a long lead was assumed by the capitalist industrial enterprise. The formidable structure of Marxian socialism was based on the assumption that this power was great and, short of revolution, immutable. As a broad historical fact such enterprise is the locus of original market power. When workers and farmers sought to develop strength in the sale of their labor power and products, they did so in markets where industrial firms had already achieved positions of original power. It would be broadly in harmony with the distinction between original and countervailing power to exclude labor and farm organizations from prosecution under the antitrust laws. This has been done. While the Sherman Act made no mention of labor, Congress did not have in mind the still modest efforts of unions to lift their bargaining power when it enacted the legislation of 1890. Subsequently, unions became subject to the law by judicial interpretation. Indeed, in the first few decades that the legislation was in effect, unions were a primary target. This led to their exclusion by name in the Clayton Act of 1914. After the Supreme Court had somewhat obdurately reincluded them in 1921 (Justices Brandeis, Holmes and Clarke dissenting) they were again and finally excluded by the Norris-LaGuardia Act of 1932 and by the subsequent and more benign decisions of a New Deal Court.

Similarly, efforts by farm co-operatives to enhance the market power of the farmer, so long as they are held within reason, are excluded by the Clayton Act of 1914, by further legislation (the Capper-Volsted Act) in 1922 and in more specific instances by the Agricultural Marketing Agreement Act of 1937. Congress has thus recognized, implicitly, that the efforts of labor and agriculture to develop market power were different from those of industrial firms. The difference — the by now plausible difference — was that these efforts were the response of workers and farmers to the power of those to whom they sold their labor or products.

A more precise and conscious use of the distinction between original and countervailing power would take account of the fact that some trade unions and some farm groups are clearly the possessors of original power. Thus workers in the building trades, although they are not highly organized or exceptionally powerful in any absolute sense, are strong in relation to the small-scale employers with whom they do business. They are clearly the possessors of original market power. The special nature of their power, as compared with that of the trade-union movement generally, explains the distress of men and women who have reacted sympathetically to the role of unions in general but who, in this uncomfortable case, have found themselves on the side of organizations that have plenary power to restrict output and enhance their own income. The obvious answer to the problem lies in the distinction between original and countervailing power. This, logically, would make restrictive practices of master plumbers or plasterers a proper object of interest by the Department of Justice while the absolutely (though not relatively) far more powerful unions in steel or automobiles who impose no similar restrictions on the supply of their labor would not be.[15]

Similarly, there are undoubted cases of exercise of original power by groups of agricultural producers. The immunity granted by existing laws is not complete — the Secretary of Agriculture is authorized to enter a complaint if, as a result of the activities of the cooperative, prices are "unduly enhanced," and a cooperative cannot merge its power with nonagricultural corporations. As a result there have been

[15] Again, government policy has shown a tendency to recognize, pragmatically, distinctions which are not recognized in the available theory. In 1940 the original power of the building trades unions was attacked by the Department of Justice. However, by eventual decision of the Supreme Court—*U.S.* v. *Hutcheson et al*, 312 U.S. 219 (1940)—the unions were held to be substantially immune.

a scattering of prosecutions of farmers' organizations — of the former California Fruit Growers' Exchange (Sunkist oranges) and of a Chicago milkshed producers' organization which was charged with being in combination in restraint of trade with milk distributors, unions and even a college professor. But such cases have been infrequent.

However, the more serious consequences of the failure to perceive the role of countervailing power have been within the fabric of industry itself. The antitrust laws have been indiscriminately invoked against firms that have succeeded in building countervailing power, while holders of original market power, against whom the countervailing power was developed, have gone unchallenged. Such action has placed the authority of law on the side of positions of monopoly power and against the interests of the public at large. The effects have been damaging to the economy and also to the prestige of the antitrust laws.

III

As the last chapter has made clear, one of the most important instruments for exercise of countervailing power is the large retail organization. These by proxy are the public's main line of defense against the market power of those who produce or process consumers' goods. We have seen that they are an American counterpart of the consumer co-operatives which, in other countries, are viewed explicitly as an instrument for countering the power of the cartels. Yet the position of the large retail organizations has been not only a general, but also in some measure a unique object of government attack. Chain stores and other large buyers have been frequent recent objects of Sherman Act prosecution and are the special target of the Robinson-Patman Act which is especially designed to inhibit their exercise of countervailing power.

Under the provisions of the Robinson-Patman Acts a chain store may receive the benefit of the demonstrably lower costs of filling the large orders which it places; it may not receive concessions that are the result of its superior bargaining power. The effect, since these concessions are important only when won from positions of original economic power, is to discriminate in favor of original power and against countervailing power.

The effects of failure to distinguish between original and countervailing power have been especially noteworthy in the several suits against the Great Atlantic and Pacific Tea Company. This company was prosecuted before the war for violation of the Robinson-Patman Act,[16] was convicted of violation of the Sherman Act in a case brought in 1944 and finally decided in 1949,[17] and was thereafter, for a period, again a defendant. In spite of its many legal misadventures, the company has not been charged with, or even seriously suspected of, exploiting the consumer. On the contrary, its crime has been too vigorous bargaining, which bargaining was, effectively, on the consumer's behalf. In the case brought in 1944 it was charged with seeking to increase its volume by reducing its margins and with bringing its bargaining power too vigorously to bear upon its suppliers in order to get price reductions. These suppliers — which included such powerful sellers as the large canning companies — had long been involved in a trial of strength with A & P over prices. They were left undisturbed. The government was in the highly equivocal position of prosecuting activities which have the effect of keeping down prices to the consumer. The positions of market power, which had given A & P its opportunity, were left untouched.

The litigation against A & P was strongly defended. Although the firm did rather less than 10 percent of the food-retailing business, had strong rivals, and was in an industry where, as observed in the last chapter, the entry of new firms is singularly easy, the danger was much stressed that it might achieve an effective monopoly of food-retailing. Nevertheless one can hardly doubt that these cases were a source of serious embarrassment to friends of the antitrust laws. No explanation, however elaborate, could quite conceal the fact that the effect of antitrust enforcement, in this case, was to the disadvantage of the public. Viewed in light of the present analysis the reason becomes evident. The prosecution, by inhibiting the exercise of countervailing power, provided protection to the very positions of market power that are anathema to the defender of the antitrust laws.[18]

[16] *Great Atlantic & Pacific Tea Co.* v. *FTC*, 106 F. 2d 667 (1939).
[17] *U.S.* v. *New York Great Atlantic & Pacific Tea Co.*, 67 F. Supplement 626 (1946). For a discussion of this case see M. A. Adelman, "The A & P Case: A Study in Applied Economic Theory," *Quarterly Journal of Economics* (May 1949), pp. 238 ff.
[18] Much of the pressure for the Robinson-Patman Act and its enforcement (and in lesser measure also the State Fair Trade laws which have a similar ultimate effect) came and continues to come from the smaller competitors of the chains who do not themselves have effective countervailing power. They have, in effect,

No one should conclude, from the foregoing, that an exemption of countervailing power should now be written into the antitrust laws. A considerable gap has always separated useful economic concepts from applicable legal ones. However, a number of conclusions, with immediate bearing on the antitrust laws, do follow from this analysis. In the first place the mere possession and exercise of market power is not a useful criterion for antitrust action. The further and very practical question must be asked: Against whom and for what purposes is the power being exercised? Unless this question is asked and the answer makes clear that the public is the victim, the antitrust laws, by attacking countervailing power, can as well enhance as reduce monopoly power.

Secondly, it is clear that some damage can be done to the economy by such legislation as the Robinson-Patman Act. This legislation is the culmination of a long and confused legal and legislative struggle dating from 1914 over what economists have come to call price discrimination. The ostensible motive of the legislation is to protect competition. The seller is prevented from giving a lower price to one customer than to another where the lower price cannot be justified by the economies associated with the particular sale and where the effect is "to injure, destroy, or prevent" competition either with the seller or between his customers. The practical effect, reinforced by recent court decisions, is to make any important price concessions to any large buyer of questionable legality.[19]

Even those who are unwavering in their belief in competition have been inclined to doubt whether this legislation does much to protect competition. What is not doubtful at all is that the legisla-

---

sought to protect their own weaker buying position by denying strength to others. This is wholly understandable but it has not been the only recourse of the independent. He has had the alternative of joining his bargaining power, as a buyer, with other independents. And, in some fields—food-retailing and department stores for example—such cooperative bargaining has enjoyed a large measure of success. A clearer view of original and countervailing power by public authority would also have made this the preferred way of protecting the position of the independent retailer. In short, the public would have been better served by a more comprehensive development of countervailing power by retailers than by a policy which sought to eliminate the advantages associated with its possession by denying it to all.

[19] Especially *FTC* v. *Morton Salt Company*, 334 U.S. 37 (1948) although a still more recent decision makes legitimate concessions to meet the price of another seller (*Standard Oil of Indiana* v. *FTC* 71 S. Ct. 240, 1951).

ion strikes directly at the effective exercise of countervailing power. To achieve price discrimination — to use bargaining power to get a differentially lower price — is the very essence of the exercise of countervailing power. In trying, with questionable effect, to preserve one of the autonomous regulators of the economy the government is seriously impairing another.

Finally, the theory of countervailing power throws important light on the advantage of different numbers of firms in an industry and on the objectives of the antitrust laws in relation thereto. One of the effects of the new ideas on market theory, as noted in Chapter IV, was to raise serious doubts whether an industry of small numbers was, in fact, socially preferable to a monopoly. Once firms had recognized their interdependence, it was believed that they would find a price, output and profit position not greatly different from that which would be achieved by a single firm. This made it doubtful whether it was worthwhile to prosecute a monopoly in order to create an oligopoly.

The examination of the relation of oligopoly to technical change and development will already have raised some questions about this conclusion. There is reason to suppose that an industry characterized by oligopoly will be more progressive than an industry controlled by one firm. Recognition of the role of countervailing power suggests a further clear advantage on the side of the oligopoly. One can hardly doubt that, in general, it will be much easier for countervailing power to break into a position of market strength maintained by an imperfect coalition of three, four or a dozen firms than into a position held by one firm. When there is more than one firm in a market there are opportunities for playing one off against another. Mistrust and uncertainty can be developed in the mind of one entrepreneur as to the intentions and good faith of others. These, in turn, can be translated into bargaining concessions. Such opportunities abruptly disappear when the number is reduced to one.

Thus the theory of countervailing power comes to the defense of the antitrust laws at what has been a very vulnerable point. Efforts to prevent or to disperse single-firm control of an industry can be defended for the greater opening they provide for the exercise of countervailing power. Similar and equally good reasons exist for resisting mergers. Those who have always believed there was something uniquely evil about monopoly are at least partly redeemed by the theory of countervailing power.

IV

It must surely be agreed that, during the present century, American economic and political life have gained in strength as the result of the improved position of workers and farmers — two important and once disadvantaged groups. A scant fifty years ago American labor relations were characterized by sullenness, anger and fear. Farmer attitudes were marked by a deep sense of insecurity and inferiority. There can be little question that these attitudes were an aspect of economic inferiority. Workers and farmers lived in the knowledge that they were subject, in one way or another, to the power of others. It was inevitable, therefore, that with the development of countervailing power these attitudes would change and they have. In place of the inferiority and insecurity has come a well-developed sense of equality and confidence. It would seem difficult, indeed, to argue that the American economy and polity is anything but stronger as a result.

That argument has been made — and vigorously since this book first appeared. Social serenity would seem to be a plausible social goal. It would seem to the common advantage that there be, at any given time, no open or suppressed revolution. However, change and innovation which have as their main purpose the relief of social tension do not have much standing in economics, at least with those whose eyes are trained on the competitive model as a social norm. There are some who would accept a little turbulence in pursuit of so admirable a goal. For others this is not a matter for the economists to worry about. They can watch the rioting from the window.

In this tradition, the sufficient and only test of social change is whether, assuming organization and technology to be given, it reduces prices to the consumer. This is not a test which countervailing power can always satisfy. The development of such power by workers or farmers may result primarily in a redistribution of returns. It may, by raising marginal costs, raise prices to the consumer.

However, apart from the error in the purely static character of this test, it is evident that it is socially limited to the point of being frivolous. The political attitudes of those who are subject to economic power are rarely benign. In numerous lands at numerous times they have been violently the reverse. Obviously the elimination of these tensions is no less a goal because it has a price. It remains to add that there is no indication that the price has ever been considerable.

A number who have accepted as desirable the development of countervailing power by previously disadvantaged groups have been nonetheless careful to point out that it is decidedly a second-best solution. Given the power of the modern industrial corporation, it is doubtless well that those who do business with it have the capacity to protect themselves. But how much better to have avoided this struggle between the behemoths. There is something frightening and possibly dangerous about this bargaining between vast aggregations. How much better to have denied power to all. The world of countervailing power may be tolerable but it is highly imperfect.

This is an appealing argument although it is not likely to appeal to anyone who is interested in results. Past efforts to extirpate economic power have been notably unavailing. One cannot suppose that they will be more successful in the future. Economic power may indeed be inherent in successful capitalism. We had better be content with restraints we have than to search for a never-never land in which they would be rendered unnecessary.

Finally, there has been special concern over the role which government has played in the development of countervailing power. As noted, farmers, workers and numerous other groups have sought and received government assistance, either in the form of direct support to their market power or in support to organization which in turn made market power possible. In short, the government has subsidized with its own power the countervailing power of workers, farmers and others. This assistance, clearly, explains some part of the self-confidence and well-being which these groups display today.

Yet few courses of policy have ever been undertaken more grudgingly and with a greater sense of guilt. One can scarcely imagine a government action which, on the record, has produced more beneficent results in practice in which less pride has been taken. Especially in the case of agriculture, all measures have, until recently, been characterized as "emergency" legislation. This is invariably our label for excusing to our consciences action which seems to be at once wise and unwise.

The principal reason for this sense of guilt, no doubt, is that the notion of a government subsidy of its power to groups seeking to develop countervailing power has never enjoyed a place in the accredited structure of American economic and political science. Accordingly the unfinished tasks of developing such power have never had a place on the reformer's calendar. The reformer, in fact, has almost invariably been overtaken by the action. When the groups in question have developed enough influence to obtain government assistance on their own behalf they have simply gone ahead and got it without blessing or benefit of doctrine. As the role of counter-vailing power comes to be understood, we can expect that much of the anxiety that is evoked by government support to the process will disappear.

We shall also view with more equanimity the extension of counter-vailing power in the economy. What has strengthened the American economy so admirably in the past must be presumed to have an unexploited potential for good in the future. There are still some millions of Americans who are without any organized expression of market power and whose standards of living and welfare are cate-gorical evidence of the consequences. These include, for example, some two million hired farm workers, the truly forgotten men of American life. They have no security in their employment—there are few that cannot be fired on a day's notice. They have only limited social security benefits; they are normally unprotected by work-men's compensation in what is a fairly hazardous occupation; many do not have a fixed place of abode; their pay, even in times when there is a strong demand for their services, is far from handsome. A share in the gains from the newly developed market power of the farmer has still to be transmitted to his hired man.

There are also the unorganized urban workers, those on the fringes of the labor movement and, perhaps most important of all, occu-pational categories which, in the past, have foresworn efforts to develop economic power. Schoolteachers, clerical workers, municipal employees and civil servants have generally avoided organization as something not quite genteel or because it was believed that em-ployers and the community at large would recognize their importance and pay accordingly. In addition the natural leaders among white-collar workers have had, as ordinary workers had not, the clear al-ternative of obtaining promotion. A 10 percent increase in pay is not of great consequence to a high-school mathematics teacher if he is soon to become principal. This self-denying ordinance by white-collar workers where organization is concerned has invariably been viewed with approval, even as a manifestation of patriotism and sound Americanism, by public authorities and private employers.

Quite possibly the white-collar groups did not suffer too severely from their lack of market power in the years before World War II.

In times of stable process the salaried worker seeks an increase in pay only for the sake of increasing his real income. His weakness is not likely — as with the wage earner contending against pay cuts — to cost him ground. A skillful negotiator can do much for himself.[20] However, in times of rising prices, market power must be exercised affirmatively if past positions are to be held. It seems to me possible that the next group to seek to assert its market power will be the genteel white-collar class. In any case, we cannot assume that efforts by presently unorganized groups to seek market power, and to seek the assistance of government in their effort, is finished business.

In the actual sequence of events, some measure of organization by the group themselves must precede any very important government subsidy to their developing market power. Not until farmers and workers achieved some organization on their own behalf were they able to get the state to reinforce their efforts. In the thirties the Farm Security Administration, an idealistic and imaginative effort to help subsistence and tenant farmers and farm workers, largely petered out because those aided lacked the organization to defend in Congress and before the public the efforts being made on their behalf. Support to countervailing power is not endowed, *ad hoc*, by government. It must be sought.

v

At this point it becomes possible to answer, at least tentatively, one of the questions with which this essay was launched. That is the meaning of the great expansion of state activity in recent decades, the expansion which conservatives have found so alarming and which many liberals have supported without knowing quite why. We can now see that a large part of the state's new activity — the farm legislation, labor legislation, minimum-wage legislation — is associated with the development of countervailing power. As such it is neither adventitious nor abnormal; the government action supports or supplements a normal economic process. Steps to strengthen countervailing power are not, in principle, different from steps to strengthen

---

[20] Though clearly this is not a simple business. The psychological crisis of the devoted but unassertive white-collar employee when he must appeal for a salary raise is one of the most reliable topics of the American cartoonist. The popularity of the theme, apart from revealing the intransigent sadism of cartoonists and their audience, suggests that the problem depicted is a real one.

competition. Given the existence of private market power in the economy, the growth of countervailing power strengthens the capacity of the economy for autonomous self-regulation and thereby lessens the amount of over-all government control or planning that is required or sought.

Two or three further points may be made. Increasingly, in our time, we may expect domestic political differences to turn on the question of supporting or not supporting efforts to develop countervailing power. Liberalism will be identified with the buttressing of weak bargaining positions in the economy; conservatism — and this may well be its proper function — will be identified with the protection of positions of original power. There will be debate over whether weak positions have been unduly strengthened. The struggle over the Taft-Hartley Act is an example of the kind of political issue which countervailing power can be expected to develop. The essential question at issue in the Taft-Hartley controversy was whether, in the process of buttressing a weak bargaining position, the government had turned it into an unduly strong one.

On the whole, the appearance of countervailing power as a political issue cannot be considered especially unhealthy although it will almost certainly be so regarded. At first glance there is something odious about the notion that the poor and the excluded improve their lot in a democracy only by winning power. But so far there has been much less reason to regret than to approve the results. The position of great groups in the community has been notably strengthened and improved. Those who lost power cannot be presumed to have enjoyed their loss. There was much outward evidence that they regretted it exceedingly. Some, however, may have lived to see that, set against the loss of their authority, is their greater prospect for an agreeable old age.

There remains, of course, the chance that power, developed and even encouraged to neutralize other power, will start on a career of its own. This is the specter which has been raised by nearly every critic of the concept of countervailing power, even the friendliest ones. This danger may exist. No one can tell. It is some comfort that those who have worked most cohesively to develop countervailing power — the unions and the major farm organizations in particular — have so far comported themselves with some restraint. This is an area, we need remind ourselves, where anything that is novel has an unparalleled aspect of danger. Economic power even in its most elementary form evokes such fears. A leading American industrialist warned in 1903 that: "Organized labor knows but one law and that is the law of physical force — the law of the Huns and the Vandals, the law of the savage. . . . Composed as it is of the men of muscle rather than the men of intelligence, and commanded by leaders who are at heart disciples of revolution, it is not strange that organized labor stands for principles that are in direct conflict with the natural laws of economics."[21] Not even the professional alarmist would voice such views of the labor movement today. It is only in light of history that our fear of the countervailing power of weaker groups dissolves, that their effort to establish their power in the market emerges as the stuff of which economic progress consists. It is by our experience, not our fears, that we should be guided.

[21] David M. Parry, President of the National Association of Manufacturers. Annual Address. *New York Times,* April 15, 1903.

BOOK

III

Theory
and
Theorist

PART ONE

THE GREAT TRIAD: A TRANSITION

Review and Preview

The Great Triad: A Transition

*I*n our pursuit of the history of an idea and the fruit it bore, we now in this Book Three reach first harvest. Let us mark the road by which we have come.

Farmboy — agricultural student — graduate student in agricultural economy and final degree in general economics — teacher — economic adviser to National Defense Advisory Board with some particular reference to agricultural economy — Administrator, Office of Price Control — as general economist, member U. S. Strategic Bombing Survey — author, particularly concerned with markets, prices, and their control. How straight the road appears in the rearview mirror.

Next in the article contributed to the Years of the Modern comes the phrase "conventional doctrine." Here for the reader, whether or not for the writer, is the moment when interest in method appears to become absorption with theory. Here is where the reader can see it happen — the birth of an idea; and from this moment its author is likely to be its guardian, its guide, and its slave, a likelihood confirmed with the publication of American Capitalism and the use of the more formal phrase: "the conventional wisdom."

An idea is like a Frankenstein monster or it may be Pygmalion's maiden. To its discoverer, it may be a garden of Eden with Eve included or a nightmare without an end — a companion, a blessing, a refuge, a guide, a terror, an addiction, a duty or a bad, bad cold, but whatever it may be and to whomever it may be what it is, it is also a lost kitten in search of a home. Feed it and it is yours. Take it to the pound, kick it out and slam the door, leave it to the sucker down the road, to caprice, compromise, and time that dulls the pangs of guilt, but if you feed it, it is yours and you belong to it. Galbraith fed it. Today, that kitten is a lion. For the writer, the creator, an "idea" is not to laugh at. It may cause life-long disappointment, "writer's block," even self-annihilation. At best it is a dangerous gift of unknown power.

For the reader, the spectator, the observer, the work of Galbraith exemplifies this drama. It is a drama of growing tensions between theorist and theory, occupation and preoccupation. It is the solemn procession of choices that is living. It does not depend upon the author or his works; rather, it is that tension itself that possesses the scene. Its necessities move all else — a bodiless force, the irresistible nature of which is seen only in the bending of the figures upon the stage. For all that, this invisible actor and his inaudible part bring life and credibility to action which in turn is illustrated and documented in the writings of Galbraith. The perception of that second play in silent silhouette adds weight, understanding and visibility to the economist's thesis which now unfolds.

If the old laws of supply and demand no longer hold, if the office of price administration has been proceeding with considerable success on empirical rules derived from practical observation, and if then there is a "conventional doctrine" that doesn't work, there must be an unconventional doctrine that does. With the statement of the negative condition, Galbraith had to have seen the inevitable positive conclusion and with it in shadow form, the architecture of a new economy.

To see in detail the structure that by necessity imposed itself upon this single penetrating glimpse required of the author three books and over twenty years of active academic, political and diplomatic life. Each useful detail derived from an intense participation in two restless decades of American history must have gathered to the central pole of theory. Thus was the author held on course. The three books are The Affluent Society, The New Industrial State, and Economics and the Public Purpose. Together they are a superb triad.

It was surely The Affluent Society that fixed Galbraith once and for all in the public consciousness. A man interested in economic theory will now reply to the challenge "Galbraith!" with the pass-words "Affluent Society." The book was an explicit attack on the establishment of classical economists. Hitherto that attack had been usually implicit, and always somewhat casual. Now it was clear that a drastic reorientation of modern economic theory lay behind that critical phrase, "the conventional wisdom," and this first volume in the triad, so memorably entitled The Affluent Society.

The three books together are in a sense one book in that they bracket economic thought from its beginnings until today and beyond. Each presents the whole but the focus shifts from book to book. No selection process can do justice to the range and depth of Galbraith's economic understanding and also, since economics is not a "pure" science, to his understanding of the men who direct its inevitable forces.

Even after the publication of The Affluent Society, there were long periods between the publication of each of its sibling titles. The Affluent Society was published in 1958, The New Industrial State in 1967 and Economics and the Public Purpose in 1973. During these periods the author completed numerous other books: two volumes of essays, a satire, a work of fiction, a memoir of his service as our ambassador to India, a book on Indian painting and another on the American Economy. They reveal the distractions and frustrations to which he was subject during this period of fifteen years. They also indicate the search for time and peace in which to reach down to the intricate mechanisms which cause the seethings in our economic life. And finally they show the compulsive need to present a formula for a good economy for our time.

It would be convenient to group the three books together in one section, but that would also be to misrepresent the growth and vary-ing experience that went into the writing of each particular volume and thus to betray the intention of this selective process, which is to present the sources and course, strewn with diversions, of a challeng-ing and complex view of commercial man in a fully developed industrial state. The selections therefore follow in the order of their publication.

PART TWO

WARM UP

SELECTION 7

I f indeed American Capitalism is an inadvertent ground-
breaking for the construction of a new understanding of modern economics, why did the author stop to dally with a nuts-and-bolts book
like The Great Crash rather than proceed at once to the first volume
in the triad, The Affluent Society.

The depression which followed the Great Crash was Galbraith's
first and sternest tutor in general economics. Throughout his early
work it is seen as a formidable element in the behavior of Americans
and thus as a factor in the reading of the national horoscope.

In Galbraith's view, the effect of the depression of the thirties was
that of a high voltage shock to the American psyche — a shock
greater than that of the First World War. The depression caused
some hardship to nearly every American; for many it was a great
hardship. By comparison the Kaiser's war affected few. The great
majority heard only the bugles, not the cannon. A decade later the
crash and depression were another matter.

The fear of a repetition of that boom and bust tempered our behavior after the Second Great War. That in turn became deceptive
evidence in later judgments about the effectiveness of measures taken
at the time to steady the postwar economy. The fear lingers with us

yet but nonetheless fades into the heroics of history beside other great landmarks of the nation's two centuries — something that cannot be that way again. Before Galbraith could attempt the outline of a better economy in the fifties he had to know exactly what happened in the thirties, and why it had not happened again. Was it even at the moment just beyond the horizon?

We have classed The Great Crash along with Money as "study" books written to assure the author that his perceptions were indeed correct. To what extent such studies were deliberate or subconscious or to what extent The Great Crash facilitated the writing of The Affluent Society even the author could not be expected to know, but when you consider the essay in Years of the Modern and later American Capitalism, it is clear that he has long been in the hands of his creation.

At any rate, here are three chapters from The Great Crash. One concerns the first days of the Crash, another its downward lethal course. Together they provide some conception of those first months of trial. A third chapter deals with causes and consequences and some measures taken in the hope of moderating any repetition.

As a codicil to the selections from The Great Crash, the editors have added an after-the-fact introduction written for a low-priced edition published in 1961 under Houghton Mifflin Company's "Sentry Editions" imprint. It seemed to us more of an afterword than a foreword, and for the generation come of age since the book was first published, it provides a startling sense of the passage of time and events that have influenced both society and Galbraith since he first looked the "Great Triad" in the eye.

We have not footnoted the piece with identification of the various senators that pass through its pages and whose names were household words at the time. Their provenance seems sufficiently suggested. If the names are lost to history, that will only emphasize the sense of another era.

The Great Crash

THE CRASH [1]

ACCORDING TO the accepted view of events, by the autumn of 1929 the economy was well into a depression. In June the indexes of industrial and of factory production both reached a peak and had turned down. By October, the Federal Reserve index of industrial production stood at 117 as compared with 126 four months earlier. Steel production declined from June on; in October freight-car loading fell. Home-building, a most mercurial industry, had been falling for several years, and it slumped still farther in 1929. Finally, down came the stock market. A penetrating student of the economic behavior of this period has said that the market slump "reflected, in the main, the change which was already apparent in the industrial situation."[2]

Thus viewed, the stock market is but a mirror which, perhaps as in this instance somewhat belatedly, provides an image of the underlying or *fundamental* economic situation. Cause and effect run from the economy to the stock market, never the reverse. In 1929, the economy was headed for trouble. Eventually that trouble was violently reflected in Wall Street.

In 1929 there were good, or at least strategic, reasons for this view, and it is easy to understand why it has become high doctrine. In Wall Street, as elsewhere in 1929, few people wanted a bad depression. In Wall Street, as elsewhere, there is deep faith in the power of incantation. When the market fell, many Wall Street citizens immediately sensed the real danger, which was that income and employment — prosperity in general — would be adversely affected.

[1] Chaper VI, "The Crash," *The Great Crash*, 1929 (London: André Deutsch, n. ed., 1973), pp. 93–112.
[2] Thomas Wilson, *Fluctuations in Income and Employment*, p. 143.

This had to be prevented. Preventive incantation required that as many important people as possible repeat as firmly as they could that it wouldn't happen. This they did. They explained how the stock market was merely the froth and that the real substance of economic life rested in production, employment and spending, all of which would remain unaffected. No one knew for sure that this was so. As an instrument of economic policy, incantation does not permit of minor doubts or scruples.

In the later years of depression it was important to continue emphasizing the unimportance of the stock market. The depression was an exceptionally disagreeable experience. Wall Street has not always been a cherished symbol in our national life. In some of the devout regions of the nation, those who speculate in stocks — the even more opprobrious term gamblers is used — are not counted the greatest moral adornments of our society. Any explanation of the depression which attributed importance to the market collapse would accordingly have been taken very seriously, and it would have meant serious trouble for Wall Street. Wall Street, no doubt, would have survived but there would have been scars. We should be clear that no deliberate conspiracy existed to minimize the consequences of the Wall Street crash for the economy. Rather, it merely appeared to everyone with an instinct for conservative survival that Wall Street had better be kept out of it. It was vulnerable.

In fact, any satisfactory explanation of the events of the autumn of 1929 and thereafter must accord a dignified role to the speculative boom and ensuing collapse. Until September or October of 1929, the decline in economic activity was very modest. As I shall argue later, until after the market crash one could reasonably assume that this downward movement might soon reverse itself, as a similar movement had reversed itself in 1927 or did subsequently in 1949. There were no reasons for expecting disaster. No one could foresee that production, prices, incomes and all other indicators would continue to shrink through three long and dismal years. Only after the market crash were there plausible grounds to suppose that things might now for a long while get a lot worse.

From the foregoing it follows that the crash did not come — as some have suggested — because the market suddenly became aware that a serious depression was in the offing. A depression, serious or otherwise, could not be foreseen when the market fell. There is still the possibility that the downturn in the indexes frightened the speculators, led them to unload their stocks and so punctured a bubble that had in any case to be punctured one day. This is more plausible. Some people who were watching the indexes may have been persuaded by this intelligence to sell, and others may then have been encouraged to follow. This is not very important, for it is in the nature of a speculative boom that almost anything can collapse it. Any serious shock to confidence can cause sales by those speculators who have always hoped to get out before the final collapse but after all possible gains from rising prices have been reaped. Their pessimism will infect those simpler souls who had thought the market might go up forever but who now will change their minds and sell. Soon there will be margin calls, and still others will be forced to sell. So the bubble breaks.

Along with the downturn of the indexes Wall Street has always attributed importance to two other events in the pricking of the bubble. In England on September 20, 1929, the enterprises of Clarence Hatry suddenly collapsed. Hatry was one of those curiously un-English figures with whom the English periodically find themselves unable to cope. Although his earlier financial history had been anything but reassuring, Hatry in the twenties had built up an industrial and financial empire of truly impressive proportions. The nucleus, all the more remarkably, was a line of coin-in-the-slot vending and automatic photograph machines. From these unprepossessing enterprises he had marched on into investment trusts and high finance. His expansion owed much to the issuance of unauthorized stock, the increase of assets by the forging of stock certificates and other equally informal financing. In the lore of 1929, the unmasking of Hatry in London is supposed to have struck a sharp blow to confidence in New York.[3]

Ranking with Hatry in this lore was the refusal on October 11 of the Massachusetts Department of Public Utilities to allow Boston Edison to split its stock four to one. As the company argued, such split-ups were much in fashion. To avoid going along was to risk being considered back in the corporate gaslight era. The refusal was unprecedented. Moreover, the Department added insult to injury by announcing an investigation of the company's rates and by suggesting that the present value of the stock, "due to the action of speculators," had reached a level where "no one, in our judgment . . . on the basis of its earnings, would find it to his advantage to buy it."

These were uncouth words. They could have been important as,

---

[3] Hatry pleaded guilty and early in 1930 was given a long jail sentence.

conceivably, could have been the exposure of Clarence Hatry. But it could also be that the inherently unstable equilibrium was shattered simply by a spontaneous decision to get out. On September 22, the financial pages of the New York papers carried an advertisement of an investment service with the arresting headline, OVERSTAYING A BULL MARKET. Its message read as follows: "Most investors make money in a bull market, only to lose all profits made — and sometimes more — in the readjustment that inevitably follows." Instead of the downturn in the Federal Reserve industrial index, the exposure of Hatry or the unnatural obstinacy of the Massachusetts Department of Public Utilities, it could have been such thoughts stirring first in dozens and then in hundreds, and finally in thousands of breasts which finally brought an end to the boom. What first stirred these doubts we do not know but neither is it very important that we know.

II

Confidence did not disintegrate at once. As noted, through September and into October, although the trend of the market was generally down, good days came with the bad. Volume was high. On the New York Stock Exchange sales were nearly always above four million and frequently above five. In September new issues appeared in even greater volume than in August, and they regularly commanded a premium over the offering price. On September 20, the *Times* noted that the stock of the recently launched Lehman Corporation which had been offered at $104 had sold the day before at $136. (In the case of this well-managed investment trust the public enthusiasm was not entirely misguided.) During September brokers' loans increased by nearly $670 million, by far the largest increase of any month to date. This showed that speculative zeal had not diminished.

Other signs indicated that the gods of the New Era were still in their temples. In its October 12 issue the *Saturday Evening Post* had a lead story by Isaac F. Marcosson on Ivar Kreuger. This was a scoop, for Kreuger had previously been inaccessible to journalists. "Kreuger," Marcosson observed, "like Hoover, is an engineer. He has consistently applied engineer precision to the welding of his far-flung industry." And this was not the only resemblance. "Like Hoover," the author added, "Kreuger rules through pure reason."

In the interview Kreuger was remarkably candid on one point. He told Mr. Marcosson: "Whatever success I have had may perhaps be attributable to three things: One is silence, the second is more silence, while the third is still: more silence." This was so. Two and a half years later Kreuger committed suicide in his Paris apartment, and shortly thereafter it was discovered that his aversion to divulging information, especially if accurate, had kept even his most intimate acquaintances in ignorance of the greatest fraud in history. His American underwriters, the eminently respectable firm of Lee, Higginson and Company of Boston, had heard nothing and knew nothing. One of the members of the firm, Donald Durant, was a member of the board of directors of the Kreuger enterprises. He had never attended a directors' meeting, and it is certain that he would have been no wiser had he done so.

During the last weeks of October, *Time* Magazine, young and not yet omniscient, also featured Kreuger on its cover — "a great admirer of Cecil Rhodes." Then a week later, as though to emphasize its faith in the New Era, it went on to Samuel Insull.[4] (A fortnight after that, its youthful illusions shattered, the weekly newsmagazine gave the place of historic honor to Warden Lawes of Sing Sing.) In these same Indian summer days, *The Wall Street Journal* took notice of the official announcement that Secretary of the Treasury Andrew Mellon woud remain in the cabinet at least until 1933 (there had been rumors that he might resign) and observed: "Optimism again prevails . . . the announcement . . . did more to restore confidence than anything else." In Germany Charles E. Mitchell[5] announced that the "industrial condition of the United States is absolutely sound," that too much attention was being paid to brokers' loans, and that "nothing can arrest the upward movement." On October 15, as he sailed for home, he enlarged on the point: "The markets generally are now in a healthy condition . . . values have a sound basis in the general prosperity of our country." That same evening Professor Irving Fisher[6] made his historic announcement about the permanently high plateau

---

[4] Operating out of Chicago, Samuel Insull, a former associate of Thomas Edison, put together in 1912 a gigantic utilities combination to supply power for the surrounding Midwest. The shaky enterprise collapsed in 1932 at the bottom of the Great Depression. Tried for embezzlement and mail fraud, Insull was acquitted in 1935.

[5] Head of the National City Bank and a director of the New York Federal Reserve Bank, Charles E. Mitchell committed $25 million of his bank's funds in support of brokers' loans before the 1929 crash. He was later acquitted on a charge of income tax evasion.

[6] Yale professor of economics. For reference on historic remark see page 75, *The Great Crash*.

and added, "I expect to see the stock market a good deal higher than it is today within a few months." Indeed, the only disturbing thing, in these October days, was the fairly steady downward drift in the market.

III

On Saturday, October 19, Washington dispatches reported that Secretary of Commerce Lamont was having trouble finding the $100,000 in public funds that would be required to pay the upkeep of the yacht *Corsair* which J. P. Morgan had just given the government. (Morgan's deprivation was not extreme: a new $3,000,000 *Corsair* was being readied at Bath, Maine.) There were other and more compelling indications of an unaccustomed stringency. The papers told of a very weak market the day before — there were heavy declines on late trading, and the *Times* industrial average had dropped about 7 points. Steel had lost 7 points; General Electric, Westinghouse and Montgomery Ward all lost 6. Meanwhile, that day's market was behaving very badly. In the second heaviest Saturday's trading in history, 3,488,100 shares were changing hands. At the close the *Times* industrials were down 12 points. The blue chips were seriously off, and speculative favorites had gone into a nose-dive. J. I. Case, for example, had fallen a full 40 points.

On Sunday the market was front-page news — the *Times* headline read, STOCKS DRIVEN DOWN AS WAVE OF SELLING ENGULFS THE MARKET, and the financial editor next day reported for perhaps the tenth time that the end had come. (He had learned, however, to hedge. "For the time at any rate," he said, "Wall Street seemed to see the reality of things.") No immediate explanation of the break was forthcoming. The Federal Reserve had long been quiet. Hatry and the Massachusetts Department of Public Utilities were from a week to a month in the past. They became explanations only later.

The papers that Sunday carried three comments which were to become familiar in the days that followed. After Saturday's trading, it was noted, quite a few margin calls went out. This meant that the value of stock which the recipients held on margin had declined to the point where it was no longer sufficient collateral for the loan that had paid for it. The speculator was being asked for more cash.

The other two observations were more reassuring. The papers agreed, and this was also the informed view on Wall Street, that the worst was over. And it was predicted that on the following day the market would begin to receive organized support. Weakness, should it appear, would be tolerated no longer.

Never was there a phrase with more magic than "organized support." Almost immediately it was on every tongue and in every news story about the market. Organized support meant that powerful people would organize to keep prices of stocks at a reasonable level. Opinions differed as to who would organize this support. Some had in mind the big operators like Cutten, Durant and Raskob. They, of all people, couldn't afford a collapse. Some thought of the bankers — Charles Mitchell had acted once before, and certainly if things got bad he would act again. Some had in mind the investment trusts. They held huge portfolios of common stocks, and obviously they could not afford to have them become cheap. Also, they had cash. So if stocks did become cheap, the investment trusts would be in the market picking up bargains. This would mean that the bargains wouldn't last. With so many people wanting to avoid a further fall, a further fall would clearly be avoided.

In the ensuing weeks the Sabbath pause had a marked tendency to breed uneasiness and doubts and pessimism and a decision to get out on Monday. This, it seems certain, was what happened on Sunday, October 20.

IV

Monday, October 21, was a very poor day. Sales totaled 6,091,870, the third greatest volume in history, and some tens of thousands who were watching the market throughout the country made a disturbing discovery. There was no way of telling what was happening. Previously on big days of the bull market the ticker had often fallen behind, and one didn't discover until well after the market closed how much richer he had become. But the experience with a falling market had been much more limited. Not since March had the ticker fallen seriously behind on declining values. Many now learned for the first time that they could be ruined, totally and forever, and not even know it. And if they were not ruined, there was a strong tendency to imagine it. From the opening on the 21st the ticker lagged, and by noon it was an hour late. Not until an hour and forty minutes after the close of the market did it record the last transaction. Every ten minutes prices of selected stocks were printed on the bond ticker, but the wide divergence between these and the prices on the tape only added to the uneasiness — and to the growing conviction that it might be best to sell.

Things, though bad, were still not hopeless. Toward the end of Monday's trading the market rallied, and final prices were above the lows for the day. The net losses were considerably less than on Saturday. Tuesday brought a somewhat shaky gain. As so often before, the market seemed to be showing its ability to come back. People got ready to record the experience as merely another setback of which there had been so many previously.

In doing so, they were helped by the two men who now were recognized as Wall Street's official prophets. On Monday in New York, Professor Irving Fisher said that the decline had represented only a "shaking out of the lunatic fringe." He went on to explain why he felt that the prices of stocks during the boom had not caught up with their real value and would go higher. Among other things, the market had not yet reflected the beneficent effects of prohibition which had made the American worker "more productive and dependable."

On Tuesday, Charles E. Mitchell dropped anchor in New York with the observation that "the decline had gone too far." (Time and sundry congressional and court proceedings were to show that Mr. Mitchell had strong personal reasons for feeling that way.) He added that the conditions were "fundamentally sound," said again that too much attention had been paid to the large volume of brokers' loans and concluded that the situation was one which would correct itself if left alone.

By Wednesday, October 23, the effect of this cheer was somehow dissipated. Instead of further gains there were heavy losses. The opening was quiet enough, but toward midmorning motor accessory stocks were sold heavily, and volume began to increase throughout the list. The last hour was quite phenomenal — 2,600,000 shares changed hands at rapidly declining prices. The *Times* industrial average for the day dropped from 415 to 384, giving up all of its gains since the end of the previous June. Tel and Tel lost 15 points; General Electric, 20; Westinghouse, 25; and J. I. Case, another 46. Again the ticker was far behind, and to add to the uncertainty an ice storm in the Middle West caused widespread disruption of communications. That afternoon and evening thousands of speculators decided to get out while — as they mistakenly supposed — the getting was good. Other thousands were told they had no choice but to get out unless they posted more collateral, for as the day's business came to an end an unprecedented volume of margin calls went out. Speaking in Washington, even Professor Fisher was fractionally less optimistic. He told a meeting of bankers that "security values *in most instances* were not inflated." However, he did not weaken on the unrealized efficiencies of prohibition.

The papers that night went to press with a souvenir of a fast departing era. Formidable advertisements announced subscription rights in a new offering of certificates in Aktiebolaget Kreuger and Toll at $23. There was also one bit of cheer. It was predicted that on the morrow the market would surely begin to receive "organized support."

v

Thursday, October 24, is the first of the days which history — such as it is on the subject — identifies with the panic of 1929. Measured by disorder, fright and confusion, it deserves to be so regarded. That day 12,894,650 shares changed hands, many of them at prices which shattered the dreams and the hopes of those who had owned them. Of all the mysteries of the stock exchange there is none so impenetrable as why there should be a buyer for everyone who seeks to sell. October 24, 1929, showed that what is mysterious is not inevitable. Often there were no buyers, and only after wide vertical declines could anyone be induced to bid.

The panic did not last all day. It was a phenomenon of the morning hours. The market opening itself was unspectacular, and for a while prices were firm. Volume, however, was very large, and soon prices began to sag. Once again the ticker dropped behind. Prices fell farther and faster, and the ticker lagged more and more. By eleven o'clock the market had degenerated into a wild, mad scramble to sell. In the crowded boardrooms across the country the ticker told of a frightful collapse. But the selected quotations coming in over the bond ticker also showed that current values were far below the ancient history of the tape. The uncertainty led more and more people to try to sell. Others, no longer able to respond to margin calls, were sold out. By eleven-thirty the market had surrendered to blind, relentless fear. This, indeed, was panic.

Outside the Exchange in Broad Street a weird roar could be heard. A crowd gathered. Police Commissioner Grover Whalen became aware that something was happening and dispatched a special police detail to Wall Street to ensure the peace. More people came and waited, though apparently no one knew for what. A workman appeared atop one of the high buildings to accomplish some repairs, and the multitude assumed he was a would-be suicide and waited impatiently for him to jump. Crowds also formed around the branch offices of brokerage firms throughout the city and, indeed, throughout the country. Word of what was happening, or what was thought to be happening, was passed out by those who were within sight of the board or the Trans-Lux. An observer thought that people's expressions showed "not so much suffering as a sort of horrified incredulity."[7] Rumor after rumor swept Wall Street and these outlying wakes. Stocks were now selling for nothing. The Chicago and Buffalo Exchanges had closed. A suicide wave was in progress, and eleven well-known speculators had already killed themselves.

At twelve-thirty the officials of the New York Stock Exchange closed the visitors gallery on the wild scenes below. One of the visitors who had just departed was showing his remarkable ability to be on hand with history. He was the former Chancellor of the Exchequer, Mr. Winston Churchill. It was he who in 1925 returned Britain to the gold standard and the overvalued pound. Accordingly, he was responsible for the strain which sent Montagu Norman to plead in New York for easier money, which caused credit to be eased at the fatal time, which, in this academy view, in turn caused the boom. Now Churchill, it could be imagined, was viewing his awful handiwork.

There is no record of anyone's having reproached him. Economics was never his strong point, so (and wisely) it seems most unlikely that he reproached himself.

VI

In New York at least the panic was over by noon. At noon the organized support appeared.

At twelve o'clock reporters learned that a meeting was convening at 23 Wall Street at the offices of J. P. Morgan and Company. The word quickly passed as to who was there — Charles E. Mitchell, the

[7] Edwin Lefèvre, "The Little Fellow in Wall Street," *The Saturday Evening Post*, January 4, 1930.

Chairman of the Board of the National City Bank, Albert H. Wiggins, the Chairman of the Chase National Bank, William C. Potter, the President of the Guaranty Trust Company, Seward Prosser, the Chairman of the Bankers Trust Company, and the host, Thomas W. Lamont, the senior partner of Morgan's. According to legend, during the panic of 1907, the elder Morgan had brought to a halt the discussion of whether to save the tottering Trust Company of America by saying that the place to stop the panic was there. It was stopped. Now, twenty-two years later, that drama was being re-enacted. The elder Morgan was dead. His son was in Europe. But equally determined men were moving in. They were the nation's most powerful financiers. They had not yet been pilloried and maligned by New Dealers. The very news that they would act would release people from the fear to which they had surrendered.

It did. A decision was quickly reached to pool resources to support the market.[8] The meeting broke up, and Thomas Lamont met with reporters. His manner was described as serious but his words were reassuring. In what Frederick Lewis Allen later called one of the most remarkable understatements of all times,[9] he told the newspapermen, "There has been a little distress selling on the Stock Exchange." He added that this was "due to a technical condition of the *market*" rather than any fundamental cause, and told the newsmen that things were "susceptible to betterment." The bankers, he let it be known, had decided to better things.

Word had already reached the floor of the Exchange that the bankers were meeting, and the news ticker had spread the magic word afield. Prices firmed at once and started to rise. Then at one-thirty Richard Whitney appeared on the floor and went to the post where steel was traded. Whitney was perhaps the best-known figure on the floor. He was one of the group of men of good background and appropriate education who, in that time, were expected to manage the affairs of the Exchange. Currently he was vice-president of the Exchange, but in the absence of E. H. H. Simmons in Hawaii he was serving as acting president. What was much more important at the

---

[8] The amounts to be contributed or otherwise committed were never specified. Frederick Lewis Allen (*Only Yesterday* [London: Hamish Hamilton, 1931], pp. 329–30) says that each of the institutions, along with George F. Baker, Jr., of the First National, who later joined the pool, put up $40 million. This total — $240 million — seems much too large to be plausible. The *New York Times* subsequently suggested (March 9, 1938) that the total was some $20 to $30 millions.
[9] *Op. cit.*, p. 330.

moment, he was known as floor trader for Morgan's, and, indeed, his older brother was a Morgan partner.

As he made his way through the teeming crowd, Whitney appeared debonair and self-confident — some later described his manner as jaunty. (His own firm dealt largely in bonds, so it is improbable that he had been much involved in the turmoil of the morning.) At the steel post he bid 205 for 10,000 shares. This was the price of the last sale, and the current bids were several points lower. In an operation that was totally devoid of normal commercial reticence, he got 200 shares and then left the rest of the order with the specialist. He continued on his way, placing similar orders for fifteen or twenty other stocks.

This was it. The bankers, obviously, had moved in. The effect was electric. Fear vanished and gave way to concern lest the new advance be missed. Prices boomed upward.

The bankers had, indeed, brought off a notable coup. Prices as they fell that morning kept crossing a large volume of stop-loss orders — orders calling for sales whenever a specified price was reached. Brokers had placed many of these orders for their own protection on the securities of customers who had not responded to calls for additional margin. Each of these stop-loss orders tripped more securities into the market and drove prices down farther. Each spasm of liquidation thus ensured that another would follow. It was this literal chain reaction which the bankers checked, and they checked it decisively.

In the closing hour, selling orders continuing to come in from across the country turned the market soft once more. Still, in its own way, the recovery on Black Thursday was as remarkable as the selling that made it so black. The *Times* industrials were off only 12 points, or a little more than a third of the loss of the previous day. Steel, the stock that Whitney had singled out to start the recovery, had opened that morning at 205½, a point or two above the previous close. At the lowest it was down to 193½ for a 12-point loss.[10] Then it recovered to close at 206 for a surprising net gain of 2 points for this day. Montgomery Ward, which had opened at 83 and gone to 50, came back to 74. General Electric was at one time 32 points below its opening price and then came back 25 points. On the Curb, Goldman Sachs Trading Corporation opened at 81, dropped to 65, and then came back to 80. J. I. Case, maintaining a reputation for

[10] Quotations have normally been rounded to the nearest whole number in this history. The steel quotation on this day seems to call for an exception.

eccentric behavior that had brought much risk capital into the threshing machine business, made a net gain of 7 points for the day. Many had good reason to be grateful to the financial leaders of Wall Street.

VII

Not everyone could be grateful to be sure. Across the country people were only dimly aware of the improvement. By early afternoon, when the market started up, the ticker was hours behind. Although the spot quotations on the bond ticker showed the improvement, the ticker itself continued to grind out the most dismal of news. And the news on the ticker was what counted. To many, many watchers it meant that they had been sold out and that their dream — in fact, their brief reality — of opulence had gone glimmering, together with home, car, furs, jewelry and reputation. That the market, after breaking them, had recovered was the most chilling of comfort.

It was eight and a half minutes past seven that night before the ticker finished recording the day's misfortunes. In the boardrooms speculators who had been sold out since morning sat silently watching the tape. The habit of months or years, however idle it had now become, could not be abandoned at once. Then, as the final trades were registered, sorrowfully or grimly, according to their nature, they made their way out into the gathering night.

In Wall Street itself lights blazed from every office as clerks struggled to come abreast of the day's business. Messengers and boardroom boys, caught up in the excitement and untroubled by losses, went skylarking through the streets until the police arrived to quell them. Representatives of thirty-five of the largest wire houses assembled at the offices of Hornblower and Weeks and told the press on departing that the market was "fundamentally sound" and "technically in better condition than it has been in months." It was the unanimous view of those present that the worst had passed. The host firm dispatched a market letter which stated that "commencing with today's trading the market should start laying the foundation for the constructive advance which we believe will characterize 1930." Charles E. Mitchell announced that the trouble was "purely technical" and that "fundamentals remained unimpaired." Senator Carter Glass said the trouble was due largely to Charles E. Mitchell. Senator Wilson of Indiana attributed the crash to Democratic resistance to a higher tariff.

VIII

On Friday and Saturday trading continued heavy — just under six million on Friday and over two million at the short session on Saturday. Prices, on the whole, were steady — the averages were a trifle up on Friday but slid off on Saturday. It was thought that the bankers were able to dispose of most of the securities they had acquired while shoring up the market on Thursday. Not only were things better but everyone was clear as to who had made them so. The bankers had shown both their courage and their power, and the people applauded warmly and generously. The financial community, the *Times* said, now felt "secure in the knowledge that the most powerful banks in the country stood ready to prevent a recurrence [of panic]." As a result it had "relaxed its anxiety."

Perhaps never before or since have so many people taken the measure of economic prospects and found them so favorable as in the two days following the Thursday disaster. The optimism even included a note of self-congratulation. Colonel Ayres in Cleveland thought that no other country could have come through such a bad crash so well. Others pointed out that the prospects for business were good and that the stock market debacle would not make them any less favorable. No one knew, but it cannot be stressed too frequently, that for effective incantation knowledge is neither necessary nor assumed.

Eugene M. Stevens, the President of the Continental Illinois Bank, said, "There is nothing in the business situation to justify any nervousness." Walter Teagle said there had been no "fundamental change" in the oil business to justify concern; Charles M. Schwab said that the steel business had been making "fundamental progress" toward stability and added that this "fundamentally sound condition" was responsible for the prosperity of the industry; Samuel Vauclain, Chairman of the Baldwin Locomotive Works, declared that "fundamentals are sound"; President Hoover said that "the fundamental business of the country, that is production and distribution of commodities, is on a sound and prosperous basis." President Hoover was asked to say something more specific about the market — for example, that stocks were now cheap — but he refused.[11]

[11] This was stated by Garet Garrett in *The Saturday Evening Post* (December 28, 1929), and it is generally confirmed by Mr. Hoover in his memoirs. According to Mr. Garrett the banker's consortium asked the President for the statement, which suggests that the reassurance, like the support, was tolerably well organized.

Many others joined in. Howard C. Hopson, the head of Associated Gas and Electric, omitted the standard reference to fundamentals and thought it was "undoubtedly beneficial to the business interests of the country to have the gambling type of speculator eliminated." (Mr. Hopson, himself a speculator, although more of the sure-thing type, was also eliminated in due course.) A Boston investment trust took space in *The Wall Street Journal* to say, "S-T-E-A-D-Y Everybody! Calm thinking is in order. Heed the words of America's greatest bankers." A single dissonant note, though great in portent, went unnoticed. Speaking in Poughkeepsie, Governor Franklin D. Roosevelt criticized the "fever of speculation."

On Sunday there were sermons suggesting that a certain measure of divine retribution had been visited on the Republic and that it had not been entirely unmerited. People had lost sight of spiritual values in their single-minded pursuit of riches. Now they had had their lesson.

Almost everyone believed that the heavenly knuckle-rapping was over and that speculation could now be resumed in earnest. The papers were full of the prospects for next week's market.

Stocks, it was agreed, were again cheap, and accordingly there would be a heavy rush to buy. Numerous stories from the brokerage houses, some of them possibly inspired, told of a fabulous volume of buying orders which was piling up in anticipation of the opening of the market. In a concerted advertising campaign in Monday's papers, stock market firms urged the wisdom of picking up these bargains promptly. "We believe," said one house, "that the investor who purchases securities at this time with the discrimination that is always a condition of prudent investing, may do so with utmost confidence." On Monday the real disaster began.

THINGS BECOME MORE SERIOUS [12]

IN THE autumn of 1929 the New York Stock Exchange, under roughly its present constitution, was 112 years old. During this lifetime it had seen some difficult days. On September 18, 1873, the firm of Jay Cooke and Company failed, and, as a more or less direct result, so did fifty-seven other stock exchange firms in the next few weeks. On October 23, 1907, call money rates reached 125 percent

[12] Chapter VII, "Things Become More Serious," *The Great Crash,* 1929, pp. 113–132.

in the panic of that year. On September 16, 1920 — the autumn months are the off season in Wall Street — a bomb exploded in front of Morgan's next door, killing thirty people and injuring a hundred more.

A common feature of all these earlier troubles was that having happened they were over. The worst was reasonably recognizable as such. The singular feature of the great crash of 1929 was that the worst continued to worsen. What looked one day like the end proved on the next day to have been only the beginning. Nothing could have been more ingeniously designed to maximize the suffering, and also to insure that as few as possible escaped the common misfortune. The fortunate speculator who had funds to answer the first margin call presently got another and equally urgent one, and if he met that there would still be another. In the end all the money he had was extracted from him and lost. The man with the smart money, who was safely out of the market when the first crash came, naturally went back in to pick up bargains. (Not only were a recorded 12,894,650 shares sold on October 24; precisely the same number were bought.) The bargains then suffered a ruinous fall. Even the man who waited out all of October and all of November, who saw the volume of trading return to normal and saw Wall Street become as placid as a produce market, and who then bought common stocks would see their value drop to a third or a fourth of the purchase price in the next twenty-four months. The Coolidge bull market was a remarkable phenomenon. The ruthlessness of its liquidation was, in its own way, equally remarkable.

II

Monday, October 28, was the first day on which this process of climax and anticlimax *ad infinitum* began to reveal itself. It was another terrible day. Volume was huge, although below the previous Thursday — nine and a quarter million shares as compared with nearly thirteen. But the losses were far more severe. The *Times* industrials were down 49 points for the day. General Electric was off 48; Westinghouse, 34; Tel and Tel, 34. Steel went down 18 points. Indeed, the decline on this one day was greater than that of all the preceding week of panic. Once again a late ticker left everyone in ignorance of what was happening, save that it was bad.

On this day there was no recovery. At one-ten Charles E. Mitchell was observed going into Morgan's, and the news ticker carried the magic word. Steel rallied and went from 194 to 198. But Richard Whitney did not materialize. It seems probable in light of later knowledge that Mitchell was on the way to float a personal loan. The market weakened again, and in the last hour a phenomenal three million shares — a big day's business before and ever since — changed hands at rapidly falling prices.

At four-thirty in the afternoon the bankers assembled once more at Morgan's, and they remained in session until six-thirty. They were described as taking a philosophical attitude, and they told the press that the situation "retained hopeful features," although these were not specified. But the statement they released after the meeting made clear what had been discussed for the two hours. It was no part of the banker's purpose, the statement said, to maintain any particular level of prices or to protect anyone's profit. Rather the aim was to have an orderly market, one in which offers would be met by bids at some price. The bankers were only concerned that "air holes," as Mr. Lamont had dubbed them, did not appear.

Like many lesser men, Mr. Lamont and his colleagues had suddenly found themselves overcommitted on a falling market. The time had come to go short on promises. Support, organized or otherwise, could not contend with the overwhelming, pathological desire to sell. The meeting had considered how to liquidate the commitment to support the market without adding to the public perturbation.

The formula that was found was a chilling one. On Thursday, Whitney had supported prices and protected profits — or stopped losses. This was what people wanted. To the man who held stock on margin, disaster had only one face and that was falling prices. But now prices were to be allowed to fall. The speculator's only comfort, henceforth, was that his ruin would be accomplished in an orderly and becoming manner.

There were no recriminations at the time. Our political life favors the extremes of speech; the man who is gifted in the arts of abuse is bound to be a notable, if not always a great figure. In business things are different. Here we are suprisingly gentle and forbearing. Even preposterous claims or excuses are normally taken, at least for all public purposes, at their face value. On the evening of the 28th no one any longer could feel "secure in the knowledge that the most powerful banks stood ready to prevent a recurrence" of panic. The market had reasserted itself as an impersonal force beyond the power of any person to control, and, while this is the way markets are supposed to be, it was horrible. But no one assailed the bankers for letting the people down. There was even some talk that on the next day the market might receive organized support.

III

Tuesday, October 29, was the most devastating day in the history of the New York stock market, and it may have been the most devastating day in the history of markets. It combined all of the bad features of all of the bad days before. Volume was immensely greater than on Black Thursday; the drop in prices was almost as great as on Monday. Uncertainty and alarm were as great as on either.

Selling began as soon as the market opened and in huge volume. Great blocks of stock were offered for what they would bring; in the first half hour sales were at a 33,000,000-a-day rate. The air holes, which the bankers were to close, opened wide. Repeatedly and in many issues there was a plethora of selling orders and no buyers at all. The stock of White Sewing Machine Company, which had reached a high of 48 in the months preceding, had closed at 11 the night before. During the day someone — according to Frederick Lewis Allen it was thought to have been a bright messenger boy for the Exchange — had the happy idea of entering a bid for a block of stock at a dollar a share. In the absence of any other bid he got it.[13] Once again, of course, the ticker lagged — at the close it was two and a half hours behind. By then, 16,410,030 sales had been recorded on the New York Stock Exchange — some certainly went unrecorded — or more than three times the number that was once considered a fabulously big day. The *Times* industrial averages were down 43 points, canceling all of the gains of the twelve wonderful months preceding.

The losses would have been worse had there not been a closing rally. Thus Steel, for which Whitney had bid 205 on Thursday, reached 167 during the course of the day, although it rallied to 174 at the close. American Can opened at 130, dropped to 110, and rose to 120. Westinghouse opened at 131 — on September 3 it had closed at 286 — and dropped to 100. Then it rallied to 126. But the worst thing that happened on this terrible day was to the investment trusts.

[13] *Only Yesterday*, p. 333.

Not only did they go down, but it became apparent that they could go practically to nothing. Goldman Sachs Trading Corporation had closed at 60 the night before. During the day it dropped to 35 and closed at that level, off by not far short of half. Blue Ridge, its offspring once removed, on which the magic of leverage was now working in reverse, did much worse. Early in September it had sold at 24. By October 24 it was down to 12, but it resisted rather well the misfortunes of that day and the day following. On the morning of October 29 it opened at 10 and promptly slipped to 3, giving up more than two-thirds of its value. It recovered later but other investment trusts did less well; their stock couldn't be sold at all.

The worst day on Wall Street came eventually to an end. Once again the lights blazed all night. Members of the Exchange, their employees, and the employees of the Stock Exchange by now were reaching the breaking point from strain and fatigue. In this condition they faced the task of recording and handling the greatest volume of transactions ever. All of this was without the previous certainty that things might get better. They might go on getting worse. In one house an employee fainted from exhaustion, was revived and put back to work again.

IV

In the first week the slaughter had been of the innocents. During this second week there is some evidence that it was the well-to-do and the wealthy who were being subjected to a leveling process comparable in magnitude and suddenness to that presided over a decade before by Lenin. The size of the blocks of stock which were offered suggested that big speculators were selling or being sold. Another indication came from the boardrooms. A week before they were crowded, now they were nearly empty. Those now in trouble had facilities for suffering in private.

The bankers met twice on the 29th — at noon and again in the evening. There was no suggestion that they were philosophical. This was hardly remarkable because, during the day, an appalling rumor had swept the Exchange. It was that the bankers' pool, so far from stabilizing the market, was actually selling stocks! The prestige of the bankers had in truth been falling even more rapidly than the market. After the evening session, Mr. Lamont met the press with the disenchanting task of denying that they had been liquidating securities — or participating in a bear raid. After explaining again, somewhat redundantly in view of the day's events, that it was not the purpose of the bankers to maintain a particular level of prices, he concluded: "The group has continued and will continue in a co-operative way to support the market and has not been a seller of stocks." In fact, as later intelligence revealed, Albert H. Wiggins of the Chase was personally short at the time to the tune of some millions. His co-operative support, which if successful would have cost him heavily, must have had an interesting element of ambivalence.

So ended the organized support. The phrase recurred during the next few days, but no one again saw in it any ground for hope. Few men ever lost position so rapidly as did the New York bankers in the five days from October 24 to October 29. The crash on October 24 was the signal for corporations and out-of-town banks, which had been luxuriating in the 10 percent and more rate of interest, to recall their money from Wall Street. Between October 23 and October 30, as values fell and margin accounts were liquidated, the volume of brokers' loans fell by over a billion. But the corporations and the out-of-town banks responded to the horrifying news from New York — although, in fact, their funds were never seriously endangered — by calling home over two billions. The New York banks stepped into the gaping hole that was left by these summer financiers, and during that first week of crisis they increased their loans by about a billion. This was a bold step. Had the New York banks succumbed to the general fright, a money panic would have been added to the other woes. Stocks would have been dumped because their owners could not have borrowed money at any price to carry them. To prevent this was a considerable achievement for which all who owned stocks should have been thankful. But the banks received no credit. People remembered only that they had bravely undertaken to stem the price collapse and had failed.

Despite a flattering supposition to the contrary, people come readily to terms with power. There is little reason to think that the power of the great bankers, while they were assumed to have it, was much resented. But as the ghosts of numerous tyrants, from Julius Caesar to Benito Mussolini will testify, people are very hard on those who, having had power, lose it or are destroyed. Then anger at past arrogance is joined with contempt for present weakness. The victim or his corpse is made to suffer all available indignities.

Such was the fate of the bankers. For the next decade they were fair game for congressional committees, courts, the press, and the comedians. The great pretensions and the great failures of these days were a cause. A banker need not be popular; indeed, a good banker in a healthy capitalist society should probably be much disliked. People do not wish to trust their money to a hail-fellow-well-met but to a misanthrope who can say no. However, a banker must not seem futile, ineffective, or vaguely foolish. In contrast with the stern power of Morgan in 1907, that was precisely how his successors seemed, or were made to seem, in 1929.

The failure of the bankers did not leave the community entirely without constructive leadership. There was Mayor James J. Walker. Appearing before a meeting of motion picture exhibitors on that Tuesday, he appealed to them to "show pictures which will reinstate courage and hope in the hearts of the people."

v

On the Exchange itself, there was a strong feeling that courage and hope might best be restored by just closing up for a while. This feeling had, in fact, been gaining force for several days. Now it derived support from the simple circumstance that everyone was badly in need of sleep. Employees of some Stock Exchange firms had not been home for days. Hotel rooms in downtown New York were at a premium, and restaurants in the financial area had gone on to a fifteen- and twenty-hour day. Nerves were bad, and mistakes were becoming increasingly common. After the close of trading on Tuesday, a broker found a large waste basket of unexecuted orders which he had set aside for early attention and had totally forgotten.[14] One customer, whose margin account was impaired, was sold out twice. A number of firms needed some time to see if they were still solvent. There were, in fact, no important failures by Stock Exchange firms during these days, although one firm had reported itself bankrupt as the result of a clerical error by an employee who was in the last stages of fatigue.[15]

Yet to close the Exchange was a serious matter. It might somehow signify that stocks had lost all their value, with consequences no one could foresee. In any case, securities would immediately be-

[14] Allen, op. cit., p. 334.
[15] The Work of the Stock Exchange in the Panic of 1929, an address by Richard Whitney before the Boston Association of Stock Exchange Firms (Boston: June 10, 1930), pp. 16, 17. Whitney's account, below, of the events of October 29 and thereafter is from the same source.

come a badly frozen asset. This would be hard on the wholly solvent investors who might need to realize on them or use them as collateral. And sooner or later a new "gutter" market would develop in which individuals would informally dispose of stocks to those increasingly exceptional individuals who still wanted to buy them.

In 1929 the New York Stock Exchange was in principle a sovereignty of its members. Apart from the general statutes relating to the conduct of business and the prevention of fraud, it was subject to no important state or federal regulation. This meant a considerable exercise of self-government. Legislation governing the conduct of trading had to be kept under review and enforced. Stocks had to be approved for listing. The building and other facilities of the Exchange had to be managed. As with the United States Congress, most of this work was done in committees. (These, in turn, were dominated by a somewhat smaller group of members who were expected and accustomed to run things.) A decision to close the Exchange had to be taken by the Governing Committee, a body of about forty members. The mere knowledge that this body was meeting would almost certainly have an unfavorable effect on the market.

Nonetheless, at noon on Tuesday, the 29th, a meeting was held. The members of the committee left the floor in twos and threes and went, not to the regular meeting room, but to the office of the President of the Stock Clearing Corporation directly below the trading floor. Some months later, Acting President Whitney described the session with considerable graphic talent. "The office they met in was never designed for large meetings of this sort, with the result that most of the Governors were compelled to stand, or to sit on tables. As the meeting proceeded, panic was raging overhead on the floor. Every few minutes the latest prices were announced, with quotations moving swiftly and irresistibly downwards. The feeling of those present was revealed by their habit of continually lighting cigarettes, taking a puff or two, putting them out and lighting new ones — a practice which soon made the narrow room blue with smoke and extremely stuffy."

The result of these nervous deliberations was a decision to meet again in the evening. By evening the late rally had occurred, and it was decided to stay open for another day. The next day a further formula was hit upon. The Exchange would stay open. But it would have some special holidays and then go on short hours, and this would be announced just as soon as the market seemed strong enough to stand it.

Many still wanted to close. Whitney said later, although no doubt with some exaggeration, that in the days to come "the authorities of the Exchange led the life of hunted things, until [eventually] the desirability of holding the market open became apparent to all."

VI

The next day those forces were at work which on occasion bring salvation precisely when salvation seems impossible. Stocks rose wonderfully, miraculously, though still on enormous volume. The *Times* industrials were up 31 points for the day, thus recouping a large part of the terrible losses of the day before. Why this recovery occurred no one will ever know. Organized support can have no credit. Organized reassurance has a somewhat better claim. On the evening of the 29th, Dr. Julius Klein, Assistant Secretary of Commerce, friend of President Hoover, and the senior apostle of the official economic view, took to the radio to remind the country that President Hoover had said that the "fundamental business of the country" was sound. He added firmly, "The main point which I want to emphasize is the fundamental soundness of [the] great mass of economic activities." On Wednesday, Waddill Catchings, of Goldman, Sachs, announced on return from a western trip that general business conditions were "unquestionably fundamentally sound." (The same, by then, could not unquestionably be said of all Goldman, Sachs.) Arthur Brisbane told Hearst readers: "To comfort yourself, if you lost, think of the people living near Mount Pelee, ordered to abandon their homes."

Most important, perhaps, from Pocantico Hills came the first public statement by John D. Rockefeller in several decades. So far as the record shows, it was spontaneous. However, someone in Wall Street — perhaps someone who knew that another appeal to President Hoover to say something specifically encouraging about stocks would be useless — may have realized that a statement from Rockefeller would, if anything, be better. The statement ran: "Believing that fundamental conditions of the country are sound . . . my son and I have for some days been purchasing sound common stocks." The statement was widely applauded, although Eddie Cantor, describing himself as Comedian, Author, Statistician, and Victim, said later, "Sure, who else had any money left?"[16]

16 *Caught Short! A Saga of Wailing Wall Street* (New York: Simon and Schuster, 1929 A.C. [After Crash]), p. 31.

The accepted Wall Street explanation of Wednesday's miracle was not the reassurance but the dividend news of the day before. This also, without much question, was somewhat organized. U.S. Steel had declared an extra dividend; American Can had not only declared an extra but had increased its regular dividend. These errant sunbeams were deeply welcome in the dark canyons of lower Manhattan.

Just before the Rockefeller statement arrived, things looked good enough on the Exchange so that Richard Whitney felt safe in announcing that the market would not open until noon the following day (Thursday) and that on Friday and Saturday it would stay shut. The announcement was greeted by cheers. Nerves were clearly past the breaking point. On La Salle Street in Chicago a boy exploded a firecracker. Like wildfire the rumor spread that gangsters whose margin accounts had been closed out were shooting up the street. Several squad cars of police arrived to make them take their losses like honest men. In New York the body of a commission merchant was fished out of the Hudson. The pockets contained $9.40 in change and some margin calls.

VII

At the short session of three hours on Thursday, October 31, well over seven million shares were traded, and the market made another good gain. The *Times* industrials were up 21 points. The weekly return of the Federal Reserve Bank showed a drop in brokers' loans by more than a billion, the largest weekly drop on record. Margin requirements had already been cut to 25 percent; now the Federal Reserve Banks lowered the rediscount rate from 6 to 5 percent. The Reserve Banks also launched vigorous open-market purchases of bonds to ease money rates and liberalize the supply of credit. The boom had collapsed; the restraint that had previously been contemplated could now give way to a policy of active encouragement to the market. On all these happy portents the market closed down for Friday, Saturday, and Sunday. They were not days of rest. Brokerage offices were fully staffed, and the Exchange floor was open for completion of trades and also for straightening out innumerable misunderstandings and mistakes. It was noted that on Friday a visitor to the galleries could not have told the market was suspended.

The weekend brought one piece of bad news. That was the announcement on Saturday of the failure of the $20,000,000 Foshay enterprises of Minneapolis. Foshay owned utilities in some twelve states, Canada, Mexico, and Central America, and an assortment of hotels, flour mills, banks, manufacturing and retail establishments wherever he had happened to buy them. The 32-story obelisk, commemorating the enterprise, which still dominates the Minneapolis skyline, had been opened with fitting ceremony by Secretary of War James W. Good, only in August. (Secretary Good had referred to it as the "Washington Monument of the Northwest.")[17] By all but the most technical of considerations, Foshay was bankrupt at that festive time. His survival depended on his ability to continue merchandising stock to the public. The market crash eliminated this source of revenue and made him dependent on the wholly inadequate earnings of his enterprises.

On all other fronts the news was all good. Alfred P. Sloan, Jr., President of the General Motors Corporation, said: "Business is sound." The Ford Motor Company emphasized a similar conviction by announcing a general reduction in its prices: ". . . we feel that such a step is the best contribution that could be made to assure a continuation of good business." The Roadster was cut from $450 to $435; the Phaeton from $460 to $440; the Tudor Sedan from $525 to $500. For the three days that the market was closed the papers carried stories of the accumulation of buying orders and, in some indefinable way, the stories had a greater ring of conviction than the week before. The market, after all, had closed after an excellent two-day rally. As Barron's pointed out, it could now be believed that stocks were selling "ex-hopes and romance." On Monday, the Commercial National Bank and Trust Company took five columns in the Times to advertise ". . . our belief and conviction that the general industrial and business condition of the country is fundamentally sound and is essentially unimpaired."

That day the market started on another ghastly slump.

VIII

Over the weekend the financial community had almost certainly been persuaded by its own organized and spontaneous efforts at cheer. The papers described the reaction of professional Wall Street

[17] Investment News, October 16, 1929, p. 538.

to Monday's market as one of stunned surprise, disbelief, and shock. Volume was smaller than the week before, but still well above six million. The whole list was weak; individual issues made big losses; the *Times* industrials were down 22 points for the day. Compared with anything but the week before, this was very bad. When measured against the bright hopes for that day, it was most distressing.

Explanations varied. The rumor recurred that the "organized support" was selling stocks, and Mr. Lamont, on meeting the press, added a minor footnote to this now completed story. He said he didn't know — the organized support was really not that well organized. The most plausible explanation is that everyone was feeling cheerful but the public. As before and later, the weekend had been a time of thought, and out of thought had come pessimism and a decision to sell. So, as on other Mondays, no matter how cheerful the superficial portents, the selling orders poured in in volume.

By now it was also evident that the investment trusts, once considered a buttress of the high plateau and a built-in defense against collapse, were really a profound source of weakness. The leverage, of which people only a fortnight before had spoken so knowledgeably and even affectionately, was now fully in reverse. With remarkable celerity it removed all of the value from the common stock of a trust. As before, the case of a typical trust, a small one, is worth contemplating. Let it be supposed that it had securities in the hands of the public which had a market value of $10,000,000 in early October. Of this, half was in common stock, half in bonds and preferred stock. These securities were fully covered by the current market value of the securities owned. In other words, the trust's portfolio contained securities with a market value also of $10,000,000.

A representative portfolio of securities owned by such a trust would, in the early days of November, have declined in value by perhaps half. (Values of many of these securities by later standards would still be handsome; on November 4, the low for Tel and Tel was still 233, for General Electric it was 234, and for Steel 183.) The new portfolio value, $5,000,000, would be only enough to cover the prior claim on assets of the bonds and preferred stock. The common stock would have nothing behind it. Apart from expectations, which were by no means bright, it was now worthless.

This geometrical ruthlessness was not exceptional. On the contrary, it was everywhere at work on the stock of the leverage trusts. By early November, the stock of most of them had become virtually unsalable. To make matters worse, many of them were traded on the Curb or the out-of-town exchanges where buyers were few and the markets thin.

Never was there a time when more people wanted more money more urgently than in those days. The word that a man had "got caught" by the market was the signal for his creditors to descend on him like locusts. Many who were having trouble meeting their margin calls wanted to sell some stocks so they could hold the rest and thus salvage something from their misfortunes. But such people now found that their investment trust securities could not be sold for any appreciable sum and perhaps not at all. They were forced, as a result, to realize on their good securities. Standard stocks like Steel, General Motors, Tel and Tel were thus dumped on the market in abnormal volume, with the effect on prices that had already been fully revealed. The great investment trust boom had ended in a unique manifestation of Gresham's Law in which the bad stocks were driving out the good.

The stabilizing effects of the huge cash resources of the investment trusts had also proved a mirage. In the early autumn the cash and liquid resources of the investment trusts were large. Many trusts had been attracted by the handsome returns in the call market. (The speculative circle had been closed. People who speculated in the stock of investment trusts were in effect investing in companies which provided the funds to finance their own speculation.) But now, as reverse leverage did its work, investment trust managements were much more concerned over the collapse in the value of their own stock than in the adverse movements in the stock list as a whole. The investment trusts had invested heavily in each other. As a result the fall in Blue Ridge hit Shenandoah, and the resulting collapse in Shenandoah was even more horrible for the Goldman Sachs Trading Corporation.

Under these circumstances, many of the trusts used their available cash in a desperate effort to support their own stock. However, there was a vast difference between buying one's stock now when the public wanted to sell and buying during the previous spring — as Goldman Sachs Trading Corporation had done — when the public wanted to buy and the resulting competition had sent prices higher and higher. Now the cash went out and the stock came in, and prices were either not perceptibly affected or not for long. What six months before had been a brilliant financial maneuver was now a form of fiscal self-immolation. In the last analysis, the purchase by a firm of its own stock is the exact opposite of the sale of stocks. It is by the sale of stock that firms ordinarily grow.

However, none of this was immediately apparent. If one has been a financial genius, faith in one's genius does not dissolve at once. To the battered but unbowed genius, support of the stock of one's own company still seemed a bold, imaginative, and effective course. Indeed, it seemed the only alternative to slow but certain death. So to the extent that their cash resources allowed, the managements of the trusts chose faster, though equally certain death. They bought their own worthless stock. Men have been swindled by other men on many occasions. The autumn of 1929 was, perhaps, the first occasion when men succeeded on a large scale in swindling themselves.

The time has now come to complete the chronicle of the last days of the crisis.

IX

Tuesday, November 5, was election day, and the market was closed all day. In the New York mayoralty race, the Democratic incumbent, James J. Walker, scored a landslide victory over his Republican opponent, F. H. La Guardia, who had been soundly denounced by the Democrats as a socialist. Babson,[18] in a statement, called for poise, discernment, judicious courage, and old-fashioned common sense. On Wednesday the market reopened for the first of a new series of short sessions of three hours. These were the compromise on the question of closing which had been reached the previous week. Nearly six million shares were traded in this session or the equivalent of ten million shares on a full day. There was another sickening slide. U.S. Steel opened at 181, and, by what one paper called a succession of "feverish dips," went to 165. Auburn Automobile lost 66 points; Otis Elevator lost 45. The *Times* industrials were off 37 points for the day, or only 6 points less than on the terrible Tuesday eight days earlier. Where would it all end?

There was also disturbing news from beyond the market. Fundamentals seemed to be turning sour. The week's figures on carloadings showed a heavy drop as compared with the year before. The steel

[18] Roger W. Babson, statistician and business expert, founder (1919) of the Babson Institute in Cambridge, Mass.

rate was significantly down from the preceding week. More serious, the slump had extended to the commodity markets. On previous days these had reacted sympathetically with the stock market. On this Wednesday they had troubles of their own. Cotton was sharply off in the heaviest trading in weeks. References were made to "panic" in the wheat market when the price dropped vertically at noon.

On Thursday the stock market was steady to higher, but on Friday it took a small drop. People had another weekend of contemplation. This time there was no talk of an accumulation of buying orders; indeed, there was little good news of any kind. On Monday, November 11, came another drastic slump. For the next two days trading was heavy — the Exchange was still on short hours — and prices went down still more. In these three days, November 11, 12, and 13, the *Times* industrials lost another 50 points.

Of all the days of the crash, these without doubt were the dreariest. Organized support had failed. For the moment even organized reassurance had been abandoned. All that could be managed was some sardonic humor. It was noted that the margin calls going out by Western Union that week carried a small sticker: "Remember them at home with a cheery Thanksgiving telegram, the American way for this American day." Clerks in downtown hotels were said to be asking guests whether they wished the room for sleeping or jumping. Two men jumped hand-in-hand from a high window in the Ritz. They had a joint account. *The Wall Street Journal*, becoming biblical, told its readers: "Verily, I say, let the fear of the market be the law of thy life, and abide by the words of the bond salesman." The financial editor of the *Times*, who by this time showed signs of being satisfied with the crash and perhaps even of feeling that it had gone too far, said: "Probably none of the present generation will be able to speak again . . . of a 'healthy reaction.' There are many signs that the phrase is entirely out of date."

CAUSE AND CONSEQUENCE[19]

AFTER THE Great Crash came the Great Depression which lasted, with varying severity, for ten years. In 1933, Gross National Product (total production of the economy) was nearly a third less than in 1929. Not until 1937 did the physical volume of production recover

[19] Chapter X, "Cause and Consequence," *The Great Crash*, 1929, pp. 173–199.

to the levels of 1929, and then it promptly slipped back again. Until 1941, the dollar value of production remained below 1929. Between 1930 and 1940, only once, in 1937, did the average number unemployed during the year drop below eight million. In 1933, nearly thirteen million were out of work, or about one in every four in the labor force. In 1938, one person in five was still out of work.[20]

It was during this dreary time that 1929 became a year of myth. People hoped that the country might get back to twenty-nine; in some industries or towns when business was phenomenally good it was almost as good as in twenty-nine; men of outstanding vision, on occasions of exceptional solemnity, were heard to say that 1929 "was no better than Americans deserve."

On the whole, the great stock market crash can be much more readily explained than the depression that followed it. And among the problems involved in assessing the causes of depression none is more intractable than the responsibility to be assigned to the stock market crash. Economics still does not allow final answers on these matters. But, as usual, something can be said.

II

As already so often emphasized, the collapse in the stock market in the autumn of 1929 was implicit in the speculation that went before. The only question concerning that speculation was how long it would last. Sometime, sooner or later, confidence in the short-run reality of increasing common stock values would weaken. When this happened, some people would sell, and this would destroy the reality of increasing values. Holding for an increase would now become meaningless; the new reality would be falling prices. There would be a rush, pellmell, to unload. This was the way past speculative orgies had ended. It was the way the end came in 1929. It is the way speculation will end in the future.

We do not know why a great speculative orgy occurred in 1928 and 1929. The long accepted explanation that credit was easy and so people were impelled to borrow money to buy common stocks on margin is obviously nonsense. On numerous occasions before and since, credit has been easy, and there has been no speculation whatever. Furthermore, much of the 1928 and 1929 speculation occurred on money borrowed at interest rates which for years before, and in

[20] *Economic Indicators: Historical and Descriptive Supplement,* Joint Committee on the Economic Report (Washington, 1953).

any period since, would have been considered exceptionally astringent. Money, by the ordinary tests, was tight in the late twenties.

Far more important than rate of interest and the supply of credit is the mood. Speculation on a large scale requires a pervasive sense of confidence and optimism and conviction that ordinary people were meant to be rich. People must also have faith in the good intentions and even in the benevolence of others, for it is by the agency of others that they will get rich. In 1929, Professor Charles Ames Dice observed: "The common folks believe in their leaders. We no longer look upon the captains of industry as magnified crooks. Have we not heard their voices over the radio? Are we not familiar with their thoughts, ambitions, and ideals as they have expressed them to us almost as a man talks to his friend?"[21] Such a feeling of trust is essential for a boom. When people are cautious, questioning, misanthropic, suspicious or mean, they are immune to speculative enthusiasms.

Savings must also be plentiful. Speculation, however it may rely on borrowed funds, must be nourished in part by those who participate. If savings are growing rapidly, people will place a lower marginal value on their accumulation; they will be willing to risk some of it against the prospect of a greatly enhanced return. Speculation, accordingly, is most likely to break out after a substantial period of prosperity, rather than in the early phases of recovery from a depression. Macaulay noted that between the Restoration and the Glorious Revolution Englishmen were at loss to know what to do with their savings and that the "natural effect of this state of things was that a crowd of projectors, ingenious and absurd, honest and knavish, employed themselves in devising new schemes for the employment of redundant capital." Bagehot and others have attributed the South Sea Bubble to roughly the same causes.[22] In 1720, England had enjoyed a long period of prosperity, enhanced in part by war expenditures, and during this time private savings are believed to have grown at an unprecedented rate. Investment outlets were also few and returns low. Accordingly, Englishmen were anxious to place their savings at the disposal of the new enterprises and were quick to believe that the prospects were not fantastic. So it was in 1928 and 1929.

Finally, a speculative outbreak has a greater or less immunizing

21 *New Levels in the Stock Market*, p. 257.
22 Walter Bagehot, *Lombard Street* (first published in London, 1873), p. 130. The quotation from Macaulay, above, is cited by Bagehot, p. 128.

effect. The ensuing collapse automatically destroys the very mood speculation requires. It follows that an outbreak of speculation provides a reasonable assurance that another outbreak will not immediately occur. With time and the dimming of memory, the immunity wears off. A recurrence becomes possible. Nothing would have induced Americans to launch a speculative adventure in the stock market in 1935. By 1955, the chances are very much better.

III

As noted, it is easier to account for the boom and crash in the market than to explain their bearing on the depression which followed. The causes of the Great Depression are still far from certain. A lack of certainty, it may also be observed, is not evident in the contemporary writing on the subject. Much of it tells what went wrong and why with marked firmness. However, this paradoxically can itself be an indication of uncertainty. When people are least sure, they are often most dogmatic. We do not know what the Russians intend, so we state with great assurance what they will do. We compensate for our inability to foretell the consequences of, say, rearming Germany by asserting positively just what the consequences will be. So it is in economics. Yet, in explaining what happened in 1929 and after, one can distinguish between explanations that might be right and those that are clearly wrong.

A great many people have always felt that a depression was inevitable in the thirties. There had been (at least) seven good years; now by an occult or biblical law of compensation there would have to be seven bad ones. Perhaps, consciously or unconsciously, an argument that was valid for the stock market was brought to bear on the economy in general. Because the market took leave of reality in 1928 and 1929, it had at some time to make a return to reality. The disenchantment was bound to be as painful as the illusions were beguiling. Similarly, the New Era prosperity would some day evaporate; in its wake would come the compensating hardship.

There is also the slightly more subtle conviction that economic life is governed by an inevitable rhythm. After a certain time prosperity destroys itself and depression corrects itself. In 1929, prosperity, in accordance with the dictates of the business cycle, had run its course. This was the faith confessed by the members of the Harvard Economic Society in the spring of 1929, when they concluded that a recession was somehow overdue.

Neither of these beliefs can be seriously supported. The twenties, by being comparatively prosperous, established no imperative that the thirties be depressed. In the past, good times have given way to less good times and less good or bad to good. But change is normal in a capitalist economy. The degree of regularity in such movements is not great, though it is often thought to be.[23] No inevitable rhythm required the collapse and stagnation of 1930–40.

Nor was the economy of the United States in 1929 subject to such physical pressure or strain as the result of its past level of performance that a depression was bound to come. The notion that the economy requires occasional rest and resuscitation has a measure of plausibility and also a marked viability. During the summer of 1954, a professional economist on President Eisenhower's personal staff explained the then current recession by saying that the economy was enjoying a brief (and presumably well-merited) rest after the exceptional exertions of preceding years. In 1929, the labor force was not tired; it could have continued to produce indefinitely at the best 1929 rate. The capital plant of the country was not depleted. In the preceding years of prosperity, plant had been renewed and improved. In fact, depletion of the capital plans occurred during the ensuing years of idleness when new investment was sharply curtailed. Raw materials in 1929 were ample for the current rate of production. Entrepreneurs were never more eupeptic. Obviously if men, materials, plant and management were all capable of continued and even enlarged exertions, a refreshing pause was not necessary.

Finally, the high production of the twenties did not, as some have suggested, outrun the wants of the people. During these years people were indeed being supplied with an increasing volume of goods. But there is no evidence that their desire for automobiles, clothing, travel, recreation or even food was sated. On the contrary, all subsequent evidence showed (given the income to spend) a capacity for a further large increase in consumption. A depression was not needed so that people's wants could catch up with their capacity to produce.

IV

What, then, are the plausible causes of the depression? The task of answering can be simplified somewhat by dividing the problem

[23] "At present it is less likely that the existence of business cycles will be denied than that their regularity will be exaggerated." Wesley Clair Mitchell, *Business Cycles and Unemployment* (New York: McGraw-Hill, 1923), p. 6.

into two parts. First there is the question of why economic activity turned down in 1929. Second there is the vastly more important question of why, having started down, it went down and down and down on this unhappy occasion and remained low for a full decade.

As noted, the Federal Reserve indexes of industrial activity and of factory production, the most comprehensive monthly measures of economic activity then available, reached a peak in June. They then turned down and continued to decline throughout the rest of the year. The turning point in other indicators — factory payrolls, freight-car loadings and department store sales — came later, and it was October or after before the trend in all of them was clearly down. Still, as economists have generally insisted, and the matter has the high authority of the National Bureau of Economic Research,[24] the economy had weakened in the early summer well before the crash.

This weakening can be variously explained. Production of industrial products for the moment had outrun consumer and investment demand for them. The most likely reason is that business concerns, in the characteristic enthusiasm of good times, misjudged the prospective increase in demand and acquired larger inventories than they later found they needed. As a result they curtailed their buying, and this led to a cutback in production. In short, the summer of 1929 marked the beginning of the familiar inventory recession. The proof is not conclusive from the (by present standards) limited figures available. Department store inventories, for which figures are available, seem not to have been out of line early in the year. But a mild slump in department store sales in April could have been a signal for curtailment.

Also there is a chance — one that students of the period have generally favored — that more deep-seated factors were at work and made themselves seriously evident for the first time during that summer. Throughout the twenties production and productivity per worker grew steadily: between 1919 and 1929, output per worker in manufacturing industries increased by about 43 percent.[25] Wages, salaries and prices all remained comparatively stable, or in any case underwent no comparable increase. Accordingly, costs fell, and with prices

[24] Geoffrey H. Moore, *Statistical Indications of Cyclical Revivals and Recessions,* *Occasional Paper* 31, National Bureau of Economic Research, Inc. (New York, 1950).

[25] H. W. Arndt, *The Economic Lessons of the Nineteen-Thirties* (London: Oxford, 1944), p. 15.

the same, profits increased. These profits sustained the spending of the well-to-do, and they also nourished at least some of the expectations behind the stock market boom. Most of all they encouraged a very high level of capital investment. During the twenties, the production of capital goods increased at an average annual rate of 6.4 percent a year; non-durable consumers' goods, a category that includes such objects of mass consumption as food and clothing, increased at a rate of only 2.8 percent.[26] (The rate of increase for durable consumers' goods such as cars, dwellings, home furnishings and the like, much of it representing expenditures of the well-off to well-to-do, was 5.9 percent.) A large and increasing investment in capital goods was, in other words, a principal device by which the profits were being spent.[27] It follows that anything that interrupted the investment outlays — anything, indeed, which kept them from showing the necessary rate of increase — could cause trouble. When this occurred, compensation through an increase in consumer spending could not automatically be expected. The effect, therefore, of insufficient investment — investment that failed to keep pace with the steady increase in profits — could be falling total demand reflected in turn in falling orders and output. Again there is no final proof of this point, for unfortunately we do not know how rapidly investment had to grow to keep abreast of the current increase in profits.[28] However, the explanation is broadly consistent with the facts.

There are other possible explanations of the downturn. Back of

[26] E. M. Hugh-Jones and E. A. Radice, *An American Experiment* (London: Oxford, 1936), 49. Cited by Arndt, *op. cit.*, p. 16.
[27] This has been widely noted. See Lionel Robbins, *The Great Depression*, p. 4, and Thomas Wilson, *Fluctuations in Income*, p. 154 ff., and J. M. Keynes, *A Treatise on Money* (London: Macmillan, 1971), II.
[28] Perhaps I may be permitted to enlarge on this in slightly more technical terms. The interruption could as well have been caused by an insufficient rate of increase in consumer spending as by a failure in the greater rate of increase of capital goods spending. Underconsumption and underinvestment are the same side of the same coin. And some force is added to this explanation by the fact that spending for one important consumers' durable, namely houses, had been declining for several years and suffered a further substantial drop in 1929. However, the investment function we still suppose to be less stable than the consumption function, even though we are less assured of the stability of the latter than we used to be. And in the present case it seems wise to attach causal significance to the part of the spending which had to maintain the largest rate of increase if total spending were to be uninterrupted. The need to maintain a specific rate of increase in investment outlay is insufficiently emphasized by Mr. Thomas Wilson in his book which I have so frequently cited and to which students of the period are indebted.

the insufficient advance in investment may have been the high interest rates. Perhaps, although less probably, trouble was transmitted to the economy as a whole from some weak sector like agriculture. Further explanations could be offered. But one thing about this experience is clear. Until well along in the autumn of 1929, the downturn was limited. The recession in business activity was modest and under-employment relatively slight. Up to November it was possible to argue that not much of anything had happened. On other occasions, as noted — in 1924 and 1927 and in 1949 — the economy has under-gone similar recession. But, unlike these other occasions, in 1929, the recession continued and continued and got violently worse. This is the unique feature of the 1929 experience. This is what we need really to understand.

V

There seems little question that in 1929, modifying a famous cliché, the economy was fundamentally unsound. This is a circum-stance of first-rate importance. Many things were wrong but five weaknesses seem to have had an especially intimate bearing on the ensuing disaster. They are:

1) The bad distribution of income. In 1929, the rich were in-dubitably rich. The figures are not entirely satisfactory, but it seems certain that the 5 percent of the population with the highest incomes in that year received approximately one-third of all personal income. The proportion of personal income received in the form of interest, dividends and rent — the income, broadly speaking, of the well-to-do — was about twice as great as in the years following the Second World War.[29]

This highly unequal income distribution meant that the economy was dependent on a high level of investment or a high level of luxury consumer spending or both. The rich cannot buy great quanti-ties of bread. If they are to dispose of what they receive, it must be on luxuries or by way of investment in new plants and new projects. Both investment and luxury spending are subject, inevitably, to more erratic influences and to wider fluctuations than the bread and rent outlays of the $25-a-week workman. This high-bracket spending

[29] Selma Goldsmith, George Jaszi, Hyman Kaitz, and Maurice Liebenberg, "Size Distribution of Income since the Mid-Thirties," *The Review of Economics and Statistics*, February 1954, pp. 16, 18.

and investment was especially suspectible, one may assume, to the crushing news from the stock market in October of 1929.

2) The bad corporate structure. In November 1929, a few weeks after the crash, the Harvard Economic Society gave as a principal reason why a depression need not be feared its reasoned judgment that "business in most lines has been conducted with prudence and conservatism."[30] The fact was that American enterprise in the twenties had opened its hospitable arms to an exceptional number of promoters, grafters, swindlers, imposters, and frauds. This, in the long history of such activities, was a kind of flood tide of corporate larceny.

The most modern corporate weakness was inherent in the vast new structure of holding companies and investment trusts. The holding companies controlled large segments of the utility, railroad, and entertainment business. Here, as with the investment trusts, was the constant danger of devastation by reverse leverage. In particular, dividends from the operating companies paid the interest on the bonds of upstream holding companies. The interruption of the dividends meant default on the bonds, bankruptcy, and the collapse of the structure. Under these circumstances, the temptation to curtail investment in operating plant in order to continue dividends was obviously strong. This added to deflationary pressures. The latter, in turn, curtailed earnings and helped bring down the corporate pyramids. When this happened, even more retrenchment was inevitable. Income was earmarked for debt repayment. Borrowing for new investment became impossible. It would be hard to imagine a corporate system better designed to continue and accentuate a deflationary spiral.

3) The bad banking structure. Since the early thirties a generation of Americans has been told, sometimes with amusement, sometimes with indignation, often with outrage, of the banking practices of the late twenties. In fact, many of these practices were made ludicrous only by the depression. Loans which would have been perfectly good were made perfectly foolish by the collapse of the borrower's prices or the markets for his goods or the value of the collateral he had posted. The most responsible bankers — those who saw that their debtors were victims of circumstances far beyond their control and sought to help — were often made to look the worst. The bankers yielded, as did others, to the blithe, optimistic and immoral mood of

[30] *Weekly Letter*, November 23, 1929.

the times but probably not more so. A depression such as that of 1929–32, were it to begin as this is written, would also be damaging to many currently impeccable banking reputations.

However, although the bankers were not unusually foolish in 1929, the banking structure was inherently weak. The weakness was implicit in the large numbers of independent units. When one bank failed, the assets of others were frozen while depositors elsewhere had a pregnant warning to go and ask for their money. Thus one failure led to other failures, and these spread with a domino effect. Even in the best of times local misfortune or isolated mismanagement could start such a chain reaction. (In the first six months of 1929, 346 banks failed in various parts of the country with aggregate deposits of nearly $115 million.)[31] When income, employment and values fell as the result of a depression, bank failures could quickly become epidemic. This happened after 1929. Again it would be hard to imagine a better arrangement for magnifying the effects of fear. The weak not only destroyed the other weak but weakened the strong. People everywhere, rich and poor, were made aware of the disaster by the persuasive intelligence that their savings had been destroyed.

Needless to say, such a banking system, once in the convulsions of failure, had a uniquely repressive effect on the spending of its depositors and the investment of its clients.

4) The dubious state of the foreign balance. This is a familiar story. During the First World War, the United States became a creditor on international account. In the decade following, the surplus of exports over imports which once had paid the interest and principal on loans from Europe continued. The high tariffs, which restricted imports and helped to create this surplus of exports remained. However, history and the traditional trading habits also accounted for the persistence of the favorable balance, so called.

Before, payments on interest and principal had in effect been deducted from the trade balance. Now that the United States was a creditor, they were added to this balance. The latter, it should be said, was not huge. In only one year (1928) did the excess of exports over imports come to as much as a billion dollars; in 1923 and 1926 it was only about $375,000,000.[32] However, large or small, this difference had to be covered. Other countries which were buying more

---

[31] Compiled from *Federal Reserve Bulletin*, monthly issues, 1929.
[32] U.S. Department of Commerce, Bureau of Foreign and Domestic Commerce, *Statistical Abstract of the United States*, 1942.

than they sold, and had debt payments to make in addition, had somehow to find the means for making up the deficit in their transactions with the United States.

During most of the twenties the difference was covered by cash— i.e., gold payments to the United States — and by new private loans by the United States to other countries. Most of the loans were to governments — national, state, or municipal bodies — and a large proportion were to Germany and Central and South America. The underwriters' margins in handling these loans were generous; the public took them up with enthusiasm; competition for the business was keen. If unfortunately corruption and bribery were required as competitive instruments, these were used. In late 1927, Juan Leguia, the son of the President of Peru, was paid $450,000 by J. and W. Seligman and Company and the National City Company (the security affiliate of the National City Bank) for his services in connection with a $50,000,000 loan which these houses marketed for Peru.[33] Juan's services, according to later testimony, were of a rather negative sort. He was paid for not blocking the deal. The Chase extended President Machado of Cuba, a dictator with a marked predisposition toward murder, a general personal line of credit which at one time reached $200,000.[34] Machado's son-in-law was employed by the Chase. The bank did a large business in Cuban bonds. In contemplating these loans, there was a tendency to pass quickly over anything that might appear to the disadvantage of the creditor. Mr. Victor Schoepperle, a vice-president of the National City Company with the responsibility for Latin American loans, made the following appraisal of Peru as a credit prospect:

> Peru: Bad debt record, adverse moral and political risk, bad internal debt situation, trade situation about as satisfactory as that of Chile in the past three years. Natural resources more varied. On economic showing Peru should go ahead rapidly in the next ten years.[35]

On such showing the National City Company floated a $15,000,000 loan for Peru, followed a few months later by a $50,000,000 loan and some ten months thereafter by a $25,000,000 issue. (Peru did prove a highly adverse political risk. President Leguia, who negotiated the

[33] *Stock Exchange Practices*, Report, 1934, pp. 220–21.
[34] *Ibid.*, p. 215.
[35] *Stock Exchange Practices*, Hearings, February–March 1933, Pt. 6, p. 2091 ff.

loans, was thrown violently out of office, and the loans went into default.)

In all respects these operations were as much a part of the New Era as Shenandoah and Blue Ridge.[36] They were also just as fragile, and once the illusions of the New Era were dissipated, they came as abruptly to an end. This, in turn, forced a fundamental revision in the foreign economic position of the United States. Countries could not cover their adverse trade balance with the United States with increased payments of gold, at least not for long. This meant that they had either to increase their exports to the United States or reduce their imports or default on their past loans. President Hoover and the Congress moved promptly to eliminate the first possibility — that the accounts would be balanced by larger imports — by sharply increasing the tariff. Accordingly, debts, including war debts, went into default, and there was a precipitate fall in American exports. The reduction was not vast in relation to total output of the American economy but it contributed to the general distress and was especially hard on farmers.

5) The poor state of economic intelligence. To regard the people of any time as particularly obtuse seems vaguely improper, and it also establishes a precedent which members of this generation might regret. Yet it seems certain that the economists and those who offered economic counsel in the late twenties and early thirties were almost uniquely perverse. In the months and years following the stock market crash, the burden of reputable economic advice was invariably on the side of measures that would make things worse. In November of 1929, Mr. Hoover announced a cut in taxes; in the great no-business conferences that followed he asked business firms to keep up their capital investment and to maintain wages. Both these measures were on the side of increasing spendable income, though unfortunately they were largely without effect. The tax reductions were negligible except in the higher income brackets; businessmen who promised to maintain investment and wages, in accordance with a well-understood convention, considered the promise binding only for the period within which it was not financially disadvantageous to do so. As a result investment outlays and wages were not reduced until circumstances would in any case have brought their reduction.

[36] Shenandoah and Blue Ridge were investment trust operations of the period promoted by Waddill Catchings along with John Foster Dulles and others. They did not survive.

Still, the effort was in the right direction. Thereafter policy was almost entirely on the side of making things worse. Asked how the government could best advance recovery, the sound and responsible adviser urged that the budget be balanced. Both parties agreed on this. For Republicans the balanced budget was, as ever, high doctrine. But the Democratic Party platform of 1932, with an explicitness that politicians rarely advise, also called for a "federal budget annually balanced on the basis of accurate executive estimates within revenues . . ."

A commitment to a balanced budget is always comprehensive. It then meant there could be no increase in government outlays to expand purchasing power and relieve distress. It meant there could be no further tax reduction. But taken literally it meant much more. From 1930 on the budget was far out of balance, and balance, therefore, meant an increase in taxes, a reduction in spending or both. The Democratic platform in 1932 called for an "immediate and drastic reduction of governmental expenditures" to accomplish at least a 25 percent decrease in the cost of government.

The balanced budget was not a subject of thought. Nor was it, as often asserted, precisely a matter of faith. Rather, it was a formula. For centuries avoidance of borrowing had protected people from slovenly or reckless public housekeeping. Slovenly or reckless keepers of the public purse had often composed complicated arguments to show why balance of income and outlay was not a mark of virtue. Experience had shown that however convenient this belief might seem in the short run, discomfort or disaster followed in the long run. Those simple precepts of a simple world did not hold amid the growing complexities of the early thirties. Mass unemployment in particular had altered the rules. Events had played a very bad trick on people but almost no one tried to think out the problem anew.

The balanced budget was not the only strait jacket on policy. There was also the bogey of "going off" the gold standard and, most surprisingly, of risking inflation. Until 1932, the United States added formidably to its gold reserves, and instead of inflation the country was experiencing the most violent deflation in the nation's history. Yet every sober adviser saw dangers here, including the danger of runaway price increases. Americans, though in years now well in the past, had shown a penchant for tinkering with the money supply and enjoying the brief but heady joys of a boom in prices. In 1931 or 1932, the danger or even the feasibility of such a

boom was nil. The advisers and counselors were not, however, analyz-
ing the danger or even the possibility. They were serving only as the
custodians of bad memories.

The fear of inflation reinforced the demand for the balanced budget. It also limited efforts to make interest rates low, credit plentiful
(or at least redundant) and borrowing as easy as possible under the
circumstances. Devaluation of the dollar was, of course, flatly ruled
out. This directly violated the gold standard rules. At best, in such
depression times, monetary policy is a feeble reed on which to lean.
The current economic clichés did not allow even the use of that frail
weapon. And again these attitudes were above party. Though himself
singularly open-minded, Roosevelt was careful not to offend or disturb
his followers. In a speech in Brooklyn toward the close of the 1932
campaign, he said:

> The Democratic platform specifically declares, "We advo-
> cate a sound currency to be preserved at all hazards." That
> is plain English. In discussing the platform on July 30,
> I said, "Sound money is an international necessity, not a
> domestic consideration for one nation alone." Far up in the
> Northwest, at Butte, I repeated the pledge . . . In Seattle
> I reaffirmed my attitude . . .[37]

The following February, Mr. Hoover set forth his view, as often
before, in a famous letter to the President-elect:

> It would steady the country greatly if there could be prompt
> assurance that there will be no tampering or inflation of
> the currency; that the budget will be unquestionably bal-
> anced even if further taxation is necessary; that the Govern-
> ment credit will be maintained by refusal to exhaust it in
> the issue of securities.[38]

The rejection of both fiscal (tax and expenditure) and monetary
policy amounted precisely to a rejection of all affirmative government economic policy. The economic advisers of the day had both

[37] Lawrence Sullivan, *Prelude to Panic* (Washington: Statesman Press, 1936),
p. 20.
[38] William Starr Myers and Walter H. Newton, *The Hoover Administration:
A Documental Narrative* (New York: Scribners, 1936), pp. 339–40.

the unanimity and the authority to force the leaders of both parties to disavow all the available steps to check deflation and depression. In its own way this was a marked achievement — a triumph of dogma over thought. The consequences were profound.

VI

It is in light of the above weaknesses of the economy that the role of the stock market crash in the great tragedy of the thirties must be seen. The years of self-depreciation by Wall Street to the contrary, the role is one of respectable importance. The collapse in securities values affected in the first instance the wealthy and the well-to-do. But we see that in the world of 1929 this was a vital group. The members disposed of a large proportion of the consumer income; they were the source of a lion's share of personal saving and investment. Anything that struck at the spending or investment by this group would of necessity have broad effects on expenditure and income in the economy at large. Precisely such a blow was struck by the stock market crash. In addition, the crash promptly removed from the economy the support that it had been deriving from the spending of stock market gains.

The stock market crash was also an exceptionally effective way of exploiting the weaknesses of the corporate structure. Operating companies at the end of the holding-company chain were forced by the crash to retrench. The subsequent collapse of these systems and also of the investment trusts effectively destroyed both the ability to borrow and the willingness to lend for investment. What have long looked like purely fiduciary effects were, in fact, quickly translated into declining orders and increasing unemployment.

The crash was also effective in bringing to an end the foreign lending by which the international accounts had been balanced. Now the accounts had, in the main, to be balanced by reduced exports. This put prompt and heavy pressure on export markets for wheat, cotton and tobacco. Perhaps the foreign loans had only delayed an adjustment in the balance which had one day to come. The stock market crash served nonetheless to precipitate the adjustment with great suddenness at a most unpropitious time. The instinct of farmers who traced their troubles to the stock market was not totally misguided.

Finally, when the misfortune had struck, the attitudes of the time kept anything from being done about it. This, perhaps, was the most disconcerting feature of all. Some people were hungry in 1930 and 1931 and 1932. Others were tortured by the fear that they might go hungry. Yet others suffered the agony of the descent from the honor and respectability that goes with income into poverty. And still others feared that they would be next. Meanwhile everyone suffered from a sense of utter hopelessness. Nothing, it seemed, could be done. And given the ideas which controlled policy, nothing could be done.

Had the economy been fundamentally sound in 1929, the effect of the great stock market crash might have been small. Alternatively, the shock to confidence and the loss of spending by those who were caught in the market might soon have worn off. But business in 1929 was not sound; on the contrary, it was exceedingly fragile. It was vulnerable to the kind of blow it received from Wall Street. Those who have emphasized this vulnerability are obviously on strong ground. Yet when a greenhouse succumbs to a hailstorm, something more than a purely passive role is normally attributed to the storm. One must accord similar significance to the typhoon which blew out of lower Manhattan in October 1929.

VII

The military historian when he has finished his chronicle is excused. He is not required to consider the chance for a renewal of war with the Indians, the Mexicans or the Confederacy. Nor will anyone press him to say how such acrimony can be prevented. But economics is taken more seriously. The economic historian, as a result, is invariably asked whether the misfortunes he describes will afflict us again and how they may be prevented.

The task of this book, as suggested on an early page, is only to tell what happened in 1929. It is not to tell whether or when the misfortunes of 1929 will recur. One of the pregnant lessons of that year will by now be plain: it is that very specific and personal misfortune awaits those who presume to believe that the future is revealed to them. Yet, without undue risk, it may be possible to gain from our view of this useful year some insights into the future. We can distinguish, in particular, between misfortunes that could happen again and others which events, many of them in the aftermath of 1929, have at least made improbable. And we can perhaps see a little of the form and magnitude of the remaining peril.

At first glance the least probable of the misadventures of the late twenties would seem to be another wild boom in the stock market with its inevitable collapse. The memory of that autumn, although now much dimmed, is not yet gone. As those days of disenchantment drew to a close, tens of thousands of Americans shook their heads and muttered, "Never again." In every considerable community there are yet a few survivors, aged but still chastened, who are still muttering and still shaking their heads. The New Era had no such guardians of sound pessimism.

Also, there are the new government measures and controls. The powers of the Federal Reserve Board — now styled the Board of Governors of the Federal Reserve System — have been strengthened both in relation to the individual Reserve banks and the member banks. The New York Federal Reserve Bank retains a measure of moral authority and autonomy but not enough to resist a strong Washington policy. Now also there is power to set margin requirements. If necessary, the speculator can be made to post the full price of the stock he buys. While this may not completely discourage him, it does mean that when the market falls, there can be no outsurge of margin calls to force further sales and ensure that the liquidation will go through continuing spasms. Finally, the Securities and Exchange Commission is a bar, one hopes effective, to large-scale market manipulation, and it also keeps rein on the devices and the salesmanship by which new speculators are recruited.

Yet, in some respects, the chances for a recurrence of a speculative orgy are rather good. No one can doubt that the American people remain susceptible to the speculative mood — to the conviction that enterprise can be attended by unlimited rewards in which they, individually, were meant to share. A rising market can still bring the reality of riches. This, in turn, can draw more and more people to participate. The government preventatives and controls are ready. In the hands of a determined government their efficacy cannot be doubted. There are, however, a hundred reasons why a government will determine not to use them. In our democracy an election is in the offing even on the day after an election. The avoidance of depression and the prevention of unemployment have become for the politician the most critical of all questions of public policy. Action to break up a boom must always be weighed against the chance that it will cause unemployment at a politically inopportune moment. Booms, it must be noted, are not stopped until after they have started. And after they have started, the action will always look, as it did to the frightened men in the Federal Reserve Board in February 1929, like a decision in favor of immediate as against ultimate death. As we have seen, the immediate death not only has the disadvantage of being immediate but of identifying the executioner.

The market will not go on a speculative rampage without some rationalization. But during the next boom some newly rediscovered virtuosity of the free enterprise system will be cited. It will be pointed out that people are justified in paying the present prices — indeed, almost any price — to have an equity position in the system. Among the first to accept these rationalizations will be some of those responsible for invoking the controls. They will say firmly that controls are not needed. The newspapers, some of them, will agree and speak harshly of those who think action might be in order. They will be called men of little faith.

VIII

A new adventure in stock market speculation sometime in the future followed by another collapse would not have the same effect on the economy as in 1929. Whether it would show the economy to be fundamentally sound or unsound is something, unfortunately, that will not be wholly evident until after the event. There can be no question, however, that many of the points of extreme weakness exposed in 1929 or soon thereafter have since been substantially strengthened. The distribution of income is no longer quite so lopsided. Between 1929 and 1948, the share of total personal income going to the 5 percent of the population with the highest income dropped from nearly a third to less than a fifth of the total. Between 1929 and 1950, the share of all family income which was received as wages, salaries, pensions and unemployment compensation increased from approximately 61 percent to approximately 71 percent. This is the income of everyday people. Although dividends, interest and rent, the income characteristically of the well-to-do, increased in total amount, the share dropped from just over 22 to just over 12 percent of total family personal income.[39]

Similarly, in the years since 1929, the great investment trust promotions have been folded up and put away, or they have become cautious and respectable. The SEC, aided by the bankruptcy laws, has

[39] These data are from Goldsmith, *et al.*, "Size of Distribution of Income," pp. 16, 18.

flattened out the great utility holding company pyramids. There has been a new age of mergers, but it does not seem yet to have produced any such Napoleonic bandits as Kreuger or so far to have encouraged illusions of destiny in stock jobbers like Hopson[40] or Insull. Federal insurance of bank deposits, even to this day, has not been given full credit for the revolution that it has worked in the nation's banking structure. With this one piece of legislation the fear which operated so efficiently to transmit weakness was dissolved. As a result the grievous defect of the old system, by which failure begot failure, was cured. Rarely has so much been accomplished by a single law.

The problem of the foreign balance is much changed from what it was twenty-five years ago. Now the United States finds itself with a propensity to buy or spend as much and more than it sells and receives. And now any disequilibrium is filled or more than filled by military aid, Export-Import and International Bank loans and economic aid. In contrast with the loans to Latin American republics and the German municipalities, these payments are relatively invulnerable to shock. A crash in the stock market would affect them but little, if at all.

Finally, there has been a modest accretion of economic knowledge. A developing depression would not now be met with a fixed determination to make it worse. Without question, no-business conferences would be assembled at the White House. We would see an explosion of reassurance and incantation. Many would urge waiting and hoping as the best policy. Not again, however, would people suppose that the best policy would be — as Secretary Mellon so infelicitously phrased it — to "liquidate labor, liquidate stocks, liquidate the farmers, liquidate real estate."[41] Our determination to deal firmly and adequately with a serious depression is still to be tested. But there is still a considerable difference between a failure to do enough that is right and a determination to do much that is wrong.

Other weaknesses in the economy have been corrected. The much maligned farm program provides a measure of security for farm income and therewith for spending by farmers. Unemployment compensation accomplishes the same result, if still inadequately, for labor. The remainder of the social security system — pensions and

[40] Less well known to the public than Insull, Howard C. Hopson also presided over a large collection of utility enterprises precariously held together by bond issues.
[41] Quoted by Herbert Hoover, *Memoirs*, p. 30.

public assistance — helps protect the income and consequently the expenditures of yet other segments of the population. The tax system is a far better servant of stability than it was in 1929. An angry god may have endowed capitalism with inherent contradictions. But at least as an afterthought he was kind enough to make social reform surprisingly consistent with improved operation of the system.

IX

Yet all this reinforcement notwithstanding, it would probably be unwise to expose the economy to the shock of another major speculative collapse. Some of the new reinforcements might buckle. Instead of the investment trusts we have the mutual funds and the contraction here would be sharp. Fissures might open at other new and perhaps unexpected places. Even the quick withdrawal from the economy of the spending that comes from stock market gains might be damaging. Any collapse, even though the further consequences were small, would not be good for the public reputation of Wall Street.

Wall Street, in recent times, has become, as a learned phrase has it, very "public relations conscious." Since a speculative collapse can only follow a speculative boom, one might expect that Wall Street would lay a heavy hand on any resurgence of speculation. The Federal Reserve would be asked by bankers and brokers to lift margins to the limit; it would be warned to enforce the requirement sternly against those who might try to borrow on their own stocks and bonds in order to buy more of them. The public would be warned sharply and often of the risks inherent in buying stocks for the rise. Those who persisted, nonetheless, would have no one to blame but themselves. The position of the Stock Exchange, its members, the banks and the financial community in general would be perfectly clear and as well protected in the event of a further collapse as sound public relations allow.

As noted, all this might logically be expected. It will not come to pass. This is not because the instinct for self-preservation in Wall Street is poorly developed. On the contrary, it is probably normal and may be above. But now, as throughout history, financial capacity and political perspicacity are inversely correlated. Long-run salvation by men of business has never been highly regarded if it means disturbance of orderly life and convenience in the present. So inaction will be advocated in the present even though it means deep trouble in the future. Here, at least equally with communism, lies the threat to capitalism. It is what causes men who know that things are going quite wrong to say that things are fundamentally sound.

INTRODUCTION TO THE 1961 EDITION[42]

THE REISSUE of a moderately well-known book provides a temptation which, I have observed, very few authors resist. That is to tell, with that combination of deprecatory modesty and evident self-approval of which Somerset Maugham was perhaps the master, just how this good thing came to be done. And I have noticed that authors who are a trifle ashamed of these exercises in self-appreciation begin them with an apology and then go right ahead anyway. And perhaps we should. Writing is a long and lonesome business; back of the problems in thought and composition hover always the awful questions: Is this the page that shows the empty shell? Is it here and now they find me out? So, like the politician when the returns are in and the prize-fighter when his glove is raised, perhaps we should be allowed our little moment. Perhaps I can be allowed mine. It is possible, moreover, that the birth pangs of this book were a little livelier than most.

I wrote this book during the summer and autumn of 1954. At the time I was engaged on the manuscript which eventually became *The Affluent Society*. Or, more precisely, after months of ineffective and frustrating labor which had produced a set of chapters so vapid in content and repulsive in style that I could not bear to read them, I was totally stalled. Suicide seemed the only answer; unfortunately it was an exceptionally lovely summer in southern Vermont. My neighbor, Arthur M. Schlesinger, Jr., had once made the modest request that I do the definitive work on the Great Depression. It would be convenient, he thought, for his work on Roosevelt. I resolved to compromise and write a book on the dramatic days that ushered the depression in.

I never enjoyed writing a book more; indeed, it is the only one I remember in no sense as a labor but as a joy. I did the research in the Baker Library at Dartmouth College, working under the Orosco murals on the ground floor. They somehow supported the mood of un-

[42] This essay was written six years after original publication of *The Great Crash, 1929*, as an Introduction to the 1961 Houghton Mifflin Sentry paperback edition.

reality, gargantuan excess and hovering disaster of the months before the crash. And, as might happen toward the end of the morning or the end of the afternoon if this mood became too overpowering, one could walk out into the sunshine, across the most exquisite village common in all New England, and have a martini and a good meal at the Hanover Inn. I scamped my teaching that autumn to work on the manuscript, when I left it with the publisher I felt that I was saying goodbye to a close and valued companion.

II

My labors during the autumn had been made to seem rather more relevant by the contemporary boom in the stock market. This was small compared with 1929; it was very small compared with the bidding up of values and the bidding down of yields that subsequently took place. But it was plain that an increasing number of persons were coming to the conclusion — the conclusion that is the common denominator of all speculative episodes — that they were predestined by luck, an unbeatable system, divine favor, access to inside information or exceptional financial acumen to become rich without work.

In the spring the boom, or boomlet, continued. The Democrats had won the Congressional elections the previous autumn; the Republicans had the White House for the first time since Hoover. It seemed worth the while of the Senate Committee on Banking and Currency to see if the boom portended another bust. Chairman William Fulbright decided that it would be a quiet and friendly investigation. I was called to testify. This was not entirely by accident. While testifying a few weeks earlier on another matter before another Committee, I used the opportunity to tell Mr. Robert A. Wallace and Mr. Myer Feldman, two of the distinguished and self-effacing men who serve the public by serving Congressmen and their Committees and then staff members of the Banking and Currency Committee, of what I had underway. An invitation to testify on the 1929 experience came promptly and was not an unbearable surprise.

I believe that almost everyone enjoys testifying before a friendly Congressional Committee or even a moderately censorious one. For the moment you are an oracle, a minor oracle to be sure, but possessed of knowledge important for the future of the Republic. Your words go down in an imperishable, if sadly unread, record. Newspapermen, one or two at least, are present to transmit your better thoughts to the world or more frequently, your worst ones, for these, being improbable, have novelty and seem more likely to merit a minor headline. An audience is on hand. Except for an exceedingly dramatic investigation, this audience is always about the same. Apart from watchdogs from the Executive Departments and one's friends, it consists of connoisseurs of the Congressional Hearings who attend them every day. Quite a few are of advanced years and none has alternative employment, and if they are not our best, they must at least be our most widely informed citizenry. Labor rackets, the missile gap, influence on the FCC, the ambassadorial ambitions of Clare Luce,[43] the economic outlook, the organization of the National Security Council are all grist for their highly diversified mill. They listen attentively and critically; any Congressional Hearing has about it a touch of theatre and this is helped by having a competent and critical house.

The witness at the Congressional Hearing is treated with courtesy and deference, which in politics is always a trifle more effusive and therefore a great deal more pleasant than in any other walk of life. He must, however, expect to be seduced into statements damaging to his case if that is beneficial to the political needs or beliefs of an interrogator. This adds interest, and the stakes are not very high. My professional colleagues occasionally complain of the time they spend in preparing for or attending these inquiries. This is strictly for the purpose of impressing the others at the Department meeting. They enjoy it and wouldn't dream of declining.

III

I testified at the morning session of the stock market hearings on Tuesday, March 8, 1955. Several witnesses from the financial world, including Mr. G. Keith Funston and a bevy of vice-commissars of the New York Stock Exchange, had preceded me. The market had reacted to their testimony with admirable equanimity perhaps because they had said nothing although they had said it very well. Nor was my testimony sensational. I had brought along the proofs of this book; I drew on them to tell what had happened twenty-five years before, in 1928 and 1929. Toward the end I suggested that history

[43] President Eisenhower's appointment as U. S. Ambassador to Brazil of Clare Boothe Luce, playwright, Congresswoman, Catholic convert and wife of *Time's* publisher Henry Luce, was the occasion of spirited public discussion.

could repeat itself, although I successfully resisted all invitations to predict when. I did urge a stiff tightening of margin requirements as a precautionary step. Similar action to minimize the use of credit for speculation had been taken during the war when the speculative enthusiasm was much less. Through it all the newspapermen sat gazing with partly open mouths at the ceiling of the Senate caucus chamber or looking down briefly to scribble a random note. An aide appeared occasionally, sidling along the wall behind the Committee, to pass a note to one of the Senators. The audience, I knew from waiting my turn on earlier occasions, was following me closely and, on occasion, exchanging a critical aside on my facts, logic, or diction. As the testimony gave way to questions, more Senators came in. This is perhaps the most trying time of any hearing. Each in his turn apologizes graciously for being late and then asks the question that has occurred to him on the way over. The question is always the same; and the Senator does not know that it has been asked before:

> Senator Robertson: *Well, Professor, we have been told by all the witnesses so far that present stock prices are not too high. What is your view on that?*
> Senator Ives: *You do not think we are faced with a bust, do you?*
> Senator Monroney: *I am wondering if there is any substance to the oft-repeated reason for the new high levels . . . That the stock market is merely catching up with the inflationary boom. . . .*
> Senator Payne: *I am sorry I came in late . . . would you want to indicate whether or not some of these increases have perhaps more truly reflected the true value of stocks in relation to their earnings?*

The experienced witness observes that the question, though it bears a resemblance to some already asked, has been formulated in a novel way. Then he gives an answer which is the same in substance but decently different in form from those offered before. The audience is especially appreciative of able handling of such details.

Toward the end of the morning, interest appeared to increase. First one and then several photographers appeared. Then a newsreel camera or two. Through the weariness that develops with even so modest a sojourn in the public eye, I thought I sensed a certain tension. I remember noticing that the normal attrition of the Committee — which on a subject such as economics can leave one in a matter of an hour or so with only the Chairman and a precautionary member of the opposition — was not taking place. All Senators were staying. And soon I was the only one in the room who did not know the reason. The stock market was taking a nasty plunge.

I still did not know the reason when the hearing recessed at 12:57, just as a harried man from CBS came dashing into the chamber followed by two beasts of burden carrying a vast poundage of electronic marvels. He had been off in another room photographing Dulles. The real history had passed him by. In response to his almost tearful plea, I repeated several minutes of my testimony to an open window. The substitution of this for the Senators led to a considerable release from inhibition. I rather let myself go with the gestures — at times grave and statesmanlike, at others perhaps a trifle flamboyant. It was this that the world and my children saw. The road from here led on and down to the $64,000 Challenge.

I still did not realize what had happened until someone handed me a paper with a big headline. The *New York Times* industrials went off 7 points on the day. Stocks lost $3 billion in value on the New York Stock Exchange.

IV

Back in Cambridge the next few days were among the most interesting in my memory. The phone rang continuously — so continuously that my secretary went home in annoyance, leaving me to answer it myself. Some of the calls were from the very great like Ed Murrow, who wanted me to extend my remarks for an even larger audience. I declined. A few wanted to know if I was likely to say anything that would affect the market in the near future. I promised them silence. The rest merely wished to denounce me for destroying their dream.

The telephone calls were supplemented, beginning the morning after the testimony, by a mountain of mail. All was unfavorable. Some was denunciatory; more was belligerent; much was prayerful. The belligerent threatened various forms of physical violence. My wife professed particular concern over five communications from a man in Florida announcing that he was on his way north to kill me. Her alarm subsided when I pointed out (having thoughtfully checked the point myself) that all were postmarked Palm Beach. The prayerful all said they were beseeching their God to have me meet with a bad accident — some were asking that I be deprived of life, some of limb, and the minimum request was that I lose all ability to open my mouth. On Wednesday night, I crawled into bed reflecting, with uncharacteristic piety, on all of the prayers that were spiraling up at that moment petitioning my dismemberment or destruction. I thought of saying a word on my own behalf and then struggled with the shattering thought that these matters might be decided by majority vote.

The next morning dawned bright and clear, and my wife and I decided to take a day away from it all. We went to Mount Snow, Vermont, to ski. Toward the end of the afternoon I turned from shaded and hard snow to some that had been softened by the sun and had a bad spill and broke my leg. The papers carried a note about my mishap. I now heard from those whose belief in the existence of a just and omnipotent God had been deeply strengthened.

A few days later, the market started up again. My mail fell off and stopped. A representative collection of the letters was posted in a seminar room and viewed admiringly by students for weeks. But there was more to come.

v

At the time, as still at this writing, the state of Indiana was represented in the Senate of the United States by Homer E. Capehart. He is a Republican, conservative and wealthy. It is possible, as partisan Democrats, at least, believe, that the people of Indiana could have a better representative. But he is not a wicked man. His colleagues find him pleasant. So had I on a previous brief encounter. These were the diminueundo days of Senator Joseph McCarthy. Unlike his colleague, William Jenner, Capehart had never been much involved in McCarthy's crusades. The senior Republican on the Banking and Currency Committee, he had not been present on the day I testified.

On March 20, in the course of a network television program, Senator Capehart announced that I would be recalled before the Committee to answer for having spoken favorably of communism and then, presumably, having advanced its cause by collapsing the market. I had had some warning. A gentleman from the Senator's office had called me a day or two before to see if I admitted to authorship of the offending encomium. The program had been filmed the day before. Also present on the program was a good and gallant friend, Senator A. S. Mike Monroney of Oklahoma. After extemporizing a brilliant defense of my dereliction, he called me to tell me what was coming.

The praise of communism had been extracted from a pamphlet of the National Planning Association dealing with problems of postwar Europe. It noted that the Communists had a better reputation for sincerity and determination in attacking old social grievances and that they also had a solution to the problem of petty nationalism by asserting the higher loyalty to the worker's state. But Senator Capehart's case was not without flaw. The kind words were marred by a caveat, expressing suspicion and distaste of communism on other grounds, which had been put into the very middle of the paragraph for the precise purpose of preventing any inconvenient use, a precaution normal in those days. The Senator had thought it necessary to delete this offending clause, a distinctly noticeable act. The pamphlet had been based on a lecture given originally at the University of Notre Dame in, of all states, Indiana. An earlier version had been published by the University. The pamphlet had been endorsed in principle by Allen Dulles, the brother of the Secretary of State, and Milton Eisenhower, the brother of the President, an underwriting which, however, could cause some doubts as to the utter originality of the ideas advanced. Even a brilliant improviser like Joe McCarthy might have wished for a better case.

A day or so later, the Senator made the further discovery that, at a meeting of the American Economic Association not long before, a conservative professional colleague had jeopardized any possible reputation for understatement by saying that I was, though perhaps unconsciously, "one of the most effective enemies of capitalism and democracy" in all the land. But this evidence did not retrieve matters as much as might have been hoped. My friend thought me dangerous because I was too soft on industrial monopoly.

Like most other liberal academicians, I had been a thoughtful observer of the methods of the Wisconsin "Titus Oates."[44] Two of these had always seemed to me worth adopting by anyone attacked. The first was to avoid defense of one's self and instead assault the accuser.

[44] The seventeenth-century conspirator who invented the story of the Popish Plot against Charles II, a fabrication that had horrid consequences for English Catholics.

The second was to avoid any suspicion, however remote, of personal modesty. I put these methods to test when I heard of the charges. I sent a telegram to the network carrying the program, to key stations, the wire services, and to important papers indicting the Senator for incompetence. I identified incompetence with failure to know my views and these I implied — indeed, I stated —were an imperishable chapter in the intellectual history of our time. I followed the wire a few days later with a press conference, which, by a fortunate accident of travel, I was able to hold in Indiana.

The effect of my efforts, I am persuaded, was to convert an attack that otherwise would have been wholly ignored into front-page news. Neither of us was ever so featured before and I trust will never be so featured again. But I have no complaint about the press. I concluded that I had been assailed for being unkind to the stock market. This it refused to condemn as seriously subversive.

The Senator then took the floor of the Senate for a further denunciation. Some of this centered on my characterization of communism as a monolithic force, which he regarded as seriously suspect. "Mr. President, 'monolithic' means like a monument, or a pillar of strength. . . . That is like describing communism as a monument or as a pillar of strength; or, as we used to say, like the Rock of Gibraltar."

But by now he was loving power. He said, handsomely, that there were things in the offending pamphlet with which "we can all agree." It was unfair, he added, to suggest that he had called me a Red. After some further bickering in the Committee, he subsided. The Senator has had no further reputation as a witch-hunter. I like to think that he himself was plucked as a brand from the burning. I filed a further and rather sanctimonious statement with the Committee but was not recalled.

VI

On April 21, 1955, the book was finally published. The publisher had some months before decided that the volume needed a good strong jacket. This turned out to be a bright and very visible red. With this color and all the excitement of the preceding weeks, it seemed certain that the interest in the book would be overwhelming. In the end the response was admirable but the early market was very orderly. Indeed, depressingly so. One evening I was coming through the old La Guardia terminal on my way back to Boston and I paused as usual to eye the window of the little bookshop on the way to the ramp. As usual there was no sign of the bright red jacket.

The lady asked me if I wanted something and I summoned all of my resources of courage and verisimilitude and said, "I seem to remember a lot of recent discussion about a book — I forget the name of the author, maybe Galbraith — but I think it was called *The Great Crash*."

She replied, "That's certainly not a title you could sell in an airport."

VII

So much for the parturition. The book was meant to be the history of an important and dramatic episode; it was no part of its purpose to predict the future or describe what must again occur. Yet I had certainly given thought to the future. I am a conservative and thus disposed to find antidotes for the suicidal tendencies of the economic system — a disposition which, by an oft-noted inversion of language, quite frequently earns a reputation as a radical. One of these damaging tendencies is the recurrent speculative orgy. This serves no useful purpose of any kind. And it subverts pecuniary motivation from ends that are ordinarily useful to those that are deeply damaging. The Great Crash of 1929 contracted the demand for goods, destroyed for a time the normal machinery for lending and investment, helped arrest economic growth, caused much hardship and, needless to say, alienated countless thousands from the economic system. The causes of the crash were all in the speculative orgy that preceded it. These speculative episodes have occurred at intervals throughout history, and the length of the interval is perhaps roughly related to the time that it takes for men to forget what happened before. The useful task of the historian is to keep the memory green.

All who read these pages and watch the world around them will on occasion see evidence of the dimming memory. Once the investment trust was the remarkable invention that brought the small and innocent investor the precious benefits of skilled investment advice and the promise of high earnings and rich capital gains. Now we have the mutual funds. So precious is the financial genius provided by these that companies are organized to supply it to the companies that actually invest the money. The profit from the sale of this counsel and also the cost of selling it being considerable, it would be illogical to assume that the investor gets the counsel at low cost. When the next collapse comes, quite a few who have committed themselves to contractual plans for investment — to putting so much money in a mutual fund each month — may discover that much of their money has gone for the genius, and the other costs, and not much remains in the stocks.

Those who read here of Ivar Kreuger will be reminded of more recent titans who ceased to be such only with the bark of a revolver or when they had left suddenly for Brazil. And the biggest and best swindlers are not discovered until last. From time to time we see exciting market operations in the old manner. One senses that, increasingly, they are being viewed with awe and admiration rather than alarm. And however frantic the market for a particular security, it is once again being said that it is based on an acute appreciation of long-term values, the exciting growth prospects of the particular industry, the certainty of increasing rewards to soundly invested risk capital, and the inevitability of continuing inflation.

Above all, it is evident that the capacity of the financial community for ignoring evidence of accumulating trouble, even of wishing devoutly that it might go unmentioned, is as great as ever. This deserves a special word.

Even in such a time of madness as the late twenties, a great many men in Wall Street remained quite sane. But they also remained very quiet. The sense of responsibility in the financial community for the community as a whole is not small. It is nearly nil. Perhaps this is inherent. In a community where the primary concern is making money, one of the necessary rules is to live and let live. To speak out against madness may be to ruin those who have succumbed to it. So the wise in Wall Street are nearly always silent. The foolish thus have the field to themselves. None rebukes them. There is always the fear, moreover, that even needful self-criticism may be an excuse for government intervention. That is the ultimate horror.

So someday, no one can tell when, there will be another speculative climax and crash. There is no chance that, as the market moves to the brink, those involved will see the nature of their illusion and so protect themselves and the system. The mad can communicate their madness; they cannot perceive it and resolve to be sane. There is some protection so long as there are people who know, when they hear it said that history is being made in this market or that a new era has been opened, that the same history has been made and the same new eras have been opened many, many times before. This acts to arrest the spread of illusion. A better sense of history is what protects Europeans if not perfectly at least more adequately from speculative excrescence.

With time, the number who are restrained by memory must decline. The historian, in a volume such as this, can hope that he provides a substitute for memory that slightly stays that decline.

PART THREE

THE TRIAD—ONE

SELECTION 8

The Affluent Society is not the society of Adam Smith. To act on the principles of Adam Smith in today's world is in certain ways like pouring oats into your gas tank and would have much the same effect.

Common convictions and social customs are usually obsolescent. In bringing up their children, parents tend to fight the last war, not the next. The realization of the present moves back and forth across society as well as onward in time. Here and there it may get stuck for centuries. Outworn custom is usually only picturesque. Outworn conviction, on the other hand, should be closely watched — in the body politic it can be carcinogenic.

It is our custom to offer our right arm to a woman because a sword was worn on the left for a right-arm draw. If the Saturday night special in the righthand coat pocket is to replace the sword, it might be better to offer the lady your left. It is important not to accept too literally the lessons of history. To act one knows not why, may be ill-advised and will certainly create a sense of insecurity because of the inability to account for one's actions.

The Affluent Society is concerned with outworn convictions in the field of economics and the effects of malignancy when it occurs.

Galbraith here officially defines his name for this anomaly and calls it "the conventional wisdom."

Excerpts from five chapters are chosen. Two have to do with the body of early nineteenth-century economic thinking which, though sound in its way and for its time, is now the conventional wisdom. The third records some American views. Galbraith's graceful outline is of interest for its own sake but it is also essential to the realization of the deep fissure that now stands, not only between two schools of economists but also — and not in small degree — between two major political parties. The last two excerpts describe two ancillary theses which follow logically upon the acceptance of the idea that the conventional wisdom is obsolete. They are "The Dependence Effect" and "The Theory of Social Balance."

The Affluent Society

THE CONCEPT OF THE CONVENTIONAL WISDOM [1]

THE FIRST requirement for an understanding of contemporary economic and social life is a clear view of the relation between events and the ideas which interpret them. For each of these has a life of its own, and much as it may seem a contradiction in terms each is capable for a considerable period of pursuing an independent course.

The reason is not difficult to discover. Economic, like other social life, does not conform to a simple and coherent pattern. On the contrary, it often seems incoherent, inchoate and intellectually frustrating. But one must have an explanation or interpretation of economic

[1] Chapter II, "The Concept of the Conventional Wisdom," *The Affluent Society* (London: André Deutsch, 3rd rev. ed., 1977), pp. 6–11.

behavior. Neither man's curiosity nor his inherent ego allows him to remain contentedly oblivious to anything that is so close to his life.

Because economic and social phenomena are so forbidding, or at least so seem, and because they yield few hard tests of what exists and what does not, they afford to the individual a luxury not given by physical phenomena. Within a considerable range he is permitted to believe what he pleases. He may hold whatever view of this world he finds most agreeable or otherwise to his taste.

As a consequence, in the interpretation of all social life there is a persistent and never-ending competition between what is relevant and what is merely acceptable. In this competition, while a strategic advantage lies with what exists, all tactical advantage is with the acceptable. Audiences of all kinds most applaud what they like best. And in social comment the test of audience approval, far more than the test of truth, comes to influence comment. The speaker or writer who addresses his audience with the proclaimed intent of telling the hard, shocking facts invariably goes on to expound what the audience most wants to hear.

Just as truth ultimately serves to create a consensus, so in the short run does acceptability. Ideas come to be organized around what the community as a whole or particular audiences find acceptable. And as the laboratory worker devotes himself to discovering scientific verities, so the ghost writer and the public relations man concern themselves with identifying the acceptable. If their clients are rewarded with applause, these artisans are qualified in their craft. If not, they have failed. However, by sampling audience reaction in advance, or by pretesting speeches, articles and other communications, the risk of failure can now be greatly minimized.

Numerous factors contribute to the acceptability of ideas. To a very large extent, of course, we associate truth with convenience — with what most closely accords with self-interest and individual well-being or promises best to avoid awkward effort or unwelcome dislocation of life. We also find highly acceptable what contributes most to self-esteem. Speakers before the United States Chamber of Commerce rarely denigrate the businessman as an economic force. Those who appear before the AFL-CIO are prone to identify social progress with a strong trade-union movement. But perhaps most important of all, people approve most of what they best understand. As just noted, economic and social behavior are complex and mentally tiring. Therefore we adhere, as though to a raft, to those ideas that represent our understanding. This is a prime manifestation of vested interest. For a vested interest in understanding is more preciously guarded than any other treasure. It is why men react, not infrequently with something akin to religious passion, to the defense of what they have so laboriously learned. Familiarity may breed contempt in some areas of human behavior but in the field of social ideas it is the touchstone of acceptability.

Because familiarity is such an important test of acceptability, the acceptable ideas have great stability. They are highly predictable. It will be convenient to have a name for the ideas which are esteemed at any time for their acceptability, and it should be a term that emphasizes this predictability. I shall refer to these ideas henceforth as the conventional wisdom.

II

The conventional wisdom is not the property of any political group. On a great many modern social issues, as we shall see in the course of this essay, the consensus is exceedingly broad. Nothing much divides those who are liberals by common political designation from those who are conservatives. The test of what is acceptable is much the same for both. On some questions, however, ideas must be accommodated to the political preferences of the particular audience. The tendency to make this adjustment, either deliberately or more often unconsciously, is not greatly different for different political groups. The conservative is led by disposition, not unmixed with pecuniary self-interest, to adhere to the familiar and the established. These underlie his test of accceptability. But the liberal brings moral fervor and passion, even a sense of righteousness, to the ideas with which he is most familiar. While the ideas he cherishes are different from those of the conservative, he is not likely to be much less emphatic in making familiarity a test of acceptability. Deviation in the form of originality is condemned as faithlessness or backsliding. A "good" liberal or a "tried and true" liberal or a "true blue" liberal is one who is adequately predictable. This means that he forswears any serious striving toward originality. In both the United States and Britain, in recent times, liberals and their British counterparts of the left have proclaimed themselves in search of new ideas. To proclaim the need for new ideas has served, in some measure, as a substitute for them.

Thus we may, as necessary, speak of the conventional wisdom of conservatives or the conventional wisdom of liberals.

The conventional wisdom is also articulated on all levels of sophistication. At the highest levels of social science scholarship, some novelty of formulation or statement is not resisted. On the contrary, considerable store is set by the device of putting an old truth in a new form, and minor heresies are much cherished. And the very vigor of minor debate makes it possible to exclude as irrelevant, and without seeming to be unscientific or parochial, any challenge to the framework itself. Moreover, with time and aided by the debate, the accepted ideas become increasingly elaborate. They have a large literature, even a mystique. The defenders are able to say that the challengers of the conventional wisdom have not mastered their intricacies. Indeed, these ideas can be appreciated only by a stable, orthodox and patient man — in brief, by someone who closely resembles the man of conventional wisdom. The conventional wisdom having been made more or less identical with sound scholarship, its position is virtually impregnable. The skeptic is disqualified by his very tendency to go brashly from the old to the new. Were he a sound scholar, he would remain with the conventional wisdom.

At the same time in the higher levels of the conventional wisdom, originality remains highly acceptable in the abstract. Here again the conventional wisdom often makes vigorous advocacy of originality a substitute for originality itself.

III

As noted, the hallmark of the conventional wisdom is acceptability. It has the approval of those to whom it is addressed. There are many reasons why people like to hear articulated that which they approve. It serves the ego: the individual has the satisfaction of knowing that other and more famous people share his conclusions. To hear what he believes is also a source of reassurance. The individual knows that he is supported in his thoughts — that he has not been left behind and alone. Further, to hear what one approves serves the evangelizing instinct. It means that others are also hearing and are thereby in the process of being persuaded.

In some measure the articulation of the conventional wisdom is a religious rite. It is an act of affirmation like reading aloud from the Scriptures or going to church. The business executive listening to a luncheon address on the virtues of free enterprise and the evils of Washington is already persuaded, and so are his fellow listeners, and all are secure in their convictions. Indeed, although a display of rapt attention is required, the executive may not feel it necessary to listen. But he does placate the gods by participating in the ritual. Having been present, maintained attention, and having applauded, he can depart feeling that the economic system is a little more secure. Scholars gather in scholarly assemblages to hear in elegant statement what all have heard before. Yet it is not a negligible rite, for its purpose is not to convey knowledge but to beatify learning and the learned.

With so extensive a demand, it follows that a very large part of our social comment — and nearly all that is well regarded — is devoted at any time to articulating the conventional wisdom. To some extent this has been professionalized. Individuals, most notably the great television and radio commentators, make a profession of knowing and saying with elegance and unction what their audience will find most acceptable. But in general the articulation of the conventional wisdom is a prerogative of academic, public or business position. Thus any individual, on being elected president of a college or university, automatically wins the right to enunciate the conventional wisdom should he choose to do so. It is one of the rewards of high academic rank, although such rank is also a reward for expounding the conventional wisdom at a properly sophisticated level.

The high public official is expected, and indeed is to some extent required, to expound the conventional wisdom. His, in many respects, is the purest case. Before assuming office, he ordinarily commands little attention. But on taking up his position, he is immediately assumed to be gifted with deep insights. He does not, except in the rarest instances, write his own speeches or articles; and these are planned, drafted and scrupulously examined to ensure their acceptability. The application of any other test, e.g., their effectiveness as a simple description of the economic or political reality, would be regarded as eccentric in the extreme.

Finally, the expounding of the conventional wisdom is the prerogative of business success. The head of almost any large corporation — the United States Steel Corporation, General Motors, the Radio Corporation of America — is entitled to do so. And he is privileged to speak not only on business policy and economics but also on the role of government in the society, the foundations of foreign policy and the nature of a liberal education. In recent years it has been urged that to expound the conventional wisdom is not only the privilege but also the obligation of the businessman. "I am convinced that businessmen must write as well as speak, in order that we may bring to people everywhere the exciting and confident message of our faith in the free enterprise way of life . . . What a change would come in this struggle for men's minds if suddenly there could pour out from the world of American business a torrent of intelligent, forward-looking thinking."[2]

ECONOMICS AND THE TRADITION OF DESPAIR[3]

II

IN THE history of economic thought Adam Smith (1723–1790), the first great figure in the central economic tradition,[4] is counted a hopeful figure. In an important sense he was. His vision was of an advancing national community, not a stagnant or declining one. His title, *An Inquiry into the Nature and Causes of the Wealth of Nations*, has an obvious overtone of opulence and well-being. He offered an all but certain formula for economic progress. This was the liberal economic society in which regulation was by competition and the market and not by the state, and in which each man, thrown on his own resources, labored effectively for the enrichment of the society.

But it was of aggregate wealth that Smith spoke. He had little hope that the distribution between merchants, manufacturers and land-lords on the one hand, and the working masses on the other, would be such as much to benefit the latter. Smith regarded this distribu-

[2] Clarence B. Randall, *A Creed for Free Enterprise* (Boston: Atlantic–Little, Brown, 1952), pp. 3, 5.
[3] Chapter III, "Economics and the Tradition of Despair," *The Affluent Society*, pp. 21–28.
[4] I have used the phrase "central tradition" to denote the main current of ideas in descent from Smith. The more common reference to the "classical tradition" is ruled out by a difference of opinion, in my view a rather futile one, as to whether classical economics should or should not be considered to have ended with John Stuart Mill and J. E. Cairnes. Another possible reference is to the orthodox tradition. But this, by implication, excludes those like Keynes who, though working in the same current of ideas, have taken sharp issue with accepted conclusions.

tion as depending in the first instance on relative bargaining strength. And he did not believe it difficult "to foresee which of the two parties must upon all ordinary occasions have the advantage in the dispute." In an admirably succinct comment on the balance of eighteenth-century economic power he added: "We have no acts of Parliament against combining to lower the price of work; but many against combining to raise it."[5] So in the normal course of events the income of the working masses would be pressed down and down. There was a floor below which they would not fall. "A man must always live by his work, and his wages must at least be sufficient to maintain him. They must even upon most occasions be somewhat more; otherwise it would be impossible for him to bring up a family, and the race of such workmen could not last beyond the first generation."[6]

But this obviously was not much. On the contrary, although Adam Smith is rarely identified with the idea, this was one of the beginnings of perhaps the most influential and certainly the most despairing dictum in the history of social comment, the notion that the income of the masses of the people — all who in one way or another worked for a living and whether in industry or agriculture — could not for very long rise very far above the minimal level necessary for the survival of the race. It is the immortal iron law which, as stiffened by Ricardo and refashioned by Marx, became the chief weapon in the eventual ideological assault on capitalism.

Smith was not categorical about the iron law — he was categorical about almost nothing, and ever since economists have always been at their best when they adhered to his example. Thus he conceded that a scarcity of workers might keep wages above the subsistence level for an indefinite time. Under conditions of rapid economic growth wages would also rise. Growth was much more important than wealth *per se* in its effect on wages. "It is not the actual greatness of national wealth, but its continual increase, which occasions a rise in the wages of labor. . . . England is certainly, in the present times, a much richer country than any part of North America. The wages of labor, however, are much higher in North America than in any part of England."[7]

[5] *Wealth of Nations*, ch. VIII. (There are so many editions of this famous work that it seems idle to cite the pages of the particular edition one happens to use.)
[6] *Ibid*.
[7] *Ibid*. Smith observes that this was written in 1773 before "the commencement of the late disturbances," meaning the American Revolution.

Smith's two great successors in the central tradition were David Ricardo (1772–1823) and Thomas Robert Malthus (1766–1834). With Adam Smith they were the founding trinity of economics, at least as the subject is known in the English-speaking countries. As the man who first gave economics its modern structure — who looked at the factors determining prices, rents, wages and profits with a sense of system that has served economists ever since — Ricardo has a special claim to have bent the twig. Marxians and non-Marxians are equally in his debt.

With Ricardo and Malthus the notion of massive privation and great inequality became a basic premise. These conclusions were never wholly unqualified. But the qualifications were only qualifications. It was to Ricardo and Malthus that Carlyle alluded when he spoke in 1850 of the "Respectable Professors of the Dismal Science" and gave to economics a name that it has never quite escaped because it was never quite undeserved.

Of Malthus it is necessary to say only a word. Through the nineteenth century and to our own day he has been intimately and all but exclusively associated with his *Essay on Population.* Though he had other and important things to say on economics which have been the subject of a latter-day rediscovery, it is for his views on population that he will be always known.

The number of people who can live in the world is obviously limited by the number that can be fed. Any increase in the supply of food would bring, in Malthus's view, an increase in the number of people to consume it. Nothing but stark need limits the numbers who are propagated and who endure. As a result, men will forever live on the verge of starvation. In the latter editions of the *Essay* Malthus hedged somewhat; the increase in response to a surplus over subsistence might be tempered by "moral restraint" and also, somewhat more ambiguously, by "vice." In other words, people might indefinitely protect their standard of living at a level above subsistence, and this would become all the more likely once both restraint and vice were abetted by effective contraceptive techniques. But as also with Ricardo, Malthus's qualifications were lost in the sweep of his central proposition. This was the inevitability of mass poverty. There was also the considerable fact that for a large part of the world, the central proposition was valid and the qualifications were unimportant. So it was and so it remains in much of Asia. Malthus, it may be noted, was professor of political economy in Haileybury College, an institution maintained by the East India Company for training its servants who would serve in India.

Since most men had always been poor, it is hardly surprising that Malthus was on the whole unperturbed by his conclusions and that he did not feel called upon to propose any remedy. (He confined himself to urging the postponement of marriage and to recommending that there be incorporated into the marriage service a warning that the husband and not the state would be responsible for the children of the union so that if these were excessive, the parents could expect to be punished by want.) "The note of gloom and pessimism which distinguished so much of the economic doctrine of the nineteenth century is in no small measure the legacy of Malthus."[8]

IV

Both Adam Smith and Malthus had an instinct for national aggregates — for the forces which acted to enrich the nation. While Malthus was concerned with showing how increased national wealth might be used up in the explosive impulse to procreate, neither was centrally concerned with how different individuals and classes might share in what the economy produced. This to David Ricardo was of primary interest. What were the laws which governed the distribution of product or income between the landlords, entrepreneurs and workers who had claim to it? "Political Economy you think is an inquiry into the nature and causes of wealth — I think it should rather be called an enquiry into the laws which determine the division of the produce of industry amongst the classes who concur in its formation."[9] These laws, as Ricardo formulated them, worked with ferocious inequality.

Like Malthus, Ricardo regarded population as a dependent variable — it "regulates itself by the funds which are to employ it, and therefore always increases or diminishes with the increase or diminution of capital."[10] Advancing wealth and productivity thus bring more people; but they do not bring more land from which to feed these

[8] Alexander Gray, *The Development of Economic Doctrine* (London: Longmans, Green, 1931), p. 163.
[9] Letter to Malthus, October 9, 1820. In *The Works and Correspondence of David Ricardo*, ed. by Piero Sraffa (Cambridge, England: Cambridge University Press, 1951), vol. VIII, p. 278.
[10] *Ibid.*, vol. I, p. 78.

people. As a result, those who own land are able to command an ever greater return, given its quality, for what is an increasingly scarce resource. Meanwhile, in Ricardo's view, profits and wages were in flat conflict for the rest of the product. An increase in profits, other things being equal, meant a reduction in wages; an increase in wages must always come out of profits. "Every rise of profits" on the other hand "is favourable to the accumulation of capital, and to the further increase of population, and therefore would, in all probability, ultimately lead to an increase of rent."[11] The effect of these compact relationships will be clear. If the country is to have increasing capital and product, profits must be good. But then as product expands, the population will increase. The food requirements of the population will press on the available land supply and force up rents to the advantage of the landowner. In other words, capitalists must prosper if there is to be progress, and landlords cannot help reaping its fruits. The children of this inescapable misfortune are the people at large. Ricardo summarized that prospect in, perhaps, the most quoted passage in economic literature: "Labour, like all other things which are purchased and sold, and which may be increased or diminished in quantity, has its natural and its market price. The natural price of labour is that price which is necessary to enable the labourers, one with another, to subsist and perpetuate their race, without either increase or diminution."[12]

This was the iron law of wages. As with Smith (and Malthus on population) Ricardo followed the proposition with qualifications. In an "improving" society the market wage might be above the natural wage for an indefinite period, and were Ricardo still alive, he could show with little difficulty that the conditions necessary for the rule of the iron law have been in abeyance ever since the nineteenth day of April, 1817, when On the Principles of Political Economy and Taxation was published. But although the truth rarely overtakes falsehood, it has winged feet as compared with a qualification in pursuit of a bold proposition. The iron law, in its uncompromised clarity, became part of the intellectual capital of the world.

Moreover, as with Malthus, nothing could be done about it. Ricardo brought his analysis to a close with the unbending observation that "These then are the laws by which wages are regulated, and by which the happiness [a word to be duly noted] of far the greatest part of every community is governed. Like all other contracts, wages

11 Ibid., p. 411.
12 Ibid., p. 93.

should be left to the fair and free competition of the market, and should never be controlled by the interference of the legislature."[13] Nor may anyone be blamed. On a number of occasions Ricardo complained that Malthus was unfairly accusing him of being hostile to landlords — "one would suppose from his language that I considered them enemies of the state."[14] The landlords were merely the passive and natural beneficiaries of their great good fortune. This was the nature of things. Such was the Ricardian legacy.

There were many contradictions and ambiguities in Adam Smith. There were also flaws in the Ricardian logic as it applied to the Ricardian world. His treatment of capital and profits left much to be desired. And he preoccupied himself with land at almost the point in history when, because of the opening of a new world, it had begun to lose its ancient preoccupying importance. Yet it is hard to think that economists ever came much closer to interpreting the world in which they lived than did Smith, Ricardo and Malthus. None was committed to preconceived doctrine. They had broken decisively with the conventional wisdom of the traditionalist and mercantilist society. They had no public opinion to appease. The result was a formidable interpretation of, and prescription for, the world as they found it.

In a world that had for so long been so poor, nothing was so important as to win an increase in wealth. The prescription — to free men from the restraints and protection of feudal and mercantilist society and put them on their own — was sound, for it was already proving itself. This was not a compassionate world. Many suffered and many were destroyed under the harsh and unpredictable rule of competition and the market. But many had always perished for one reason or another. Now some were flourishing. This was what counted. One looked not at the peril and misfortune, for there had always been peril and misfortune, but at the opportunity. In any case, nothing could be done about the inequality, for it was not rooted in mutable social institutions but in biology. This was fortunate, for the state was excluded from intervention by its prior commitment to freedom of enterprise.

Remarkably little that concerned contemporary economic society was left unbuttoned. It is hardly surprising that a system, seemingly so complete and practical and so subject to test against the realities of the world, made an indelible dent on men's minds.

13 *Ibid.*, p. 105.
14 *Ibid.*, vol. II, p. 117.

V

For thirty years following the death of Ricardo the development of economics continued firmly in the tradition he had established. Lesser men together with the conscientious and immeasurably learned John Stuart Mill refined, developed and organized the ideas. Their thoughts remained centered on the liberal economic society — that in which economic life was regulated by the market and not by the state. On the continent men did talk about socialism but in England and in the Anglo-Saxon tradition they took the market very nearly for granted.

Then at mid-century the economic ideas in the descent from Ricardo came to the great divide. The central tradition continued in its course. It continued to provide the skeletal framework for economic ideas down to our own day. In so doing, it gave them system and continuity and went far to make economic life comprehensible. But now, branching off to the left but with a common debt to Ricardo, was the revolutionary tradition of Karl Marx. Henceforth, in shaping attitudes toward economic life, it was both a massive competitor of, and a powerful influence on, the central tradition.

The purpose of these chapters is not to trace the evolution of the individual ideas. That is the task of other volumes and even more of other authors. Rather, it is to see what economics assumed in its origins about the ordinary individual and his fate. As between the early Ricardian world and that of Marx, there was in this respect no difference. For both, the prospect, given the uninterrupted working out of the underlying forces, combined peril with hopelessness. The difference was that Ricardo and his immediate followers expected the system to survive and Marx did not. But for Ricardo the system survived not because it served the ordinary man. Obviously it did not. It survived only because there was no evident alternative and certainly none that was better. Any effort to modify it made it less efficient.

THE AMERICAN MOOD [15]

ONLY WITHIN very narrow limits can one speak of a separate American tradition in economics. Ideas do not respect national frontiers, and this is especially so where language and other traditions

[15] Chapter V, "The American Mood," *The Affluent Society*, pp. 41–51.

are in common. The precepts of the central tradition were accepted equally by Englishmen and Americans. It was from Smith, Ricardo, Mill and Marshall that American economic ideas were derived. The ideas were written by Americans into the textbooks and enlarged or amended as to detail. But in the last century not much was added by American theorists. Just as the ideas were common to both countries, so were the worries, uncertainties and doubts which the ideas engendered.

This is not to say there were no distinctively American figures but, as compared with the majestic authority of the central tradition, their influence was comparatively small. There would be a measure of agreement on who were the three that were most heard. They were not the total of the American voice but they were also far more than a mere sample. Of the three, two did nothing to offset the presumption of privation and the sense of foreboding that lingered in the central tradition. On the contrary, they did a good deal to accentuate it.

The exception was Henry Charles Carey (1793–1879) who did voice the buoyant optimism which one is obliged to think appropriate to the new republic. Ricardo, he observed, had never seen from his window the progress of a new settlement; had he done so, he would have had a different view of the prospects for mankind. Drawing on such observation, he argued that, with the passage of time, men were not forced, as Ricardo claimed, to poorer and poorer land with ever lower return to their labor and, for any land that was better than the worst, ever higher rents to the landlords. On the contrary, they first cultivated the thin but unencumbered soil on top of the hills. Then at a later period they tackled the thick vegetation in the valleys; having cleared away the trees, they proceeded to work this richer alluvial soil. The returns to their toil were not less but more. In his first book in 1835, which, like those of his English contemporaries, centered on the problem of wages and thus as ever on the mass prospect for poverty or well-being, he argued that real wages during the previous forty years had shown a tendency to rise. This, too, was in contrast with Ricardian expectations.

But even Carey was not an unqualified optimist. He more than half agreed with Malthus on the procreative power of mankind, and in his earlier books he hazarded the guess that the time might come when "there will not even be standing room."[16] And the influence of Carey, whether as an optimist or pessimist, was not great. Of this he

16 Quoted by Gray, *The Development of Economic Doctrine*, p. 256.

himself was aware. He complained bitterly of the small attention that was paid to his ideas in his own country. In Europe he felt that he was discussed more seriously, and this may well have been so.[17] Little or nothing of Carey passed into the tradition of American economic thought. His books moldered and died. In the last fifty years he has been mentioned only as a curiosity — an early American economist who had the fortitude to disagree with Ricardo on rent and with Adam Smith on the virtues of free trade.

II

The two other distinctively American figures had more enduring influence. These were Henry George and Thorstein Veblen. But so far from manifesting the exuberant attitudes of the frontier, both were prophets of a gloom that was, in some respects, more profound than that of Ricardo. Henry George (1839–1897) was, like Marx, the founder of a faith, and the faithful still assemble to do honor to their prophet. Like Adam Smith he made clear his view of the social prospect in the title of his remarkable book: *Progress and Poverty. An Inquiry into the Cause of Industrial Depressions and of Increase of Want with Increase of Wealth.* In the opening chapter he posed his basic questions: Why in a time of general economic advance — he was writing in the depression years following 1873 — should so much labor "be condemned to involuntary idleness," should there be so much "pecuniary distress among businessmen," and so much "want, suffering and anxiety among the working classes."[18] Why, to press things further, should there be so little gain to the poorest classes from increased productive power. "Nay, more," why should its effect be "still further to suppress the condition of the lowest classes."[19]

The reason for this perverse aspect of progress was again part of the almost infinite legacy of Ricardo. Labor and capital increased in productivity; the land supply remained constant in quality and amount. Rents, as a result, increased more than proportionately and made the landlords the undeserving beneficiaries of advance. The anticipation of rent increases and attendant speculation in land values was also the cause of depression. (It is worth recalling that the nine-

---

[17] See Joseph Dorfman, *The Economic Mind in American Civilization, 1606–1865* (New York: Viking, 1946), p. 804.
[18] Henry George, *Progress and Poverty* (Fiftieth Anniversary Ed.; New York: Robert Shalkenbach Foundation, 1933), p. 5.
[19] *Ibid.*, p. 9.

teenth century was marked by recurrent outbreaks of real estate speculation, especially in the West, and that Henry George spent much of his life in California. Economic ideas, as ever, have their nexus with their environment.) So long as there was private property in land, poverty and depressions were the prospect. Progress would make them worse.

In one respect, Henry George was radically more optimistic than Ricardo. On his title page were the further words *The Remedy*; this phrase had no place in the Ricardian lexicon. If land were nationalized — more precisely if a tax were imposed equal to the annual use value of real property *ex* its improvements, so that it would now have no net earnings and hence no capital value — progress would be orderly and its fruits would be equitably shared. But this, obviously, was a very drastic prescription. Were the remedy not applied, and this was a reasonable prospect given the predictable reaction of property owners to the proposal, then the consequence would be continuing poverty combined with increasing inequality and increasing insecurity. If this was the American dream, it had little to commend it as compared with the meager classical prospect. And, in fact, the mood of Henry George's followers was often one of misanthropic or frustrated radicalism.

III

In the tradition of American popular radicalism there were other influential figures besides Henry George — Henry Demarest Lloyd and Edward Bellamy come especially to mind as important figures of the latter decades of the last century. Their conclusions, however, were broadly similar: great inequality and great poverty were inevitable in the absence of great reform. And unlike Henry George their words mostly died with them. There remains, however, the man whom many regard as the uniquely American economist, Thorstein Veblen (1857–1929).[20]

For the eager search for reassurance that followed the Ricardian

[20] A case might be made for the influence of three other men who were generally outside the central tradition; namely, Simon N. Patten (1852–1922), John R. Commons, (1862–1945), and Wesley C. Mitchell (1874–1948). However, Patten, a singularly interesting and original figure, has joined Carey in the neglect reserved for American heretics. Commons and Mitchell, as a matter of principle or method, largely avoided any overall theoretical formulation of man's prospects and hence could not be said to have contributed to the attitudes with which we are here concerned.

gloom, Veblen substituted a grandiloquent iconoclasm. Ricardo had forecast a disagreeable fate for most of mankind. His followers hoped against hope that it might not be. Veblen took a position above the debate. The fate of man was something with which, at least for purposes of posture, he chose not to identify himself. But he also made clear his view that those who talked of progress were mostly idiots or frauds.

To this end, he made specific many of the misfortunes that lurked in the background of the central tradition. Poverty, or more accurately both the moral and material debasement of man, was part of the system and would become worse with progress. There is an inescapable conflict between industry and business — between the "excessive prevalence and efficiency of the machine industry" and its "deplorable" tendency to overproduce and thus to threaten the basic goal of business which is to make money.[21] In this conflict business always wins. Monopolistic restrictions are imposed where, on purely technical grounds, there could be abundance. This channels income to the owners. The public pays with relative impoverishment.

The economic costs of progress are, however, even less severe than its cultural consequences. Machine industry does not necessarily call for less intelligence on the part of the workers. But it does require a peculiarly narrow and mechanical process of thought, and it discourages all other. It also undermines family and church and (here the unions play a key role) the ancient foundations of law and order. The massing together of the workers is a great inducement to "socialist iconoclasm" which is the threshold to anarchy.

Serious depressions are not accidental misfortunes. They are inherent in the conflict between industry and business and hence are organic aspects of the system. They occur "in the regular course of business."[22]

Finally, in his immortal *The Theory of the Leisure Class*,[23] Veblen dramatized, as no one before or since, the spectacle of inequality. The rich and successful were divorced from any serious economic function and denied the dignity of even a serious or indignant attack. They became, instead, a subject for detached, bemused and perhaps subtly contemptuous observation. One observes the struggle between hens

---

[21] Thorstein Veblen, *The Theory of Business Enterprise* (1932 ed; New York: Scribner), p. 234.

[22] *Ibid.*, p. 183. The conclusions sketched above are principally developed in *The Theory of Business Enterprise*.

[23] Originally published in 1899.

for social pre-eminence in the chicken yard as an interesting phenomenon but in so doing, one does not do much to underwrite the social values of the birds. So with Veblen on the rich.

But equally with Ricardo, wealth and poverty were made inherent. And so, moreover, were their least ingratiating aspects. The ostentation, waste, idleness and immorality of the rich were all purposeful: they were the advertisements of success in the pecuniary culture. Work, by contrast, was merely a caste mark of inferiority. "During the predatory culture labour comes to be associated in men's habits of thought with weakness and subjection to a master. It is, therefore, a mark of inferiority, and, therefore, comes to be accounted unworthy of man in his best estate."[24] In the central tradition the worker was accorded the glory of honest toil. Veblen denied him even that.

Nor was there any hope for change. These things were part of the pecuniary culture. Where Marx looked forward hopefully to revolutionary reconstruction, Veblen did not. In his latter years he comforted himself only with the thought that the evolving economic society was destroying not only itself, but all civilization as well. Such was the view of the greatest voice from the frontier.

There will always be debate as to how influential Veblen was. He is the indubitably indigenous figure in American economic thought. This has always commended him to those who — failing to see the enormous authority of the orthodox-classical tradition — have supposed that the dominating influence in American thought must be an American.[25] This must still be true even though, as in the case of Veblen, no one could worse fit the cultural stereotype of the optimistic, extrovert American. In fact, Veblen's strictly economic conclusions were not widely read or taught. They never entered the textbooks in competition with the ideas of the central tradition. Yet he was no Carey. He influenced a generation of scholars, writers and teachers. These, in turn, brought something of his iconoclasm to the ideas of the time. Teachers influenced by Veblen taught the doctrines of the central tradition but they brought to it a disbelief, even a contempt, for the notion that economic progress could much benefit the masses or, indeed, that there was such a thing. Veblen thus precipitated the doubts and pessimism which lurked in the central tradition. In American social thought before the Great Depression

[24] *Ibid.*, p. 36.
[25] This is a criticism which, I think, can fairly be made of Professor Henry Steele Commager. Cf. his discussion of Veblen in *The American Mind* (New Haven: Yale University Press, 1950), pp. 227–246.

there was a strong feeling, manifested for example in such liberal journals as *The Nation* and *The New Republic*, that the hard-headed intellectual was never beguiled by notions of reform or advance under capitalism. These when offered were either a façade, a trap or an illusion which would quickly bring disenchantment. These attitudes faded with the New Deal but not until the Roosevelt reforms had been similarly and repeatedly discussed and dismissed. These attitudes were in no small measure the legacy of Veblen.

IV

Such was the distinctively American contribution. However, we must take note of the impact of another set of social ideas — ideas, which though not American in origin, came almost uniquely to root in the American soil. Toward the close of the last century and in the early years of this, they deeply influenced attitudes on the fate of the ordinary man. These were the doctrines of the Social Darwinists.

Ricardo and Malthus did not conceal from anyone that theirs was a world of struggle. In that struggle some, and perhaps many, succumbed, and there was no hope in public measures to ameliorate the lot of those who were to fall. Speaking of the poor laws, then supported by a fund subscribed by each parish for the support of the indigent, Ricardo concluded that no scheme for their amendment "merits the least attention, which has not their abolition for its ultimate object," adding that "the principle of gravitation is not more certain than the tendency of such laws to change wealth and power into misery and weakness."[26]

However, Ricardo's case for leaving everything to the market — for not allowing compassion to interfere with economic process — was essentially functional. Idleness not being subsidized and substance not being wasted, more was produced and the general well-being would thus be raised. Struggle and misfortune were not themselves to be welcomed.

The position of the Social Darwinists was different. Economic society was an arena in which men met to compete. The terms of the struggle were established by the market. Those who won were rewarded with survival and, if they survived brilliantly, with riches. Those who lost went to the lions. This competition not only selected the strong but developed their faculties and ensured their perpetuation. And in eliminating the weak, it ensured that they would not

[26] *Principles of Political Economy* (Cambridge: University Press for the Royal Economic Society, 1951), pp. 107–8.

reproduce their kind. Thus the struggle was socially benign, and, to a point at least, the more merciless the more benign its effects, for the more weaklings it combed out.

The birthplace of these ideas was nineteenth-century England, and their principal source and protagonist was Herbert Spencer (1820–1903). It was Spencer and not Charles Darwin who gave the world the phrase "the survival of the fittest," and it was first applied not to the lower animals but to mankind. Spencer believed that acquired as well as inherited traits were genetically transmitted.

Spencer was a decidedly uncompromising exponent of a very uncompromising creed. He opposed state ownership of the post office and the mint. He was opposed to public education, for it interfered with parental choice between different schools and, indeed, with the choice between wisdom and ignorance for their children. Public aid to the needy and even public sanitation tended to perpetuate the more vulnerable members of the race.

> *Partly by weeding out those of lowest development, and partly by subjecting those who remain to the never ceasing discipline of experience, nature secures the growth of a race who shall both understand the conditions of existence and be able to act up to them. It is impossible in any degree to suspend this discipline by stepping in between ignorance and its consequences, without, to a corresponding degree, suspending the progress. If to be ignorant were as safe as to be wise, no one would become wise.*[27]

Spencer was restrained from a condemnation of all private charity only by the disturbing thought that this would abridge the liberty of the giver as surely as it would winnow out the weaklings of the race. Misery and misfortune are not misery and misfortune alone but the rungs of a ladder up which man makes his ascent. To seek to mitigate misery was to put in abeyance the fundamental arrangements by which nature ensured progress. "What can be a more extreme absurdity than that of proposing to improve social life by breaking the fundamental law of social life."[28]

Although Spencer was an Englishman, Social Darwinism had much of its greatest success in the United States. Here, in William Graham Sumner (1840–1910) of Yale, it found its major prophet. Here too it

[27] *Social Statics* (New York: D. Appleton, 1865), p. 413.
[28] *Principles of Ethics*, vol. II (New York: D. Appleton & Co., 1897), p. 60.

found a host of minor ones. Spencer's own books were widely read, or at least widely discussed, in the closing decades of the nineteenth century and the opening years of the present one. When Spencer visited the United States in 1882, he was accorded a welcome by the faithful befitting a messiah. In 1904, when the Supreme Court struck down a New York State law limiting the hours of labor of bakers to ten a day, Justice Holmes observed that "The Fourteenth Amendment does not enact Mr. Herbert Spencer's Social Statics."[29] It was a dissenting opinion.

There were a number of reasons for his popularity in the new republic. By the time of Spencer, England was already moving away from the unhampered rule of the market. Unions, factory inspection, the regulation of the hours of women and children had gained acceptance. In the United States the race was still being more ruthlessly improved.

And there were many who wished to see the improvement continue with all it implied for those who had been selected. "The peculiar condition of American society," Henry Ward Beecher told Spencer as early as 1866, "has made your writings far more quickening here than in Europe."[30] In fact, ideas were never more marvelously in the service of circumstance.

The rise of Social Darwinism in the United States coincided with the rise of the great fortunes. It was a time not only of heroic inequality but of incredible ostentation. Great limestone mansions were rising in New York. Even more stately pleasure domes were being built in Newport. Mrs. William K. Vanderbilt gave her $250,000 ball in 1883. That of the Bradley Martins in 1897 was rather more lavish. For this the ballroom of the old Waldorf-Astoria was transformed into a replica of Versailles. One guest appeared in a suit of gold inlaid armor valued at an estimated $10,000. A little earlier at Delmonico's — where Spencer had been entertained — guests were given cigarettes wrapped in hundred-dollar bills which they lighted with a legitimate sense of affluence.

It was also a time of widespread poverty and degradation. The distant workers who supported this wealth lived in noisome slums. There were numerous beggars near at hand. Nor could it always be said that the wealth was being acquired without cost to others. The techniques were sometimes very rude. But none of this need lie on anyone's

[29] Lochner v. New York, 1904.
[30] Quoted by Richard Hofstadter, *Social Darwinism in American Thought* (Boston: Beacon Press, 1955), p. 31.

conscience. Natural selection was at work. The rich could regard themselves as the product of its handiwork — as Chauncey Depew was pleased to remind those who attended one of the great dinners of the successful in New York. So, an important point, could their sons, for the superior qualities were genetically transmitted. This legitimized inherited wealth, for it blessed only the biologically superior. The problem of poverty, meanwhile, was being solved by the only means by which it could be solved. The unfit were being weeded out. Public and even private succor, which if compelled by compassion could be inconveniently expensive, was banned not by callousness but by a perceptive adherence to the laws of nature. "The law of the survival of the fittest was not made by man. We can only by interfering with it produce the survival of the unfittest."[31] How much better to resist taxation and charity and, incidentally, keep one's money. To this day the man who refuses a beggar and righteously observes, "I'm told it's the worst thing you can do," is still finding useful the inspired formula of Spencer and Sumner.

Nor need one reflect, uncomfortably, on the methods by which growth had been achieved and wealth acquired. As John D. Rockefeller explained to a fortunate Sunday School class: "The growth of a large business is merely the survival of the fittest. . . . The American Beauty rose can be produced in the splendor and fragrance which bring cheer to its beholder only by sacrificing the early buds which grow up around it." As with the rose, so with the Standard Oil Company. "This is not an evil tendency in business. It is merely the working-out of a law of nature and a law of God."[32] This aligned God and the American Beauty rose with railroad rebates, exclusive control of pipelines, systematic price discrimination and some other remarkably aggressive business practices.

THE DEPENDENCE EFFECT [33]

IV

AS A society becomes increasingly affluent, wants are increasingly created by the process by which they are satisfied. This may operate passively. Increases in consumption, the counterpart of increases in

[31] William Graham Sumner, *Essays in Political and Social Science* (New York: Henry Holt, 1885), p. 85.
[32] Hofstadter, *Social Darwinism in American Thought*, p. 45.
[33] Chapter XI, "The Dependence Effect," *The Affluent Society*, pp. 131–133.

production, act by suggestion or emulation to create wants. Or producers may proceed actively to create wants through advertising and salesmanship. Wants thus come to depend on output. In technical terms, it can no longer be assumed that welfare is greater at an all-round higher level of production than at a lower one. It may be the same. The higher level of production has, merely, a higher level of want creation necessitating a higher level of want satisfaction. There will be frequent occasion to refer to the way wants depend on the process by which they are satisfied. It will be convenient to call it the Dependence Effect.

We may now contemplate briefly the conclusions to which this analysis has brought us.

Plainly, the theory of consumer demand is a peculiarly treacherous friend of the present goals of economics. At first glance, it seems to defend the continuing urgency of production and our preoccupation with it as a goal. The economist does not enter into the dubious moral arguments about the importance or virtue of the wants to be satisfied. He doesn't pretend to compare mental states of the same or different people at different times and to suggest that one is less urgent than another. The desire is there. That for him is sufficient. He sets about in a workmanlike way to satisfy desire, and accordingly, he sets the proper store by the production that does. Like woman's, his work is never done.

But this rationalization, handsomely though it seems to serve, turns destructively on those who advance it once it is conceded that wants are themselves both passively and deliberately the fruits of the process by which they are satisfied. Then the production of goods satisfies the wants that the consumption of these goods creates or that the producers of goods synthesize. Production induces more wants and the need for more production. So far, in a major tour de force, the implications have been ignored. But this obviously is a perilous solution. It cannot long survive discussion.

Among the many models of the good society, no one has urged the squirrel wheel. Moreover, as we shall see presently, the wheel is not one that revolves with perfect smoothness. Aside from its dubious cultural charm, there are serious structural weaknesses which may one day embarrass us. For the moment, however, it is sufficient to reflect on the difficult terrain which we are traversing. In previous pages we have seen how deeply we were committed to production for reasons of economic security. Not the goods but the employment provided by their production was the thing by which we set ultimate store. Now we find our concern for goods further undermined. It does not arise in spontaneous consumer need. Rather, the dependence effect means that it grows out of the process of production itself. If production is to increase, the wants must be effectively contrived. In the absence of the contrivance, the increase would not occur. This is not true of all goods, but that it is true of a substantial part is sufficient. It means that since the demand for this part would not exist, were it not contrived, its utility or urgency, *ex* contrivance, is zero. If we regard this production as marginal, we may say that the marginal utility of present aggregate output, *ex* advertising and salesmanship, is zero. Clearly the attitudes and values which make production the central achievement of our society have some exceptionally twisted roots.

Perhaps the thing most evident of all is how new and varied become the problems we must ponder when we break the nexus with the work of Ricardo and face the economics of affluence of the world in which we live. It is easy to see why the conventional wisdom resists so stoutly such change. It is a far, far better thing to have a firm anchor in nonsense than to put out on the troubled seas of thought.

THE THEORY OF SOCIAL BALANCE [34]

> *It is not till it is discovered that high individual incomes will not purchase the mass of mankind immunity from cholera, typhus, and ignorance, still less secure them the positive advantages of educational opportunity and economic security, that slowly and reluctantly, amid prophecies of moral degeneration and economic disaster, society begins to make collective provision for needs which no ordinary individual, even if he works overtime all his life, can provide himself.*
>
> — R. H. TAWNEY [35]

THE FINAL problem of the productive society is what it produces. This manifests itself in an implacable tendency to provide an opulent supply of some things and a niggardly yield of others. This disparity

[34] Chapter XVII, "The Theory of Social Balance," *The Affluent Society*, pp. 190–204.
[35] *Equality* (4th revised ed.; London: Allen & Unwin, 1952), pp. 134–35.

carries to the point where it is a cause of social discomfort and social unhealth. The line which divides our area of wealth from our area of poverty is roughly that which divides privately produced and marketed goods and services from publicly rendered services. Our wealth in the first is not only in startling contrast with the meagerness of the latter but our wealth in privately produced goods is, to a marked degree, the cause of crisis in the supply of public services. For we have failed to see the importance, indeed the urgent need, of maintaining a balance between the two.

This disparity between our flow of private and public goods and services is no matter of subjective judgment. On the contrary, it is the source of the most extensive comment which only stops short of the direct contrast being made here. In the years following World War II, the papers of any major city — those of New York were an excellent example — told daily of the shortages and shortcomings in the elementary municipal and metropolitan services. The schools were old and overcrowded. The police force was under strength and underpaid. The parks and playgrounds were insufficient. Streets and empty lots were filthy, and the sanitation staff was underequipped and in need of men. Access to the city by those who work there was uncertain and painful and becoming more so. Internal transportation was overcrowded, unhealthful and dirty. So was the air. Parking on the streets should have been prohibited but there was no space elsewhere. These deficiencies were not in new and novel services but in old and established ones. Cities have long swept their streets, helped their people move around, educated them, kept order and provided horse rails for equipages which sought to pause. That their residents should have a nontoxic supply of air suggests no revolutionary dalliance with socialism.

The discussion of this public poverty competed, on the whole successfully, with the stories of ever-increasing opulence in privately produced goods. The Gross National Product was rising. So were retail sales. So was personal income. Labor productivity had also advanced. The automobiles that could not be parked were being produced at an expanded rate. The children, though without schools, subject in the playgrounds to the affectionate interest of adults with odd tastes and disposed to increasingly imaginative forms of delinquency, were admirably equipped with television sets. We had difficulty finding storage space for the great surpluses of food despite a national disposition to obesity. Food was grown and packaged under private auspices. The care and refreshment of the mind, in contrast with the stomach, was principally in the public domain. Our colleges and universities were often severely overcrowded and underprovided, and the same was even more often true of the mental hospitals.

The contrast was and remains evident not alone to those who read. The family which takes its mauve and cerise, air-conditioned, power-steered and power-breaked automobile out for a tour passes through cities that are badly paved, made hideous by litter, blighted buildings, billboards and posts for wires that should long since have been put underground. They pass on into a countryside that has been rendered largely invisible by commercial art. (The goods which the latter advertise have an absolute priority in our value system. Such aesthetic considerations as a view of the countryside accordingly come second. On such matters, we are consistent.) They picnic on exquisitely packaged food from a portable icebox by a polluted stream and go on to spend the night at a park which is a menace to public health and morals. Just before dozing off on an air mattress, beneath a nylon tent, amid the stench of decaying refuse, they may reflect vaguely on the curious unevenness of their blessings. Is this, indeed, the American genius?

II

In the production of goods within the private economy, it has long been recognized that a tolerably close relationship must be maintained between the production of various kinds of products. The output of steel and oil and machine tools is related to the production of automobiles. Investment in transportation must keep abreast of the output of goods to be transported. The supply of power must be abreast of the growth of industries requiring it. The existence of these relationships — coefficients to the economist — has made possible the construction of the input-output table which shows how changes in the production in one industry will increase or diminish the demands on other industries. To this table, and more especially to its ingenious author, Professor Wassily Leontief, the world is indebted for one of its most important of modern insights into economic relationships. If expansion in one part of the economy were not matched by the requisite expansion in other parts — were the need for balance not respected — then bottlenecks and shortages, speculative hoarding of scarce supplies and sharply increasing costs would ensue. Fortunately in peacetime the market system combined with considerable planning serves to maintain this balance, and this, together with the existence of stocks and some flexibility in the coefficients as a result of substitution, ensures that no serious difficulties will arise. We are reminded of the problem only by noticing how serious it is for those countries which seek to solve it by a more inflexible planning and with a much smaller supply of resources.

Just as there must be balance in what a community produces, so there must also be balance in what the community consumes. An increase in the use of one product creates, ineluctably, a requirement for others. If we are to consume more automobiles, we must have more gasoline. There must be more insurance for them as well as more space on which to operate them. Beyond a certain point, more and better food appears to mean increased need for medical services. This is the certain result of the increased consumption of tobacco and alcohol. More vacations require more hotels and more fishing rods. And so forth. With rare exceptions — shortages of doctors and some kinds of private transportation facilities are exceptions which suggest the rule — this balance is also maintained quite effortlessly so far as goods for private sale and consumption are concerned.

However, the relationships we are here discussing are not confined to the private economy. They operate comprehensively over the whole span of private and public services. As surely as an increase in the output of automobiles puts new demands on the steel industry so, also, it places new demands on public services. Similarly, every increase in the consumption of private goods will normally mean some facilitating or protective step by the state. In all cases if these services are not forthcoming, the consequences will be in some degree ill. It will be convenient to have a term which suggests a satisfactory relationship between the supply of privately produced goods and services and those of the state, and we may call it social balance.

The problem of social balance is ubiquitous, and frequently it is obtrusive. As noted, an increase in the consumption of automobiles requires a facilitating supply of streets, highways, traffic control and parking space. The protective services of the police and the highway patrols must also be available, as must those of the hospitals. Although the need for balance here is extraordinarily clear, our use of privately produced vehicles has, on occasion, got far out of line with the supply of the related public services. The result has been hideous road congestion, an annual massacre of impressive proportions and chronic colitis in the cities. As on the ground, so also in the air. Planes are endlessly delayed or collide over cities with disquieting consequences for passengers when the public provision for air traffic control fails to keep pace with private use of the airways.

But the auto and the airplane, versus the space to use them, are merely an exceptionally visible example of a requirement that is pervasive. The more goods people procure, the more packages they discard and the more trash that must be carried away. If the appropriate sanitation services are not provided, the counterpart of increasing opulence will be deepening filth. The greater the wealth, the thicker will be the dirt. This indubitably describes a tendency of our time. As more goods are produced and owned, the greater are the opportunities for fraud and the more property that must be protected. If the provision of public law enforcement services does not keep pace, the counterpart of increased well-being will, we may be certain, be increased crime.

The city of Los Angeles, in modern times, is a near-classic study in the problem of social balance. Magnificently efficient factories and oil refineries, a lavish supply of automobiles, a vast consumption of handsomely packaged products, coupled for many years with the absence of a municipal trash collection service which forced the use of home incinerators, made the air nearly unbreathable for an appreciable part of each year. Air pollution could be controlled only by a complex and highly developed set of public services — by better knowledge of causes stemming from more public research, public requirement of pollution-control devices on cars, a municipal trash collection service and possibly the assertion of the priority of clean air over the production of goods. These were long in coming. The agony of a city without usable air was the result.

The issue of social balance can be identified in many other current problems. Thus, an aspect of increasing private production is the appearance of an extraordinary number of things which lay claim to the interest of the young. Motion pictures, television, automobiles and the vast opportunities which go with mobility, together with such less enchanting merchandise as narcotics, comic books and pornographia, are all included in an advancing Gross National Product. The child of a less opulent as well as a technologically more primitive age had far fewer such diversions. The red schoolhouse is remembered mainly because it had a paramount position in the lives of those who attended it that no modern school can hope to attain.

In a well-run and well-regulated community, with a sound school system, good recreational opportunities and a good police force — in short, a community where public services have kept pace with private production — the diversionary forces operating on the modern juvenile may do no great damage. Television and the violent mores of Hollywood and Madison Avenue must contend with the intellectual discipline of the school. The social, athletic, dramatic and like attractions of the school also claim the attention of the child. These, together with the other recreational opportunities of the community, minimize the tendency to delinquency. Experiments with violence and immorality are checked by an effective law enforcement system before they become epidemic.

In a community where public services have failed to keep abreast of private consumption, things are very different. Here, in an atmosphere of private opulence and public squalor, the private goods have full sway. Schools do not compete with television and the movies. The dubious heroes of the latter, not Miss Jones, become the idols of the young. The hot rod and the wild ride take the place of more sedentary sports for which there are inadequate facilities or provision. Comic books, alcohol, narcotics and switchblade knives are, as noted, part of the increased flow of goods, and there is nothing to dispute their enjoyment. There is an ample supply of private wealth to be appropriated and not much to be feared from the police. An austere community is free from temptation. It can be austere in its public services. Not so a rich one.

Moreover, in a society which sets large store by production, and which has highly effective machinery for synthesizing private wants, there are strong pressures to have as many wage earners in the family as possible. As always, all social behavior is part of a piece. If both parents are engaged in private production, the burden on the public services is further increased. Children, in effect, become the charge of the community for an appreciable part of the time. If the services of the community do not keep pace, this will be another source of disorder.

Residential housing also illustrates the problem of the social balance, although in a somewhat complex form. Few would wish to contend that, in the lower or even the middle-income brackets, Americans are munificently supplied with housing. A great many families would like better-located or merely more houseroom, and no advertising is necessary to persuade them of their wish. And the provision of housing is in the private domain. At first glance at least, the line we draw between private and public seems not to be preventing a satisfactory allocation of resources to housing.

On closer examination, however, the problem turns out to be not greatly different from that of education. It is improbable that the housing industry is greatly more incompetent or inefficient in the United States than in those countries — Scandinavia, Holland, or (for the most part) England — where slums have been largely eliminated and where *minimum* standards of cleanliness and comfort are well above our own. As the experience of these countries shows, and as we have also been learning, the housing industry functions well only in combination with a large, complex and costly array of public services. These include land purchase and clearance for redevelopment; good neighborhood and city planning and effective and well-enforced zoning; a variety of financing and other aids to the housebuilder and owner; publicly supported research and architectural services for an industry which, by its nature, is equipped to do little on its own; and a considerable amount of direct or assisted public construction for families in the lowest income brackets. The quality of the housing depends not on the industry, which is given, but on what is invested in these supplements and supports.

III

The case for social balance has, so far, been put negatively. Failure to keep public services in minimal relation to private production and use of goods is a cause of social disorder or impairs economic performance. The matter may now be put affirmatively. By failing to exploit the opportunity to expand public production, we are missing opportunities for enjoyment which otherwise we might have had. Presumably a community can be as well rewarded by buying better schools or better parks as by buying bigger automobiles. By concentrating on the latter rather than the former, it is failing to maximize its satisfactions. As with schools in the community, so with public services over the country at large. It is scarcely sensible that we should satisfy our wants in private goods with reckless abundance, while in the case of public goods, on the evidence of the eye, we practice extreme self-denial. So, far from systematically exploiting the opportunities to derive use and pleasure from these services, we do not supply what would keep us out of trouble.

The conventional wisdom holds that the community, large or small, makes a decision as to how much it will devote to its public services. This decision is arrived at by democratic process. Subject to the imperfections and uncertainties of democracy, people decide how much of their private income and goods they will surrender in order to have public services of which they are in greater need. Thus there is a balance, however rough, in the enjoyments to be had from private goods and services and those rendered by public authority.

It will be obvious, however, that this view depends on the notion of independently determined consumer wants. In such a world, one could with some reason defend the doctrine that the consumer, as a voter, makes an independent choice between public and private goods. But given the dependence effect — given that consumer wants are created by the process by which they are satisfied — the consumer makes no such choice. He is subject to the forces of advertising and emulation by which production creates its own demand. Advertising operates exclusively, and emulation mainly, on behalf of privately produced goods and services.[36] Since management and emulative effects operate on behalf of private production, public services will have an inherent tendency to lag behind. Automobile demand which is expensively synthesized will inevitably have a much larger claim on income than parks or public health or even roads where no such influence operates. The engines of mass communication, in their highest state of development, assail the eyes and ears of the community on behalf of more beer but not of more schools. Even in the conventional wisdom it will scarcely be contended that this leads to an equal choice between the two.

The competition is especially unequal for new products and services. Every corner of the public psyche is canvassed by some of the nation's most talented citizens to see if the desire for some merchantable product can be cultivated. No similar process operates on behalf of the nonmerchantable services of the state. Indeed, while we take the cultivation of new private wants for granted, we would be measurably shocked to see it applied to public services. The scientist or engineer or advertising man who devotes himself to developing

[36] Emulation does operate between communities. A new school in one community does exert pressure on others to remain abreast. However, as compared with the pervasive effects of emulation in extending the demand for privately produced consumers' goods, there will be agreement, I think, that this intercommunity effect is probably small.

a new carburetor, cleanser or depilatory for which the public recognizes no need and will feel none until an advertising campaign arouses it, is one of the valued members of our society. A politician or a public servant who dreams up a new public service is a wastrel. Few public offenses are more reprehensible.

So much for the influences which operate on the decision between public and private production. The calm decision between public and private consumption pictured by the conventional wisdom is, in fact, a remarkable example of the error which arises from viewing social behavior out of context. The inherent tendency will always be for public services to fall behind private production. We have here the first of the causes of social imbalance.

IV

Social balance is also the victim of two further features of our society — the truce on inequality and the tendency to inflation. Since these are now part of our context, their effect comes quickly into view.

With rare exceptions such as the postal service, public services do not carry a price ticket to be paid for by the individual user. By their nature, they must, ordinarily, be available to all. As a result, when they are improved or new services are initiated, there is the ancient and troublesome question of who is to pay. This, in turn, provokes to life the collateral but irrelevant debate over inequality. As with the use of taxation as an instrument of fiscal policy, the truce on inequality is broken. Liberals are obliged to argue that the services be paid for by progressive taxation which will reduce inequality. Committed as they are to the urgency of goods (and also, as we shall see in a later chapter, to a somewhat mechanical view of the way in which the level of output can be kept most secure), they must oppose sales and excise taxes. Conservatives rally to the defense of inequality — although without ever quite committing themselves in such uncouth terms — and oppose the use of income taxes. They, in effect, oppose the expenditure not on the merits of the service but on the demerits of the tax system. Since the debate over inequality cannot be resolved, the money is frequently not appropriated and the service not performed. It is a casualty of the economic goals of both liberals and conservatives for both of whom the questions of social balance are subordinate to those of production and, when it is evoked, of inequality.

In practice, matters are better as well as worse than this description of the basic forces suggests. Given the tax structure, the revenues of all levels of government grow with the growth of the economy. Services can be maintained and sometimes even improved out of this automatic accretion.

However, this effect is highly unequal. The revenues of the federal government, because of its heavy reliance on income taxes, increase more than proportionately with private economic growth. In addition, although the conventional wisdom greatly deplores the fact, federal appropriations have only an indirect bearing on taxation. Public services are considered and voted on in accordance with their seeming urgency. Initiation or improvement of a particular service is rarely, except for purposes of oratory, set against the specific effect on taxes. Tax policy, in turn, is decided on the basis of the level of economic activity, the resulting revenues, expediency and other considerations. Among these, the total of the thousands of individually considered appropriations is but one factor. In this process, the ultimate tax consequence of any individual appropriation is *de minimus*, and the tendency to ignore it reflects the simple mathematics of the situation. Thus it is possible for the Congress to make decisions affecting the social balance without invoking the question of inequality.

Things are made worse, however, by the fact that a large proportion of the federal revenues are pre-empted by defense. The increase in defense costs has also tended to absorb a large share of the normal increase in tax revenues. The position of the federal government for improving the social balance has also been weakened since World War II by the strong, although receding, conviction that its taxes were at artificial wartime levels and that a tacit commitment exists to reduce taxes at the earliest opportunity.

In the states and localities, the problem of social balance is much more severe. Here tax revenues — this is especially true of the General Property Tax — increase less than proportionately with increased private production. Budgeting too is far more closely circumscribed than in the case of the federal government — only the monetary authority enjoys the pleasant privilege of underwriting its own loans. Because of this, increased services for states and localities regularly pose the question of more revenues and more taxes. And here, with great regularity, the question of social balance is lost in the debate over equality and social equity.

Thus we currently find by far the most serious social imbalance in the services performed by local governments. The F.B.I. comes much more easily by funds than the city police force. The Department of Agriculture can more easily keep its pest control abreast of expanding agricultural output than the average city health service can keep up with the needs of an expanding industrial population. One consequence is that the federal government remains under constant and highly desirable pressure to use its superior revenue position to help redress the balance at the lower levels of government.

v

Finally, social imbalance is the natural offspring of persistent inflation. Inflation by its nature strikes different individuals and groups with highly discriminatory effects. The most nearly unrelieved victims, apart from those living on pensions or other fixed provision for personal security, are those who work for the state. In the private economy, the firm which sells goods has, in general, an immediate accommodation to the inflationary movement. Its price increases are the inflation. The incomes of its owners and proprietors are automatically accommodated to the upward movement. To the extent that wage increases are part of the inflationary process, this is also true of organized industrial workers. Even unorganized white collar workers are in a milieu where prices and incomes are moving up. The adaptation of their incomes, if less rapid than that of the industrial workers, is often reasonably prompt.

The position of the public employee is at the other extreme. His pay scales are highly formalized, and traditionally they have been subject to revision only at lengthy intervals. In states and localities, inflation does not automatically bring added revenues to pay higher salaries and incomes. Pay revision for all public workers is subject to the temptation to wait and see if the inflation isn't coming to an end. There will be some fear — this seems to have been more of a factor in England than in the United States — that advances in public wages will set a bad example for private employers and unions.

Inflation means that employment is pressing on the labor supply and that private wage and salary incomes are rising. Thus the opportunities for moving from public to private employment are especially favorable. Public employment, moreover, once had as a principal attraction a high measure of social security. Industrial workers were subject to the formidable threat of unemployment during depression. Public employees were comparatively secure, and this security was worth an adverse salary differential. But with improving economic security in general, this advantage has diminished. Private employment thus has come to provide better protection against inflation and little worse protection against other hazards. Though the dedicated may stay in public posts, the alert go.

The deterioration of the public services in the years of inflation has not gone unremarked. However, there has been a strong tendency to regard it as an adventitious misfortune — something which, like a nasty shower at a picnic, happened to blight a generally good time. Salaries were allowed to lag, more or less by neglect. This is a very inadequate view. Discrimination against the public services is an organic feature of inflation. Nothing so weakens government as persistent inflation. The public administrations of France for many years, of Italy until recent times, and of other European and numerous South American countries were deeply sapped and eroded by the effects of long-continued inflation. Social imbalance reflects itself in inability to enforce laws, including significantly those which protect and advance basic social justice, and in failure to maintain and improve essential services. One outgrowth of the resulting imbalance has been frustration and pervasive discontent. Over much of the world, there is a rough and not accidental correlation between the strength of indigenous Communist parties or the frequency of revolutions and the persistence of inflation.

VI

A feature of the years immediately following World War II was a remarkable attack on the notion of expanding and improving public services. During the depression years, such services had been elaborated and improved partly in order to fill some small part of the vacuum left by the shrinkage of private production. During the war years, the role of government was vastly expanded. After that came the reaction. Much of it, unquestionably, was motivated by a desire to rehabilitate the prestige of private production and therewith of producers. No doubt some who joined the attack hoped, at least tacitly, that it might be possible to sidestep the truce on taxation vis-à-vis equality by having less taxation of all kinds. For a time, the notion that our public services had somehow become inflated and excessive was all but axiomatic. Even liberal politicians did not seriously protest. They found it necessary to aver that they were in favor of public economy too.

In this discussion, a certain mystique was attributed to the satisfaction of privately supplied wants. A community decision to have a new school means that the individual surrenders the necessary amount, willy-nilly, in his taxes. But if he is left with that income, he is a free man. He can decide between a better car or a television set. This was advanced with some solemnity as an argument for the TV set. The difficulty is that this argument leaves the community with no way of preferring the school. All private wants, where the individual can choose, are inherently superior to all public desires which must be paid for by taxation and with an inevitable component of compulsion.

The cost of public services was also held to be a desolating burden on private production, although this was at a time when the private production was burgeoning. Urgent warnings were issued of the unfavorable effects of taxation on investment — "I don't know of a surer way of killing off the incentive to invest than by imposing taxes which are regarded by people as punitive."[37] This was at a time when the inflationary effect of a very high level of investment was causing concern. The same individuals who were warning about the inimical effects of taxes were strongly advocating a monetary policy designed to reduce investment. However, an understanding of our economic discourse requires an appreciation of one of its basic rules: men of high position are allowed, by a special act of grace, to accommodate their reasoning to the answer they need. Logic is only required in those of lesser rank.

Finally, it was argued, with no little vigor, that expanding government posed a grave threat to individual liberties. "Where distinction and rank is achieved almost exclusively by becoming a civil servant of the state . . . it is too much to expect that many will long prefer freedom to security."[38]

With time, this attack on public services has subsided. The disorder associated with social imbalance has become visible even if the need for balance between private and public services is still imperfectly appreciated.

Freedom also seemed to be surviving. Perhaps it was realized that all organized activity requires concessions by the individual to the group. This is true of the policeman who joins the police force, the

[37] Arthur F. Burns, Chairman of the President's Council of Economic Advisers, *U.S. News and World Report*, May 6, 1955.
[38] F. A. von Hayek, *The Road to Serfdom* (London: George Routledge & Sons, 1944), p. 98.

teacher who gets a job at the high school and the executive who makes his way up in the hierarchy of General Motors. If there are differences between public and private organization, they are of kind rather than of degree. As this is written, the pendulum has in fact swung back. Our liberties are now menaced by the conformity exacted by the large corporation and its impulse to create, for its own purposes, the organization man.

Nonetheless, the postwar onslaught on the public services left a lasting imprint. To suggest that we canvass our public wants to see where happiness can be improved by more and better services has a sharply radical tone. Even public services to avoid disorder must be defended. By contrast, the man who devises a nostrum for a non-existent need and then successfully promotes both remains one of nature's noblemen.

BOOK
IV

Theory and Theorist

Round II

PART ONE

"HOLIDAY WRITING"

SELECTIONS

A necessary ingredient of the natural writer is that he shall like to write, in the sense that he feels better when things are put down. This is true of any experience, any train of thought. What he has written has been completed, put away in his mind for convenient reference. For such people and for minor reflections, the essay is the perfect package. It follows that Galbraith is an occasional essayist. Two volumes of his essays have been published. They are The Liberal Hour (1960) and Economics, Peace and Laughter (1971). Both of course belong in the category of "holiday books."

"Farming an Abandoned Farm" is one such essay. It was written for the New York Times magazine in 1953 though not published in book form until much later. In it the instincts of the countryman and the mind of the· economist have most happily collaborated — a collaboration recorded not only in the essay which follows but also in the shaping of a certain small bit of Vermont landscape.

In the late forties with a prophetic eye to increasing their scanty store of peace and time, the Galbraiths had bought an abandoned farm in Newfane, a village in southeastern Vermont. It must have been a kind of return to Iona Station — if not in the conformation of the land, at least in the conformation of the profiles of some of its inhabitants. One way or another, Newfane must have looked like home ground.

The farm once bought, it becomes most interesting to consider how the talents of the Ontario farmboy, the agriculturist, the economist, the Washington bureaucrat and even the future diplomat were called into play to meet the specifications laid down for the ideal abandoned farm. Galbraith dealt with his problem in a style that could only have won the dazzled admiration of his Vermont neighbors. The property lies at the end of a maze of country cart-tracks which leads, or rather misleads, the traveler through a pleasant hardwood forest. Those who have been privileged with the gift of the combination to this maze or with second sight or both eventually come to a cottage farm house in an ample clearing of contiguous meadows. Some partitions have been removed from the cottage and a not inconsiderable wing has been added. There is nothing about the addition to suggest that it was not built by the first owners sometime in the early nineteenth century, to house a happily growing family, and for ought the editors have been able to ascertain that is true.

When the city greenhorn in search of pastoral peace sets out to buy an abandoned farm, he will have, as Galbraith points out, two things much in mind: his newfound paradise must have a brook and a view; but he will not for example insist on a good well, fertile soil, or cleared land. We can safely assume on the other hand that the graduate agriculturalist well understood the paramount value of water and soil and that the economist was not likely to ignore the importance of such amenities as brooks and views in figuring his resale value and the consequent desirability of his property.

There is a brook on the Galbraith farm; but it is not a well-directed, jolly-up, rattling story-book brook. Here the talents of the farmboy, the agriculturalist, the general economist and even the Washington official must all have been brought into play. Surely it was the farmboy who struck up an acquaintance with a young beaver couple; and it must have been the future ambassador who persuaded them of the beauties, privacy and fringe benefits of housekeeping on the Galbraith property. Beavers are protected by federal law and have only recently returned to their native homes in Vermont. There is no escaping the fact that the Galbraith pond was built by government wards at government expense.

As for the view, we have heard that it is there when the leaves are off the trees, the grass in the ample meadows green again and the *hills navy-blue against the November sky, but the instincts of the Canadian Scotch do not die. Galbraith is a farmer at heart, in this case a tree farmer. Why destroy a part of the crop just to have a view that God will provide six months in every year anyway?*

Farming an Abandoned Farm[1]

FOR SOME YEARS I have been conducting an informal and highly unprofessional investigation of the New England farm real estate market. My interest, like that of nearly all the customers for such property, has been in the farms that cannot or should not be farmed. It has occurred to me that I should make these findings more generally available but I do so without any intention of trying to save the prospective purchaser money. I would like to see him invest in New England real estate — I regard this as good for New England, for the value of some land that I own myself, and also good for the purchaser. However, while I have a few suggestions about how to keep the investment within reasonable bounds, anyone for whom saving money is a paramount consideration should keep it in the bank.

II

Each autumn in this part of southern Vermont people who visited friends in the country in the summer decide that they must have a place of their own by next year. They owe it to the children, and there is no nicer time to look than on autumn weekends when the maples are turning. To this seasonal demand for country real estate is added that of two other groups, more or less permanently in the market.

The first and most numerous of the nonseasonal home-seekers con-

[1] "Farming an Abandoned Farm," *The Liberal Hour* (London: Hamish Hamilton, 1960). Previously published in the *New York Times* magazine, 1953.

sists of people who are in retreat from the city, mostly from New York. Local real estate men realize that their fortunes are tied up with New York City's traffic congestion and the state of its transit system. In the line of duty they read the New York papers and view the future with confidence.

Along with the fugitives from the subway come the advance refugees from the bombs — those who have convinced themselves that it might be possible to sustain life for a month or two in the New England hills after New York, Boston, and maybe also Brattleboro, Vermont and Keene, New Hampshire, have been vaporized. This demand fluctuates with the warmth of the cold war, and of late — in spite of the stern warnings from Washington that we must not relax — it has been falling off. However, with the world as it is, this recession may be only temporary.

III

Unlike the futures market, which most people merely do not understand, the trouble with the New England Abandoned Farms Market is that most of what is understood is wrong.

First, there is the notion that the hills and valleys of New England have now been combed over and all the nice old houses with a view have been snatched up. It is true that you can no longer find a lovely old colonial, shabby but sound, with four fireplaces, nice meadows, stately maples, a brook and a distant mountain for fifteen hundred dollars. However, there is still an abundance of less graceful houses with a view that, if unspectacular, is better than anything in the East Sixties. With the land thrown in, they offer, for these days, exceptionally inexpensive if somewhat imperfect shelter. In Vermont and New Hampshire the person with from nothing to, say, seven thousand dollars doesn't have much choice. If he has from eight to twelve thousand dollars, he can spend many happy days traveling around the back roads with the local real estate men, confident in the knowledge that he is a very decent prospect.

The market is also still being replenished. New England is no longer a declining agricultural region. The long period of decay which started in 1825 when the Erie Canal began admitting cheap Ohio grain to the East has been arrested for twenty-five years or more. But while dairying, broiler raising and fruit, vegetable and tobacco production have been expanding in favored locations, farm abandonment in the hill towns has continued. Most of the houses, to be frank, are pretty tacky by the time the last occupant dies or moves to town. But so, originally, was that darling place the Greens bought and fixed up.

IV

A second misconception is that buying real estate is an outrageously risky business. For the first two or three centuries of our history it was taken for granted that city people were smarter than country folk. Countless yokels were victimized each year by accomplished urban students of devious if somewhat stylized fraud. Now, with O. Henry, the chronicler of this larceny, only fifty years in his grave, the tables have been completely turned. The city man, and especially the New Yorker, is regarded as a commercial cretin. And he so regards himself. He does not think for a moment that he is a match for the amiable villager whose rough-hewn and battered exterior masks a capacity for the deepest guile. To buy real estate from such a man is, he feels, to risk total expropriation.

There is always a chance that in buying an old farm one will fall into the hands of some rural Raffles,[2] but the danger is not great. For one thing, the risks in buying an old farm dwelling are minor. Warnings about morbid beams, rotten sills and leaky roofs have been greatly overdone. If anything is seriously wrong, it will be evident to the eye even of the most innocent purchaser. If something goes wrong, it can either be left that way or if — like a leak in the roof — it is too uncomfortable, it can be patched.

And much can be wrong without being fatal. I had a Harvard colleague who spent each summer enjoying a breathtaking view of the Green Mountains from a house that had had no maintenance of any kind for at least fifty years. Something fell off each year. And the house looked as though it might fall in — visiting assistant professors were reported as feeling encouraged about their chances for early promotion. But it didn't fall in and won't.

It is true that rural real estate men ask marvelously inflated prices from their suburban colleagues on the bare chance that an utter idiot will come along and pay the first sum mentioned. But a little inquiry in the neighborhood will always establish a consensus on what the old place is worth. The neighbors will help, partly because they don't

[2] The fictional, gentleman thief, not to be confused with the nineteenth-century gentleman administrator who acquired Singapore for the East India Company.

want to see anyone get robbed and partly because they have a deep mistrust of the real estate man who makes a living without decent labor.

v

The grave threat to your pocketbook comes not from the seller or his much maligned agent but from yourself, and the dangerous time is after you have bought. Once you are in possession, you will yield to the impulse to improve. This means a water system, a better kitchen, the removal of a partition or two, sanding to bring out the "natural beauty" of the old floors, a terrace, a rambler rose, a workshop and a dam.

The impulse to improve cannot be resisted; it is American and doubtless made us what we are today. The only hope is to divert it into inexpensive channels. The best thing is paint. Paint is not expensive; the results of an hour's work are admirably visible to the naked eye. Structural flaws, when well-groomed, may acquire an antiquarian interest.

An inexpensive alternative to painting is cutting brush. Among the marvels of New England is its phenomenal procreation of young trees — "God loves this country," an old neighbor of mine remarks, "and He is always trying to get it back." Once you are persuaded that brush anywhere in the near or middle distance is an eyesore and have equipped yourself with a brushhook, you are also tolerably well protected from spending money.

Thus, the urge to improve need not be resisted, for it can be sublimated. The urge to farm, though less universal, is fiscally much more dangerous. It must be checked and checked with the utmost firmness.

The reasons for not trying to revive an abandoned farm would seem to be fairly apparent. After all, it was abandoned. The last farmer may not have been the kind of operator on whom the county agent dotes but if the farm had been good, he might have been a better farmer. Or a better farmer might have rescued the farm. Instead it went out of business. So have thousands of New England farms. Yet typically it is only a short step from the acquisition of an old farm to a state of deep sorrow that such beautiful terrain should lie commercially derelict. The new owner resolves, with far more heroism than he suspects, to hold a bridgehead against those inscrutable economic forces which have been returning New England to timber.

If the decision is to tackle dairying or chickens, one cannot absolutely predict failure. In the right locations and in the hands of competent managers dairying and poultry raising do succeed. However, the entrepreneur's success would be considerably more probable if he were not a new arrival and had selected the farm initially with these enterprises in mind.

But dairying and modern poultry husbandry are demanding and — because of somewhat undignified chores — unromantic agriculture. Accordingly, the man who has caught the fatal vision of redeeming New England from the birch and maple and pine and wild cherry is much more likely to think of a herd of Aberdeen Angus cattle or a flock of Shropshire sheep moving placidly over his meadows. Or if he prides himself on his imagination, his mind may leap on to some really novel enterprise — an apiary or a nursery or geese.

Here one can be dogmatic. If a particular type of agriculture is not being practiced in New England, it is roughly a hundred to one that it is because it doesn't pay. And it is at least a thousand to one that any successful new enterprise will be hit upon by some intelligent and skillful local farmer in consultation with the Extension Service and not by a new arrival from town.

VI

Take the case of sheep. Except on a few mixed farms in northern New England, the sheep population of this area is negligible. Every year several hundred new arrivals from town are stunned by this oversight. They see plenty of rough pasture everywhere. Sheep, they know, are notoriously untroubled by steep hillsides, stones and streams. The yield of forage on such pasture is anywhere from five to fifty times that which supports the flocks that once supported Senator McCarran.[3] Sheep leave the meadows clipped and groomed and free of brush — "Remember how beautiful the hills in the Lake Country around Windermere are?"

As an agricultural economist, in the face of the advantages just listed, I have never succeeded in making a case against sheep raising to any determined sheep raiser. Still, there are a few disadvantages to be mentioned.

New England pastures, while lush in the summer, are singularly

[3] Patrick McCarran, Democratic senator from Nevada, reactionary and demagogic in his attitudes and frequently an ally of Senator Joseph McCarthy, was for many years chairman of the Senate Judiciary Committee. He was particularly active in the loyalty disputes of the Forties and Fifties.

unavailable in the winter. That means New England must compete
with areas that have year-round pasture or, at least, do not have to
go in for prolonged winter feeding. Since New England produces
almost no grain, concentrates for finishing lambs must be imported
from the Midwest, whereas Iowa farms can fatten lambs on grain
grown in the adjacent field.

Fencing is also necessary — a stone wall is no barrier to a determined
ewe — and this is expensive. Fences will not keep out dogs, of which
New England has an unusually dense population, and their owners
dislike having them shot. In the Mountain and Midwestern States
men who can shear sheep or lend an experienced hand at lambing
time can be found, but these arts are all but unknown in the Berk-
shires and the Green Mountains.

Finally, sheep husbandry is a declining industry in the nation at
large. While Nevada has a decided edge on New Hampshire, it
competes poorly with Australia. In Canada, when I was a youngster,
a good flock of sheep would pay the taxes. The most that can be
expected of them in New England is a sizable income tax deduction.

If resistance to ostensible land utilization is out of the question,
the owner of abandoned farm land has one possibility that will cost
little. That is to grow trees. The investment in forest management is
small; the return is reasonably secure. There is a county forester who
will advise. It also makes sense, something which does not impress
visitors but often increases a man's stature in the eyes of his neighbors.

VII

With self-control and an enlightened preference for forestry over
agriculture, the cost of owning an old farm in New England need not
greatly exceed that of owning and garaging an automobile in New
York City. (Taxes are still low — those on a hundred acres and an
old house will rarely be as much as the insurance on the car.)

It is the peculiar good fortune of the New Yorker, and indeed
of everyone who lives along the Eastern seaboard, that he is close
to an erstwhile agricultural region. Poor land makes good scenery.
An ancient farmhouse as a weekend or holiday retreat is in wonderfully mellow contrast with the raw log-and-shingle affairs which people
must build for themselves among the Minnesota lakes or in the national forests. It is most unlikely that anyone who ever bought one
didn't become sublimely proud both of himself and his property.

SELECTION 10

The McLandress Dimension was originally published under the pseudonym of Mark Epernay. That was in 1962. In 1968 a low-priced edition was published by New American Library. For that edition Galbraith wrote a retrospective introduction. He had decided to acknowledge the paternity of Epernay and legitimize that gentleman's place among the "G's" in the Galbraith library.

In that introduction the author gives some account of life behind a false moustache and his reasons for assuming the insignia of the distinguished order of the ANON.

The opening sentences of the introduction suggest the therapeutic nature of the "holiday" book. The sentence describes the state of the author's health at the time of its writing. "In the spring of 1962, while I was Ambassador to India, I was convalescing from what the Navy doctors at Bethesda thought was some form of jaundice and the Army doctors at Tripler General Hospital in Hawaii thought was the result of poor Navy medical practice and what I, secretly, felt might be a reaction to a dangerously prolonged exposure to the Secretary and Department of State." We now proceed to the circumstances that gave rise to the birth of Epernay.

[265]

The question now arose of whether an Ambassador could publish contrivance under his own name. There seemed to be no rule against it. On the contrary there were certain precedents in favor. But the question of payment obtruded. The precedents involved speeches and articles in *Foreign Affairs* or *The Foreign Service Journal* which, from all superficial evidence, involved compensation not to the author but the reverse. I concluded that I could certainly take payment if I published under a pseudonym — then no one would suppose I was exploiting official position in order to merchandise my stuff. And to be on the safe side I addressed a letter of inquiry to the Attorney General of the United States, then Mr. Robert F. Kennedy. The problem was obviously a difficult one for I received no answer. Later after some prodding, I received an answer from an assistant telling me to be guided by my own conscience. My conscience was completely pliable. I used the name Mark Epernay — Mark, borrowed from another famous pseudonym; Epernay, because I happened to be reading a book about the Franco-Prussian War. Before Sedan the Emperor Napoleon had his headquarters at Epernay.

Two passages describe the later life of Mark Epernay, and his final demise.

An Ambassador has far more time on his hands than members of this privileged profession allow anyone except their immediate subordinates to suppose. At any given moment you are likely to be waiting for an appointment, waiting for someone who has an appointment with you or — what is often equally a hiatus — keeping these appointments. Or, as I have said often before, you are listening to dull and interminable speeches, including your own. Having discovered Epernay, I kept him busy. . . . One or two stories I wrote especially for the volume which was published in 1963 shortly after I left India. Until then my authorship was a fairly well-kept secret. Thereafter I no longer bothered.

Once while I was still in India, I received a rather peremptory telegram from *Newsweek* which said: "Are you Mark Epernay? Please confirm or deny." I replied collect: "Who is Mark Epernay?" I never heard further from them.

The editors chose "McLandress Dimension" to represent the Mc-Landress essays because it was the title piece and as such set the keynote of mad probability that pervades the book. There was however a second piece that we found ourselves tempted to add: "The Fully Automated Foreign Policy."
In the end we decided against it.
A second of Galbraith's "holiday books" deals wholly with his savage contempt for the management of the State Department under Dean Rusk and the tradition of prompt inaction that he represented. That book is a satirical novel entitled The Triumph. Though many read it, it appears to have fallen short of its apparent mark as a declaration of the desperate need for reform of the methods and attitude of the department of state. We did not want the farcical "Fully Automated Foreign Policy" to share the stage with its sister satire which appears further along in this volume and which is, in sum, both a more serious and more constructive comment.

The McLandress Dimension[1]

THE McLANDRESS Dimension, as it is known to scientists, is a new line of mensuration in the assessment of human behavior patterns. It allows the reliable sorting and classification of behavioral tendencies, and it has already caught the attention of seasoned professionals as a possible way of predicting political and other career success. It owes its origins to the scientifically imaginative work of Herschel McLandress, former Professor of Psychiatric Measurement

[1] "The McLandress Dimension," The McLandress Dimension (London: Hamish Hamilton, 1964), pp. 1–14. Previously published in Esquire, 1962.

at the Harvard Medical School and now chief consultant to the Noonan Psychiatric Clinic in Boston. Because of his simple but searching insights, Dr. McLandress's work has long appealed to a small but devoted group of disciples, including a goodly number of informed and discerning laymen. With the McLandress Dimension, in the view of well-qualified observers, he is firmly destined for a place among the scientific and medical immortals. Certainly it will be among the best-remembered of his contributions.

The dimension along which McLandress has sought to measure human behavior is that of the individual's relation to self. The unit of measurement which he employs, called the McLandress Coefficient, reflects the intensity of the individual's identification with his own personality. No modern scientific tool is ever simple, and the McLandress Coefficient — in scientific circles it is referred to as the McL–C (pronounced Mack-el-see) — is a thing of some complexity. But in essence it is the arithmetic mean or average of the intervals of time during which a subject's thoughts remain centered on some substantive phenomenon other than his own personality. By way of illustration, a twenty-minute coefficient — a McL–C of twenty minutes — means that an individual's thoughts remain diverted from his own personality for periods of average duration of twenty minutes. A sixty-minute McL–C, a fairly large coefficient according to Dr. McLandress's researches, would mean that an individual's thoughts are diverted from himself for intervals averaging one hour. The McL–C, it should be noted, refers only to waking time. "The focus of the dream consciousness," Dr. McLandress has said, "is an important area of research but it is not my present scientific preoccupation."

The McL–C for an individual is established by someone who is trained in Dr. McLandress's methods, and the individual may or may not know that he is being subject to psychometric measurement. Many of the ratings have been done by newspapermen who, after a brief but intensive period of training in Dr. McLandress's clinic, do the interviews under the guise of obtaining news. The subject is encouraged to talk with minimum restraint. By various depth-perception techniques, including such simple indicators as substantive references to the first person singular, the intervals of thought-distraction are measured. They are registered by means of a recording stopwatch carried unobtrusively in the researchers' jacket pocket. Interviews are supplemented by what is called secondary communications research, which means, principally, a detailed study of the individual's oral and written expression — his books, articles, speeches, sermons and interviews. Experience has shown that where published expression is adequate, the interview can be omitted and the coefficient established on the basis of such secondary material without loss of accuracy.

Although he is careful to say that his work is still in a preliminary state, Dr. McLandress has already established McL–C's for a sizable number of people. This is not a random sample; his concern has been quite frankly with people who are prominent in the political, scientific, academic, artistic, literary and business life of the United States and Britain. Early drafts of his manuscript, abstracts of which will appear in the autumn number of the *Journal of Psychiatric Measurement*, have been circulated for comment and criticism, and it is these that have provoked much of the recent discussion. When the full volume is published, Veritan Press, Inc., of Raleigh, North Carolina, will almost certainly have on its lists the first medico-scientific bestseller since the famed Kinsey reports.

Interest will center, inevitably, on the coefficients that have been established for men and women who are prominent in public life. Dr. McLandress is careful to point out that these coefficients are "value-free." A low coefficient, one in the lower minute range, implies a close and diligent concern by the individual for matters pertaining to his own personality but Dr. McLandress is careful to insist that this suggests neither superiority nor inferiority as compared with the individual with a higher coefficient. Nor can it yet be concluded that the person with a low rating is more effective or efficient than a person whose mental processes are less precisely concentrated. While Dr. McLandress occasionally hints at lines of thought emerging from his researches, he is careful to say, "The task of the scientist is to classify and measure and, on occasion, to propose fecund lines of speculation but it is never his function to decide what is good or bad."

Many of the coefficients will not be thought entirely surprising. Thus, theater people have uniformly low McL–C's — the representatives of Broadway and Hollywood are nearly always in the minute range. Writers and playwrights, though with many exceptions, have higher coefficients than actors and actresses, and there are no significant differences between the latter. Both Mr. Arthur Miller and Mr. Tennessee Williams have a rating of thirty-five minutes. Mr. Gore

Vidal, by contrast, has a rating of twelve and a half minutes. Among actors and actresses, Mr. Danny Kaye is something of a theatrical phenomenon with a McL–C of fifty-five minutes. Mr. Bob Hope's is eighteen minutes. At the other extreme, Mr. Mort Sahl has a rating of four minutes and Miss Elizabeth Taylor of three. By coincidence, Miss Taylor's coefficient is the same as that of Mr. David Susskind, the television impresario. This is impressively low. By further and quite innocent coincidence, Mr. Susskind's coefficient is the same as that of Mr. Nikita Khrushchev, whom he once interviewed on his television program. Mr. Khrushchev was rated from secondary written and verbal expressions and is the only Communist leader with a sufficient volume of personal expression to be handled in this way. No interview with Mr. Susskind was necessary.

Writers and journalists tend also to have low scores. At the upper extreme are Mr. Art Buchwald at two hours and Mr. Richard H. Rovere, *The New Yorker* writer and author of the recent volume of *The American Establishment,* with a rating of one hour and fifty-five minutes. Nearly all other writers and journalists are in the minute range: James Reston, ten minutes; Truman Capote, ten minutes; Dean Acheson, ten minutes; Vladimir Nabokov, ten minutes; Mary McCarthy, nine minutes; Ian Fleming, nine minutes; Kenneth Tynan, eight minutes; Max Ascoli, four minutes; Norman Cousins, three minutes; H. Trevor-Roper (the English historian) two and a half minutes. One writer and journalist conspicuously missing is Mr. Joseph Alsop. Dr. McLandress, in an amusing footnote, tells of his effort to interview Mr. Alsop in the course of personally establishing his coefficient. Dr. McLandress found himself deeply preoccupied with defending his methods against Mr. Alsop's strongly held views as to more appropriate procedures. Mr. Alsop also urgently advanced the hypothesis that men with high ratings would not face nuclear crisis with adequate equanimity. As a result, the measurement of Mr. Alsop was never completed. Dr. McLandress hazards the guess that it is in the low minute range.

As might be expected, Dr. McLandress has established coefficents for a large number of his academic and scientific colleagues. For these, as also for ministers of the gospel, generalization is difficult — the range is from a few minutes to several hours. Thus, the Reverend Martin Luther King, Jr., has a rating of four hours; by way of contrast, both the Reverend Dr. Norman Vincent Peale and the Reverend Billy Graham turn up in the middle minute range. The nature of the pre-emptive character of spiritual preoccupation is, Dr. McLandress believes, a subject for further research. A similar dispersion characterizes the scientific community. Dr. Robert Oppenheimer has a remarkable coefficient of three hours and thirty minutes, and Dr. McLandress suggests "as a further line of speculation" that this may well have been related to his problems as a security risk. "When a really first-rate mind is so divorced from self, it is certain to range rather widely. And we cannot be wholly surprised if this causes it occasionally to invade what many will regard as dangerous territory." Dr. Edward Teller, contemporary of Dr. Oppenheimer in the development of nuclear fission, has the much more conservative coefficient of three minutes, ten seconds.

In the academic world there is not only a wide dispersion in ratings, but also a considerable unpredictability. Dr. McLandress cites but tactfully refrains from giving the name of a Harvard Professor with a community-wide reputation for absentmindedness. On fine days he carries an umbrella; it is invariably left home in inclement weather. His Radcliffe students have not been the only ones to observe the occasionally embarrassing disarray of his attire. His McL–C was exactly two minutes.

Reflecting their strong interest in the McLandress work, which has had university as well as foundation[2] support, the Presidents of both Harvard and the Massachusetts Institute of Technology asked to be rated and will have their coefficients included in the forthcoming volume.[3] Both, incidentally, are a highly unspectacular forty-five minutes.

There is little doubt that it will be the McLandress ratings for political and other public figures that will provoke the most comment when they appear. And possibly with this in mind, Dr. McLandress has gone into greatest detail in this department. Political leaders, like actors, tend to low ratings. Some that are surprises at first glance seem much more reasonable on analysis.

The President of the United States, rated during a long and highly

---

[2] Dr. McLandress acknowledges his indebtedness to the Ford Foundation, the Carnegie Corporation of New York, the Rockefeller Institute, the Overbrook Foundation, the Shelter Rock Foundation, Inc., the George M. and Pamela S. Humphrey Fund and the Aadland Trust.

[3] Only a small sample of Dr. McLandress' coefficients, offered purely by way of illustration, are given here.

cooperative interview, has a McL–C of twenty-nine minutes. Prime Minister Harold Macmillan, who was similarly cooperative, has twelve minutes. In discussing the coefficients of these two political leaders, Dr. McLandress makes some allowance for the possibility of change. He hazards the guess that the President's coefficient may be higher than when he was serving as senator. The Macmillan rating, he feels, has recently gone down.

The British Royal Family, much of which had to be rated from rather sparse secondary expression, provides few surprises. One is the coefficient of Antony Armstrong-Jones, now Lord Snowdon, who is far above all other members of the family with forty-eight minutes. Dr. McLandress, who is intrigued by the relation of royal lineage to McL–C, thinks that this may be the highest royal rating since Queen Victoria's consort, Prince Albert. People with a position in the court, as also in London and Washington society, have a uniformly low rating. Association with the great leads, evidently, to reflection less on the great associate than on the association. So thought returns to self. Two Washington hostesses of the Truman-Eisenhower era, Mrs. Perle Mesta and Mrs. Gwen Cafritz, who, surprisingly enough, caught Dr. McLandress' attention, are in the lower minute range. So were all Washington diplomats included in the study and Vice President Lyndon Johnson.

Rated from secondary oral and written communication — Dr. McLandress attaches considerable importance to the appearance of the first person singular and plural in such material — Winston Churchill has a coefficient of eight minutes. One of the few French leaders rated is President Charles de Gaulle. He has the surprisingly high rating (for a political leader) of seven hours and thirty minutes. Dr. McLandress, who has a high reputation in Paris medical circles and who has lectured at the Sorbonne and the Ecole de Médecine de Lyon, suggests that in de Gaulle's case the rating is misleading. The subject's thoughts are constantly on France, and France has, in a sense, become the surrogate of his own personality. Thus, when he thinks of France, he thinks of himself and vice versa. Recalculated, with appropriate substitutions, de Gaulle turns out to have a McL–C of one minute, thirty seconds.

The McL–C of Churchill's old friend, Lord Beaverbrook, is two minutes. Lord Beaverbrook's coefficient is matched on this side of the water by an American elder statesman, Mr. Bernard Baruch. Speaking of Beaverbrook and Baruch, Dr. McLandress offers the thought that ratings decline with advancing age.

Other publishers are within range of Lord Beaverbrook, although there is none that matches his score. Mr. John Hay Whitney, owner of the *New York Herald Tribune,* has a McL–C of one hour, twenty-seven minutes. (Mr. Whitney and Mr. Roger Blough of the United States Steel Corporation, one hour, thirty minutes, are both examples, according to Dr. McLandress, of men whose relatively high McL–C is associated with the diverting effect of a single strong external attraction. In the case of Mr. Whitney, this would appear to be the earnings statement of his newspaper; in the case of Mr. Blough, it is the historic comments of the President of the United States on the steel industry.) The McL–C for Mr. Alfred Knopf is seven minutes; that of another publisher, Mr. Bennet Cerf, is one minute and seven seconds.

In the immediate field of American politics, only one member of the United States Senate has a McL–C of more than fifteen minutes. That is Senator Everett McKinley Dirksen, who has a McL–C of three hours, twenty-five minutes. In this connection — the question seems also to have arisen in the case of Mr. James Reston — Dr. McLandress has been asked if a subject sufficiently gifted in verisimilitude could contrive to give investigators the impression of a much greater McL–C than he really has. Dr. McLandress discounts the possibility. He attributes Senator Dirksen's politically high McL–C to an almost unique inability to divert his thoughts from the public interest.

Honors for the lowest coefficient in the Senate are evenly divided between Democrats and Republicans and the East and West Coasts. This is the result of a tie between Senator Wayne Morse of Oregon and Senator Jacob Javits of New York, each with a coefficient of four minutes. A large number of the more devoted and diligent members of the Senate are within the four- to eight-minute range. Senatorial coefficients are also subject to some variation over time. Senators facing re-election had a lower rating than those recently returned for a six-year term.

Coefficients in the Executive Branch tend also to be low and to fall rapidly in the higher reaches of the civil service and political hierarchy. Dr. McLandress does not attribute this entirely to personal insecurity. In his view, men in senior positions in the government are generally more intelligent and thus have a more sensitive appreciation of the various contingencies and accidents that may await the person in public position in the United States. Coefficients are extremely low in the upper levels of the Department of State, the U.S. Information Agency and in sections of the Department of Agriculture. Ratings are also low in the White House.

High ratings were found in the Department of Commerce, the National Archives and the Interstate Commerce Commission. Reflecting, according to Dr. McLandress, the natural concern of the judge with the problems of other people, the highest McL–C in the Federal Government was that of Chief Justice Earl Warren at four hours, thirty minutes. The lowest was that of Professor J. K. Galbraith, the then American Ambassador to India, at one minute, fifteen seconds. Noting the natural tendency of people to think that a diplomat's attention should be centered on his country rather than himself, Dr. McLandress warns once more against hasty conclusions. As instanced by General de Gaulle, there is an omnipresent tendency for people in important public office to confuse the two, and the tendency in the case of noncareer diplomats is especially marked.

An incumbent and a onetime candidate for governor had the distinction of two of the three lowest McL–C's that Dr. McLandress had encountered at the time of his researches. The governor was Mr. Nelson Rockefeller of New York and one of the two men to break into what Dr. McLandress calls the "second range." Governor Rockefeller has a McL–C of forty-five seconds. This is very low, but ceases to seem so in comparison with Mr. Richard Nixon's coefficient which, at the time he was rated, was only three seconds. It should be noted, incidentally, that both of these ratings are based on a wealth of oral material and are thought by Dr. McLandress to be exceptionally reliable. A third public figure with a low McL–C is Mr. Lewis Strauss. First giving him a McL–C of thirty-eight seconds, Dr. McLandress re-evaluated him on the basis of his personal memoirs and put him in the high milli-second range.

These very low ratings for prominent political figures have led to the discussion of the advantages or disadvantages of a low McL–C for people seeking political preferment. In Dr. McLandress's view, concentration of attention on inward factors of personality is an advantage in politics, and he adduces impressive empirical evidence to support his thesis. He has made an extensve case study of a New York congressional fight in 1960 between two closely matched contenders, Mr. John V. Lindsay and Mr. William vanden Heuvel. Equal in all other respects, Mr. Lindsay has a McL–C of fourteen minutes as compared with Mr. vanden Heuvel's of one hour and thirty-six minutes. Mr. Lindsay was the victor. Similarly in gaining office in New York State, Mr. Rockefeller was matching his 45-second McL–C against Governor Averell Harriman's 12.5 minutes. Governor Harriman was, of course, unseated. Dr. McLandress implies, and many will agree, that in the face of this evidence, undue significance cannot be attached to the last Presidential election when the relatively low-rated Mr. Kennedy nosed out the phenomenally low-rated Mr. Nixon. Other factors — the predominantly Democratic temper of the country, the close identification of the Democrats with the masses, the natural Democratic bias of the American newspapermen, the "me too" campaign of the Republicans — were all working for Kennedy. The almost total concentration of purpose implicit in his coefficient may well have been what enabled Mr. Nixon to do as well as he did. Dr. McLandress's informal advice to both political parties is to be extremely cautious about selecting any man with a coefficient of more than five minutes. In anticipation of the 1964 campaign, both parties are now quietly rating prospective congressional and gubernatorial — and in the case of the Republicans also presidential — candidates. Informed observers say, however, that this has not yet led to the exclusion of a large amount of potential talent.

PART TWO

THE TRIAD—TWO

SELECTION

11. The New Industrial State

SELECTION *11*

*N*ine years elapsed between the publication of The
Affluent Society and the appearance of this sister volume. The New
Industrial State is the central volume in the triad, the keystone of the
arch and the peak of the argument. It gives weight to the two sibling
volumes of the triad and locks them into place as its necessary
supports.

As the first line in the selections which follow shows, Galbraith
clearly foresaw the necessity of writing The New Industrial State even
before he had completed The Affluent Society: and yet during the
nine years, in addition to The Liberal Hour and The McLandress
Dimension, Galbraith also wrote The Scotch and a series of lectures
presented while on duty in India and later published under the title
of Economic Development. Likewise he kept a full diary of his daily
experiences while in India — edited and published later as Ambassador's Journal. Meanwhile, of course, he conducted the affairs of
the Embassy during a difficult period which included the Chinese-
Indian War and, when that assignment was completed the duties of
his professorship at Harvard.

Five books, completed or nearly so, an ambassadorship and then
the professorship seem a rather elaborate way of avoiding the writing

of a book that had announced itself now so long ago. Why this delay?

It is most likely that by now theory and theorist had come to understand each other pretty well. Galbraith tells us in the introduction to The Great Crash that he wrote that book during a summer that he had intended to spend writing The Affluent Society. Though he does not say so one is nonetheless tempted to think that, consciously or otherwise, he found it impossible to write about an affluent society without first restudying the causes of that society's remarkable decade of depression. The result was The Great Crash. Theoretical scholarship is a creative process and as such, its nature still unplumbed, it remains something to be conjured, immune to all command. Both theory and theorist, monster and master, must have learned from that experience with The Affluent Society a tolerance for the caprices and perversities of literary production.

Whereas The Affluent Society deals with the unfortunate results of applying horse-and-buggy rules to the internal combustion engine, The New Industrial State is devoted solely to the more modern forms of horsepower and the new instruction book that is required for their effective use. The excerpts included here will do no more than tell you where the steering wheel, gas pedal and brakes are. There are two complete chapters and parts of three more.

The centerpiece of the book is the chapter that describes the technostructure. This is the chain of specialists on which all corporate judgments of ultimate feasibility depend. Here are the market analysts, the pollsters, the chemists and physicists, promotors and designers, the lawyers and labor negotiators. They seldom meet as a single group. No one knows all the others. Each holds a power of veto. Here responsibility is more than diffused. In such a situation it is nonexistent. Action depends on a long string of lights, all green. If by some chance a design for a low-priced, disposable, combination cigarette lighter and pocket death-ray were to be put into the system and draw from the binomial computer a unanimous green, it would be made.

Gone are the captains of industry. They have made a perfect thing and are no longer needed. What is good for big business is very good for big business. There is but that one question and the system will answer it. There is no second question such as: "Yes, but is it good?" That system is the technostructure, Galbraith's villain-hero. Together with the numberless armies of men and machines of which it is the firing mechanism; it is in Galbraith's phrase the new "industrial system." It makes step-by-step decisions the outcome of which perhaps few of its members individually would agree with if they knew what final decisions were being made. Each separate step is a figure in a long column which is never added up.

Galbraith's war is against this robotry of management in the new industrial state. The first step is to identify the weakness which so effectively admits this invasion of judgment. That work is done in this book from which we have made the selections which follow. Though diagnosis may be the better part of cure there nonetheless remains much to be done. Two bracketing chapters tell of the world that brought the technostructure to birth and of what its rewards in that world seem to be.

The New Industrial State

FOREWORD [1]

I STARTED this book nearly ten years ago and, in a sense, it started itself. What was to become *The Affluent Society* was nearing completion. Presently another and larger world began obtruding itself on my thoughts. This was a world of great corporations in which people increasingly served the convenience of these organizations which were meant to serve *them*. It was a world in which the motives of organization members seemed not to fit the standard textbook mold. Nor did the relationship between business and state. Nor did markets. Especially markets. So far from being the controlling power in the economy, markets were more and more accommodated to the needs and convenience of business organizations. Numerous writers had dealt with parts of this reality but without assuming larger

[1] "Foreword," *The New Industrial State* (London: André Deutsch, rev. ed., 1972), pp. vii–ix.

change. I became persuaded, reluctantly, that these parts belonged, indeed, to a much greater and very closely articulated process of change.

I resisted these thoughts. The book on which I was working was too obviously one part of this movement. And, however unscientifically, one must accommodate task to talent. I went ahead and published *The Affluent Society* and then settled down to try to see what I had only glimpsed.

I had nearly finished a preliminary draft of this book when President Kennedy asked me to go to India as his ambassador in 1961. With some misgiving I put the manuscript away in the vault of the bank. Only men of considerable vanity write books; consistently therewith, I worried lest the world were exchanging an irreplaceable author for a more easily purchasable diplomat. The danger was not as great as I imagined. I returned from India with some new thoughts and, in the end, a better view of the problem.

I must again remind the reader that this book had its origins alongside *The Affluent Society*. It stands in relation to that book as a house to a window. This is the structure; the earlier book allowed the first glimpse inside.

THE IMPERATIVES OF TECHNOLOGY [2]

ON JUNE 16, 1903, after some months of preparation which included negotiation of contracts for various components, the Ford Motor Company was formed for the manufacture of automobiles. Production was to be whatever number could be sold. The first car reached the market that October. The firm had an authorized capital of $150,000. However, only $100,000 worth of stock was issued, and only $28,500 of this was for cash. Although it does not bear on the present discussion, the company made a handsome profit that year and did not fail to do so for many years thereafter. Employment in 1903 averaged 125 men.[3]

Sixty-one years later, in the spring of 1964, the Ford Motor Company introduced what is now called a new automobile. In accordance

[2] Chapter II, "The Imperatives of Technology," *The New Industrial State*, pp. 11–20.
[3] Allan Nevins, *Ford, The Times, The Man, The Company* (New York: Scribner, 1954), pp. 220 ff., and appendix.

with current fashion in automobile nomenclature, it was called, one assumes inappropriately, a Mustang. The public was well prepared for the new vehicle. Plans carefully specified prospective output and sales; they erred, as plans do, and in this case by being too modest. These preparations required three and a half years. From late in the autumn of 1962, when the design was settled, until the spring of 1964, there was a fairly firm commitment to the particular car that eventually emerged. Engineering and "styling" costs were $9 million; the cost of tooling up for the production of the Mustang was $50 million.[4] In 1964, employment in the Ford Motor Company averaged 317,000. Assets at that time were approximately $6 billion.[5]

Virtually all of the effects of increased use of technology are revealed by these comparisons. We may pass them in preliminary review.

II

Technology means the systematic application of scientific or other organized knowledge to practical tasks. Its most important consequence, at least for purposes of economics, is in forcing the division and subdivision of any such task into its component parts. Thus, and only thus, can organized knowledge be brought to bear on performance.

Specifically, there is no way that organized knowledge can be brought to bear on the production of an automobile as a whole or even on the manufacture of a body or chassis. It can only be applied if the task is so subdivided that it begins to be coterminous with some established area of scientific or engineering knowledge. Though metallurgical knowledge cannot be applied to the manufacture of the whole vehicle, it can be used in the design of the cooling system or the engine block. While knowledge of mechanical engineering cannot be brought to bear on the manufacture of the vehicle, it can be applied

[4] I am grateful to Mr. Walter T. Murphy of the Ford Motor Company for providing these details. In this and subsequent chapters, I have also drawn on earlier help of Robert McNamara which he gave when he was still an executive of Ford. I wish here, at the outset, not only to concede but to emphasize that one may have planning without precision of result and that there will also be occasional failures. Accordingly, to cite a failure — another Ford creation, the Edsel, will come automatically to the mind of the more impulsive critic — is not to disprove this argument.

[5] *Fortune*, August 1964.

to the machining of the crankshaft. While chemistry cannot be applied to the composition of the car as a whole, it can be used to decide on the composition of the finish or trim.

Nor do matters stop here. Metallurgical knowledge is brought to bear not on steel but on the characteristics of special steels for particular functions, and chemistry not on paints or plastics but on particular molecular structures and their rearrangement as required.[6]

Nearly all of the consequences of technology, and much of the shape of modern industry, derive from this need to divide and subdivide tasks and from the further need to bring knowledge to bear on these fractions and from the final need to combine the finished elements of the task into the finished product as a whole. Six consequences are of immediate importance.

First. An increasing span of time separates the beginning from the completion of any task. Knowledge is brought to bear on the ultimate microfraction of the task; then on that in combination with some other fraction; then on some further combination and thus on to final completion. The process stretches back in time as the root system of a plant goes down into the ground. The longest of the filaments determines the total time required in production. The more thoroughgoing the application of technology — in common or at least frequent language, the more sophisticated the production process — the farther back the application of knowledge will be carried. The longer, accordingly, will be the time between the initiation and completion of the task.

The manufacture of the first Ford was not an exacting process. Metallurgy was an academic concept. Ordinary steels were used that could be obtained from the warehouse in the morning and shaped that afternoon. In consequence, the span of time between initiation and completion of a car was very slight.

The provision of steel for the modern vehicle, in contrast, reaches

---

[6] The notion of division of labor, an old one in economics, is a rudimentary and partial application of the ideas here outlined. As one breaks down a mechanical operation, such as the manufacture of Adam Smith's immortal pins, it resolves itself into simpler and simpler movements, as in putting the head or the point on the pin. This is the same as saying that the problem is susceptible to increasingly homogeneous mechanical knowledge.

However, the subdivision of tasks to accord with the area of organized knowledge is not confined to, nor has it any special relevance to, mechanical processes. It occurs in medicine, business management, building design, child and dog rearing and every other problem that involves an agglomerate of scientific knowledge.

back to specifications prepared by the designers or the laboratory, and proceeds through orders to the steel mill, parallel provision for the appropriate metal-working machinery, delivery, testing and use.

Second. There is an increase in the capital that is committed to production aside from that occasioned by increased output. The increased time, and therewith the increased investment in goods in process, costs money. So does the knowledge which is applied to the various elements of the task. The application of knowledge to an element of a manufacturing problem will also typically involve the development of a machine for performing the function. (The word technology brings to mind machines; this is not surprising, for machinery is one of its most visible manifestations.) This too involves investment as does equipment for integrating the various elements of the task into the final product.

The investment in making the original Ford was larger than the $28,500 paid in, for some of it was in the plant, inventory and machinery of those who, like the Dodge Brothers, supplied the components. But investment in the factory itself was infinitesimal. Materials and parts were there only briefly; no expensive specialists gave them attention; only elementary machinery was used to assemble them into the car. It helped that the frame of the car could be lifted by two men.

Third. With increasing technology the commitment of time and money tends to be made ever more inflexibly to the performance of a particular task. That task must be precisely defined before it is divided and subdivided into its component parts. Knowledge and equipment are then brought to bear on these fractions, and they are useful only for the task as it was initially defined. If that task is changed, new knowledge and new equipment will have to be brought to bear.

Little thought needed to be given to the Dodge Brothers' machine shop, which made the engine and chassis of the original Ford, as an instrument for automobile manufacture. It was unspecialized as to task. It could have worked as well on bicycles, steam engines or carriage gear and, indeed, had been so employed. Had Ford and his associates decided, at any point, to shift from gasoline to steam power, the machine shop could have accommodated itself to the change in a few hours.

By contrast, all parts of the Mustang, the tools and equipment that worked on these parts, and the steel and other materials going into these parts were designed to serve efficiently their ultimate function.

They could serve only that function. Were the car appreciably altered, were it shaped, instead of as a Mustang, as a Barracuda or were it a Serpent, Scorpion or Roach, as one day one will be, much of this work would have to be redone. Thus the firm commitment to this particular vehicle for some eighteen months prior to its appearance.

Fourth. Technology requires specialized manpower. This will be evident. Organized knowledge can be brought to bear, not surprisingly, only by those who possess it. However, technology does not make the only claim on manpower; planning, to be mentioned in a moment, also requires a comparatively high level of specialized talent. To foresee the future in all its dimensions and to design the appropriate action does not necessarily require high scientific qualification. It does require ability to organize and employ information or capacity to react intuitively to relevant experience.

These requirements do not necessarily reflect, on some absolute scale, a higher order of talent than was required in a less technically advanced era. The makers of the original Ford were men of talent. The Dodge Brothers had previously invented a bicycle and a steam launch. Their machine shop made a wide variety of products, and Detroit legend also celebrated their exuberance when drunk. Alexander Malcolmson, who was Ford's immediate partner in getting the business under way, was a successful coal merchant. James Couzens, who may well have had more to do with the success of the enterprise than Henry Ford,[7] had a background in railroading and the coal business and went on from Ford to be Police Commissioner and Mayor of Detroit, a notable Republican Senator from Michigan and an undeviating supporter of Franklin D. Roosevelt. Not all of the present Ford organization would claim as much reach. But its members do have a considerably deeper knowledge of the more specialized matters for which they are severally responsible.

Fifth. The inevitable counterpart of specialization is organization. This is what brings the work of specialists to a coherent result. If there are many specialists, this coordination will be a major task. So complex, indeed, will be the job of organizing specialists that there will be specialists on organization. More even than machinery, massive and complex business organizations are the tangible manifestation of advanced technology.

Sixth. From the time and capital that must be committed, the

[7] A case I have argued elsewhere. Cf. "Was Ford a Fraud? in *The Liberal Hour* (London: Hamish Hamilton, 1960).

[284]

inflexibility of this commitment, the needs of large organization and the problems of market performance under conditions of advanced technology, comes the necessity for planning. Tasks must be performed so that they are right not for the present but for that time in the future when, companion and related work having also been done, the whole job is completed. And the amount of capital that, meanwhile, will have been committed adds urgency to this need to be right. So conditions at the time of completion of the whole task must be foreseen as must developments along the way. And steps must be taken to prevent, offset or otherwise neutralize the effect of adverse developments and to ensure that what is ultimately foreseen eventuates in fact.

In the early days of Ford, the future was very near at hand. Only days elapsed between the commitment of machinery and materials to production and their appearance as a car. If the future is near, it can be assumed that it will be very much like the present. If the car did not meet the approval of the customers, it could quickly be changed. The briefness of the time in process allowed this; so did the unspecialized character of manpower, materials and machinery.

Changes were needed. The earliest cars, as they came on the market, did not meet with complete customer approval: there were complaints that the cooling system did not cool, the brakes did not brake, the carburetor did not feed fuel to the engine, and a Los Angeles dealer reported the disconcerting discovery that, when steered, "Front wheels turn wrong."[8] These defects were promptly remedied. They did the reputation of the car no lasting harm.

Such shortcomings in the Mustang would have invited reproach. And they would have been subject to no such quick, simple and inexpensive remedy. The machinery, materials, manpower and components of the original Ford, being all unspecialized, could be quickly procured on the open market. Accordingly, there was no need to anticipate possible shortages of these requirements and take steps to prevent them. For the more highly specialized requirements of the Mustang, foresight and associated action were indispensable. In Detroit, when the first Ford was projected, anything on wheels that was connected with a motor was assured of acceptance. Acceptance of the Mustang could not be so assumed. The prospect had to be carefully studied. And customers had to be carefully conditioned to want this blessing. Thus the need for planning.

[8] Nevins, p. 248.

III

The more sophisticated the technology, the greater, in general, will be all of the foregoing requirements. This will be true of simple products as they come to be produced by more refined processes or as they develop imaginative containers or unopenable packaging. With very intricate technology, such as that associated with modern weapons and weaponry, there will be a quantum change in these requirements. This will be especially so if, as under modern peacetime conditions, cost and time are not decisive considerations.

Thus when Philip II settled on the redemption of England at the end of March 1587, he was not unduly troubled by the seemingly serious circumstance that Spain had no navy. Some men-of-war were available from newly conquered Portugal but, in the main, merchant ships would suffice.[9] A navy, in other words, could then be bought in the market. Nor was the destruction of a large number of the available ships by Drake at Cadiz three weeks later a fatal blow. Despite what historians have usually described as unconscionable inefficiency, the Armada sailed in a strength of 130 ships a little over a year later on May 18, 1588. The cost, though considerable, was well within the resources of the Empire. Matters did not change greatly in the next three hundred years. The *Victory*, from which Nelson called Englishmen to their duty at Trafalgar, though an excellent fighting ship, was a full forty years old at the time. The exiguous flying machines of World War I, built only to carry a man or two and a weapon, were designed and put in combat in a matter of months.

To create a modern fleet of the numerical size of the Armada, with aircraft carriers and appropriate complement of aircraft, nuclear submarines and missiles, auxiliary and supporting craft and bases and communications would take a first-rate industrial power a minimum of twenty years. Though modern Spain is rich beyond the dreams of its monarchs in its most expansive age, it could not for a moment contemplate such an enterprise. In World War II, no combat plane that had not been substantially designed before the outbreak of hostilities saw major service. Since then the lead time for comparable matériel has become yet greater. In general, individuals in late middle

[9] Instructions issued from the Escorial on March 31. Cf. Garrett Mattingly, *The Armada* (London: Cape, n. ed., 1970). Philip had, of course, been contemplating the enterprise for some years.

age stand in little danger of weapons now being designed; they are a menace only to the unborn and the uncontemplated.

IV

It is a commonplace of modern technology that there is a high measure of certainty that problems have solutions before there is knowledge of how they are to be solved. It was known in the early sixties with reasonable certainty that men could land on the moon by the end of the decade. But many, perhaps most, of the details for accomplishing this journey remained to be worked out.

If methods of performing the specified task are uncertain, the need for bringing organized intelligence to bear will be much greater than if the methods are known. This uncertainty will also lead to increased time and cost, and the increase can be very great. Uncertainty as to the properties of the metal to be used for the skin of a supersonic transport; uncertainty therefore as to the proper way of handling and working the metal; uncertainty therefore as to the character and design of the equipment required to work it can add extravagantly to the time and cost of obtaining such a vehicle. This problem-solving, with its high costs in time and money, is a recognized feature of modern technology. It graces all modern economic discussion under the cachet of "Research and Development."

The need for planning, it has been said, arises from the long period of time that elapses during the production process, the high investment that is involved and the inflexible commitment of that investment to the particular task. In the case of advanced military equipment, time, cost and inflexibility of commitment are all very great. Time and outlay will be even greater where — a common characteristic of weaponry — design is uncertain and where, accordingly, there must be added expenditure for research and development. In these circumstances, planning is both essential and difficult. It is essential because of the time that is involved, the money that is at risk, the number of things that can go wrong and the magnitude of the possible ensuing disaster. It is difficult because of the number and size of the eventualities that must be controlled.

One answer is to have the state absorb the major risks. It can provide or guarantee a market for the product. And it can underwrite the costs of development so that if they increase beyond expectation the firm will not have to carry them. Or it can pay for and make available the necessary technical knowledge. The drift of this argument will be evident. Technology, under all circumstances, leads to planning; in its higher manifestations it may put the problems of planning beyond the reach of the industrial firm. Technological compulsions, and not ideology or political wile, will require the firm to seek the help and protection of the state. This is a consequence of advanced technology of no small interest, and to which we shall return.

In examining the intricate complex of economic change, technology, having an initiative of its own, is the logical point at which to break in. But technology not only causes change, it is a response to change. Though it forces specialization, it is also the result of specialization. Though it requires extensive organization, it is also the result of organization. The changes stimulated by technology, slightly reordered for purposes of exposition, are nonetheless the themes of the ensuing chapters.

THE TECHNOSTRUCTURE [10]

"... the prevalence of group, instead of individual, action is a striking characteristic of management organization in the large corporations."

R. A. Gordon, *Business Leadership in the Large Corporation*

THE INDIVIDUAL has far more standing in our culture than the group. An individual has a presumption of accomplishment; a committee has a presumption of inaction.[11] We react sympathetically to the individual who seeks to safeguard his personality from engulfment by the mass. We call for proof, at least in principle, before curbing his aggressions. Individuals have souls; corporations are notably soulless. The entrepreneur — individualistic, restless, with vision, guile and courage — has been the economists' only hero. The great business organization arouses no similar admiration. Admission to

[10] Chapter VI, "The Technostructure," *The New Industrial State*, pp. 59–71.
[11] "Of the various mechanisms of management, none is more controversial than committees . . . Despite their alleged shortcomings, committees are an important device of administrations." Paul E. Holden, Lounsbury S. Fish and Hubert L. Smith, *Top Management Organization and Control* (Maidenhead: McGraw-Hill, 1968), p. 59.

heaven is individually and by families; the top management even of an enterprise with an excellent corporate image cannot yet go in as a group. To have, in pursuit of truth, to assert the superiority of the organization over the individual for important social tasks is a taxing prospect.

Yet it is a necessary task. It is not to individuals but to organizations that power in the business enterprise and power in the society has passed. And modern economic society can only be understood as an effort, wholly successful, to synthesize by organization a group personality far superior *for its purposes* to a natural person and with the added advantage of immortality.

The need for such a group personality begins with the circumstance that in modern industry a large number of decisions, and *all* that are important, draw on information possessed by more than one man. Typically they draw on the specialized scientific and technical knowledge, the accumulated information or experience and the artistic or intuitive sense of many persons. And this is guided by further information which is assembled, analyzed and interpreted by professionals using highly technical equipment. The final decision will be informed only as it draws systematically on all those whose information is relevant. Nor, human beings what they are, can it take all of the information that is offered at face value. There must, additionally, be a mechanism for testing each person's contribution for its relevance and reliability as it is brought to bear on the decision.

II

The need to draw on, and appraise, the information of numerous individuals in modern industrial decision-making has three principal points of origin. It derives, first, from the technological requirements of modern industry. It is not that these are always inordinately sophisticated; a man of moderate genius could, quite conceivably, provide himself with the knowledge of the various branches of metallurgy and chemistry, and of engineering, procurement, production management, quality control, labor relations, styling and merchandising which are involved in the development of a modern motorcar. But even moderate genius is in unpredictable supply, and to keep abreast of all these branches of science, engineering and art would be time-consuming even for a genius. The elementary solution, which allows of the use of far more common talent and with far greater predictability of result, is to have men who are appropriately qualified or experienced in each limited area of specialized knowledge or art. Their information is then combined for carrying out the design and production of the vehicle. It is a common public impression, not discouraged by scientists, engineers and industrialists, that modern scientific, engineering and industrial achievements are the work of a new and quite remarkable race of men. This is pure vanity; were it so, there would be few such achievements. The real accomplishment of modern science and technology consists in taking ordinary men, informing them narrowly and deeply and then, through appropriate organization, arranging to have their knowledge combined with that of other specialized but equally ordinary men. This dispenses with the need for genius. The resulting performance, though less inspiring, is far more predictable. No individual genius arranged the flights to the moon. It was the work of organization — bureaucracy. And the men walking on the moon and contemplating their return could be glad it was so.

The second factor requiring the combination of specialized talent derives from advanced technology, the associated use of capital and the resulting need for planning with its accompanying control of environment. The market is, in remarkable degree, an intellectually unndemanding institution. The Wisconsin farmer need not anticipate his requirements for fertilizers, pesticides or even machine parts; the market stocks and supplies them. The cost of these is substantially the same for the man of intelligence and for his neighbor who, under medical examination, shows daylight in either ear. And the farmer need have no price or selling strategy; the market takes all his milk at the ruling price. Much of the appeal of the market, to economists at least, has been from the way it seems to simplify life. Better orderly error than complex truth.

For complexity enters with planning and is endemic thereto. The manufacturer of missiles, space vehicles or modern aircraft must foresee the requirements for specialized plant, specialized manpower, exotic materials and intricate components and take steps to ensure their availability when they are needed. For procuring such things, we have seen, the market is either unreliable or unavailable. And there is no open market for the finished product. Everything here depends on the care and skill with which contracts are sought and nurtured in Washington or in Whitehall or Paris.

The same foresight and responding action are required, in lesser

degree, from manufacturers of automobiles, processed foods and detergents. They too must foresee requirements and manage markets.
Planning, in short, requires a great variety of information. It requires
variously informed men and men who are suitably specialized in
obtaining the requisite information. There must be men whose
knowledge allows them to foresee need and to ensure a supply of
labor, materials and other production requirements; those who have
knowledge to plan price strategies and see that customers are suitably
persuaded to buy at these prices; those who, at higher levels of technology, are informed that they can work effectively with the state
to see that it is suitably guided; and those who can organize the flow
of information that the above tasks and many others require. Thus, to
the requirements of technology for specialized technical and scientific
talent are added the very large further requirements of the planning
that technology makes necessary.

Finally, following from the need for this variety of specialized
talent, is the need for its coordination. Talent must be brought to
bear on the common purpose. More specifically, on large and small
matters, information must be extracted from the various specialists,
tested for its reliability and relevance, and made to yield a decision.
This process, which is much misunderstood, requires a special word.

III

The modern business organization, or that part which has to do
with guidance and direction, consists of numerous individuals who are
engaged, at any given time, in obtaining, digesting or exchanging
and testing information. A very large part of the exchange and testing
of information is by word of mouth — a discussion in an office, at
lunch or over the telephone. But the most typical procedure is
through the committee and the committee meeting. One can do
worse than think of a business organization as a hierarchy of committees. Coordination, in turn, consists in assigning the appropriate
talent to committees, intervening on occasion to force a decision,
and, as the case may be, announcing the decision or carrying it as
information for a yet further decision by a yet higher committee.

Nor should it be supposed that this is an inefficient procedure. On
the contrary it is, normally, the only efficient procedure. Association
in a committee enables each member to come to know the intellectual
resources and the reliability of his colleagues. Committee discussion
enables members to pool information under circumstances which

allow, also, of immediate probing to assess the relevance and reliability of the information offered. Uncertainty about one's information or error is revealed as in no other way. There is also, no doubt, considerable stimulus to mental effort from such association. One may enjoy torpor in private but not so comfortably in public, at least during working hours. Men who believe themselves deeply engaged in private thought are usually doing nothing. Committees are condemned by those who have been captured by the cliché that individual effort is somehow superior to group effort; by those who guiltily suspect that since group effort is more congenial, it must be less productive; and by those who do not see that the process of extracting, and especially of testing, information has necessarily a somewhat undirected quality — briskly conducted meetings invariably decide matters previously decided; and by those who fail to realize that highly paid men, when sitting around a table as a committee, are not necessarily wasting more time than, in the aggregate, they would each waste in private by themselves.[12] Forthright and determined administrators frequently react to belief in the superior capacity of individuals for decision by abolishing all committees. They then constitute working parties, task forces or executive groups in order to avoid the one truly disastrous consequence of their action which would be that they should make the decisions themselves.

Thus decision in the modern business enterprise is the product not of individuals but of groups. The groups are numerous, as often informal as formal and subject to constant change in composition. Each contains the men possessed of the information, or with access to the information, that bears on the particular decision together with those whose skill consists in extracting and testing this information and obtaining a conclusion. This is how men act successfully on matters where no single one, however exalted or intelligent, has more than a fraction of the necessary knowledge. It is what makes modern business possible, and in other contexts it is what makes modern government

[12] Also committees are not, as commonly supposed, alike. Some are constituted not to pool and test information and offer a decision but to accord representation to diverse bureaucratic, pecuniary, political, ideological or other interests. And a particular committee may have some of both purposes. A committee with representational functions will proceed much less expeditiously, for its ability to reach a conclusion depends on the susceptibility of participants to compromise, attrition and cupidity. The representational committee, in its present form, is engaged in a zero sum game, which is to say that some win, others lose. Pooling and testing information is nonzero sum — all participants end with a larger score.

possible. It is fortunate that men of limited knowledge are so constituted that they can work together in this way. Were it otherwise, business and government, at any given moment, would be at a standstill awaiting the appearance of a man with the requisite breadth of knowledge to resolve the problem presently at hand. Some further characteristics of group decision-making must now be noticed.

IV

Group decision-making extends deeply into the business enterprise. Effective participation is not closely related to rank in the formal hierarchy of the organization. This takes an effort of mind to grasp. Everyone is influenced by the stereotyped organization chart of the business enterprise. At its top is the Board of Directors and the Board Chairman; next comes the President; next comes the Executive Vice President; thereafter come the Department or Divisional heads — those who preside over the Chevrolet division, the large-generators division, the computer division. Power is assumed to pass down from the pinnacle. Those at the top give orders; those below relay them on or respond.

This happens, but only in very simple organizations — the peacetime drill of the National Guard or a troop of Boy Scouts moving out on Saturday maneuvers. Elsewhere the decision will require information. Some power will then pass to the person or persons who have this information. If this knowledge is highly particular to themselves, then their power becomes very great. In Los Alamos, during the development of the atomic bomb, Enrico Fermi rode a bicycle up the hill to work; Major General Leslie R. Groves[13] presided in grandeur over the entire Manhattan District. In association with a handful of others Fermi could, at various early stages, have brought the entire enterprise to an end.[14] No such power resided with Groves. At any moment he could have been replaced without loss.

[13] General Leslie R. Groves, Army Corps of Engineers, was head of the Manhattan District project that developed the atom bomb. He is known especially for his role in the controversial hearings that removed security clearance from the distinguished physicist J. Robert Oppenheimer during the later hydrogen bomb program.
[14] He was head of the Advanced Development Division of the Los Alamos Laboratory. His slightly earlier work was central to the conclusion that a self-sustaining chain reaction was possible. Cf. Henry De Wolfe Smyth, *Atomic Energy for Military Purposes* (London: Oxford University Press, 1946), Chapter 6.

When power is exercised by a group, not only does it pass into the organization but it passes irrevocably. If an individual has taken a decision, he can be called before another individual, who is his superior in the hierarchy, his information can be examined and his decision reversed by the greater wisdom or experience of the superior. But if the decision required the combined information of a group, it cannot be safely reversed by an individual. He will have to get the judgment of other specialists. This returns the power once more to the organization.

No one should insist, in these matters, on pure cases. There will often be instances when an individual has the knowledge to modify or change the finding of a group. But the broad rule holds: If a decision requires the specialized knowledge of a group of men, it is subject to safe review only by the similar knowledge of a similar group. Group decision, unless acted upon by another group, tends to be absolute.[15]

V

Next, it must not be supposed that group decision is important only in such evident instances as nuclear technology or space mechanics. Simple products are made and packaged by sophisticated processes. And the most massive programs of market control, together with the most specialized marketing talent, are used on behalf of soap, detergents, cigarettes, aspirin, packaged cereals and gasoline. These, beyond others, are the valued advertising accounts. The simplicity and uniformity of these products require the investment of compensatingly elaborate science and art to suppress market influences and make prices and amounts sold subject to the largest possible measure of control. For these products too, decision passes to a group which combines specialized and esoteric knowledge. Here too power goes deeply and more or less irrevocably into the organization.

For purposes of pedagogy, I have sometimes illustrated these tendencies by reference to a technically uncomplicated product, which, unaccountably, neither General Electric nor Westinghouse has yet

---

[15] I reached some of these conclusions during World War II when, in the early years, I was in charge of price control. Decisions on prices — to fix, raise, rearrange or, very rarely, to lower them — came to my office after an extensive exercise in group decision-making in which lawyers, economists, accountants, men knowledgeable of the product and industry and specialists in public righteousness had all participated. Alone, one was nearly helpless to alter such decisions; hours

placed on the market.[16] It is a toaster of standard performance, the pop-up kind, except that it etches on the surface of the toast, in darker carbon, one of a selection of standard messages or designs. For the elegant, an attractive monogram would be available or a coat of arms; for the devout, at breakfast there would be an appropriate devotional message from the Reverend Billy Graham; for the patriotic or worried, there would be an aphorism urging vigilance from Mr. J. Edgar Hoover; for modern painters and economists, there would be a purely abstract design. A restaurant version would sell advertising.

Conceivably this is a vision that could come from the head of General Electric. But the systematic proliferation of such ideas is the designated function of much more lowly men who are charged with product development. At an early stage in the development of the toaster the participation of specialists in engineering, production, styling and design and possibly philosophy, art and spelling would have to be sought. No one in position to authorize the product would do so without a judgment on how the problems of inscription were to be solved and at what cost. Nor, ordinarily, would an adverse finding on technical and economic feasibility be overridden. At some stage, further development would become contingent on the findings of market researchers and merchandise experts on whether the toaster could be sold and at what price. Nor would an adverse decision by this group be overruled. In the end there would be a comprehensive finding on the feasibility of the innovation. If unfavorable this would not be overruled. Nor, given the notoriety that attaches to lost opportunity, would be the more plausible contingency of a favorable recommendation. It will be evident that nearly all powers — initiation, character of development, rejection or acceptance — are exercised

---

or days of investigation would be required, and, in the meantime, a dozen other decisions would have been made. Given what is commonly called an "adequate" staff, one could have exercised control. But an adequate staff would be one that largely duplicated the decision-making group with adverse effect on the good nature and sense of responsibility of the latter and the time required for decision. To have responsibility for all the prices in the United States was awesome; to discover how slight was one's power in face of group decision-making was sobering. President Kennedy enjoyed responding to proposals for public action by saying, "I agree but I don't know whether the government will agree."

16 Since the first edition of this book appeared, I have been advised by a number of people that they have had the same inspiration. A British engineer informed me that he developed the device while on fire watch in London in World War II.

deep in the company. It is not the managers who decide. Effective power of decision is lodged deeply in the technical, planning and other specialized staff.

VI

We must notice next that this exercise of group power can be rendered unreliable or ineffective by external interference. Not only does power pass into the organization but the quality of decision can easily be impaired by the efforts of an individual to retain control over the decision-making process.

Specifically the group reaches decision by receiving and evaluating the specialized information of its members. If it is to act responsibly, it must be accorded responsibility. It cannot be arbitrarily or capriciously overruled. If it is, it will develop the same tendencies to irresponsibility as an individual similarly treated.

But the tendency will be far more damaging. The efficiency of the group and the quality of its decisions depend on the quality of the information provided and the precision with which it is tested. The last increases greatly as men work together. It comes to be known that some are reliable and that some, though useful, are at a tacit discount. All information offered must be so weighed. The sudden intervention of a superior introduces information, often of dubious quality, that is not subject to this testing. His reliability, as a newcomer, is unknown; his information, since he is boss, may be automatically exempt from the proper discount; or his intervention may take the form of an instruction and thus be outside the process of group decision in a matter where only group decision incorporating the required specialized judgments is reliable. In all cases the intrusion is damaging.

It follows both from the tendency for decision-making to pass down into organization and the need to protect the autonomy of the group that those who hold high formal rank in an organization — the President of General Motors or General Electric — exercise only modest powers of substantive decision. This power is certainly less than conventional obeisance, professional public relations or, on occasion, personal vanity insist. Decision and ratification are often confused. The first is important; the second is not. There is a tendency to associate power with any decision, however routine, that involves a good deal of money. Business protocol requires that money be treated with solemnity and respect and likewise the man who passes on its use. The nominal head of a large corporation, though with slight power, and perhaps in the first stages of retirement, is visible, tangible and comprehensible. It is tempting and perhaps valuable for the corporate personality to attribute to him power of decision that, in fact, belongs to a dull and not easily comprehended collectivity. Nor is it a valid explanation that the boss, though impotent on specific questions, acts on broad issues of policy. Such issues of policy, if genuine, are pre-eminently the ones that require the specialized information of the group.

Leadership assigns tasks to committtes from which decisions emerge. In doing so, it breaks usefully with the routine into which organization tends to fall. And it selects the men who comprise the groups that make the decisions, and it constitutes and reconstitutes these groups in accordance with changing need. This is, perhaps, its most important function. In an economy where organized intelligence is the decisive factor of production, the selection of the intelligence so organized is of central importance. But it cannot be supposed that a boss can replace or even second-guess organized intelligence on substantive decisions.

VII

In the past, leadership in business organizations was identified with the entrepreneur — the individual who united ownership or control of capital with capacity for organizing the other factors of production and, in most contexts, with a further capacity for innovation.[17] With the rise of the modern corporation, the emergence of the organization required by modern technology and planning and the divorce of the owner of the capital from control of the enterprise, the entrepreneur no longer exists as an individual person in the mature industrial enterprise.[18] Everyday discourse, except in the economics textbooks, recognizes this change. It replaces the entrepreneur, as the directing force of the enterprise, with management. This is a collective and imperfectly defined entity; in the large corporation it embraces chairman, president, those vice presidents with important staff or de-

---

[17] "To act with confidence beyond the range of familiar beacons and to overcome that resistance requires aptitudes that are present in only a small fraction of the population and [they] define the entrepreneurial type as well as the entrepreneurial function." Joseph A. Schumpeter, *Capitalism, Socialism and Democracy*, 2nd Edition (London: Allen & Unwin, 1965).

[18] He is still, of course, to be found in smaller firms and in larger ones that have yet to reach full maturity of organizations.

partmental responsibility, occupants of other major staff positions and, perhaps, division or department heads not included above. It includes, however, only a small proportion of those who, as participants, contribute information to group decisions. This latter group is very large; it extends from the most senior officials of the corporation to where it meets, at the outer perimeter, the white- and blue-collar workers whose function is to conform more or less mechanically to instruction or routine. It embraces all who bring specialized knowledge, talent or experience to group decision-making. This, not the management, is the guiding intelligence — the brain — of the enterprise. There is no name for all who participate in group decision-making or the organization which they form. I propose to call this organization the Technostructure.

THE GENERAL THEORY
OF MOTIVATION [19]

II

THE MOST famous definition of an organization holds it to be a "system of consciously coordinated activities or forces of two or more persons."[20] The most important word here is coordination. It means that the participating individuals are persuaded to set aside their individual purposes or goals and pursue those of the organization. All having done so, all work to the common goals. They are coordinated. Motivation is the means or inducements by which such coordination is effected — the means or inducements by which individuals are led to abandon their own goals and, with greater or less vigor, to pursue those of the organization.

The essentials of the matter are evident when a group of men dig a ditch. Ditch-digging is an unlikely passion for the average person. A useful completed excavation is a plausible goal of a group or organization. The problem is to win the surrender of individual preference in favor of the disciplined wielding of a spade. This can be brought about in the following ways:

(1) The group may compel the acceptance of its goals. Behind

[19] Chapter XI, "The General Theory of Motivation," *The New Industrial State*, pp. 130–139.
[20] Chester I. Barnard, *The Functions of the Executive* (London: Oxford University Press, 1939).

the man with the spade is another with a club. Failure to accept the goals of the group brings the negative reward of punishment. Without extravagant novelty, this motivation may be called *compulsion*.

(2) The acceptance of the common goal may be purchased — at the end of the trench is a man with money. Acceptance of the goals of the organization brings not a negative but an affirmative reward. In return for this inducement, the individual "offers the organization . . . undifferentiated time and effort."[21] Such is pecuniary motivation.

(3) The individual, on becoming associated with the group, may conclude that its goals are superior to his own. In the case of ditch-digging the likelihood is less than in a chamber music group, a political conspiracy or the Marine Corps. Yet it exists. If the ditch drains a particularly nauseous and malarial swamp, the individual on associating himself with the excavators may then become aware of the utility of their enterprise. This is to say that he finds the goals of the group superior to his own previous purposes and so he joins. "Humans, in contrast to machines, evaluate their own positions in relation to the value of others and come to accept others' goals as their own."[22] Such an exchange is not compelled. Neither is it purchased, although it is not inconsistent with compensation. Following Professor Herbert Simon, this motivating influence may be called identification.[23]

(4) Finally, the individual may serve the organization not because he considers its goals superior to his own but because he hopes to make them accord more closely with his own. By being a member of

---

[21] Herbert A. Simon, *Administrative Behavior*, Second Edition (London: Collier-Macmillan, 1965).

[22] James G. March and Herbert A. Simon, *Organizations* (Chichester: Wiley, 1958), p. 65.

[23] This term which has overtones of suburban psychology is not entirely satisfactory. When first working out these ideas, I used the word *conformance* — and this will appear in past, and presumably long unread, lecture notes of my students. Its tone implies, however, that the individual is somehow pressed or forced to conform, and this is not the meaning sought. Identification has no connotation of compulsion and has the claim of prior use. I should like to acknowledge my debt to Professor Simon and his associates. The literature dealing with organization and organization theory is of singular aridity. By far the most distinguished of the exceptions is the work of Herbert A. Simon and his past and present colleagues at the Carnegie Institute of Technology. The two key volumes are *Administrative Behavior* and *Organizations*. Everyone professionally concerned with organization should become acquainted with these difficult but rewarding books.

the ditch-digging organization, he can hope for a ditch that, in capacity, depth or direction, conforms more closely to his ideal.

But once again the ditch-digger is not the most powerful case. The cabinet officer who serves, and on occasion concurs, in action that he finds repugnant in order to advance measures of which he approves, is a better one. So is the politician who would rather influence modestly the policies of a great party than be in full command of a one man movement. And so is the corporation executive who strings along with much that he thinks routine and unenterprising in the hope of winning support for a few new ideas of his own.

The pursuit of the goals of organization because of the prospect or in the hope of accommodating these goals more closely to the participant's preference is an important motivation. But unlike compulsion, pecuniary compensation or even identification, it has also much less standing in the theory of organization. A name for it must be coined, and I propose to call it *adaptation*. Adaptation, it will be evident, has much to do with the urge for power in a world of organization.

Compulsion, pecuniary compensation, identification and adaptation can motivate an individual either separately or in combination. Their collective influence I shall refer to as the motivating system. The strength of any given motivation or of the motivating system will be measured by the effectiveness with which it aligns the individual with the goals of the organization. The motivating system varies greatly in power depending on the motivations that are combined. Some motivations clash and so neutralize each other. Some combine passively. Some strongly reinforce each other. What is called an effective organization is one which, in substantial measure, has a motivational system that is internally reinforcing. The goals of the organization are thus pursued with the greatest possible effect. I turn now to the relation between the several motivating forces.

III

Compulsion and pecuniary compensation exist in varying degrees of association with each other. Those who are compelled to accept the goals of organization by fear of punishment — of negative reward — always have some affirmative compensation for such acceptance. The slave got the whip when he did not work; he got food and shelter of a sort when he did. As we shall see presently, varying amounts of compulsion are associated with pecuniary compensation.

Compulsion is inconsistent with either identification or adaptation. If a person is compelled to accept the goals of an organization, he is unlikely, at least so long as he is under the sense of compulsion, to find them superior to his own. The conflict is not quite absolute. Household slaves — in contrast with field-hands — were believed to accept the goals of their masters. In consequence, they were thought unreliable material for insurrections. The reluctant draftee may come, in time, to relish the barracks and parade ground. But the broad rule holds: What is compelled cannot be a matter of choice. Alienation, not identification, will be the normal result. Bondsmen and serfs have regularly been held to love their masters — to have identified themselves deeply with their masters' goals. This has rarely prevented them, when the opportunity arose, from asserting their own very different goals, frequently after burning the master's house, together with its occupants, or showing some similar manifestation of distaste.

Nor is compulsion consistent with adaptation. If the individual is obliged to accept the goals of organization, he will not embrace them in the hope of accommodating them more closely to his own. When his acceptance is forced, he will understand that he has no power over the goals to which he is compelled. The serf, slave or prison occupant takes the goals of the organization with which he is associated as given and, eccentric cases apart, is alienated from them all. He does only what avoids punishment. Similarly, the oldest rule of the reluctant soldier is to take life as it comes and never volunteer.

Pecuniary motivation may be associated in greater or less measure with compulsion. This will depend on the level of the compensation and the nature of the individual's alternatives. If the element of compulsion is high, it follows that pecuniary motivation will then be inconsistent with identification and adaptation. If it is low, they are readily reconciled. The difference here is of great importance for understanding modern economic behavior.

The worker in a Calcutta jute mill who loses his job — like his American counterpart during the Great Depression — has no high prospect of ever finding another. He has no savings. Nor does he have unemployment insurance. The alternative to his present employment, accordingly, is slow but definitive starvation. The fate of a defecting southern slave before the Civil War or a serf before Alexander II was not appreciably more painful. The choice between hunger and flogging may well be a matter of taste. The aversion to the organization that compels the acceptance of its goals will be much the same in each instance. This aversion excludes identification. To repeat, the fact that the worker serves because he is compelled sufficiently reveals to him his powerlessness vis-à-vis the organization and its goals. Adaptation is thus also excluded.

The modern industrial employee who loses or abandons his job has, by contrast, every expectation of finding another. In the meantime he has unemployment compensation and perhaps some personal resources, and, if the worst comes to the worst, he can obtain welfare support. The danger of physical discomfort has been much reduced and therewith, in general, the element of compulsion. In higher income brackets, as a rule, it will be yet lower. As compulsion as an aspect of pecuniary compensation diminishes or disappears, so do the barriers to identification and adaptation.

IV

The diminishing role of compulsion in pecuniary compensation has been a force of no small historical importance. Among other things it goes far to explain the disappearance of slavery. Until two centuries ago the motivation of the wage laborer in most parts of the world was not radically different from that of the bondsman. Both got little; both toiled in fear of the alternative.

The slave, accordingly, had no reason to regard the free wage worker with much envy. He did not press aggressively to change his position. Nor did society on his behalf. But as the wage worker improved his material position, the element of compulsion to which he was subject diminished. Then the contrast between free man and slave deepened and slavery became untenable. In the absence of the Civil War, slavery in the United States could have lasted only a few more years. For, in a relatively short time, industrialization and rising living standards in the North together with improving communications would have made it increasingly difficult to keep the slaves in the fields. And the cost of patrols and the machinery for redeeming fugitives, together with the capital loss from those who made good their escape into northern employments, would have been intolerable. Planters would have been forced to pay inducements, i.e., wages, to hold their men. As in other countries, at a roughly similar stage in economic development, slavery would have been given up. The reform would have been attributed to the innate humanity of man to man. By 1880 or 1890 at the latest, the more respected philosophers would have been congratulating the nation on having accomplished peacefully what men once feared could only have been done by war.

As it is wrong to deny the role of conscience in human affairs, it is also an error to minimize that of economics. Speaking to the same subject, when bondsmen were still valuable property, Adam Smith observed: "The late resolution of the Quakers in Pennsylvania to set at liberty their negro slaves, may satisfy us that their number cannnot be very great."[24]

V

As compulsion and pecuniary compensation are associated in varying mix, so also are identification and adaptation. The two are highly complementary. An individual, on becoming associated with an organization, will be more likely to adopt its goals in place of his own if he has hope of changing those he finds unsatisfactory or repugnant. And if he is strongly identified with the goals of an organization, he will be moved all the more strongly to try to improve it — to alter (i.e. adapt) any unsatisfactory goals so that they accord with his own. A member will identify himself more enthusiastically with a political party if he feels that he has some power to influence its platform; he will work more diligently to influence the platform if he is generally in accord with the party's goals.

The relation of identification to adaptation is partly a matter of temperament; the disposition of some on associating themselves with an organization is to accept its goals and of others to improve them. Some college presidents and diplomats, by disposition, accept the goals of their respective institutions; others seek to advance the purposes of education or peace. Adaptation is also partly a matter of position. It more strongly motivates a President of the United States than a postman making his rounds, more strongly the general manager than the receptionist, the pastor than the sexton.

VI

Pecuniary motivation cannot be combined with identification and adaptation when the element of compulsion is large. It can be when the element of compulsion is small. This means that the motivational system will be different in the poor country as compared with the

[24] Adam Smith, *Wealth of Nations*, Book III, Chapter II.

rich, and different for the poor man as compared with the well-to-do. And what begins as a difference in degree widens, ultimately, into a difference in kind.

In the poor country, and among the poorly paid, labor relations will, in general, be harsh and angry. The compulsion associated with low compensation alienates the worker from the employer. This being so, the employer does not seek to cultivate his employee's loyalty — to encourage his identification with the firm — for this he knows to be impossible. There being nothing to lose, nothing is lost by arrogant or offensive behavior. The worker, not being identified with the employer, will be receptive to the goals of the union. He will also be vulnerable to threats from the employer that he will be fired if he joins, for this is precisely the hardship he fears and which compels his effort. The stage is thus set for disagreeable behavior on both sides. Those concerned have rarely failed to conform to expectation.

In the richer country, and among the well-to-do, everything is more benign. Compulsion will have receded. In consequence, there is little or no alienation; the way is open for the worker to accept the goals of the organization. The worker will have less inducement to join a union but much less to fear in doing so. The employer will seek to encourage the identification of the worker with the firm; the worker having less to fear, the employer will find it less useful to play on his fears. The worker being more identified with the firm, the union has less enmity to arouse. On both sides the motivational system both allows and rewards more agreeable behavior. This mellowing of industrial relations, the result of wealth, will, however, be attributed to more humane instincts, greater employer enlightenment, more responsible unions and the spread of industrial statesmanship.

The paradox of pecuniary motivation is that, in general, the higher the amount the less its importance in relation to other motivations. This is not because of the declining marginal utility of money, although, along with progressive income taxation, this may reduce its capacity to buy effort. Rather it is because with higher incomes there is, under most circumstances, a lessened dependence on a particular employment. So there is a lessened element of compulsion, and this paves the way for identification and adaptation. These supplement and may transcend pecuniary compensation in their importance in the motivational system.

It will be clear that we have here a solution, or in any case a clue, to the contradictions encountered in the last chapter. Pecuniary compensation need not be the main motivation of members of the technostructure. Identification and adaptation may be driving forces. Above a certain level these may operate independently of income. Maximization of income for the technostructure is neither needed nor sought. The question of what goals members of the technostructure identify themselves with, and to what personal goals they seek adaptation, remains. But it will be clear that there is no necessary conflict with the stockholders as there would be if both were seeking to maximize pecuniary return.

VII

One test of sound social analysis is that it explains small matters as well as great. One of the most puzzling pleas of the American business executive, regularly echoed in public rituals, is for lower taxes to encourage initiative and effort. The puzzle lies in the fact that few executives would ever admit to putting forth less than their best effort for their present income after taxes. To suggest such malingering would be considered a gross insult.[25]

An explanation is now at hand. The reference to incentives is traditional, a hangover from a more primitive association of income and effort. It accords seeming respectability and social utility to the desire for lower taxes or the natural wish to shift more of the existing burden to the poor. But the reality is that the executive's present level of income allows for identification and adaptation. These are the operative motivations. They are also the only personally reputable ones: the executive cannot afford to have it thought that his commitment to the goals of the corporation is less than complete or that he is at all indifferent to his opportunity to shape these goals. To suggest that he subordinates these latter motives to his response to pay would be to confess that he is an inferior executive.

A FURTHER SUMMARY[26]

THE PRINCIPAL TOPOGRAPHY of the industrial system is now in view. Most will think it a formidable sight. Few will minimize the complexity of its probable social effect; the only man who

[25] A recent study under the auspices of the Brookings Institution, Washington, fully affirms the point: *The Economic Behavior of the Affluent* by Robin Barlow, Harvey E. Brazer and James N. Morgan, 1966.
[26] Chapter XXVIII, "A Further Summary," *The New Industrial State*, pp. 320–324.

must surely be wrong about the industrial system is the one who essays a simple judgment upon it.

The system produces goods and renders services in vast and increasing volume. There are many poor people left in the industrial countries, and notably in the United States. The fact that they are not the central theme of this treatise should not be taken as proof either of ignorance of their existence or indifference to their fate. But the poor, by any applicable tests, are outside the industrial system. They are those who have not been drawn into its service or who cannot qualify. And not only has the industrial system — its boundaries as here defined are to be kept in mind — eliminated poverty for those who have been drawn into its embrace but it has also greatly reduced the burden of manual toil. Only those who have never experienced hard and tedious labor, one imagines, can be wholly indifferent to its elimination.

Once it was imagined that the economic system provided man with the artifacts by which he has anciently surrounded himself in response to his original and sovereign desires. This source of economic motivation is still celebrated in the formal liturgy of the system. But, as we have sufficiently seen, the system, if it accommodates to man's wants, also and increasingly accommodates men to its needs. And it must. This latter accommodation is no trivial exercise in salesmanship. It is deeply organic. High technology and heavy capital use cannot be subordinate to the ebb and flow of market demand. They require planning; it is the essence of planning that public behavior be made predictable — that it be subject to control.

And from this control flow further important consequences. It ensures that men and numerous women will work with undiminished effort however great their supply of goods. And it helps ensure that the society will measure its accomplishment by its annual increase in production. Nothing would be more discomfiting for economic discipline than were men to establish goals for themselves and on reaching them say, "I've got what I need. That is all for this week." Not by accident is such behavior thought irresponsible and feckless. It would mean that increased output would no longer have high social urgency. Enough would be enough. The achievement of the society could then no longer be measured by the annual increase in Gross National Product. And if increased production ceased to be of prime importance, the needs of the industrial system would no longer be accorded automatic priority. The required readjustment in social attitudes would be appalling.

The management to which we are subject is not onerous. It works not on the body but on the mind. It first wins acquiescence or belief; action is in response to this mental conditioning and thus devoid of any sense of compulsion. It is not that we are required to have a newly configured automobile or a novel reverse-action laxative; it is because we believe that we must have them. It is open to anyone who can resist belief to contract out of this control. But we are no less managed because we are not physically compelled. On the contrary, though this is poorly understood, physical compulsion would have a far lower order of efficiency.

II

The industrial system has brought its supply of capital, and in substantial measure also its labor supply, within its control, and thus within the ambit of its planning. And it has extended its influence deeply into the state. Those policies of the state that are vital for the industrial system — regulation of aggregate demand, maintenance of the large public (if preferably technical) sector on which this regulation depends, underwriting of advanced technology and provision of an increasing volume of trained and educated manpower — are believed to be of the highest social urgency. This belief accords with the needs of the system. And the influence of the technostructure of the mature firm extends to shaping the demand for its particular product or range of products. Individual members of the technostructure identify themselves with the design, development and production of items purchased by the government as the technostructure identifies itself with the social goal (say) of an effective national defense. And the members of the technostructure adapt design, development or need for items procured by the government to what accords with their own goals. These goals reflect, inevitably, the needs of the technostructure and of its planning.

Paralleling these changes, partly as a result and partly as a cause, has been a profound shift in the locus of economic and political power. The financier and the union leader are dwindling influences in the society. They are honored more for their past eminence than for their present power. The technostructure exercises much less direct political power than did the antecedent entrepreneur. But that is because it has far more influence as an arm of the bureaucracy and in its influence on the larger climate of belief. The scientific, technical, organizational and planning needs of the technostructure have brought into being a large educational and scientific estate. And, while the commitment of the culture, under the tutelage of the industrial system, to a single-minded preoccupation with the production of goods is strong, it is not complete. Rising income also nurtures a further artistic and intellectual community outside of the industrial system.

III

Such in briefest sketch are the principal results of this pilgrimage. Two questions inevitably follow: Where does it take us? How should it be guided?

Neither question is, in fact, as important as those already considered, and, one hopes, resolved. Agreeable as it is to know where one is proceeding, it is far more important to know where one has arrived. And while there will always be resistance to accepting what has come to exist — a resistance nurtured by nostalgia, vested interest in painfully acquired error which is thus understandably precious, and the omnipresent need to sustain belief in what is convenient as distinct from what is real — one has, where the present is concerned, appellate rights in two great courts, namely the internal consistency of the ideas and their coherence with what can be seen. It will perhaps be agreed that these have rendered good service here. When one turns to the future, these guides are lost. There are wise and foolish predictions but the difference between them is not so clear.

There are also difficulties in talking, at the same time, about what will happen and what should happen. Marx must on occasion have wondered, if revolution were inevitable, as he proclaimed, why it required the passionate and unrelenting advocacy which he accorded it. Should baleful tendencies be predicted when one hopes that popular understanding will bring the reaction that reverses them? No one who believes in ideas and their advocacy can ever persuade himself that they are uninfluential. Nor are they. And those who deal in ideas, if they are wise, will welcome attack. Only a peaceful passage should dismay them, for it proves that the ideas do not affect anyone very much. I have hopes that popular understanding will reverse some of the less agreeable tendencies of the industrial system and invalidate, therewith, the predictions that proceed from these tendencies. And I am not without hope for the controversy that attests the importance of such change.

BOOK
V

Theory and Theorist

Round III

and Truce

PART ONE

GETTING INDIA FILED

SELECTION *12*

The Triumph was a successful book—a satirical novel with a very sharp point. Looking at it in retrospect one is inclined to recall La Rochefoucauld's witticism to the effect that the trouble with a penetrating remark is that it exceeds its target. The Triumph passed through the body politic leaving behind a wound so fine and clean that it was healed almost as soon as made.

Galbraith's asides, in both The McLandress Dimension and Ambassador's Journal, sufficiently justify us in not mistaking the intent of The Triumph. However, 1968 was not the year for an A.D.A. Democrat to give aid and comfort to the Nixon rooters by openly attacking the conduct of foreign relations under a recent Democratic administration. In the circumstance surely fiction was the only form allowed, but fiction was not the best weapon for the purpose.

It would be irrelevant to attempt to present the plot of The Triumph in any detail. The novel is short and extremely compact; the action takes place in both North and South America; though the characters are surprisingly varied and numerous for so short a book, the reader has little trouble in keeping them clearly in mind. For presentation here, we have chosen two meetings of two very different kinds. The contrast between the two is striking. They stand near opposite ends of the book and record the opening and the closing of the action. The first is between two men, the wise old finance minister of the "republic" of Puerto Santos and an American newspaper man whose ardent voice has long been muffled by that world weariness that is the occupational malady of good men who have too often observed the triumph of darkness. It takes place in a club in Flores, the capital city of Puerto Santos. The second meeting is in the office of the Assistant Secretary of State in Washington, D.C. It is attended by a score of representatives from various departments of our government and requires the dramatis personae which precedes the text.

The dramatis personae:

DR. GRANT WORTHING CAMPBELL, the Assistant Secretary, who favored a policy of "watchful waiting," so long as that did not interfere with waiting for promotion and watching out for his public image.

AMBASSADOR PETHWICK, U. S. Ambassador to Puerto Santos, who pursued the policies of his superior — subect to the same limitations.

SYMES JONES, Pethwick's First Secretary, an able but unambitious man long since defeated by the policy of permanent watching and permanent waiting.

WILLIAM O'DONNELL, on the staff of O.A.S.; Acting Director of the Office of Centrals American and Caribbean Affairs. He would rather take a chance on the new than suffer the degenerate old.

JOSÉ MARÍA MIRÓ-SÁNCHEZ (Miro), the liberal, young usurper who desperately needs U. S. support to continue the fight against the ousted dictator.

PRESIDENT LUIS MIGUEL MARTÍNEZ-OBREGÓN (Martínez), the despotic old dictator who had used American handouts to maintain himself in senile dissipation and his nation in total misery.

DR. RICHARD WILLIAM KENT, a busybody from AID; Special Consultant on Primary and Secondary Educational Methods and Programs for the Agency of International Development; full of verbose "-isms" suited only for a society of moderate literacy — if for anything at all — who had been sent to report on the progress of educational science under the new government. He could not understand that the people of Puerto Santos were largely illiterate or that there was no money at all in the treasury.

CAPTAIN GONZALEZ, Assistant Attaché for the U. S. Flores, inclined to think that to watch and wait was to leave the unbearable to become the impossible.

The scene: the office of the Assistant Secretary of State for Inter-
American Affairs in the New State Department Building, Washington, D. C.

The time: 3 P.M., the hour announced for the meeting called by the
Assistant Secretary to discuss recognition by the U. S. of a new
government in a small, seedy Graustarkian republic in South
America situated perhaps along the southern margin of the Caribbean Sea, well within the West Indian girdle. The country is
Puerto Santos, its capital city is Flores. The new government is
headed by a young reformer of leftist tendencies who has requested
financial, advisory and moral support for his regime. The Assistant
Secretary has been told to get a proper consensus on the subject
from the appropriate department of his government.

The Triumph[1]

THE BEARING of the Martínez wealth on the survival of the regime,
was, oddly enough, the subject of discussion at the Santos Club —
the Club, possibly misnamed, of the Saints — on the night that his
enemies closed in on the dictator.

Many think this building, on the square opposite the cathedral,
the most beautiful in Flores, and possibly in what was once New
Spain. The main structure dates from colonial times, but it was greatly
extended and improved early in the present century when rich sugar
and coffee planters, Flores merchants and an occasional cattleman
felt a need for a congenial resort where they might restore themselves
after a lonely vigil on their land or a long day in the counting room.
In those days, neither politicians nor army officers were allowed to
belong, and the barrier has never been entirely lifted. However, in
recent times, it has been understood that if the President of the Re-

[1] *The Triumph: A Novel of Modern Diplomacy* (London: Hamish Hamilton, 1968),
pp. 38–44; 205–217.

public insists, a man must be admitted. This has not often happened, and the club has never been popular with the Martínez regime.

In inspiration the club is Venetian not Spanish, and the high chaste walls with the scalloped fringe along the top are solid and have withstood well the rains. So has the great nail-studded door although its metal has not been polished for many years and has tarnished to a dull green. Within, the red tile floors are laid on a thick footing of mortar and crushed rock and are still level, cool and clean. There is more than a trace of grandeur in the large central patio to which the building is open and which it seems to surround almost as an after-thought. The chairs are angular and solid, the seats are large sheets of leather and from the heavy refectory tables one imagines that monks might eat. It is all shabby but still very strong and beautiful. The bar is fully fifty feet long, and the occasional visitors are still shown a bullet hole where the bullet is still lodged after passing through the alleged seducer of the daughter of a rich and angry coffee planter. Acting on a hasty and rather general description, the rancher had shot the leading Flores pharmacist by mistake. Visitors are less likely to be shown the table where, in the late twenties, the American Minister drank himself to death. A former Republican State Chairman from South Dakota, his pleasure in his unexpected escape from prohibition knew no bounds. Once he solemnly mounted the bar and announced his intention of riding it all the way back to Sioux Falls. The stories of his final delirium are of slight clinical interest and not entirely pleasant, but his widow gave a handsome stained-glass window to the Protestant chapel in his honor. Nor do members like to recall the more recent occasions when the Martínez police have entered to arrest a member suspected of plotting against the regime, or whose sudden departure, it had been decided, would be a useful warning to those who probably were.

The number of such arrests has not been large, for the club in recent times has not had many members. The rich and the well-to-do who once graced its rolls are those, naturally enough, who aroused the acquisitive instinct of Martínez. They are gone from Puerto Santos, and those who wish to get along under the regime find the club of no help. Once the bar featured every alcoholic beverage known to the Americas — tequila, pisco sour, planter's punch, *aguardiente*, whiskey sour with bourbon, scotch and soda, gin and tonic, Jack Daniels, Four Roses, Schlitz. Now the single aging waiter searches under the bar for a bottle and shuffles out to the kitchen for some ice. The food is far from good and frequently, and for good reason, has a warmed-over taste. None of the regular patrons is under sixty, but for a score or so beyond this age it is a much-loved link with a much better past. They will be sorry when, as all recognize must eventually happen, the club finally closes its doors.

The Setting: The Patio of the Santos Club

On this night none of the shabbiness and only a little of the beauty of the club were visible, for here too the electricity was off. And only indistinctly visible in the light reflected from the half-moon rising in the night sky were the two elderly men who sat at a table in the big patio. One seemed to be rather somberly dressed in what might have been dark tropical worsted. The other was in crumpled white. There were some sounds of movement from the direction of the bar or kitchen; otherwise they were alone. Neither had spoken for several minutes, but finally the man in dark observed: "It seems that the firing has stopped."

"I expect Martínez has things under control," his companion replied. "Anyway, we will know soon enough. I realize that you have a contrary opinion."

"Contrary and, I believe, correct," the man in dark replied. Martínez is finished. It is only that it has taken a certain time for people to make this interesting and important discovery."

"I have still to be persuaded. He has soldiers. He has police. Both impress me. I confess to regretting the temperament which caused me to accept your invitation to join you here tonight. Besides there is very little to see."

"Don't be alarmed. Age is a great protection. Men do not respect years, but they instinctively feel that with a little patience the appropriate punishment will come from other and more authoritative sources. Why waste energy or run risk for what the Lord will accomplish in a few years? So we are spared." The man in dark took a sip from a glass or cup, put it back on the table and listened to the sounds beyond the walls for a moment. There were distant shouts but still no shooting. He continued in a rather didactic tone.

"You would be more sanguine, I believe, if you understood the nature of power. And exceptional too, for in my experience it is not even understood by those who wield it. There is, of course, the power of love, which, in the case of Luis Martínez, can reasonably be excluded. For the rest, it is merely a matter of reward and punishment. Men can pay others to accept their will or they can punish them for failing to do so. These are the sources of power, and it is a remarkable fact that when the ability to reward disappears so does the ability to punish. Martínez has now lost both. Accordingly, he will disappear, and, in my view, that will happen this evening."

"You are eloquent and logical as always, my friend. But I fail to see why Martínez is so suddenly assailed by this weakness."

"It was not sudden. He has been living on borrowed time, and any serious opposition was certain to topple him. Fairly certain, perhaps I should say. Once the members of this club were rich and numerous and most of them wanted to be richer still. Their wealth and their avarice were the source of the Martínez power to punish and reward. They did his bidding lest he take away their money or their chance to make more. Thus his power of punishment. And he could take away enough to give other people jobs, graft and trips to the United States. Thus his power to reward. Now the wealth is gone, the people are gone and the taxes are gone. Is it surprising that his power has also gone?" . . .

"He has money from the Americans."

"I admit that the Americans are a problem. They are defending freedom and resisting Communism, and it is a great tragedy when this takes place in a small country like ours with a dictator like Martínez. We have not been the first so to suffer. But I think it is now too late even for the American money. Also, others have been saying that they could get more. But pardon me, I wonder if the revolution isn't approaching our door."

The old man got up and listened again. There were still no shots, but unmistakably there was a sound of crowded footsteps and occasional shouts and commands outside. Presently there was a pounding on the door. "Perhaps you will excuse me. I made certain arrangements for our friends to use the club as a command post, possibly even as a place of detention. It was good of you to keep me company. I trust that my predictions are sound and that they are not seeking asylum." The old man disappeared into the darkness in the direction of the door. Presently flashlights and then a lantern pierced the gloom.

The Setting: The Office of the Assistant Secretary in Washington, D.C.

The meeting assembled in Worth Campbell's office at 3 P.M. Earlier there is too much danger of interruption by late-comers hurriedly and apologetically making their entrance after an unduly prolonged lunch. Symes Jones's copies were available for distribution. Each was marked *Secret* and *Draft* and was numbered in ink in Symes's handwriting. Each recipient was requested to return his copy at the end of the meeting. These were a trifle more than normal precautions. But it was Worth Campbell's practice to take White House business with the utmost seriousness, and this also explained why copies had not been circulated in advance. This last also eliminated the danger that the recipients would come in with a great many unnecessary amendments.

A meeting such as this, Worth Campbell had years ago learned, cannot be small. Too many agencies have a legitimate concern, and, in any case, Campbell wanted to be sure everyone had a fair hearing. That was what the White House wanted. So when everyone was present, the big room was more than comfortably full. Three men shared the leather sofa, their knees rising awkwardly to the level of their chins. Three more were in the big leather armchairs to which Worth Campbell always moved from his desk for informal conversations with a visiting envoy. These six were either amateurs or men with little real interest in the proceedings. However admirable for easy talk, no man can address a meeting with authority from the depths of a sofa or armchair. The determined or articulate men had chosen the plain leather chairs or the even more Spartan metal ones that lined the walls. They put their briefcases on the floor between the chair legs; to relax, they tipped back against the walls. When their eyes wandered from the speaker, they looked at the framed and autographed photos on the wall behind Worth Campbell's chair — Lucius Clay, John J. McCloy, John Foster Dulles, Allen Welsh Dulles, Paul Hoffman, Averell Harriman, Clare Boothe Luce, Herbert Hoover, Jr., Nathan Pusey, several more who could not be so readily identified. The meeting could have been moved to a conference room, but Worth Campbell was more at home in his office and more immediately accessible by telephone in case of emergency. He also had a somewhat greater feeling of command. Present were one civilian and three officers, all in civilian clothes, from the office of the Assistant Secretary of Defense (International Affairs), including the Deputy Assistant Secretary (Far East and Latin American Affairs) and the Regional Director (Western Hemisphere). The Special Assistant for Counter Insurgency and Special Activities was also there from the Joint Staff of the Joint Chiefs of Staff together with two deputies. Two men were present from CIA and two from USIA. Two had come from AID including Dr. Richard Williams Kent. Dr. Kent had some difficulty in concealing his eagerness and also his nervousness. He swallowed frequently. It was the first meeting of such importance to which he had ever been invited. A Deputy Assistant Secretary of State for Educational and Cultural Affairs had been asked because Dr. Kent had been asked. This was to maintain parity. Were education in Puerto Santos to come up, someone from that shop would have a legitimate claim to be heard. Two men were present from the office of the Assistant Secretary of State for Intelligence and Research and two from the office of the Assistant Secretary of State for Economic Affairs. The scruffy-looking man in the tweed jacket from Policy Planning was there along with an assistant. His dandruff seemed worse. Pethwick was present. So in addition to Symes Jones were Bill O'Donnell and two younger men from O'Donnell's office including the well-tailored youngster whose name gave Worth Campbell trouble. The head of the Sugar Policy Staff of the Agricultural Stabilization and Conservation Service of the Department of Agriculture was there and also the Director of the American Republics Division of the Department of Commerce. The Treasury was to have been represented by the Director, Office of Developing Nations, but he did not show up. Alone among the departments of government, the Treasury cannot be counted upon to cover all meetings of importance. At the beginning of the meeting, the Ambassador to the Organization of American States was also missing. He came in five minutes late, very apologetic and even more so when everyone, including those deep in the couches, stood up until a seat was found for him.

One of the girls in the Assistant Secretary's office was present by the corner of his desk with a pad to take notes. The Assistant Secretary opened the meeting by thanking everyone present and briefly explaining its purpose. He stressed especially his desire for a free, frank dialogue with — as he smilingly said — "no holds barred." No policy was sacred; certainly none could be so regarded when the White House asked for review. Nothing was off limits for the dialogue. He would say a brief word on the present policy. It was not a rigid policy; it was one of keeping a close eye on developments, one, in a word, of watchful waiting. We wanted to minimize the risk of Communism, we tried to be sure that we did business with governments that had, in a sense, proved themselves. No one, he supposed, and certainly not the President, wanted our aid and diplomatic support to be used to build a Communist regime. There would be agreement on this; he would not say more for he did not want to seem to be prejudging the issue. He asked for a general dialogue. It got off to a slow start. Nearly everyone, however, was impressed by Campbell's open-mindedness.

In concerting their strategy the evening before, Bill O'Donnell and the Ambassador to the OAS had decided that the latter should lead off. People associated with diplomacy have a tendency to defer to age and rank, especially rank. Also O'Donnell was not a persuasive man. His choice of language regularly confirmed his opposition in the rightness and even the righteousness of its views. It was also understood that they would hold their fire. Both were experienced men and knew that all meetings in the Department of State open on a highly undirected note. No serious argument can usefully be offered until this period has passed.

Things went reasonably to form. After a few moments' silence with everyone looking a little uneasily at everyone else, the untidy man from Policy Planning asked if it would not be useful at the outset to define the American and free world interest in Puerto Santos. When no one responded, he took this as agreement and proceeded. Everyone recognized the irrelevance of his remarks but pretended, nonetheless, to listen closely. It appeared, generally, that Puerto Santos was not of primary and not of secondary but because of its proximity to the Canal was of more than tertiary interest to free world security. Under no circumstance should the Communists be allowed to cross the Rostow truce line at this point. He went on to urge that we be prepared at all times to rethink our policy and to regear our planning and reorient our programs accordingly. His colleague from Policy Planning looked uncomfortable. It was speeches like this that gave the organization a bad name. Before the speaker had begun to show any perceptible loss of power, the Assistant Secretary's secretary came in with a note. Peering through his glasses, Campbell selected from a choice of buttons on the console and picked up the telephone. A hush fell over the room.

The conversation which none could hear was very brief, but quite a few noticed that the Assistant Secretary's manner was even firmer and more decisive over the telephone than in the meeting. He was a man, obviously, with reserves of strength. It was an emergency call from Mrs. Campbell. Their boy had beeen picked up for speeding in Falls Church, and the police officer had promised to give him a hard time. The man from Policy Planning resumed but with visibly less authority. During the interruption his colleague had slipped him a note saying, "It might be good strategy to cut it a little short— if you agree." A few observations on general nuclear strategy, a reference to the parallels between the present position of Communism and that of the Confederacy after Fort Sumter and a plea that everyone be guided "by the numbers in this situation," and he was finished.

Soon the meeting was well under way. A lean, healthy-looking man from the Joint Staff sketched in succinct terms the present thinking on military action to prevent a Communist take-over. The Air Force had agreed to a plan for bombing communications with Flores, and it was now before the Chiefs. It contained an important change in thinking. Reflecting the present assessment of the Communist threat. bombing was now designed not to keep the Communists out of the capital city but to keep them in. It would need to be combined, they recognized, with maximum emphasis on winning the hearts and minds of the people. Accordingly, the closest liaison would be maintained with the Agency for International Development (AID) and the U.S. Information Agency. The men from the latter agencies bowed in general acknowledgment of their need.

The Sugar Policy man from the Department of Agriculture then said that, given the present attitudes on the Hill toward the Miró Administration, it would be tough to keep the present sugar quota. He implied, without quite saying so, that Miró would do well to get himself an experienced Washington lawyer and learn a few things from Martínez about how things were done in this town. "You don't get sugar quotas up there outa love." Interest sharpened. Here was the world of political legerdemain which most of those present knew only from reading Drew Pearson and about Senator Thomas J. Dodd. Also, the man from Agriculture depended not so much on words as on a succession of confidential winks, meaningful twistings of the mouth, and thumbs and fingers made into a circle and punched knowingly with an index finger. This required close attention. The Ambassador, studying the man's age and accent, allowed himself to imagine he had come in with Huey Long. Worth Campbell thanked the sugar man when he showed signs of launching an unduly lengthy eulogy of Senator Allen J. Ellender. He suggested that perhaps they should get even closer to the subject. He asked the senior CIA man for their current estimate of Communist infiltration in the government of Puerto Santos and the resulting threat to the free world.

This was slightly dangerous. The Agency was not as alarmed as the Assistant Secretary would have wished. Their younger men were showing the same uncertainty of mission that was to be found in so many other places. And their man in Puerto Santos was clearly under the influence of Joe Hurd. But early in such a meeting one must have the intelligence position. Bypassing it would be noticed. And as it developed, Campbell's worries were groundless. The gist of the Agency position was that the situation was unclear. They did not estimate an early Communist take-over, but when pressed a little by Campbell, their man, after a whispered consultation with his colleague, said that it could not be excluded. He summarized by saying that the Agency regarded the situation as unclear. He asked all to keep in mind that these matters were highly classified.

The Ambassador to the OAS judged that the time had come to intervene.

"These people had thirty years of the dictatorship of Martínez. Now they seem to have a good and decent government. I have known some of these people, either personally or their families, and I think they want to be friends of ours. I say we should recognize this government and give it some help — the kind of help we gave to Martínez. Mr. O'Donnell here, who has followed things closely, agrees with me. The President is leaning that way which is why we are having this meeting. I've read the cables, and there seems to be full agreement" — here the Ambassador paused for emphasis and repeated himself — "there is full agreement among our people on the spot on supporting the Miró Administration. People who do things usually get called Communists. That is something they probably learned from us, so it's no objection. If we don't support Miró, we will get something worse."

It was a very effective speech. The Ambassador knew how to hit the right note of authority. For just a moment even Campbell felt a twinge of uneasiness. Could the meeting be swung around so that it did something foolish? He saw with more alarm that Pethwick was moving in.

Campbell gave the floor to Pethwick and then held him off for a word first. He said he hoped the Ambassador did not suggest that anyone was making any loose charges about Communism. They would all agree on not countenancing that sort of thing. But they would also have to agree that Communists did exist and were active. They were a danger just as McCarthyism was a danger. Their task was to avoid the one without resorting to the other. He might make one other point. They had before them the old problem of giving proper weight but not excessive weight to the views of those on the ground. There was the matter of perspective. There was also the old disease of clientitis — the tendency to see things through the eyes of the government to which you were accredited. He supposed that he had suffered from that himself, that he had sometimes pulled an oar for Adenauer and Jean Monnet. And unanimity of view down there could be discounted a little bit; they all worked closely together, and in fact all of their recommendations had come in at the same time yesterday couched in almost exactly the same language. One guessed that they had been pretty well discussed — which was as it should be. But their views should be weighed. He didn't go so far as Winston Churchill who once said that the British Empire was built on two principles: "Never trust the man on the spot; never yield to anything but force." It was another of Campbell's rare resorts to the lighter touch. There was an appreciative titter which promptly stopped as Pethwick got under way.

Pethwick was still angry at what the Ambassador had said. It took him some time to say what he had to say for he repeated himself with some frequency. But the gist was not complex. Martínez had given that country thirty years of stable government, and from being there he knew the people had been happy. (Pethwick had evidently not been impressed by Churchill.) As for Miró he could only say that "Miró was . . . was a dog!"

Pethwick was not persuasive. However, he was helped by O'Donnell. O'Donnell said Pethwick's views on Miró like those on Martínez's popular support were not to be trusted. In proof he recalled the telegrams predicting Martínez's survival and implied, not too obliquely, that Pethwick had brown-nosed the dictator to the point of acute sinusitis. All this was true. But its vigor diverted attention from the case that the old Ambassador had made. And it violated a cardinal rule of American diplomacy which is that one never dwells in public on the mistakes of another man. This is a sensible rule. Mistakes are inevitable. If they are not allowed to others, they will not be allowed to you. So reciprocity is essential. At this juncture one of the men from the Office of the Assistant Secretary of Defense (International

Affairs) broke in to say "purely for the record" that the Air Force plans on bombing and counter-insurgency action had not been approved by the Office of the Secretary of Defense. One of his assistants, an Army colonel, then volunteered his purely personal opinion that they might not be as effective as the Air Force expected.

The military were questioned knowledgeably on the point by several civilians, and then the discussion returned to the sugar quotas and to land reform. Campbell's stenographer walked over to the door and turned on the lights. A vicious winter rain was beating on the windows above and behind the leather couch. Campbell listened impassively, patiently.

In the course of every meeting, Worth Campbell knew, there comes a time when impatience and even boredom induce tractability. Decisions that might earlier be deplored will now be accepted by men who are tired, have engagements, want to pee, or are incipient alcoholics. That time would come soon. Presently he suggested that it was time "to redefine the issue." To what extent, he asked, could we exclude the danger of a Communist take-over if we gave Miró all-out backing. The Ambassador and Bill O'Donnell both protested that this was not the issue. The issue was whether Miró was a reasonable risk. Campbell asked, with almost deliberate gentleness, if, where Communism was concerned, it wasn't a good principle to try to minimize risk. He would welcome an indication of dissent. Heads nodded in general approval. Campbell then asked if this could be taken as agreement, in principle, that they should continue the present policy of watchful waiting. He would welcome a preliminary indication of feeling. Who disagreed? People looked rather uneasily at the Ambassador and Bill O'Donnell who, with the man from the Sugar Policy Staff, were the only ones immediately to indicate opposition. All held up their hands. However, after a moment they were joined by one of Bill O'Donnell's boys, a man from the Bureau of Intelligence and Research, and, more ambiguously, by one of the men from CIA. He put up his hand and then, after a glance around the room and at his colleague, took it down again. There was a more stalwart dissenting vote from one of the officers from the office of the Assistant Secretary of Defense. Captain González's initiative had not been entirely without effect. The man from Agriculture insisted on explaining his vote. Watchful waiting was a policy of inaction; he was, he said, by nature a man of action. The Ambassador asked Campbell to put the question affirmatively: How many thought it would be wise to support the Miró Administration now that we had six months' experience with it? Campbell said he thought everyone would perhaps agree that there had been a fairly full and free chance for expression of opinion ending with a vote on the policy as presently defined. He ignored a request from O'Donnell that he ask how many had no position, and several present looked at O'Donnell with mild hostility. Campbell then said he did not wish to rush matters, but perhaps they should get down to work on the piece of paper. There are many kinds of managed democracy.

Numerous suggestions were now forthcoming on how to clarify the language, sharpen the dialogue, be more constructive, emphasize the essential point, avoid being "quite so categorical on matters where we cannot be entirely sure" and on how "to leave ourselves a little avenue of escape without hedging the point unduly." The man from Commerce asked for insertion of a sentence stressing the importance of "a free flow of private trade and capital regardless of what government we might be backing." The Assistant Secretary listened attentively to all these suggestions and asked Symes Jones to see that they were fully considered. The Ambassador to OAS asked if it could be made clear that the decision against supporting Miró — as he took it to be — was not unanimous. Worth Campbell replied: "Of course, sir. There is no coercion here." From time to time a man excused himself and looking at his watch or frowning hurried away. Presently the meeting came to an end.

The Ambassador and O'Donnell were unhappy but not surprised. Dr. Richard Williams Kent was merely unhappy. He hadn't enjoyed the meeting for, in spite of himself, he had kept going over his speech about Roberto Ryan. And he hadn't been asked to say a word. At dinner that evening even his wife noticed that he seemed depressed.

Before I left Washington for India in 1961, President Kennedy asked me to write him occasionally and tell him what an ambassador does. Quite possibly I took this request more seriously than he intended; in any case, at frequent though irregular intervals, I told him of what I was doing in India, and of my anxieties and instinct for reform on Vietnam, Laos, Berlin, and also domestic tax reduction which I opposed. I tried to avoid tedium in these; there is certainly competition for the President's eye.

*T*his paragraph is from Galbraith's introduction to his *Ambassador's Journal and appears in context in the following pages. It provides a basis for our choice of the passages selected from the Journal. These letters to Kennedy fulfill the assignment. They record a world of crisis, war, and social trivia, of imperial privilege, backstage scramble and dusty detail. They range over questions of national welfare and administrative policy. For the President they must have provided an invaluable triangulating view, and nevertheless they read* curiously like letters home. They are concise, sure-footed, clear-headed, bold and imaginative, and yet there is a vitality and innocence that seems to come from another age. They speak to us from across the new frontier.

More than half of these "letters home" are therefore given here, along with some pages from Mrs. Galbraith's brief companion account of that Indian experience which was first published in the Atlantic Monthly and later reprinted in an appendix to this volume. It is mysteriously supplementary to Galbraith's account and leaves the reader sure that he has seen India through a stereoscope.

Two parts of the story are not included in Galbraith's letters from India. They are of course what happened at home before he left and after his return. Selections from the Journal here complete the story.

Regardless of our politics, few of us will deny the sense of waking in a dew-covered, apple-blossomed, May morning that came with the Inauguration of the New Frontier. Perhaps in retrospect the day, tarnished by heat and haze, did not quite fulfill the promise of that morning, and surely it did not have a happy ending. The day is nonetheless here as it should be—dawn to sudden dark. The letters seem like the records of a legendary court when there was time to keep a journal, invent McLandress and remember Iona Station. The whole glows like one of the Indian miniatures that Galbraith admired when he was Ambassador.

Not represented in this collection is yet another book which has its roots in Galbraith's Indian years. Written with the collaboration of M. S. Randawa and published in 1968, it was entitled Indian Painting. It was about the work of the miniaturists who came in search of work to the courts of the Indian princes. Though the miniatures record heroic scenes of medieval wealth and luxury, each would fit on a page of this book. They are brilliant and jewel-like, and their splendors linger even in today's India. On a two-year leave from Harvard, garbed in the implicit magnificence of a representative from a still greater nation, here was the clansman as Cinderella. In spite of all the humdrummery, Galbraith's backward view of those years, distilled by the lapse of time, must begin to look like one of those miniatures crowded with microscopic history, sparkling and rich and sad. Set in the hopes and disappointments of diplomacy, bounded by the Inauguration and the assassination, attested to in portions of no less than five books, that tiny picture hanging in the hall of memory must have an ever-deepening effect upon the work of the economist.

Ambassador's Journal

INTRODUCTION[1]

NOW I MUST give the reader some information on our personal
ménage and economy and some other details which will help in
understanding the pages that follow.

Our family at the time of our departure for India numbered six.
In addition to my wife, Catherine Atwater, usually called Kitty, we
had our three sons, Alan, twenty, at Harvard, Peter, ten, and James,
nine, who were in school in Cambridge and who continued at the
American International School in New Delhi, and Emily G. Wilson
who for twenty years, with authority backed by competence and
love, had managed our children, household, cooking and any number
of other matters associated with our existence. In New Delhi when
we arrived, the Ambassador's house on Ratendone Road, a modest-
size bungalow from the days of the British Raj, was much too small
to hold all this family. Accordingly, Emily and the two younger boys
lived in half of another house down the street. Alan, after an initial
summer in India, returned to Harvard. A year and a half later we
were all able to house ourselves in the new Residence designed by
Edward Durell Stone immediately adjacent to the Chancery, also and
even more famously of his design.

Our houses required a remarkably ample staff for their operation —
bearer, which in India roughly is a butler, assistant bearers, cook and
assistant cooks, sweepers, gardeners, guards, drivers, laundrymen and
more. Some were on the payroll of the Embassy, some were charged to
the Ambassador, and the basis for this financially interesting distinction was never clear. Except where food was involved, all were toler-

[1] Introduction to *Ambassador's Journal: A Personal Account of the Kennedy Years*
(London: Hamish Hamilton, 1969), pp. xvii–xx.

[327]

ably efficient. The Indian-style food which was usually, although not exclusively, served at receptions was not bad. Food prepared in European style was uniquely inedible. Our principal predecessors in office had been, in order, Chester Bowles, John Sherman Cooper and Ellsworth Bunker. Between these civilized men and their even more remarkable wives and the household staff, there had been a deep bond of respect and affection. Few inheritances could have been more important in easing our life in our new and exotic land and occupation.

New Delhi has, roughly speaking, three seasons. From October to March, the days are sunny and warm, the nights cool. Around Christmastime, a fire is welcome and even necessary. From April through June, it is hot beyond belief — a dry searing heat that led Kipling to speak of a pile of sand under a burning glass. From June to September, it rains — not steadily but recurrently and often for two or three days at a time. While it is raining, it is moderately cool; when the rain stops, it is hot and humid. This disquisition is necessary for, although American and Indian officials live and work in air conditioning, it is impossible to write about India without mentioning the weather. In this journal, it compels comment as it did in Scott's account of his journey to the South Pole and for the same reason.

An embassy is rather like a state government — it is organized to function with good leadership, in the absence of leadership and in spite of it. The New Delhi Mission staff was very good. It had been selected with discrimination by my predecessors, and India is not the type of place where the time-serving, socially ambitious or John O'Hara type of officer aims to be. To go there he must have something in mind. The Ambassador in New Delhi operates from a large, light, pleasant office in the New Stone Chancery. Most business was done not at the desk but around a low coffee table on which there was always a bowl of flowers selected and arranged with great chromatic and geometric precision. There is no view from the windows because Edward Stone's screen surrounds the building. Could one look out, it would be to the Chinese Embassy on one side, the British across and the Soviet Embassy on the other side. Office work is conducted with only the rarest recourse to the telephone. Washington does not call because when it is noon in Washington it is midnight in New Delhi, give or take an hour or so, and the line is not secure. And the local system, though good, is not extensive. Also for the reason that few people in Washington ring up the President, so in New Delhi there is a certain reluctance in ringing up the American Ambassador. Rank or anyhow formal grandeur has its advantages.

The most important man in an Embassy, not excluding the Ambassador, is often the Deputy Chief of Mission, as these pages suggest. He deputizes for the Ambassador, provides professional continuity, directs subordinate officers and, with suitable tact, tells his superior what he should do. Benson E. L. (Lane) Timmons, my D.C.M. during nearly all of my tour, had an office interconnecting with mine through a lavatory. The Political Counselor of the Embassy supervises and keeps track of all relations with the government to which the Ambassador is accredited. In New Delhi, an Economic Minister combined general supervision of economic questions with administration of the AID program. Other counselors and attachés and their staffs — commercial, consular, press, agricultural, scientific and military — deal with their special subjects and, on occasion, have trouble keeping busy. In New Delhi, the Air and Naval Attachés, out of the infinitely greater wealth of the Pentagon, possessed planes and provided transportation for the Ambassador. Two secretaries of extraordinary competence, Aloha Baguley and Helen Eisenman, presided over the Ambassador's outer office, and I think of them with affection. One of Helen Eisenman's extracurricular assignments was to type this journal. She always said she enjoyed it and even if she didn't, it was good of her to say so. A young Foreign Service Officer is always assigned to the Ambassador as his personal assistant on everything from planning travel to purchasing newspapers. It is a job that must cause a great many young men to think again about their choice of career. The United States Marine Corps, as most must know, provides a guard detachment for our Missions abroad. Its members also with ferocious enthusiasm inspect offices to make sure that no one has left any classified papers on top of his desk.

In Washington, Indian matters were handled or otherwise by a hierarchy of officials. At the top, below the Secretary, was the Chief of the Bureau of Middle East and South Asian Affairs, in my time the unstalwart Talbot whose frightened retreat from liberalism to the Cold War is adequately chronicled in the pages that follow. An officer embracing the South Asian countries of India, Pakistan, Ceylon and Nepal was next below, and one or two further rungs down was a harried man who was called the India Desk Officer. With exceptions, these lesser officers were hard-working, informed and capable. That their resulting performance left something to be desired they would, with suitable discretion, concede. The State Department, to a remarkable degree, is the sum of less than its parts.

I have identified nearly everyone whose name appears in this journal. Americans need to be reminded as to who even quite famous Indians are and what they do. I've assumed the converse even as regards Robert McNamara.

Bachelors can be ambassadors. Perhaps once it was an advantage, given the diverse forms of persuasion that were held to be used. In New Delhi, it would have been inconceivable. The household, entertainment, a wide range of protocol activities, concern for the problems of the American community, association with wives and families of my Indian and diplomatic associates, cultivation of the arts and representation of the Ambassador at a succession of functions during my absence were all accomplished by my wife. She even found time to learn Hindi to the point of making a quite acceptable speech in the language. There is little about this in the present diary for, in truth, I knew little about it — I was rather astonished at the scope of her activities when she recounted them in an article in *The Atlantic Monthly* of May 1963. It would be wrong, therefore, for anyone to assume that, as regards all an Ambassador and his family do, this journal is complete.

John Kenneth Galbraith
Newfame, Vermonth
Summer 1968

BEFORE THE CURTAIN[2]

December 17 — Cambridge
A letter dated December 10 from J.F.K. arrived and proposed that I come to Florida. It had taken eight days from Washington to Cambridge. An earlier letter also took eight days and led me to suggest to J.F.K. that the Post Office was a key sport in his administration. (He later cited this time lag in appointing Ed Day the new Postmaster General.)

December 24 — Cambridge
Yesterday I went to Palm Beach. I went to New York the night before, on to Florida on the ten o'clock jet and arrived (slightly late) about one o'clock. I taxied over to the Kennedy house and on the way heard a call on the cab radio for a cab to go to that address to

[2] Chapter I, "Before the Curtain," *Ambassador's Journal*, pp. 5–14.

pick up "a Mr. Heller." That told me Walter Heller's appointment to the Council of Economic Advisers must have gone through. I am much pleased for, with others, I have urged him for the post.

The house, a long, white, vaguely Spanish and not unhandsome structure designed by Mizner, fronts directly on the ocean. One enters from the street. After being duly checked by the Secret Service, I found the President-elect with Mr. Joseph P. Kennedy and J.B.K. in the living room. We had a drink together and then Jackie disappeared. She was not feeling well but was much pleased by some books that I had brought her — a couple of volumes of about-to-be-published verse from Houghton Mifflin. I had also collected some history volumes and novels for J.F.K. He was attracted by a volume by J. H. Plumb on Walpole, but I don't suppose he will have time to do much aimless reading in the near future.[3] We had lunch on the terrace, talked, and then I had a nap while the President-elect and his father played golf. Then I went for a walk on the ocean side and talked with a Secret Service man who was studying marine biology. He was examining beach crabs with the field glasses he had with him to spot approaching assassins. Then I met Caroline and the baby and talked further with J.F.K. We were joined by Bob and Ethel for a family dinner. Thereafter I talked again with the President-elect and at midnight was driven back to the airport. I was somewhat tired and more so when I got to Boston at breakfast time.

We refought the election — J.F.K. is not persuaded that being a Catholic was an advantage. Nixon was less alert, less effective than he had expected. And he was also less willing to take risks; thus he sat out the jailing of Martin Luther King while J.F.K. called Mrs. King to express sympathy, and Bob called the judge. Incidentally, the brothers acted individually; neither knew what the other was doing. J.F.K.: "The finest strategies are usually the result of accidents." Bob shares my view that Henry Cabot Lodge's[4] faux pas — the offer of a cabinet position to a Negro in Harlem, its withdrawal the next day in Virginia — was one of the classic errors of politics. If one is wrong on some vital questions of foreign policy, the opposition must still explain why it is an error. But no citizen is so benighted that he could not see that this was stupid. And it was equally damaging in both the North and the South which takes skill. Bob Kennedy thought that Nixon was saved from serious trouble over his brother's

---

[3] J.B.K., writing to thank me for the poetry a few days later, said that her husband had finished it the same night.

[4] Nixon's Vice-Presidential running mate.

involvement with Howard Hughes — a big loan on a not very valuable corner covered by a service station — only because he had a generally sympathetic and hence not very penetrating press. I received credit for raising the alarm signals over New Jersey a few days before the election.[5] J.F.K. thought his only serious mistake was in not spending more time in California and less in New York when it became clear that New York was certain. I urged my final view — that he was the only Democrat who could have won and Nixon the only Republican who could have lost.

Our talks during the day ranged over a great number of matters. The problem of filling the subordinate positions in the Federal Executive is appalling. Several hundred important and fairly influential jobs must be filled within the next few weeks if the Government is to function effectively. J.F.K. thinks there must be some better way. "I must make the appointments now; a year hence I will know who I really want to appoint."

He obviously devoted a great amount of time to thought and discussion of cabinetmaking, and this is reflected in his choices. Bill Fulbright,[6] incidentally, was his primary choice for State although he is well pleased by Rusk. Bob talked him out of appointing Fulbright — the objection of Negroes and the use that the Russians might make of the appointment being, in his view, decisive. One of the leading candidates for Agriculture — Fred Heinkel of Missouri — destroyed himself by his interview. He slumped down in a chair, and when J.F.K. asked him what he would do about overproduction, he replied, "That is a terrible problem. I suppose we shall just have to give it away abroad." I had predicted this general reaction to Heinkel, who is a very good farm leader, to Sargent Shriver.[7] Orville Freeman[8] is much more Kennedy's type. He asked especially that I work with Freeman during the next few weeks.

On the issue of economic recession and a tax cut, I urged that needed public expenditures be pressed first as an anti-recession measure. Thereafter, if unemployment was still high, taxes could be re-

[5] As the result of campaigning in northern New Jersey, I concluded that the state, contrary to assumption, was far from safe. Kennedy thereupon scheduled a further visit.
[6] Then, as at this writing, Chairman of the Senate Foreign Relations Committee.
[7] Brother-in-law of the President, the first Director of the Peace Corps and then, concurrently, Director of the Office of Economic Opportunity. At the time of writing, he is Ambassador to France.
[8] Then Secretary-designate of Agriculture, after being defeated by a narrow margin for reelection as Governor of Minnesota.

duced. I believe J.F.K. agrees. He faces trouble with William McChesney Martin, Jr., Chariman of the Federal Reserve, and dislikes the prospect of a fight with him — which he thinks may be inevitable. Martin has been in office for a long time and, in his chosen sphere, obviously regards himself as superior to the President. It is the old notion that money gives a man position above politics and that banking, like the judiciary, is a separate power. I doubt, however, that in a showdown the President would be without resources. I would rather welcome this row were I in the White House.

In the last eight years, the Eisenhower Administration has swept problems under the rug. Now they must have attention. But, one senses, our liberal friends have not got down to hard cases — to what should be done about wage-price stabilization, foreign aid, disarmament, Far Eastern policy and a dozen other matters. The various New Frontier papers being prepared for the Administration are vague and unspecific. Not much is in tight, programmatic form that can be submitted to Congress. J.F.K. says at the moment his only major new idea is the Peace Corps. "If Scotty Reston[9] finds out that this is all there is on the New Frontier, he will write quite a story." Some hard work must obviously be done in these next few weeks.

On India, he asked me if I were happy. I told him entirely so. He then proposed letting it stand for a while—certainly until after the Inauguration—while I pitched in on more current matters. I agreed and told him before leaving in the evening that if these continued to be pressing, he could count on me for as long as I was needed. "I can give help on a new AID program from Cambridge but not from New Delhi." I did tell him that I was averse to a desk job in Washington.

J.F.K. is functioning as President-elect from a small library off the living room of the Palm Beach house — a chintz and bookish office about fifteen feet square. He was putting in his own long distance calls and giving a credit card number. Once he looked for a letter from Harold Macmillan to show me; he was struck by its elegance, information and style. It could not be found, and I suggested that after he became President, he might want to have a special filing cabinet for communications from other heads of state. He said the idea was constructive and hazarded the guess that Caroline had walked off with this one.

Eisenhower was pleasant at the time of J.F.K.'s visit early this

[9] James Reston, then chief Washington correspondent for the New York Times.

month. There were no papers on his desk, and J.F.K. asked him what he did with them after he had read them. He was sorry he asked, for Ike seemed embarrassed. Eisenhower said that Adenauer was an oriental figure, and he had some similar characterization for de Gaulle. He told Kennedy he would refrain from criticizing him except in the event of fiscal irresponsibility or the recognition of Red China.

December 30 — St. Paul

This morning I pulled myself out of bed after only a few hours sleep — a dreary meeting of the Executive Committee of the American Economic Association had lasted until after midnight — and caught a plane to St. Paul–Minneapolis. After hedge-hopping stops at Des Moines, Waterloo and Rochester, I arrived a little before noon and was picked up by Governor Freeman's car and taken to the Capitol. Freeman's office was full of the disorder and confusion of last-minute packing. Some of the files, I noticed, were going into empty whiskey cartons.

I had been asked by J.F.K. at Palm Beach to go out and have a talk with Freeman — he was uncertain of Freeman's ideas on agriculture but knew something of mine. Freeeman and I talked for several hours—the general farm program, the organization of the USDA,[10] the people and who would be loyal to the Secretary and who primarily to themselves, the possibility of hanky-panky in the commodity stabilization operations and a dozen other matters.

Freeman is enormously able, very enthusiastic about the job and still unaware of what he had ahead of him. The misfortune of a defeated politician is that his field of choice narrows so drastically. So poor bastard, he may have to be a Secretary of Agriculture.

The trouble with this post is not that the problem is beyond solution. With strong action — firm controls, cross-compliance so that controls on one crop do not shove farmers into another, production payments as the basic technique of support and a few other steps — the farm problem would disappear. But there is well-dug-in opposition to every one of these steps. If one takes account of this opposition, he will end up doing nothing. Freeman sees this clearly enough.[11]

Toward the end of the afternoon, we drove out to a beautiful house of some friends — the Jacobsons — overlooking a lake. The latter is

10 United States Department of Agriculture.
11 And to a remarkable extent he overcame the opposition and solved the farm surplus problem as for thirty years it had been known.

called Lake Farquar which Freeman explained was an Indian name. I told him I assumed that he had lost the Scottish vote. There we discussed a few novelties. I think better nutrition should be a part of Robert Kennedy's fitness program (something on which he had dwelt at Palm Beach.) Surely no youngster should play touch football on a diet of beans and prunes. Why shouldn't a food allotment be a standard supplement to unemployment compensation?

In the late afternoon, a State highway patrolman drove me back to the airport. He has been driving the Governor for years. Now, he told me, he faces a return to the force or the risks of a new post in Washington. We always reflect on how the fortunes of politics affect the life of the first man. The change and uncertainty is much greater for those below.

The trip back was shortened by fewer stops and total weariness. On the way up, I had concentrated on the adventures of Arabella Trefoil and Senator Gotobed. On the way back, even this mental effort was far too great.

January 9, 1961 — Cambridge
The President-elect was here today, and I am reported as having been closeted with him. In fact, I did not see him. However, I learned from one of his aides that the Indian Government has given its *agrément* to my appointment with much enthusiasm. (This could not have been true unless by most informal query.) This is very amusing. A fortnight ago, I dropped a pleasant note to Dean Rusk congratulating him on his appointment and saying, anent the rumors of my going to India, that perhaps a word might go to Ellsworth Bunker. He has been a good and loyal servant; I had heard that Rusk wanted to keep him in the Department; he might be told what was pending but that the rumors portended no immediate change. I got back a very stiffly worded letter from Rusk saying that he had asked the people around Kennedy to talk less about the ambassadorial posts, that only a president and not a president-elect could ask for the *agrément* of the government to which the ambassador would be accredited, and that none of this had any reflection on my abilities. I dictated a rather nasty retort, saying I did not need instruction on these matters, especially from one who had not shared perceptibly in the effort that elected Kennedy, and that I was not seeking the place. Eventually I was persuaded not to send it. Or rather I compromised on a less tart version. But now, evidently, the Indian Government

has been sounded out — if not formally asked. Anyhow, Reuters has carried the story from New Delhi, and I have been receiving cables of congratulation.

One of the few people in the United States who can think about foreign policy — and not merely reflect what isn't necessarily so — is Walt Rostow.[12] He had been promised, more or less, that he would be Assistant Secretary of State for Policy Planning. Now Rusk wishes to put George McGhee[13] in the job. George is an old friend of mine and was in the Truman State Department as Ambassador to Turkey. His qualifications as a planner are somewhat exiguous. Walt is upset. However, he had a very good breakfast with the President-elect today and has been promised a useful role.[14]

January 10 — Cambridge

The *Globe* yesterday ran my picture as the next Ambassador to India. Theodore Sorensen[15] asked me to give him a hand on domestic matters "until your appointment is confirmed." I have decided to stop being enigmatic, inscrutable or coy and admit it all.

I have been wondering what to do about Harvard. It is a trifle disconcerting to give up a lifetime post, and we all like life in Cambridge. My first thought was to ask for a leave of absence. But that is limited to two years, and I couldn't promise absolutely to be back in that time. And there is something cowardly in trying to protect oneself against every eventuality. The university professor who thinks deeply of how to secure his own future regularly ends up thinking of nothing else. So I have decided to resign and tell President Pusey that if I am not worth rehiring, I shouldn't have been kept in the absence of an ambassadorship. The courage required is not so enormous. If not Harvard, there is M.I.T., Tufts, Fletcher, Brandeis, Wellesley and possibly Shady Hill. If I do not teach, I could write more. And we probably have enough money so I would not be reduced to trade. Having made the decision to resign, I feel rather good about it.[16]

12 Not, in later times on Vietnam, a man whose views enlisted my sympathy.
13 He became head of the Policy Planning Staff, subsequently Undersecretary of State, then Ambassador to the Federal Republic of Germany.
14 He was taken into the White House on Bundy's staff, went later to State as Chief of the Policy Planning Council where he made peace with Rusk, and was brought back to the White House by President Johnson as an adviser on National Security Affairs.
15 Special Counsel to President Kennedy.
16 Later, after all this, I did find myself much more reluctant to resign and obtained a leave of absence.

January 11 — Cambridge

This morning at 9:30 A.M., I visited Mr. Pusey to tell him that, in the event of being offered the post in India — which I said I deemed likely — I planned to resign. He received the news with great equanimity and said that he hoped it might be early in the term so there would be a minimum of academic disturbance. (The interview, the only one I have ever had with him, took about five minutes.) I am a little comforted by the greater regret of my colleagues. Alex Gerschenkron[17] called me this evening much distressed and tried to persuade me to ask for a leave of absence. I stood fast.

A university, in our society, acts as a prop to the individual. As a member of the university community, he is much; divorced from it, he is on his own and maybe much less. So resignation seems a remarkably formidable step. But if one has strength in his own right, he does not need the crutch. I hope that is my situation. I am susceptible to doubts, however. On occasion in these last days, I have wondered if I have been reckless.

January 18 — Washington

There was a long and interesting meeting last evening at David Bell's[18] office in the Old State Building — Douglas Dillon,[19] Joe Fowler,[20] Ted Sorensen,[21] George Ball,[22] Walter Heller,[23] James Tobin[24] — to consider the Economic Report of the President. This must go up to the Congress early in February. The notion is to use it to spell out rather specifically the legislative program of the new session.

The discussion was dominated — too much I thought — by the problem of gold outflow. It is a symptom rather than a cause. If we can remedy the present shortcomings in the balance of payments, we will, of course, have no gold problem. Otherwise gold outflows will continue. Elementary since Adam Smith. Jim Tobin and Douglas Dillon pressed the case for legislation to reduce the reserve require-

[17] Professor of Economics at Harvard and longtime friend.
[18] The newly designated Director of the Bureau of the Budget.
[19] Secretary-designate of the Treasury.
[20] Henry H. Fowler, Undersecretary-designate of the Treasury.
[21] See page 336.
[22] Undersecretary-designate of State for Economic Affairs and close personal friend. He later very briefly became Ambassador to the United Nations.
[23] See page 331.
[24] Professor of Economics at Yale and a newly designated member of the Council of Economic Advisers.

ment — the gold coverage of the currency. I argued strongly against. The new administration would be thought to be tampering with the currency in a most alarming way. No one could explain otherwise. The gold outflow would increase. And the reform itself was not fundamental. I was joined by George Ball and others, and in the end the proposal was more or less shelved.

I am undertaking to second Ted Sorensen on the problem and will help with the drafting. Immediately I am going to pursue the agricultural, labor and defense aspects of the message.

THE BEGINNING[25]

January 22 — Washington
The Inaugural, the equivalent of a four-day carnival, is now over. Kitty came down and we housed ourselves with the George Balls. At first, I struggled against increasingly hopeless odds to get Commerce, Agriculture and Labor to work on their proposals for the economic message. The new cabinet members, with the singular exception of Arthur Goldberg,[26] were highly unclear about what they wanted to do. So were their next men. One could not bypass them to deal with the permanent civil service, for the latter wished guidance from their new bosses or thought it polite to ask. In the end I decided that more time would simply be required for the message and concentrated instead on the festivities. One minor problem was that everyone was moving, hard to reach on the telephone and impossible to find at home.

On Wednesday night (January 18), at J.F.K.'s request, I went to the Hill to see the final draft of the Inaugural Address. (I had written a draft which I had taken to Palm Beach and turned in a revision when J.F.K. visited Cambridge.) I was late and dashed through the Kennedy office to Ted Sorensen's, shouldering a pleasant, rather chubby man somewhat perfunctorily aside. He introduced himself, rather apologetically, as the new Senator from Massachusetts.

The address bore little resemblance to my contributions although some of the language and tone survived. It was short, economical of words and said something. My phrases about aid to the under-

25 Chapter II, "The Beginning," *Ambassador's Journal*, pp. 15–18.
26 Secretary of Labor — later, of course, Supreme Court Justice and Ambassador to the United Nations.

developed lands being given "not to defeat communism, not to win votes, but because it is right" survived as did my suggestion that we should never negotiate out of fear but never fear to negotiate. In going over it, I added the sentence, "Let us begin" at one point to give proper cadence, and a day or two later it was mildly historic. A low score but not completely negligible. A ghost-writer is like an unloved dog in a poor family. He must be content with scraps. The Kennedy-Sorensen draft, though less daring, was probably a lot wiser than mine. I made a number of suggestions, mostly cosmetic, though I urged the elimination of a mildly hectoring tone toward the allies and the poor countries. These were accepted with the exception of a line about those who mount the tiger ending up inside. I thought it out of tune. Others differed.

There must have been a party that night, but I forget where. The next day I worked, against the handicap of a frightful headache, until early afternoon and then went home and to bed. Before going, I responded to the depression of the scene and my head by writing out a draft letter withdrawing my name from consideration as Ambassador. I couldn't believe I wanted it; during the day, the new Secretary of State was cited as resenting all the political appointments.

On the night before the Inaugural came a thick snowstorm. In 1933 when Roosevelt was inaugurated, all the banks were inoperative. In 1961, it was the automobiles. The New Frontier began, most appropriately, with the greatest traffic jam in human history. We made our way around Georgetown on foot and were among the few to arrive at parties on time. The Kennedys were snowbound and failed entirely to arrive at a party at Philip Graham's.[27] We were there for a while, then went on to dinner with Chester Bowles. Chet was much upset at the newspaper reporting on Senate questioning on where he stood on recognizing Red China. The *Star* had him opposing; the *Post* advocating. I told him I thought it showed considerable skill.

Inauguration Day was bright, clear and very cold. My wife and I were covered from dawn to dark by a television team. They were doing a documentary on the events as seen through our eyes. Nothing could have added more to our status than the cameras. The television people also provided us with a car and chauffeur so they could record our observations.

Our seats were just close enough to the podium so that we could

[27] Philip L. Graham, publisher of the *Washington Post*.

not see the proceedings. The prayers were of exceptional length, especially that of the Cardinal[28] who began by exhorting God and ended by instructing Him. John Steinbeck, who accompanied us, claimed afterward that he had a conversation with the Almighty who said, "I hadn't realized there was anything much going on in the United States until around noon, and then I received one hell of a blast." The Inaugural speech was well received.

It took a couple of hours to get uptown, and we missed the early part of the parade. The rest was tedious. Each state had a governor, a stereotyped football band with drum majorettes, a hideous float and a National Guard, police or other marching unit. All looked alike; none took my mind off the bitter cold. We had fine seats in front of the White House. But we were still cold. About four we went to the Bowleses' for drinks and on to a number of other parties ending up around eleven at the Inaugural Ball in the Armory. To reach the latter, we walked the last half-dozen blocks; those who didn't were confined to their cars for upwards of two hours.

The ball was a vast conclave of seeming strangers whom, it turned out, one mostly knew. Most of the men were in tails; the women were mostly overdressed. No one did much dancing. However, our television team attracted the attention of other cameras, and we were challenged to perform. I felt, and I think looked, fairly muscle-bound. In a singularly uninspiring ceremony, the members of the Cabinet and their wives walked across the dance floor in the direction of the Kennedy box. It proved that all could walk. Stevenson received the most applause. By a combination of walking and riding, we arrived home about 4 A.M. At the ball, Mac Bundy urged me to go to India — and swallow my pride re Rusk.

Saturday, I was briefed formally on India in the morning and then went to a fine luncheon party at Phil Stern's[29] in Alexandria. There I learned that Bowles had taken literally my withdrawal and had removed my name from the ambassadorial list. Thomas Farmer had then intervened to have it restored. More afternoon parties and then an all-night costume party by Marie Ridder and Scotty Lanahan[30] in McLean, Virginia, near the CIA. All the liberal establish-

[28] Richard Cardinal Cushing of Boston.
[29] Philip M. Stern, economist and author, was on Stevenson's staff in 1952 and was about to join the State Department as Deputy Assistant Secretary for Public Affairs. He did not long remain on companionable terms with Dean Rusk.
[30] Washington writers and newspaperwomen. Mrs. Lanahan, now Mrs. Clinton Grove Smith, an accomplished writer, is the daughter of F. Scott Fitzgerald.

ment was present without exception. (I wore my kilt. Dining in Georgetown beforehand we heard someone say, "It's what you can expect from now on.") Sunday, we talked more about ambassadorial life with the Penfields[31] and came home to a dinner party in Cambridge.

My principal impression of the week was the gaiety of the crowds. Everyone seems to be intensely pleased with both the Kennedys and themselves.

LETTERS TO PRESIDENT KENNEDY[32]

New Delhi, India
April 17, 1961

Dear Mr. President:

As I once told you, I think, I propose to revive the ancient and admirable custom of an occasional letter from the envoy if not to his sovereign at least to his sovereign source of authority.[33] Since, however, this practice could easily bitch up modern procedure (to borrow from the stately language of Metternich) I will avoid matters where I am in need of advice or action. These I will put in channels or, in high-level emergency, in a special letter. The present communications . . . will be modestly informative and conceivably entertaining and you can read them (or not read them) in the secure knowledge that you will neither encounter (nor miss) any crisis. If I have anything in mind it will be simply to let you see something of India and Asia and of its leaders and its problems through the eyes of your ambassador.

[31] James K. Penfield, a Foreign Service Officer, was one of the few old China hands to survive the mistake of predicting that the Communists would defeat Chiang Kai-shek. A distinguished and liberal man, I asked for him as my Deputy Chief of Mission. Possibly to prevent having two like-minded men in one place, the Department promptly made him Ambassador to Iceland.

[32] Taken from Chapter IV, "India at First," pp. 73–77; Chapter V, "Settling In," pp. 89–111; Chapter VII, "More Education," pp. 151–154; Chapter X, "Berlin, China, Laos, Kashmir," pp. 195–196; Chapter XVI, "Great Fun," pp. 341–344; Chapter XVII, "Mountain Journey," pp. 372–375; Chapter XVIII, "Interlude— Mostly Dull," pp. 393–397; Chapter XIX, "Aid Train," pp. 424–426; in *Ambassador's Journal*.

[33] This wording implies that the idea of the letters came from me. However, my memory is quite clear that the President proposed them — following, though I am less certain of this, some expression of doubt as to how an ambassador really employed himself.

We have been here now for a week. I have lunched or dined with all of my senior officers, had lengthy sessions on the various embassy enterprises — politics, economics, aid, USIS, labor, science and other — spoken to the staff, seen Nehru for a lengthy talk, called on the senior Foreign Office officials and encountered a few of my Indian friends. Some of this is legally a bit premature for I do not present my credentials for another day or two.

We were, of course, given an amiable welcome and the radio carried in full my remarks on arrival which, faithful to the fraud of modern communications, I recorded in Beirut and never gave at all. Some fifteen or twenty pounds of garlands were laid on in a manner that must have rejoiced the local florists. Our physical arrangements are enchanting. The residence, a one-time bungalow of the British raj, is small — only three bedrooms — and the principal wall decorations are some large gilt mirrors left behind possibly by Lord Curzon. Some of the furniture was discarded from the White House by Mrs. Warren G. Harding. But basically it is a charming house with a large loggia and a reach of thick green lawn, floral borders in violent color and great trees that are a constant delight. The staff is of alarming size but considerable competence, and the cook, while in no danger of being stolen by you, is anxious to please. Your new man may be better on sauces but cannot touch mine in reproducing the Taj Mahal in macaroons. The new Ed Stone Chancery is even more of a delight. Some complain that it is highly unfunctional — water fountains, water gardens and even a few ducks but no office space. You certainly can't please everyone.

The new Chancery is located in an uninviting stretch of terrain on the edge of town which has been set aside for embassies. It is flat, dusty and barren. The junior Americans and their Indian staff live in adjacent quarters with slight protection from sun, dust and heat. At this time of the year it is around 90 at midday but before long it will get warm. The Russian embassy and quarters are on one side; on the other side are the British. In both compounds the youngsters splash happily in swimming pools; one was once contemplated for ours but abandoned lest it seem un-American. I have asked for the development of plans. Most of the cost, I might add, will be paid for out of the abundant PL 480 counterpart so that your budget will suffer no more than from a very minor Nubian temple.[34]

[34] I had taken up with him, as had others, the matter of rescuing the Nubian monuments, including Abu Simbel, from the Nile waters rising behind the new Aswan Dam.

The size of the total staff — 300 Americans, 726 Indians —came to me rather as a shock. My preliminary impression is of well-mannered, competent and hard-working people of good morale. From my deputy, Edward Maffitt, I have had firm and courteous guidance and good judgment in the tradition of the true professional. Past experience of the staff with ambassadors has been favorable so it is favorably disposed toward us. We are, to be sure, expected to combine the best qualities of the Bowleses, the Coopers and the Bunkers but that ought to be easy. I am not quite sure where the line falls in this business between dignity and stuffiness. I shall try to combine decorum and discipline with a reasonably relaxed attitude toward rank but, of course, without descending to the raffish informality of the White House.

The senior officials of the Foreign Ministry are intelligent and on easy terms with the Embassy. Communications seem to involve a minimum of restraint. My first talk with Nehru was not quite so easy — I am not entirely at home in his presence and I rather wonder if anyone is. (A strong political leader is, I think, one who raises a certain moral threshold against disagreement.) He read your letter with obvious enjoyment (and later circulated it to his officials) and we talked for a bit about books, the number of bicycles as an index of progress, and other trivia. Then he turned to the Congo which is very much on his mind. His principal concern here was the delay in getting the troops from Dar-es-Salaam and getting out the Belgian and white irregulars. (Dayal and Timberlake came up but less centrally.) I have reported on all this to the Department. One general point struck me hard. The Indian Government feels that it has committed itself deeply with this contingent and is worried about it. The U.N. was faltering and is very important in Indian eyes and to Indian policy. The troops shored up the U.N. position, may well save it, but the domestic risks now seem more considerable.

We talked in Nehru's Parliament office — a smallish, rather shabby room, indifferently furnished, not far from the floor of Parliament. He is usually here when the House is sitting; this is an aspect of his determination to get parliamentary habits firmly fixed during his lifetime. The central Parliament functions at least as efficiently and equably as the Senate. In the provincial capitals, however, they throw things in their moments of truth. I could not see that Nehru had aged since I saw him last — about two years ago. His face is smooth and unlined and handsome. When I left, he asked that my new role not prevent me from continuing as an economic adviser to his government. I told him I hoped it wouldn't but that my voice might now be a trifle muted.

When I was first here in 1956, the tension between the United States and India — and between Americans and Indians — was evident, palpable. Three years later in 1959, things were much easier. Now I would sense a still further relaxation — it is necessary now that at least some members of the government remind themselves that they are neutral. Things being so I doubt that I can make much of a score.

In the next letter or so I will give you among other things some working impressions of the Indian economy — I must find out whether the Central Bank is maintaining its independence or could use Martin[35] and on some of the strength and weaknesses of Embassy operations.

Yours faithfully,
JOHN KENNETH GALBRAITH

THE PRESIDENT
THE WHITE HOUSE

•

New Delhi, India
April 27, 1961

Dear Mr. President:

The last week wasn't the best in the history of the frontier and I haven't found much comfort in contemplating your problems. However I think I can offer a word or two of cheer — and since you know how I felt about this adventure, as well as my mean tendencies, you won't imagine that I am glossing things over. New Delhi was, I imagine, the worst station. The papers had carried the full newspaper accounts of our Cuban involvement with all available exaggeration. There are lots of people here who love to make life difficult for us — and who think we have been doing too well these last two or three years. And, perhaps not less than the Latin Americans, the Indians see their protection (in particular to the North) in the principle of nonintervention. This attitude is a most important force in the unpowerful part of the world, where it is naturally regarded as a vital protection. The result was a bad setting and much pressure on Nehru to give us the business.

[35] William McChesney Martin, Jr. Currently, as before and since, there was much discussion of the independence of the Federal Reserve System and Martin's insistence thereon.

We did not escape unscathed but it was no disaster. I kept our explanations simple and short; there is nothing worse than windy arguments. At a press conference, which came as these damn things always do on the worst day, I repeated you and then contented myself with running over our history of alleged misdeameanors in undermining Cuban despots as seen by the latter from the complaints of Spain to the present. Castro I made merely the last troublesome chapter on the list.

As much by good luck as good management I saw Nehru almost every day during the business — once during a long family lunch at his house — and this helped take a great deal of the sting out of the situation. At the beginning he made a rather unhappy statement in the House. But he ended last Saturday with a speech minimizing our role, stressing that no Americans had been involved and citing a point that I had urged in our conversations, namely that 100,000 Cuban refugees were bound to cause us trouble. The episode is now over. Do keep it muted at the Washington end.

In the next few days I am going to write a detailed policy paper on how to balance prospective accomplishment and risk in matters of this sort and on the realities as distinct from the slogans of social revolution.[36] We must be more learned on these matters than we are. Would you have an eye out for these thoughts?

I am engaged, these days, in making my calls on the other ambassadors. This is an incredible waste of time. As you can imagine New Delhi is not the place where (say) Peru[37] sends its best man or the best man wants to come. Paris suits the Latin and Levantine temperament better and so does New York. One Levantine, who is accredited to a half dozen Asian governments, I suspect of being in the black market and possibly in the white slave trade. As a result he does seem rather more affluent than the common run. Many of the other diplomats obviously get along on a shoestring. They live in hideous houses decorated by some expressionist of the rural Nepal school. I do note one redeeming feature: the more underdeveloped the country the more overdeveloped the women. Still after meeting many of my diplomatic colleagues I think better of . . . conversations with Foster Furcolo.[38] Nehru suggested that I call on the big countries because of their vanity, the small ones because of their sensibility

[36] It never got written.
[37] A tactful reference, for Peru does not accredit an ambassador to India.
[38] Recently retired Governor of Massachusetts.

and omit those in between. However I shall struggle nobly on — for a while. Fulbright should know, incidentally, that the Soviet Ambassador next door, though he understands, does not speak . . . English.[39] He has given me five jars of caviar, and I have given him a copy of one of my books. I hope you do as well trading with Khrushchev.

I did pick up one useful bit of information yesterday. An Indian told me that when they recently played a game of ordinary or non-touch football with the Indonesians in Djarkarta, the latter got a medicine man to the stadium early in the morning to insure by incantation and other well-established techniques that the citizen-supporters of our friend Sukarno would win. I asked if it worked. My Indian friend replied, "Of course not. We had the better team and anyhow our astrologists had picked the day."

I am still looking into Embassy operations. Next week after welcoming Sarge,[40] I shall give you a view of this operation.

Faithfully,
JOHN KENNETH GALBRAITH

THE PRESIDENT
THE WHITE HOUSE

•

New Delhi, India
May 10, 1961

Dear Mr. President:

The last two weeks have been very busy, mostly over Laos. The ceasefire now seems firm. Thus I have my first diplomatic triumph. However, my satisfaction is slightly dimmed by the fact that at no point can I see the slightest relation between my stupendous effort and the result.

I have reached two conclusions as the result of my concern with Laos and the Congo. These jungle regimes, where the writ of government runs only as far as the airport, are going to be a hideous problem for us in the months ahead. . . . The rulers do not control or particularly influence their own people; and they neither have nor warrant their people's support. As a military ally the entire Laos nation is clearly inferior to a battalion of conscientious objectors

[39] Senator Fulbright had long insisted that American ambassadors be competent in the language of the country to which they were going.
[40] Sargent Shriver, Director of the Peace Corps, who was arriving to launch this activity in India.

from World War I. We get nothing from their support, and I must say I wonder what the Communists get. One answer, no doubt, is that the Communists will do a better job of organizing existing leaders out. Nevertheless I am convinced that in these primitive countries we cannot always back winners and we cannot be sure that the winners we back will stay on our side. For the same reason we should never assume that anyone is lost to the Communists. We must above all face the probability of gains and losses and certainly no single loss will be decisive. Most of all we must not allow ourselves or the country to imagine that gains or losses in these incoherent lands are the same as gains or losses in the organized world, that of France or Italy — or India.

A second thought I have been trying out provisionally on the Indian officials. It is that our friends must one day recognize that there has been a change in our attitude toward these regimes. In Dulles' day our efforts to save them from Communism did have elements of a holy crusade. Perhaps there was occasion then for some alarm over our (or rather Dulles') zeal. But we are getting more practical. Those who get alarmed over what we do need to ask themselves whether they would prefer total inaction. Would India be happy were we to wash our hands of Nepal, South Vietnam or the Congo? Would they wish that we were neutral too?

In spite of Laos and the ceremonial preoccupations of this task, I have begun to get a fair view of the operation of this Embassy. I doubt that you would wish to acquaint yourself with all features of all your Missions. But perhaps you should know about one. And India probably reveals the common strength and weaknesses with the further advantage that it is exceedingly important in itself.

With the exception of some [matters] . . . which do not lend themselves to these letters (but about which I will have much to say when I see you and others in June) the affairs of the Embassy can, like Gaul, and most everything else, be divided into three parts: (1) the traditional political, economic and administrative tasks of the Embassy proper; (2) the technical assistance and other economic aid functions; and (3) the United States Information Service. Two and Three, i.e., technical aid and USIS, are very important and very large — the largest, indeed, of any overseas headquarters.

The central Embassy staff, the whole show in your London youth, and including the political and economic ministers, counsellors and secretaries, are hard-working, competent and admirably committed to the interest of the United States without being humorlessly enslaved by any particular line or theology. They respect the Indians and are respected in turn. The political sophistication of the younger officers seems higher than when I knew the Service fifteen years ago. I am well pleased with this part of the enterprise.

The USIS runs libraries, publishes three or four magazines, distributes books, arranges exhibits, books American cultural enterprises and gets your speeches to the intellectually starving masses. It is a large operation; the current budget is $3,466,261. My impression of this is less happy. The people here are hardworking and dedicated. The various activities are conducted with reasonable efficiency. The libraries handle an enormous traffic. (At the end of the month the McGraw-Hill bakery magazine is grubby from its many avid readers.) What is missing is spirit or lift. The organization lacks excitement. Everyday tasks are not even very expertly done. The magazines and other publications are poorly written and edited with unattractive layouts and fairly dull material. Our upper middle-brow magazine is so far inferior to what the Poles distribute as to make one cry. (The latter very rarely mentions Communism and can even outstrip us on an article on ecclesiastical architecture.) The book presentation program for libraries has not, in the past, thought it wise to distribute your books or Schlesinger's or even very many of mine.

Much of the trouble is from the Washington support. You cannot imagine how bad this is. Each morning, over the air, comes the day's American story. I can no longer read it for simple reasons of health; five minutes of this wireless file and one loses his breakfast and cannot eat the rest of the day. In two weeks it caused me to lose twenty pounds and I have prescribed it for the Saudi Arabian Ambassador who is badly overweight. Apart from some useful speech texts it consists in equal parts of utterly irrelevant pieces about the progress of the grass silage industry, tedious and execrably written articles on the American economy (I attach today's thought which brilliantly likens the nation to a large corporation. You would have saved yourself trouble if you had held out for the Merchandise Mart[41] — or uninspired thoughts of the lesser members of the bureaucracy, or diatribes against Communism. The latter are perhaps the dreariest feature of all. I cannot read them without pausing to consider whether the Communists have something, and Murrow may well be turning me into a security risk. Lately I have been sending him samples of

[41] In Chicago. Owned by the Kennedy family.

this gaseous diffusion with a note of personal congratulation.[42]

I am going to need a new head of the USIS organization here. So far I have been shown only a worthy but broken-arch bureaucrat. Outsiders are opposed in the interest of upholding the merit system. I am puzzled as to why a merit system is important in the absence of merit, but you are President and will understand better. Or perhaps you could ask Larry O'Brien[43] to explain.

The technical assistance program, and related economic aid activities, also produce no cheering. In the old Dulles days, the Indian Government regarded the technical assistance activities — agriculture, public health, education and so forth — with considerable suspicion. It seemed an invasion of sovereignty, a possible cover for cold war penetration. And there was feeling that some of our experts we were sending were less than leaders in their chosen fields — a suspicion that was amply confirmed when at intervals some truly remarkable stumble-bums were off-loaded at the local airport. As a consequence of all this, whenever the Indian Government asked for help there was a great effort to respond — "at least they were asking us." No effort was made to fit the particular expert into a sense-making program or even to be sure that what he did made sense. And the Indians in turn subjected our talent to a scrutiny that regularly took and still takes months. So our technical assistance is a hit-and-miss affair, helping here and missing there, and maybe even doing occasional damage by diverting attention from first essentials. On the essentials, for example technical assistance to improve Indian agriculture, the effort is spread very, very thin — so thin that I cannot think it will have any appreciable impact before the Second or possibly the Third Coming. The experts range from very good and very skilled to indifferent. Vacancies remain unfilled for many months and by the time a man is cleared for appointment, if he is any good, he is no longer available. Quite a few experts still come for short tours of duty and afflict the Mission and the government with the divine

[42] The President, as I later learned, read this to Ed Murrow over the telephone in what Ed described as the most difficult single telephone call of his life. It pleased the President to imply that Murrow had written it personally. Presently the file diminished radically in size. Previously anything that might offend a right-wing congressman was deleted. Now anything that might offend me had also to go. Not much was left between.
[43] Special Assistant to President Kennedy for Congressional Relations and since then Postmaster General and manager of presidential election campaigns.

revelations of every newcomer to India. It may be debated in the matter of religion but no one seems to question the doctrine of immaculate conception where ideas on economic development are involved.

The leadership of the economic and technical aid program, if not inspired, seems sound. I have already asked for a thorough restudy of operation, and I have given my thoughts on needed reform. These include concentration of our energies on first essentials, the elimination of frills, and a clear indication to the Indian Government that we will henceforth provide assistance only when it is seriously wanted. This being so we will expect our judgment on people to be accepted and will undertake to ensure performance. This means we will have to provide people of first-rate ability.

Shriver was here last week and did exceedingly well. The Prime Minister liked him and he seems even to have charmed Krishna Menon[44] whom I sent him to visit. Krishna Menon is an odd and difficult character. But some small part of the problem, I think, is that the Republicans treated him with all the warmth and tact of a Brahmin encountering a leprous untouchable at his table. I am routing all visitors through K.M.'s office.

This includes Lyndon who arrives next week with two airplanes, a party of fifty, a communications unit, and other minor accoutrements of modern democracy. . . .

Faithfully,
JOHN KENNETH GALBRAITH

THE PRESIDENT
  THE WHITE HOUSE

•

New Delhi, India
July 11, 1961

Dear Mr. President:

I have been back about three weeks and from day to day I have been planning to pass along some thoughts on matters in Washington and here. I must say that the trip was reasonably exhausting with my time divided almost equally between asking for things that I needed and asking not to have things that I don't need. On occasion I am appalled at the money possessed by the United States Government for things that aren't necessary. A few more years and I could easily become as penurious as I learn you already are.

---

[44] Krishna Menon, then Indian Defense Minister and long a power in Indian public life, had a talent for harboring and generating suspicion. He played a highly controversial part in the mountain war with China in 1962.

Thus I have just successfully arrested a Commerce [Department] plan to send a high level trade commission to India — officials, businessmen, staff to spend several weeks touring India to acquaint the natives[45] with the virtues of American products. They do not sell, only expound. It was all but settled when I learned about it. I discover that there have been six such missions in the last six years. I learn further that the results of all have been nil or negative except as described by the participants or the unduly polite. The Indians operate a water-tight system of exchange control and import licenses, with our encouragement, to save dollars. However admirable American goods they cannot be bought without a license and licenses are available only to the extent that dollars are. Some dollars do get spent in other countries not because of ignorance but because our goods are too expensive. The cost of our goods incidentally is the major problem of our trade and our balance-of-payments. Ultimately it will be the major problem of our foreign policy for the latter costs a lot of money which we must earn.

I do discover that past missions have raised hopes in the minds of numerous Indian entrepreneurs that they might be allowed to import our gear grinders and garter belts — "The Americans must know what they are doing" — only to have their hopes dashed when they sought the licenses. So much for this. I cite it not for its importance but as an example of excessive affluence.

As you may have seen from my cables I discharged your commissions with Nehru on Berlin and testing and, I think, made some impression. More on testing than Berlin, I think. The press dust-up over a new China policy started just as I got back so I concluded that I had better postpone any talk with the Chinese (Com) Ambassador.[46] There is an off-chance that it might have become known with muddying effect. When it seems safe I will raise the matter.

From here the discussions over Berlin have an Alice-in-Wonderland quality which, sadly, I can only suppose is improved by distance. When I wonder about our ability to conduct a successful foreign policy, which is often, it is usually because of our tendency to take an issue and simplify it to the point of absurdity. The two favorite

---

[45] This usage, I should perhaps explain to Indian readers, bears no relation to nineteenth-century imperial language. It is an American slang form. "You were in Boston. How did you find the natives?"

[46] A proposal by the President that we open up a new channel of communication with Peking. For various reasons, the matter was not pursued. The "dust-up" refers to rumors that the Administration was moving to revise the China policy.

absurdities consist (1) in reducing all matters to a choice between whether we win or lose and (2) to whether we are hard or soft.

In Laos, for example, our problem has long been to escape from an impossible position with a certain amount of grace. Any escape will be good and one may still be possible. But according to the official simplifiers, we have already suffered an overwhelming loss. We never, so far as I can see, had a chance to win — not anyhow since we arrived. And if we are convinced we have lost I can't see how the Communists can fail to take the hint.

In the Berlin discussions the simplification is between hard and soft. Nothing could be more irrelevant. Were the Russians determined to have a war they could doubtless force one upon us. And similarly if we were so bent. So at some point we are both hard. There is no need to demonstrate this point for it is evident. Since the contingency is one which presumably we both seek to avoid the problem is to find a solution tolerable to us in between.

Those who talk about hard solutions divert all thought from solutions by asking only that we advertise our willingness to risk a deep thermonuclear burn. In their souls they know that this is an eventuality which a President cannot accept. And they always protect themselves with their public by saying that, of course, it won't really happen. So they happily exploit the antipathy toward the Russians, strike impressively heroic poses, feel personally secure nonetheless, and, when the inevitable bargain is struck, are free to condemn it as a defeat. It is only when one spells it out that one comes to realize how tactically unassailable are those who argue such tactics. I can't think that you find them very helpful.

This brings me to my suggestion of the day. In making appointments there are three qualifications which, in one way or another, rate a measure of consideration. These are *ability, political acceptability* and *personal loyalty.* It is my impression that in key positions you have put more or less the inevitable stress on political acceptability and that you have stressed ability at the expense of personal loyalty. I would not argue that ability is a wholly negligible asset. But it is often combined with a tendency to think of one's self first, one's agency second and the President last. In the end the best Roosevelt men were not the smartest but those who thought of F.D.R. first and themselves and their agencies second. Hopkins,[47] a man of second class wit, was a case in point . . .

[47] Harry L. Hopkins, chief aide to Roosevelt.

I suspect in these days it is almost as important to know what isn't serious as to know what is. The current flare-up in Pakistan of which you will be getting an earful strikes me as unserious. Kashmir is an involved and troublesome matter with no solution in sight but I think most of the present flare-up is political posturing.

On the other hand South Vietnam is exceedingly bad. I hope, incidentally, that your information from there is good and I have an uneasy feeling that what comes in regular channels is very bad. Unless I am mistaken Diem has alienated his people to a far greater extent than we allow ourselves to know. This is our old mistake. We take the ruler's word and that of our own people who have become committed to him. The opponents are thieves and bandits; the problem is to get the police. I am sure the problem in Vietnam is partly the means to preserve law and order. But I fear that we have one more government which, on present form, no one will support.

The monsoon has come and it is wet and almost cool. I am starting out next week to make a tour of the major cities and a few speeches. I am avoiding the Indo-American Societies, the Rotary Clubs and the other usual American forums to see if I can make some dent on the university audiences. These are influential and also rather suspicious.

Yours faithfully,
John Kenneth Galbraith

The President
The White House

•

New Delhi, India
August 26, 1961

Dear Mr. President:

I am a good deal worried about our negotiating position on admission of the Chinese Communists to the United Nations. I know as a politician rather than as a diplomat exactly how difficult this situation is and how difficult you know it to be. Indeed, some years ago I concluded that I would speak my mind on what I deemed to be inevitable and have had some experience of the consequences. I am not reacting now to the merits of the case but to the reputation and posture of the Administration and the United States.

The experts have cooked up a device which they think will keep the Chicoms[48] out for another year. This, as you certainly know, is to

---

[48] An offensive official usage for which I weep.

have Chinese representation made an "important question" which, if adopted by a majority vote, would make the decision to change from Formosa to Peking subject to a two-thirds majority vote. The tactic is patently transparent. Debate over whether it is an "imporant question" will straightaway become a debate on admission. We will have gone out on a limb for what seems to be a clever maneuver and will be defeated. At the meeting of the South Asian Ambassadors a fortnight ago not a soul thought we could promote a majority for exclusion. This morning Maffitt, my DCM, and I discussed the tactic with Desai at the Foreign Office. Since I could easily be considered a prejudiced party I let Maffitt carry the ball which he did very cleverly. He got nowhere. Desai simply said, "There would have to be a majority vote and it is our position that the seat belongs to the Chinese mainland." He was willing to consider charter revision as an interesting idea. But this tactic would greatly alarm me for it would give the Russians a hunting license on the office of Secretary-General.

As I say, I see no chance of lining up a majority. What seems to me inevitable is that we shall have a minority consisting of the more dubious figures in the world — Salazar,[49] Chiang,[50] Sarit.[51] We won't have Ayub.[52] The New Frontier will get credit only for continuing the Old Frontier policy with the difference that with us it failed. And even should we win, we will have the issue back with us again a year hence and an election to boot. There is no happy solution to this problem but wise men have long been told of the proper reaction to inevitable rape. I would urge that we take a passive attitude on the Chicoms, making a token vote against them but no impassioned pleas. Our prestige should not be put on the block. Then let us put our energies into keeping Formosa in the General Assembly. Here we are acting on behalf of an old ally and no one will doubt our good will. We might even get a majority for this although I confess to being uncertain about the precise legal procedures.

I have put all these matters in a pointed telegram to the State Department. The result was not entirely disappointing. It produced one of the rudest responses in the history of diplomacy.

Yours faithfully,

JOHN KENNETH GALBRAITH

[49] Then Prime Minister of Portugal.
[50] General Chiang Kai-Shek, then controlling China's United Nations seat from Taiwan.
[51] Then Prime Minister of Thailand.
[52] Then Prime Minister of Pakistan.

THE PRESIDENT
THE WHITE HOUSE

•

April 5, 1962

Dear Mr. President:

I have put in a lot of time the last three or four days on the scene
of my well-known guerrilla activities, namely, South Vietnam. This
included a long and most reassuring discussion with Bob McNamara.
We are in basic agreement on most matters and for the rest I think
Bob appreciated having some arguments from my side of the fence.
I also had two or three long discussions with Averell and the attached
memorandum, which is of no breathtaking novelty, comes close to reflecting our combined views. I think I can safely spare you another
eloquent restatement of what you have already heard from me several
times before. However, I do pray that in addition to reading the attached memorandum you see Governor Harriman at some early date.

I am leaving this afternoon for New York and tomorrow night for
India. There are no pressing Indian issues I need to cover with you.
Kashmir will continue to simmer. This is not the time for any brilliant
initiatives and the best we can do is to press both sides to keep their
behavior in low key and keep above the obscene politics ourselves. As
I told you attitudes on the Hill toward India seem mellower than I
had expected. I am coming back on a very brief private trip in early
June to get an honorary degree and make a speech. I will try and
give A.I.D. and India a lift before the Senate if, as Fulbright and
some others believe, it may then be needed.

Last, but not least, I must tell you how much I enjoyed the other
evening at Glen Ora, our survey of the problems of the nation and
the world, and the chance to reflect on the unique capacity of your
advisers to solve them.

Affectionately,
JOHN KENNETH GALBRAITH

THE PRESIDENT
THE WHITE HOUSE

•

April 4, 1962

MEMORANDUM FOR THE PRESIDENT
Subject: Vietnam

The following considerations influence our thinking on Vietnam:
1. We have a growing military commitment. This could expand

step by step into a major, long drawn-out, indecisive military involvement.

2. We are backing a weak and, on the record, ineffectual government and a leader who as a politician may be beyond the point of no return.

3. There is consequent danger we shall replace the French as the colonial force in the area and bleed as the French did.

4. The political effects of some of the measures which pacification requires, or is believed to require, including the concentration of population, relocation of villages, and the burning of old villages, may be damaging to those and especially to Westerns associated with it.

5. We fear that at some point in the involvement there will be a major political outburst about the new Korea and the new war into which the Democrats as so often before have precipitated us.

6. It seems at least possible that the Soviets are not particularly desirous of trouble in this part of the world and that our military reaction with the need to fall back on Chinese protection may be causing concern in Hanoi.

In the light of the foregoing we urge the following:

1. That it be our policy to keep open the door for political solution. We should welcome as a solution any broadly based non-Communist government that is free from external interference. It should have the requisites for internal law and order. We should not require that it be militarily identified with the United States.

2. We shall find it useful in achieving this result if we seize any good opportunity to involve other countries and world opinion in settlement and its guarantee. This is a useful exposure and pressure on the Communist bloc countries and a useful antidote for the argument that this is a private American military adventure.

3. We should measurably reduce our commitment to the particular leadership of the government of South Vietnam.

To accomplish the foregoing, we recommend the following specific steps:

1. In the next fortnight or so the I.C.C. will present a report which we are confidentially advised will accuse North Vietnam of subversion and the Government of Vietnam in conjunction with the United States of not notifying the introduction of men and material as prescribed by the Geneva accords. We should respond by asking the co-chairmen to initiate steps to re-establish compliance with the Geneva accords. Pending specific recommendations, which

might at some stage include a conference of signatories, we should demand a suspension of Vietcong activity and agree to a standstill on an introduction of men and material.

2. Additionally, Governor Harriman should be instructed to approach the Russians to express our concern about the increasingly dangerous situation that the Vietcong is forcing in Southeast Asia. They should be told of our determination not to let the Vietcong overthrow the present government while at the same time to look without relish on the dangers that this military build-up is causing in the area. The Soviets should be asked to ascertain whether Hanoi can and will call off the Vietcong activity in return for phased American withdrawal, liberalization in the trade relations between the two parts of the country and general and non-specific agreement to talk about reunification after some period of tranquility.

3. Alternatively, the Indians should be asked to make such an approach to Hanoi under the same terms of reference.

4. It must be recognized that our long-run position cannot involve an unconditional commitment to Diem. Our support is to non-Communist and progressively democratic government not to individuals. We cannot ourselves replace Diem. But we should be clear in our mind that almost any non-Communist change would probably be beneficial and this should be the guiding rule for our diplomatic representation in the area.

In the meantime policy should *continue* to be guided by the following:

1. We should resist all steps which commit American troops to combat action and impress upon all concerned the importance of keeping American forces out of actual combat commitment.

2. We should disassociate ourselves from action, however necessary, which seems to be directed at the villagers, such as the new concentration program. If the action is one that is peculiarly identified with Americans, such as defoliation, it should not be undertaken in the absence of most compelling reasons. Americans in their various roles should be as invisible as the situation permits.

•

Bombay, India
May 7, 1962

Dear Mr. President:

It is some time since you have had one of these reports, a gap to be related more or less equally to the state of my stomach, the pressure of other tasks including most recently the need to complete some travel before the heat here becomes unbearable, and the absence of any information for which, by my best assessment, you could have an incontrollable thirst.

I am writing from Bombay where I have just spent an hour or two with your Secretary of State. We had a useful and agreeable session. While I still do not find him the easy, confident, forth-coming, eclectic and commanding figure with which in my imagination I associate the diplomacy of the New Frontier, we get along much better than hitherto. This is partly because, in some indefinable way, our foreign policy does seem to me to show increasing evidence of thought. But as you are aware I grow mellower by the month.

My most recent major worry has been over testing[53] and the danger of a major anti-American explosion with some serious effect on fundamental public and political attitudes. However, we have come through all right. We are getting only a few strictly C.P.[54] demonstrations. The press, politicians and public are not aroused even in this congenial environment. Partly it is the general good management by the Kennedy Administration. We have managed to establish our reputation for good sense and restraint; we obviously responded to the Soviet initiative with reluctance; we have managed to keep in focus the simple fact that the Russians did it first.

I suspect also that this is the reward for a lot of patient and tedious effort. Clearly the government, press, students and pundits do not want to embarrass us on the issue. And one reason is that our cultivation of the universities and press, your unrewarding hours with Nehru last autumn, Jackie's visit and other efforts have persuaded the Indians that we are good people and they have no righteous obligation to embarrass us.

Incidentally, I hope the series will be run as rapidly through to conclusion as possible. Time deepens the effect and engages passions. I also strongly endorse the policy of the minimum of needful publicity and avoidance of comment on the destructive virtuosity of the gadgets we are testing.

One of my current problems is Ayub's compulsively repeated statements that he will use American arms against India if the need arise. He said it again last week and, naturally, the Indian press reacted joyously. It greatly helps those who want to buy Soviet aircraft, an enterprise I am trying to stand off. There was never such a drastic

---

[53] The reference here is to the resumption of nuclear testing.
[54] Communist Party.

misadventure in modern diplomacy as these minor alliances of Dulles. Machiavelli warned weak princes against joining with a strong one. In my forthcoming revision of his work, I will warn all strong states against weak ones. Since weak states are weak, the strong state gets no added strength out of its alliance. But the weak state can use its stronger ally for its own purposes. Since the state is small and weak, its purposes will be small and undignified. To these the large state becomes a party and such is our present fate. From the Portuguese to General Phoumi[55] our indigent allies are principally concerned with how to use the U.S. to promote their puny affairs.

In fact the United States should stand in majesty and grandeur above such matters. Involved we lose our influence. Above we could have great influence. The major N.A.T.O. powers apart, I cannot think of anything so important as that we have a gradual but inflexible will to remove ourselves from special relationships with the Albanias of the world and be prepared, instead, to help and treat all alike. There is of course nothing in the experience of being Ambassador to India which argues against this view. But this was always our instinct and it shouldn't surprise us that we were right.

One feature of the State Department mind on which I find I have not mellowed is its profound moral conviction that established policy is to be preferred to the one that is best for the United States.

I am coming back more or less privately for a few days in early June to get on honorary degree and possibly get some more of the medical advice for which I am becoming a kind of global customer. I plan in a speech to develop the point you raised at Glen Ora; namely, what, on candid view, are the advantages and disadvantages of communism as compared with our mixture from the viewpoint of the new and developing country. Thought, as distinct from *obiter dicta*, will show I think that we do have some important advantages and more than incidentally, that we have some faults that if remedied would add to our margin of advantage. In accordance with established procedures, I will send you a copy.

My recent travels have taken me up along the Chinese frontier and back to the Burma border. In addition to their better-publicized problems with the Chinese, the Indians are having very serious trouble in living with people within their own borders. This is an area with a large number of ethnically separate groups and all are unhappy in their present relations with the Indians. The Nagas are in open revolt

---

[55] A CIA-backed puppet in Laos.

and tie down a couple of divisions but they are only the extreme case. A half dozen other ethnic or linguistic groups are asking what they can have in the way of independence, autonomy or self-determination.[56]

Yours faithfully,
JOHN KENNETH GALBRAITH

THE PRESIDENT
THE WHITE HOUSE

•

New Delhi, India
July 10, 1962

Dear Mr. President:

I read with a good deal of concern about the pressure that is mounting on taxes. I also sense that your instinct is to resist and I hope you continue to do so. I submit the following thoughts:

(1) A very large part of American conservative and business opinion is simply against taxes regardless. It will thus argue with great enthusiasm for tax reduction, quite apart from the consequences fiscal and otherwise about which they couldn't care less. Of course, after the taxes are reduced, these people will not hesitate to attack you for an unbalanced budget. Some of them may be sophisticated enough to hope the new lower tax revenues will set a new lower ceiling on spending. The rest welcome the liberal initiative as assistance from an unexpected quarter.

(2) The momentary alliance with my friends is more apparent than real.[57] The people who are simply anti-tax will want an across-the-board and upper brackets reduction including, though less urgently, the corporation tax. The liberals and unions will want relief in the withholding brackets and here, of course, it would have its effect on spending. (The effect of upper bracket and corporation tax on business outlays and spending will be slight or negligible.) So a proposal to reduce taxes, while it looks simple and fast, will produce a nasty Congressional brawl with a disagreeable aftermath. What will satisfy the liberals will outrage the rich and vice versa. Both, in the end, will be angry at the Administration.

(3) From this distance I don't see that the condition of the economy is all that bad. Personal income seems to be holding up very well. The investment plans seem not to have been seriously revised. The stock market is steadier for the moment at a safer level.

---

[56] A final untactful sentence was deleted from this letter.
[57] Meaning the conservatives mentioned in paragraph (1) above, with the Keynesians in the Administration.

Unemployment, is, to be sure, substantial. But without excusing it, it remains that we have been living with something like this volume of unemployment for a long while. Once we would have thought it creditably low.

(4) Most of what I read on the politics of this situation makes no sense at all. While you are aware of my reluctance to lecture you on this curious subject, perhaps I could make three points (a) No tax cut has the slightest chance of having the slightest effect on the economy by November. (b) The unemployed are (to their misfortune) a small minority and few can be so silly as to suppose they will do better under the Republicans. (c) The unemployed stiff may have become extremely well educated in recent months, but I still can't imagine him applauding the Kennedy Administration for helping him by reducing the taxes of the guy who has a job or the fellow he would be working for if he had a job.

(5) I needn't remind you (but nevertheless I always deem it wise) that the glories of the Kennedy Era will be written not in the rate of economic growth or even in the level of unemployment. Nor, I venture, is this where its political rewards lie. Its glory and reward will be from the way it tackles the infinity of problems that beset a growing population and an increasingly complex society in an increasingly competitive world. To do this well costs the money that the tax reducers would deny.

If the economic outlook for next year is not good, this means that economists and planners should now get down to work on how men can be employed if jobs are needed. Then when next year comes there will be no reason to say that spending for the things that society so desperately needs is too time-consuming a remedy.

With this, I turn my thoughts back to the local scene.

Yours faithfully,

JOHN KENNETH GALBRAITH

THE PRESIDENT
THE WHITE HOUSE

•

New Delhi, India
July 13, 1962

Dear Mr. President:

Carl[58] has sent me a letter with a penetrating item by Ruth

[58] Carl Kaysen. The enclosures criticized the Administration for too much aid and attention to India for too small a reward. I was asked to comment, the implication being the President partly agreed. The President some time before was said to have banished the *New York Herald Tribune* from the White House.

Montgomery which could lead me to hope that you might cut off the *Journal-American* too. However, my further thought is that perhaps I should give you a succinct view of exactly what I am doing here. I sense a remote but discouraging tendency for you to imagine (a) that I have become a financial arm of the Indian Government; (b) that my task is to defend the Indians to the United States; (c) that I yearn to be loved. None, not even the last, reflects in fact my preoccupation. In fact, I find Indian politics depressing and not less so on continued contact. The thought crosses my mind more often than you might think as to why Galbraith cultivates this particular vineyard. I also spend my time trying to persuade the Indians of our problems and point of view, but, since I need no particular help in this, it is not in my recurrent advice to the State Department. Here is what concerns me:

India is a peasant and bourgeois, property-owning and, in the aggregate, conservative community. It is held to the West by ties of language and tradition of considerable strength. Most of the effective political leaders are on our side — a distinct oddity as the world goes. Their position depends on their history in the independence movement, the inherent conservatism of the country, the fact that our food eliminates the desperation that would result from hunger, and because planning plus our aid gives a semblance of progress.

Working against these conservative influences is a combination of the Communist, the angry, the frustrated, the xenophobic, and the anti-Moslem. Increasingly in recent years, and rapidly in recent months, they have been coalescing around Menon. And Menon with great brilliance has made himself the custodian of the particular inflammatory issues — Goa, arms aid to Pakistan, Kashmir — which put us automatically on the other side.

A disaster in this part of the world, as I see it, would be considerably worse not only for the United States but for the political reputation of the New Frontier than a disaster in Indo-China. Accordingly, as your man hereabouts, I assume I should seek to prevent it. Aid is a substantial part of my armory and that is my interest. I don't exclude a certain compassion for poor people. If one lacked compassion, he would not see the full importance of our assistance.

I am equally concerned to arrest the impulse of the State Department and my old friend Adlai Stevenson to show mighty indignation on irrelevant issues. That is why I was so anxious to cut our losses on Portuguese colonialism. It is why we simply cannot have another debate on Kashmir and State must be prevented from drifting on in to it. It is also why our arms aid to Pakistan is a two-edged sword that cuts principally on the wrong side.

Yours faithfully,
JOHN KENNETH GALBRAITH

THE PRESIDENT
THE WHITE HOUSE

•

New Delhi, India
October 16, 1962

Dear Mr. President:

I remember when I was running price control the only news ever passed up to me was of major disasters. The intelligence reaching your office must be much the same. In recent weeks things here have been going sufficiently better so that it requires a major act of will to talk about them. However, perhaps you need a moment's relaxation.

My policy on the border conflict,[59] in the convenient absence of instructions, is to express quiet sympathy, make clear that we hope for settlement here as elsewhere, and not to feel any urgency about offering help. It will be far better if the Indians have to ask. They must not think we are yearning for an opportunity to line them up on our side and save them.

I have just completed an interesting and rather encouraging experiment. I took some twenty or thirty Indian newspapermen and photographers plus two American television crews and a newsreel crew on a ten-day tour of American-aided projects in India. We traveled by special train — a delight in itself and, I hasten to say, at no expense either to balance of payments or the United States taxpayer. (We have enough rupees available for United States use to last well into John Jr.'s second term.) Apart from a major University speech at Lucknow, another center of antipathetic attitudes toward the United States, the hegira included (by way of illustration) the new Indian Institute of Technology at Kanpur, support for which we announced a year ago; several power plants which we are financing; two coal washeries, which may well be the least fascinating industrial processes in the world; a huge dam near Hyderabad which is being financed by Public Law 480 rupees on which 100,000 people (sic) are employed; all kinds of agricultural betterment; a big fertilizer plant; an automobile and truck plant; a school for training mechanics and draftsmen and two schools for the training of young

---

[59] Between China and India then in incipient stage.

workers in the operation and care of bulldozers, steam shovels and the like.

Everywhere there was a lively appreciation of the scource of the aid. Invariably there was a sign saying it was being done with the cooperation of the United States. And there was a good deal of enthusiasm on the part of those who were on the payroll. The tour got a great deal of national attention and it blanketed the local papers. I held a more or less continuous seminar on economic development which must have been highly rewarding to all listeners.

Many things about AID still worry me. While I have been trying to do fewer things and making sure that these are the most important, there is still room for further concentration. We still need to move more of our people out of Delhi — it is like pulling teeth to accomplish this. Some very odd people get recruited. The Indian industrial management is highly bureaucratic — at a big fertilizer plant outside Bombay they had — characteristically — put up a vast office building before they had started excavations for the plant itself. Still there is much that is good. A lot of the projects selected by my predecessors were exceedingly sound and the program could easily suffer from too much reform. Out in Kotah (a Godforsaken[60] desert community in Rajasthan) I encountered a Californian by the name of Childs married to a Japanese wife who for four years has been the only American in town. He has done a superb job of organizing a school for training in the operation and maintenance of bulldozers, graders, heavy trucks and so forth and is just about ready to turn it over to Indian direction. There are many other such cases.

I have been following the aid legislation in the Congress this year with a good deal of misgiving. I would gather there is even more serious trouble ahead in the future. I have a suggestion for giving it a new lift which I will put to you when I am back — that is, if I can catch you for a few minutes between whistle stops. I am in Washington week after next — October 30 to November 6.

The Mississippi affair[61] seemed from here to have been superbly handled. Without question it greatly raised our stock in this part of the world. Not even the Communists now seriously accuse us of evasion.

Yours faithfully,
JOHN KENNETH GALBRAITH

[60] An unkind adjective justified only by the bad state of my digestive tract that day and for which I apologize to all citizens of that city. I do not believe that God has forsaken it.
[61] The insertion of James Meredith into the University of Mississippi.

THE PRESIDENT
THE WHITE HOUSE

•

IT WAS ALL OVER[62]

November 26, 1963

This journal was to have ended with the last entry in Madras. Now a last, sad chapter must be added.

In August, at the President's request, I returned to Washington to spend five or six weeks, first negotiating a settlement of an ancient airline dispute with the Canadians. After Kashmir, it was pleasant to find an issue where only naked financial self-interest was involved.[63] Then, a more interesting task, I made a new survey of the balance-of-payments problem. I wrote a stiff paper on the subject which was taken up at a couple of meetings in the White House, but it led to no real action. We ended with an agreement to limit capital exports which had been already accomplished pro tem by the interest equalization tax the Treasury had proposed to levy retroactively earlier in the summer.

Between these tasks, I worked on the book on the Scotch,[64] corrected the final proofs on Dr. McLandress and began a series of articles for *Look* for which they are paying me $5,000 each for three.[65] And of course when autumn came, I resumed teaching here at Harvard. My classes were sizable with a fair number of tourists looking in at least briefly to see one of the local sights.

Last Friday, November 22, I went to New York to have lunch with Kay Graham, now the directing head of the *Washington Post* and *Newsweek*.[66] Arthur Schlesinger was to join us and also some *Newsweek* editors. Arthur and Kay were flying up from Washington together. They arrived late, and I drank tomato juice in Kay's office while the *Newsweek* editors had Old-Fashioneds. Arthur and Kay arrived and ordered drinks and they had just picked them up when

---

[62] Chapter XXVII, "It Was All Over," *Ambassador's Journal*, pp. 587–597.

[63] The problem, that of allowing Canadian airlines to fly to destinations deep in the United States in return for similar rights in Canada (complicated by the fact that all Canadian cities are close to the border), was eventually resolved to the reasonable satisfaction of all concerned.

[64] *Made to Last* (London: Hamish Hamilton, 1964).

[65] None ever appeared in *Look*. One, "The American Ambassador," was published in the *Foreign Service Journal* of June 1969.

[66] Philip Graham having died a few weeks earlier.

a staff man of the magazine opened the door rather tentatively, almost apologetically, and said, "I think I should interrupt. President Kennedy has just been shot in Dallas." There was a moment of horrified silence; someone said, "It couldn't be." Kay's face suddenly looked haggard. We went out to the newsroom and to the tickers where everyone was gathered around a radio. The further word was that he had been shot in the head. It all sounded much too real to be a mistake, and I confess at this juncture that I gave up hope. Imagining what it means to be shot in the head, mentally destroyed, I wished momentarily that the news might have been that he was dead. Then the radio reported that a Secret Service man traveling with Mrs. Kennedy by the name of Clint Hill had said, "The President is dead." Clint Hill was the advance man on Mrs. Kennedy's trip to India. He is a well-organized and thoughtful man who would never in any emergency be wrong. His reaction, if accurately reported, was bound to be right.

For half an hour, we alternated between Kay's office, the radio and the television. Now I found myself hoping it was just a wound, even a bad wound. Word came that two priests had gone into the hospital. Further word came that blood was being sent in. Finally, these details were interrupted with the annoucement that the President of the United States was dead.

Kay had come up in the *Washington Post* plane. We went down to the car, over to the Century Club to pick up my bags and out to the Marine Terminal at LaGuardia and flew back to Washington. My strongest thought was that we were paying the price for the poisonous hatred stirred up so casually by the extreme right. Somehow or other, national indignation should have intervened to shut them up and thus to have excluded the incitement to violence for those whose mental discrimination is too slight. We all three took for granted that it was done by right-wing extremists. Stevenson had been roughed up in Dallas only a few weeks before. Lyndon Johnson and his wife had been pummeled there during the 1960 campaign. For a brief moment, there was word that Johnson had been wounded also.

At Washington, we went to the White House and Ralph Dungan's office where preliminary efforts were being made to organize life. There is in the United States a great latent capacity for self-organization. Some people take charge; some take orders. This was already beginning to make itself felt. Dungan was organizing the arrangements for the return of the President's body and the new President and J.B.K. to Andrews Field. Most of the members of the Cabinet were over the Pacific on their way to a meeting in Japan; sub-Cabinet members were gathering at the White House. In the early evening — I did not make any note of exact times — we got into helicopters and White House cars and made our way to Andrews Field. Bob Roosa, Undersecretary of the Treasury, and Clarence Martin,[67] one of the Undersecretaries of Commerce, were my companions in one of the cars. We had a motorcycle escort through the home-going traffic and we had only a few moments to wait at Andrews Field before Air Force-I came in. There was already a considerable crowd of on-lookers on the way and near the airfield, and quite a number of Congressmen and Senators had arrived. A lift arrangement of the kind that is used to put food aboard a commercial plane was wheeled up to the jet as it came abreast of the ramp, and after a little time the coffin was maneuvered out, brought down and put into a gray Navy hearse. The lift arrangement, truck and all, was not over-whelming in its dignity.

Then Robert Kennedy brought Jackie off the plane followed by President Johnson and the rest of the party. J.B.K. was pale but otherwise in control. Evidently it had been intended that she should go to the White House by helicopter. Instead she went in the hearse to the Bethesda Naval Hospital. We went back to the White House. Arthur and I had our first meal of the day in the White House Mess, and I went on to Averell Harriman's. George Backer[68] was there and one or two others. I can rarely remember an evening when a deadlier or drearier pall fell over a group. No one had anything to say or indeed seemed to wish to talk. Presently Arthur Schlesinger, who had come with me, disappeared and soon I had a call from him, asking me to come down to the White House. Two problems were being resolved: one, the arrangement for the stationing of the coffin in the East Room which was Bill Walton's responsibility; and the other, the preparation of the lists of people to be invited to view the coffin the next day at various times which Sarge Shriver was handling. These were the two natural leaders of the evening.

On the first, there were plans available to the White House, updated as recently as 1958 (evidently at the time of one of Ike's illnesses) for the funeral of a President while in office. Walton got

[67] Until we were nearly at the field, I thought Martin was Franklin D. Roosevelt, Jr. My mind simply had not registered.
[68] Friend, journalist and fellow amateur novelist. A longtime leader in New York Democratic politics.

out books and pictures showing how the East Room had been decorated for Lincoln's funeral but decided that the taste in crepe of that era was too extravagant. He contented himself with some simple black drapes. Word was sent out to arrest the inflow of flowers, and he set himself to standing off the undertakers and the Catholics. The undertakers had numerous artifacts and rich satin backgrounds to display; some churchmen felt that this was a time for a considerable ceremonial and liturgical exercise. The Kennedy family supported a control of both of these extravagances and, in the end, everything was simple, in good proportion and in good taste.

The problem of deciding who would visit the White House at various times was more difficult. One had the conflicting claims of politics, officialdom and friendship and the possibility that some individuals would fall between all stools. In a way, politics and officialdom fell into fairly straightforward categories. One invited all governors and officials above a certain rank as a matter of course. The friends and faithful supporters were more difficult, but this problem was partly resolved when we got a list of people who had been invited to Kennedy dinners.

It was midnight or one o'clock when I got home to Kay Graham's. Others waited for the coffin to come from the Bethesda Hospital. The work of the evening was therapeutic.

During the afternoon, Al Friendly of the *Washington Post,* in response to a not fully considered suggestion that I would be willing, asked me to write an appreciation of Kennedy. On second thought, I declined, but next morning, though I woke up under the drugged effect of too many sleeping pills, I changed my mind again. I wrote most of it in bed before breakfast and then reworked it the rest of the morning. I gave it no title and the *Post* called it merely "A Communication." I avoided the mistake of other writers who tried to assess Kennedy in his whole person and in his relation to history. I confined myself to a single facet of his personality — his intelligence, wit and information.[69]

At noon, I went down with Kitty, who had meanwhile arrived, to Blair House and the White House to visit the bier. This was the first of several times when my emotions were severely taxed. We were, however, almost alone at the time. The article had kept me until after most of the friends of the family had disappeared. From the East Room of the White House, we went to Arthur Schlesinger's

[69] The article is at the end of this Journal.

office and then on to the Occidental for lunch. The Sam Beers,[70] Seymour Harris,[71] Paul Samuelson,[72] Bill Walton and one or two others were present for lunch. Arthur (naturally enough) was in a rather poor mood. But like most people interested in politics, he was reacting too much to the chemistry of the moment.

Walter Heller, who was at the lunch, left early for Johnson's first Cabinet meeting and the rest of us made our more leisurely way back to the White House. I went over to the West Basement to say a word to Ted Sorensen who was badly broken up. In some ways, he had invested more in John F. Kennedy than anyone else. His personal life, everything else had been subordinated to the Kennedy career.

From there, I went on to the Executive Office Building to see Robert Komer and look at the India cables. I was waiting meanwhile for the galley proofs to come back from the *Post* for correction. However, I decided halfway to Komer's office that I had no heart to talk about India and returned to get a White House car to go to the Grahams'. As I turned, I encountered President Johnson who told me he had just sent for me. He asked me to come to his office. When we got there, he threw out a waiting Texas judge and made a strong plea for support.[73] He also asked me to work with Sorensen on the message for a joint session of Congress to be given on Wednesday. He asked how I worked with Sorensen and I answered that I got along with him very well. Johnson then said he wanted to continue the Kennedy policies, reminded me he was a Roosevelt liberal, and said that he was going to affirm his support for the Kennedy programs. I asked specifically about civil rights. He said he was for civil rights, not out of loyalty to the President but out of loyalty to the idea. I told him that I was a Democrat as well as a friend and would, of course, give him any help I could.

The incident had an interesting relation to the problem of the change in power. Like the other members of the Kennedy group, I

[70] Past National Chairman of A.D.A. and Professor of Government at Harvard.
[71] Harvard Professor.
[72] M.I.T. Professor.
[73] He also asked me what problems I thought he faced. I told him by far the most serious was in foreign policy. And this would be the tendency of the foreign policy establishment, which had gone along reluctantly with Kennedy, to relapse into Cold War adventures. The point evidently seemed sufficiently commonplace, even banal at the time, so that I did not bother to mention it in these notes. In the light of later history, it is more interesting. However, I do not want to exaggerate its importance. Neither President Johnson nor any other man could have registered mentally all of the advice being given in those days.

had become accustomed to wandering through the White House and through the press without anyone paying the slightest attention. Johnson had been seen taking me into his office so when I came out, I was overwhelmed by newspapermen and photographers. I brushed them off.

I tried my hand at the speech that afternoon and showed it to Arthur. He was appalled by it. His judgment was in fact clearer than mine. I had drafted out a liberal program; it was pretty bad. He correctly said that this was not what the occasion called for.

Kitty and I had dinner at the Grahams' with the Graham children who were down from Radcliffe and Harvard for the occasion, and then went briefly to the Harrimans'. Arthur divided the community in Washington into two categories, the realists and the loyalists. The loyalists would resign and try to find an alternative to Johnson. The realists, a group to which, alas, I was assigned, took the Democratic Party in earnest and would continue to give their best to it, however little that might be.

I went home early and went to bed.

Sunday morning, I concluded that the speech was in fact very bad and wrote a new and better version. It was balanced and liberal and set about the right tone. I finished it just in time to go to the White House to join the White House staff to go to the Capitol. We drove down by a circuitous route, went up the Capitol steps and into the Rotunda where a catafalque had been prepared in the center. After a little, in came Congressmen, Senators, members of the Supreme Court and various officials. The Congressmen who were immediately adjacent to us seemed principally concerned in their conversation with whether or not they were to be invited to the funeral the next day. They obviously couldn't be since the Cathedral holds only some fifteen hundred people, and by this time it was evident that most of the chiefs of state of the world were flying in for the occasion. Otherwise, the conversation was on the weather, the identity of various people in the crowd and funerals in general. News was just beginning to circulate in this weekend of Texas violence that Lee Oswald, the President's presumed assassin, had also been shot. This, I must say, struck me in some ways as the most unforgivable thing of all. Perhaps it is impossible to prevent a madman from getting a rifle and striking down the President but surely peace officers should be able to protect a prisoner in their own custody.

Then an honor guard came in, followed by six soldiers — actually, Navy, Marine, Air and Army enlisted men — carrying the coffin. Their approach was quiet and impressive. Speeches followed. Mike

Mansfield had a poem; the symbolism had to do with a ring on a finger, gaiety, wit, stillness, and it was good. John McCormack, now (as Speaker) next in line for the Presidency, left much to be desired. The Chief Justice gave a magnificent talk and he said the one thing that needed to be said, namely that while few will advocate assassination, many will contribute to the climate which causes men to contemplate it.

J.B.K. had come in with the coffin and with the two youngsters. However, John, Jr., had become restless and a Marine guard took him away. At the conclusion of the speeches, she came forward with Caroline and with silent eloquence knelt and kissed the coffin. Then President Johnson came forward a bit haltingly and put a large wreath of roses before the coffin. We then went back to the White House. It was almost midafternoon.

At the White House, I encountered Lee Radziwill who asked me if I had seen J.B.K., and she said she thought she wanted to see me. I went upstairs to one end of the central hall where she was resting and still in perfect control. She asked me if I wouldn't have a drink; I broke down for the first time in a long while to have one. We talked a little bit about the events of the morning and more about the funeral the next day. She was holding firm to her determination that J.F.K.'s sense of pageantry would be respected. All sorts of suggestions that people ride in cars for security reasons were being made. She was determined that the coffin would be drawn on a caisson, that people would follow on foot, and that bands and soldiers would add as much stately solemnity to the occasion as might be possible. The Ormsby Gores were there and she recalled how much J.F.K. had enjoyed the visit of the Black Watch a few days before. He offered to get them back to Washington for the occasion.

In moments of this sort, what seem to be simple matters assume enormously difficult proportions. J.B.K., it developed, had no place to go on leaving the White House. Her parents had no accommodations large enough for her substantial household. It was necessary for her to have a place to which members of the Kennedy political entourage would have reasonably easy access. It had to be in Washington. And, money apart, you cannot buy a house on the spur of the moment and move in. I took this on. It occurred to me that Averell Harriman, who has more real estate than he knows what to do with, could offer her his house. At this time of year, Marie Harriman usually goes to New York or Hobe Sound. It is a large, comfortable house in the most agreeable part of Georgetown and has the particular advantage of some of the best impressionist paintings in the world.

After seeing J.B.K. and a session with Sorensen, some more work on the speech took me until early evening. I then went back to the Grahams' for dinner — I had had no lunch. After dining, I went over to Harriman's to brace him on the real estate question. This proved to be no problem, and he straightaway called Jackie to make the offer. She, however, had gone to bed and so he made it through Lee. I then talked the matter over with Bob Kennedy who was delighted with this resolution.

In the general resolution of the funeral arrangements, Kitty's name and mine had been on no list. This was not remarkable in fact because my only qualification was in the category of friends — or possibly as a sometime member of the White House staff. Except possibly for Roswell Gilpatric,[74] not even those of the rank of Undersecretary were invited. There must have been a considerable number of damaged feelings. When Bob learned of the oversight, he had it corrected with great speed and not without some expressions of anger. Arthur, meanwhile, took on the problem of Averell Harriman who had similarly been excluded, the offer of the house to J.B.K. notwithstanding.

Yesterday, which was the day of the funeral, I did a final version of the speech. My piece appeared in the *Washington Post*. I think on the whole it was quite good, and this, I believe, was the common view. I got some satisfaction from having done it.

We gathered in the lobby of the White House at 10:30 A.M. where the great from all countries were now arriving. Lord Home, Prince Philip, Mikoyan, Pearson,[75] all lined up to sign the book as though waiting for their hats and coats. The caisson with the coffin came from the Capitol, and as it passed through the White House grounds, we fell in behind. My companions for the march up Connecticut Avenue were Lem Billings[76] and Nathan Pusey. Kitty and Marian Schlesinger had gone ahead to the Cathedral. The weather was beautiful. Soldiers and airmen lined the route. The crowds were huge and utterly somber. Far ahead, we heard occasionally the piping of the Black Watch. I had little impression of the pageantry in fact. Anyone watching from the sidelines saw much more.

The church when we arrived was full, and I squeezed into a seat

---

[74] His rank was, in fact, that of Deputy Secretary of Defense.
[75] Leaders from England, Russia and Canada.
[76] Lemoyne Billings, close personal friend of the President.

with the Harrimans, Marian and Kitty. The funeral service itself, my first experience with a full Catholic mass, was long and very formal. The only secular part was a reading from the Inaugural Address. At the end, the coffin was wheeled out; J.B.K. followed with Bob. Then the other members of the family and then the heads of state. I imagine no one ever looked down a narrow aisle and saw quite so many before: de Gaulle, Home, Pearson, U Thant, Erhard, the Japanese Foreign Minister, Belgians, Dutch, on and on. Eventually we made our way out, on down the steps to our cars and began the long ride out to Arlington. The caisson by this time was well on its way, and we gradually closed up with it. We came to the gates just as the flypast was marking the beginning of the graveside ceremony.

The ceremony at Arlington was the most heartrending time of all. The sky was blue and bright, and one had the impression of a day that had very little to do with death. People were massed on the hillside with flowers scattered everywhere. There was a prayer by Cardinal Cushing, not eloquent but full of emotion. The twenty-one gun salute sounded and the muskets fired from the brilliantly polished ranks of soldiers, sailors and Marines. The music from the band was impressive and the playing of Last Post almost unbearably so. At the end, the flag was folded and given to J.B.K. It was over.

"MOTHER DOESN'T DO MUCH"[77]
By Catherine A. Galbraith

IT IS EXCITING to be in India now, for one can see the old beside the new. India's history goes back thousands of years. At the time the Pilgrims were building log cabins in Salem, Shah Jahan was building the Taj Mahal. But India became an independent nation a decade and a half ago. The contrasts are striking. In Delhi, buses, scooter taxis, and bicycles weave in among the tongas and oxcarts. New housing developments spring up around old tombs and ancient forts, those monuments are so familiar and numerous that no one can tell you for whom or when they were built. You go to a village, even on the outskirts of a city, and you see how life has gone on in the same way for centuries. There are the same wooden plows and plodding bullocks, the same cow-dung fires and Persian waterwheels,

[77] Appendix I, "Mother Doesn't Do Much," *Ambassador's Journal*, pp. 609–616. This article first appeared in *The Atlantic Monthly* in May 1963. Copyright © 1963 by the Atlantic Monthly Company.

the same bright saris bending over the rice fields—though the ubiquitous black umbrellas used for sunshades must have come in with the British. You think there has been no change, and then you discover that the village now has a small dispensary, very simple by our standards; a handful of nurses and a doctor serve thousands of patients. Or there is an eye clinic, set up in tents so that it can be moved from district to district; two hundred thin old men and women lie on charpoys waiting for operations for glaucoma. Each operation takes about ten minutes, and the doctors are busy all day. Or a farmer comes proudly to show off his new crop of peas; they are much fatter and sweeter than before, because of improved varieties, irrigation and fertilizer.

But it has become a time of peril for India. Its problems are very great. With half the area of the United States, it has nearly three times the population. People are everywhere — in the lonely jungle, clinging to the steep Himalayas, sleeping on the city streets, and clustered all over the plains. Most of these people are poor, customs are diverse, and many tensions have threatened to disunite the nation. India so far has kept a full parliamentary system of government, its heritage from the British, but the Chinese have already marched. In its plans for development India counted on peace. Will the cost of war to a poor country be disaster, or will the need for preparation hasten progress? Right now people are donating their gold bangles, their life savings, their blood; women are forming knitting parties, and girls in saris are training on the rifle range. In the villages the people are asking what they can do. There is a sense of urgency and national purpose, and also, initially, bewilderment. The Chinese action was a great jolt.

Since Independence progress has been made, though the answers to India's problems are not simple. For instance, DDT has checked malaria, but the decline in disease has raised the birthrate. The solution to poverty can start with small things — a new well, better seeds, an outside market for village handwork, a teacher and a little school. It can also start with big things — dams and power plants and factories. The United States has helped with both.

One of our great privileges has been the opportunity to travel and to see what is going on. Usually we fly in one of our Embassy planes — a Convair if the airfields are 4,500 feet long, otherwise a DC-3, which can land even on the meadow in the narrow Kulu Valley. The Convair is comfortable for long distances. In addition to seats for sixteen passengers, it has a rear section for the Ambassador, with two couches, a large leather lounge chair, a table and desk.

When we arrive at the airport on official visits we are garlanded, photographed and driven off to the governor's mansion or the state guesthouse. Usually a police inspector rides in the front seat. (Once, outside Calcutta, our protector jammed his finger in the car door and fainted; my husband picked up his bodyguard and laid him gently on the nearest table.) We call on the governor, the chief minister, the mayor; attend receptions, cultural programs, and dinners at which we forgather in good academic fashion, men on one side, wives on the other. We shop hurriedly for handicrafts at the government emporium, and, if we are lucky, have a little time for sightseeing. I may have a special schedule arranged by worthy women's organizations. There are press conferences, and my husband often speaks. By now he has lectured at most of the leading universities in India.

At major functions my husband makes the speeches while I sit quietly in the platform and share the garlands. But if he is not around to talk, then I must. This can happen without warning. The first time was at a girls' school in Cochin, where, having been invited to pay an informal call, I was led to the platform in front of the entire student body, seated on a red plush chair between the principal and the archbishop, and handed a printed program which read "Speech by Mrs. Galbraith."

Twice I have presented mobile kitchens (jeeps with trailers) from Wheat Associates to be used to teach the village women how to cook the wheat we give them when the rice crop fails. I have judged floats in parades, distributed sweets to children, awarded prizes. In one village, after inspecting a neat little hospital, I was handed a baby spotted deer which promptly began to munch the flowers around my neck.

I have even undertaken trips on my own, to celebrate, as a state guest, the harvest festival in Kerala, when they have the wonderful snake-boat processions and the noisiest fireworks, and to visit the first Peace Corps group in the Punjab. That was in August, and it was hot. But despite the wearing heat, minor discouragements and a few amoebas, they were hard at work raising chickens, designing housing for villages, teaching, studying and demonstrating methods of farming. Every one of them was enthusiastic about being in India, and no one complained of the simple living conditions. They were a good group, glad for what they were learning and eager to be of more service. They have already won the regard of their Indian neighbors.

Our travels have covered most of India, from the lush coconut groves of Kerala to the cool valleys of Kashmir, and from the monumental Gateway of India in Bombay to the small Naga villages beyond Assam. Our two weeks in April 1962 near the North East Frontier now seem to have been planned with special prescience.

On this trip we stayed at a cinchona plantation near Kalimpong and feasted on roast sheep and beer made by pouring hot water over millet in bamboo mugs; it ferments while you wait. Next we visited the Maharajah of Sikkim in the tiny mountain capital of Gangtok, where we were protected by five-foot palace guards in uniforms which make Hollywood seem real. In Shillong, the capital of Assam, we stayed with the Governor in a large Tudor-style mansion, and then we crossed the Brahmaputra River to go to a game preserve just over the border in Bhutan. This little frontier country is so remote that it did not then even have a postal system; the first Bhutanese stamps were issued last October. We thought we would be roughing it, but we found that three hundred people had worked fourteen days to build us a camp on a bluff above the rushing Manas River. Out of split bamboo they had created a village of basketweave houses which they had furnished with real beds, new sheets, full-length-mirror dressing tables, all brought in by dugout for our two-night stay. We, too, were poled up the river in dugouts and were met on the opposite shore by six large elephants which carried us the rest of the way along a path lined with bright prayer flags. The riverbank on which we stayed is now one of the danger routes into India. It all seemed very peaceful then.

Our final stop was Manipur, in the green hills by the Burmese border. It was here that we saw polo played by men on little ponies, and danced with the Naga tribes, my husband wearing a headband with peacock feathers and I a golden cardboard crown. The valley people are a different lot, easygoing and gentle. Women do all the work, but they also control the purse strings and, being independent, are free to change or discard a husband when convenient. The Naga tribes, not long ago headhunters, are mostly in the hills. They were a happy, graceful people, fond of bright clothes and dancing. Now they are close to the fighting.

We travel in order to get acquainted with regional problems and politics, and also to highlight American aid. Of course, this help is not new; Americans have been contributing for years to agricultural and industrial development, to medicine and to education, through our government, our foundations and other agencies. We do not believe, however, that such work should be done in secret. In Kerala, the most literate and the most unsettled politically of all the Indian states, my husband not long ago announced a loan for two vast dams which will more than double the present supply of electricity. In Calcutta, too, a loan was announced for a thermal power plant. On this occasion everything went wrong with the ceremony. It began with a cloudburst. The two speakers, my husband and the late Dr. B. C. Roy, got there by jeep, but the audience bogged down in the mud, so the speeches were not made. The teacups blew away, and when my husband planted the symbolic gulmohar tree he dug with such enthusiasm that the silver trowel broke in half. He symbolically watered the tree while it rained an inch an hour. However, all these disasters served to make a better story.

Some of the most heartwarming work is what we have done for children. This is largely accomplished through CARE. In Mussoorie, in the mountains north of Delhi, I visited a Tibetan refugee camp; the triple-decker cots, as many as seventy in a room, and much of the kitchen supplies had come from CARE. In Madras we met a ship which was unloading four million pounds of powdered milk from the United States Government for CARE. One of our most beautiful mornings was spent at a school just outside Trivandrum in Kerala which was inaugurating a school-lunch program for several hundred children, with food also provided by the United States Government through CARE. Girls in bright blue skirts and white blouses greeted us with coconut lamps, flower petals and garlands, and under the *shamiana* (colorful awning) which had been set up for the ceremony were chandeliers made of fragrant white tuberoses. Meanwhile, outside, little boys and girls sat patiently in rows, their leaf plates and brass cups in front of them, waiting for the end of the speeches so that they could eat. We were told that the school lunches do away with the truant officer; sometimes this is the only meal these children get in twenty-four hours. The program starts with the first grade, and poor parents have been advancing the ages of their four-year-olds to get them into school early so they will be fed. We have recently also opened another school-lunch program for 500,000 children in Rajasthan.

In early October we went by special train through central India on a ten-day U.S. AID tour. Our party of fifty included twenty-eight Indian and American journalists, for by showing them our projects first hand, we thought they would become aware of the contribution of the United States to Indian development. Our train had nine cars — three of air-conditioned bedroom compartments, two dining cars, two baggage cars, a car for the officials of the railway accompanying us, and the Ambassador's special coach, belonging to the president of the railway. Divisional superintendents were instructed to ensure "stabling" at quiet sidings, to keep platforms and surroundings scrupulously clean and the staff on duty tidy, to supply chilled boiled water and ice, and hot water for baths, good food, laundry facilities and a doctor "equipped to meet any emergency" throughout the journey.

To go across India in this way, just after the monsoon, protected from the hubbub of the highways, is in itself a delightful experience. As the sun rises in the rain-clear sky you see the farmer already out in the bright green rice fields driving his white bullocks and the women in blue or red or green saris coming from the well with shining brass water jugs on their heads, and in the remote stretches where only the railway tracks pass, the villages with their red-tiled roofs look very well kept.

We were busy. We visited power plants, a coal washery, the docks at Bombay where American wheat was being unloaded, training centers for teaching the use and maintenance of heavy equipment, a district experimenting in raising food production by putting into practice modern agricultural techniques and the new Indian Institute of Technology, now being started with the help of some of our leading professors, that aspires to equal M.I.T. South of Hyderabad we inspected a huge dam which, except for two tall U.S. cranes, is being built like the pyramids of old, by thousands of workmen, some of them children (though that is illegal), carrying concrete on their heads up zigzag bamboo ramps. For buildings up to the height of 120 feet we were told that human labor is cheaper than machines. It must always be remembered that this is a country of many poor people, and many people need jobs.

We also paid a visit to Literacy Village in Lucknow, the dream come true of a remarkable American, Mrs. Welthy Fisher, now over eighty. Here young women are trained to go out into the villages to teach reading, books are written, and ways of communicating new ideas to illiterates are devised. A favorite method is through puppets. We were treated to a skit on family planning, the romance of Birju and Chanda, whose happy marriage turns to despair when in five years they have five children. The bride has become an old woman, the children fight and one who is ill vomits yellow liquid over the edge of the stage. When Chanda whispers to Birju that she is expecting yet another baby, he rushes out to hang himself, but is rescued by the village-level worker, who sends him to the doctor at the block head-quarters for much-needed advice.

The trip accomplished its purpose. Many articles were written about our work in India. A week later the Chinese marched into the North East Frontier. After that, there was hardly any need to emphasize American aid. When my husband went to the Lok Sabha one day, even his car was garlanded, and strangers rushed up to thank him as though he were providing the assistance from his own pocket. But the appreciation of U.S. generosity and compassion is no sudden thing. It has existed for a long time, even in out-of-the-way places. On our way to Bhutan across the hot dusty roads of Assam, where we had not met another car for miles, my husband was dozing in the back seat of the car with his shoes off when I noticed ahead of us crowds of people gathering as though for a fair. But they came to see us. In this poor little village they had heard we were passing through; they stopped the car to give us a letter, written in longhand and framed, expressing their warm friendship for the United States.

In spite of differences of opinion that arise, our relations with India rest on respect. The Indians know that we help them not because we are richer and want power but because we care and because we believe, as they do, in the value of human life and in the freedom and dignity of the individual. It is to our mutual advantage and interest to stand by one another since we hold the same faith.

PART TWO

THE TRIAD—THREE

SELECTION

14. *Economics and the
Public Purpose*

"*T*his book is in descent, the last in the line from two earlier volumes. . . ." Thus Galbraith begins his introduction to Economics and the Public Purpose, the third and final book in what we have called "the triad." He then continues ". . . The earlier volumes were centrally concerned with the world of the great corporations . . . there is also the world of the farmer, repairman, retailer, small manufacturer. . . . This book seeks to bring them fully into the scene." That much Galbraith surely does, but in the third section of the book, he also goes much further. In that last section the author proposes an economic system for our time. Herein, this book differs emphatically from its sister volumes and must be weighed on a different set of scales. The first two books are descriptive and interpretive; this one is conjectural and constructive and in being so is much more susceptible to hostile criticism and misunderstanding, while being at the same time probably the boldest and most essential of the three.

In our attempt to show the part that this book plays in the long crescendo of Galbraith's writing, we have selected a chapter each from the first two sections. The first reviews the complexities, needs and importance of the great corporate conglomerates. The second delineates the hazards and hardships of little businesses and depicts the skills and values that separate it from the metallic jungles of contemporary industrial society. Little business is an endangered species searching for nineteenth-century security. It is essential to big business, but it is also essentially separate as are barnyards to General Foods.

The positive third section points to the course of treatments we shall have to prescribe for ourselves if we are to hope for continuing economic health. Here no single chapter does justice to the cure, and we have in consequence selected passages from three chapters. One defines the ineffectiveness and undesirability of present remedies and suggests public ownership as preferable; the second points to the folly of trying to keep up with the Joneses; the last lays down some steps and standards required for a better balance of power within the community and brings home the point: there is little room for choice.

The thinking in the triad as a whole is eloquently bracketed by two paragraphs in this third book. The first comes at the end of the author's introduction. Its key sentence reads as follows: "Left to themselves, economic forces do not work out for the best except perhaps for the powerful." The second is near the beginning of the next to last chapter: "One cannot have a socially excellent economic system without having an economic system." To one who had completed his reading of Economics and the Public Purpose, Galbraith might hold these truths to be self-evident.

Indeed, they sum up the liberal democratic dilemma. You cannot have the efficiencies, the comforts and the securities of the industrial state unless a few single management-blocks exercise enormous and rigorous control over the state resources in labor and material for considerable periods of time. Some of our great corporate conglomerates already wield more power than our smaller states. Spreading across the boundaries of states and nations, they can only be federally controlled. To reduce their size would only destroy the strength of our economy.

Yet corporations by their nature act only for themselves. There must be a greater force to secure the welfare of the nation from which the corporations in their turn draw their strength. This force can only be the government in Washington, in turn dependent on an informed electorate — the final countervailing power. Here then, at last, is the element missing in that first ancestral volume — the last three fingers on the baseball bat.

The chain of logic is complete. We as voters may argue about what measures are best adapted to achieve the end, but the future of General Motors must no longer be determined by the technocratic teams of General Motors nor in the councils of the U.A.W. The whole nation, not just parts of it, must prosper. That prospering can only be achieved if the electorate understands the problem and its cure and it is to that understanding that the whole triad, and this third book in particular, is addressed. It is the last book in the triad, but it is only the brave beginning of reform.

Economics and the Public Purpose

FOREWORD[1]

THIS BOOK is in descent, the last in the line, from two earlier volumes — *The Affluent Society* and *The New Industrial State*. There are also some genes, though not many, from yet another volume — *American Capitalism*. The principal precursors each dealt with a part of the economic system; this one seeks to put it all together, to give the whole system. The earlier volumes were centrally concerned with the world of the great corporations — with the decisive part of the economy which the established or neoclassical economics has never ingested. There is also the world of the farmer, repairman, retailer, small manufacturer, plumber, television repairman, service station operator, medical practitioner, artist, actress, photographer and pornographer. Together these businesses supply about half of all we use or consume. This book seeks to bring them fully into the scene. In economics as in anatomy the whole is much more than the sum of the parts. This is certainly so when the parts are in support of each other or in conflict with each other or are otherwise shaped by the fact of their common existence. Also, a lesser point, the earlier books stopped at the water's edge. This one gives the first elements of the international system.

[1] Foreword to *Economics and the Public Purpose* (London: André Deutsch, 1974), pp. ix–xiii.

The New Industrial State pictures the world of the large corporation as the outgrowth of the neoclassical world of monopoly and
oligopoly. At least by implication what was left behind was the
world of the competitive market. That also I here correct; what is left
behind is, in fact, something resembling the neoclassical admixture of
entrepreneurial monopoly, oligopoly and competition. The consequence of so seeing matters is a better explanation of the behavior
of the entrepreneurial firm and what I here call the market system.
It shows, also, that the world of the large corporation is something
new — that it is a clear break with what is described by traditional
doctrine.

The traditional economics assumes that economic institutions and
the motivation of the people who comprise them change but slowly.
As with physics or botany economic truth once established is largely
immutable. This is agreeable but not so. Economic institutions
change rather rapidly; the large corporation and its relations with the
community and state are especially in flux. And with such change
comes new information, new insight. In consequence the rate of
obsolescence in economic knowledge is high. On many smaller matters such change and such information have nurtured a view that
differs from that of the earlier volumes. And I must remind the reader,
and more painfully myself, that on the present views time will also
have its way.

There is also the disconcerting business, half euphoric, half de-
pressant, of discovering what you did not see before. One such matter
is central. Dominating this book as a drumbeat is the theme of unequal development and the associated inequality in income. The
unequal development is unrelated to need; the inequality in income
bears no necessary relation to productivity or efficiency. Both are the
result of unequal deployment of power. Both are socially damaging.
In the established economics these tendencies are mostly concealed
and where not concealed are misconstrued. But I did not see them
with sufficient clarity in the earlier books. In *The Affluent Society* I
dealt with the starvation of the public services as though all services
were alike. I did not see that this deprivation was great where public
needs were involved, nonexistent where powerful industry pressed its
requirements on the state. And perhaps partly because I was dealing
only with the world of the large corporation, I did not identify adequately the systemic inequality in product and income as between
different parts of the so-called private economy. Nor did I identify
sufficiently the problem, unknown to orthodox economics but en-

demic to planning, of matching performance in related parts of the economy and the consequences of failure to do so. From this failure come blackouts and energy crises of which we will hear much more before we hear less.

2

This book also speaks in a somewhat different mood to a somewhat different audience. In recent years the ideas in the earlier books have won a certain measure of professional acceptance, especially among a younger generation of economists. It would be nice to think that this was the result of the logical force and clarity of the argument; more of my debt, alas, is to circumstance. In the earlier books I argued that the quality of our life would suffer from a single-minded concentration on the production of salable goods as a social goal; that the environment would be a casualty; that we would suffer especially from the disparate development of the services of the private economy and those of the state; and that some exceedingly somber problems were inherent in the growth of the power of the great private and public bureaucracies and their exercise of that power, including that over weaponry and other technical development, in their own interest. This bureaucratic power, not that classically associated with the sovereignty of the consumer, was now the decisive force in economic and political life.

The initial reaction to this argument, at a time when the prospect seemed more benign than now, was less than enthusiastic. Important economists, including many whose self-regard is widely shared, were sharply averse. They judged the traditional ideas to have survived intact. But events intervened, and with a force which I did not foresee. Problems inherent in my case — the decay of services and therewith of life in the great cities, pollution and environmental disharmony, the extravagances and dangers of the weapons culture, the seeming indifference to the public will of the great corporations — became ever more visible and the staple subjects of oratory and, on occasion, even of action. For being right, one may perhaps conclude, it is better to have the support of events than of the higher scholarship.

The notion that power in the modern economy lies increasingly with the great organizations and increasingly less with the supposedly sovereign consumer and citizen has also been making its way into the textbooks. Something here is owing to a vacuum. In recent years there has been a rapidly growing discontent with the established or-neoclassical model of economic and political life. The way was open for an alternative. Still the inertial forces are great. The textbook writer is naturally a cautious fellow. Like liberal candidates for public office he must always have one eye for what is reputable and salable as distinct from what is true. And, as these pages will sufficiently emphasize, economics is not primarily an expository science; it also serves the controlling eceonomic interest. It cultivates the beliefs and therewith the behavior that such interest requires. I would like to see economic instruction reflect the current reality. And it should be no part of its purpose to propagate the convenient belief. In writing this book, I have had the general reader in view. But I've also had the emancipation of the student from the textbook very much in mind.

Not that one can escape entirely from the textbook. Economics now brings its communicants to conclusions that are convenient for the great corporation but painful for the society. But the economic concepts and institutions that are explained by the texbooks — capital, rent, Gross National Product, index numbers, money supply, income tax, the capital market, the purposes of the Federal Reserve System — are essential knowledge. So is the capacity to visualize an economic system, provided always that one does not become a captive of a particular image. So we must still have textbooks — though hopefully we will not always have their present view of the economic system. And we must not be limited to the textbooks.

Perhaps it should be added that we must also still have diligence. In recent times the politically emancipated, or those who so regard themselves, have tended to identify difficult matters with the obscurantism of the Establishment. Study is a tedious disguise for wickedness, a way of diverting people from the simple disconcerting truth. This does not arouse my sympathy. It would not, the more radical may be reminded, have aroused the sympathy of Marx, for his was a notably demanding intellectual tradition. It is one thing to liberate man from physical toil. To exempt him from mental effort is premature.

3

As noted, this book seeks to bring the market sector of the economy and therewith the whole economic system into focus. But if we are to see the whole, the highly organized sector with which I dealt in *The New Industrial State* must also be here. In consequence some chapters go over ground covered in the earlier book. Such repetition rightly arouses suspicion — few things are more tempting to a writer than to repeat, admiringly, what he has said before. Yet there was no alternative. Pleas to the reader to go back to an earlier book are poorly obeyed. However, I've greatly abbreviated the previous argument and, as noted, also altered the tone. Before, I was seeking to establish a bridgehead in existing belief. This, unless I am greatly mistaken, has now, at least partly, been won. Accordingly, where the earlier book argued (and in some degree shamed or cajoled), this one assumes a receptive audience and explains.

Once I considered publishing the part of this book dealing with the theory of reform as a separate volume. (For better or for worse I am a reformer and not a revolutionist.) It is a terrible and sobering fact that the first part of any book, and especially one on economics, is likely to be better read than the last. But I could not have two books without prefacing the second with a detailed and repetitious summary of the first. This would have been a heavy trial for the reader and a dubious enjoyment for the writer. (I recapitulate at intervals in this volume not for pleasure but because such reminder is recurrently necessary if the further argument is to be persuasive.) Had there been two books, moreover, I would have had to end the first with a request to the reader to buy another. Again one doubts the response. So there is only one book. But I beg the reader not to give up after the first twenty or so chapters. It is then that the book gets on to the questions of what to do. By these I set much store. For on no conclusion is this book more clear: Left to themselves, economic forces do not work out for the best except perhaps for the powerful.

THE GENERAL THEORY OF ADVANCED DEVELOPMENT[2]

IN THE NEOCLASSICAL model oligopoly — the market shared by a few firms — is the only concession to the existence of the large firm. In fact it reflects a small step in a giant process which moves much of economic life dramatically away from this model. The oligopolist can fix prices, control production. But much more than this is involved when firms become large; in fact a transformation of the very nature of economic society occurs.

The critical instrument of transformation is not the state or the

---

[2] Chapter V, "The General Theory of Advanced Development," *Economics and the Public Purpose*, pp. 38–51.

individual but the modern corporation. It is the moving force in the change. But all social life is a fabric of tightly interwoven threads. The change of which the corporation is the driving force is a complex process in which many things are altered at the same time and in which cause becomes consequence and cause again. No description is uniquely correct; much depends on where one breaks into this matrix.[3] But a starting point which has application over the whole development is technology and its yet more important counterpart which is organization.

Technology — the development and application of scientific or systematic knowledge to practical tasks — is a central feature of modern economic development. It comes to bear on both products and services and on the processes by which these are made or rendered. Organization goes hand in hand with technical advance. Little use can be made of technology from the knowledge available to any one man; all but invariably its employment requires the shared knowledge of several or numerous specialists — in short, of an organization. But this is only the beginning. To make technology effective, capital is required — plant, machinery, assembly lines, power, instrumentation, computers, all the tangible embodiment of technology. The management of this equipment also requires specialists and more organization.

With rare exceptions the more technical the process or product, the greater the gestation period that is involved — the greater the elapse of time between the initial investment and the final emergence of a usable product. Goods being in process for a greater time, the investment in working capital is greater. Steps must be taken to ensure that initial decisions are not ruined and capital lost by events that occur before the results are achieved. The capital that is now at risk and the organization that now exists must be paid for — are an overhead cost. It is incurred or persists whatever the level of output. This adds to the need to control intervening events. Things that might go wrong and jeopardize sales and therewith the return to capital or the revenue that is needed to pay for organization must be prevented from going wrong; things that need to go right must be made to go right.

In specific terms this means that prices must, if possible, be under control; that decisive costs must also be under control or so managed

[3] See *The New Industrial State*, 2nd ed., rev. (London: André Deutsch, 1972), p. 45.

that adverse movements can be offset by the controlled prices; that effort must be made to ensure that the consumer responds favorably to the product; that if the state is the customer, it will remain committed to the product or its development; that other needed state action is arranged and any adverse government action prevented; that other uncertainties external to the firm are minimized and other external needs assured. In other words the firm is required, with increasingly technical products and processes, increasing capital, a lengthened gestation period and an increasingly large and complex organization, to control or seek to control the social environment in which it functions — or any part which impinges upon it. It must plan not only its own operations; it must also, to the extent possible, plan the behavior of people and the state as these affect it. This is a matter not of ambition but of necessity.

For any given level and use of technology there is, no doubt, a technically optimum size of firm — the size which most economically sustains the requisite specialists, the counterpart organization and the associated capital investment. But the need to control environment — to exclude untoward events — encourages much greater size. The larger the firm, the larger it will be in its industry. The greater, accordingly, will be its influence in setting prices and costs. And the greater, in general, will be its influence on consumers, the community and the state — the greater, in short, will be its ability to influence, i.e., plan, its environment.

More important, as organization develops and becomes more elaborate, the greater will be its freedom from external interference. In the small, uncomplicated enterprise authority derives from the ownership of capital — of the means of production. In the large and highly organized firm authority passes to organization itself — to the technostructure of the corporation. At the highest level of development — that exemplified by the General Motors Corporation, General Electric, Shell, Unilever, IBM — the power of the technostructure, so long as the firm is making money, is plenary. That of the owners of capital, i.e., the stockholders, is nil.

As organization acquires power, it uses that power, not surprisingly, to serve the ends of those involved. These ends — job security, pay, promotion, prestige, company plane and private washroom, the charm of collectively exercised power — are all strongly served by the growth of the enterprise. So growth both enhances power over prices, costs, consumers, suppliers, the community and the state and also rewards in a very personal way those who bring it about. Not surprisingly the growth of the firm is a dominant tendency of advanced economic development.

This growth, with the associated exercise of power, is the primal force by which economic society is altered. In its practical manifestation, however, it is singularly uneven. In some parts of the economy such growth by the firm is subject to no clear upper limit. In other parts it is subject to severe limits or it proceeds against increasing resistance. Where the growth is stunted, so, of course, is the capacity to persuade consumers as to products, and the state as to products and needs, and so is the technical competence that goes with organization. These are facts of the first importance for understanding the modern economy. This is why, in some parts of the economy, production and the associated blessings are great or excessive and in other parts deficient. It is why the rewards to workers and other participants are far more favorable in some parts of the economy than others. It explains, as we shall see, much else.

2

As noted, the normal thrust for growth is aborted or stunted in numerous industries. This is a fact of prime importance, and the point at which growth is arrested is exceptionally clear. It is where direction by an individual, either an owner or his immediate agent, would have to give way to direction by an organization. Some tasks can be performed by organization, some cannot. In those industries where organization is inapplicable or ineffective the firm remains at a size which allows its operations to be performed or guided by a single individual. Four factors exclude organization, make necessary individual performance or direction.

Organization is excluded where the task is unstandardized and geographically dispersed. In such a case central supervision cannot easily or economically be maintained, and, the scale of operations at each geographical point being necessarily small, no very sophisticated technology with associated capital equipment can be brought to bear. In these instances there is no substitute for the incentive which accords a primary share of the return (or the lack of it) to the skill, intelligence and effort expended by an individual. Adding to the advantage of the individual in such instances is the frequent opportunity for exploiting himself and on occasion his family or immediate employees. Organizations are subject to rules as to pay and how hard or how long people are worked; individuals in relation to themselves or their families are not. For this reason they can flourish where organizations do not.

The second factor confining the firm to the authority of an individual person is the surviving demand for explicitly personal service. Where one person pays for the personal attention of another person, technology is ordinarily limited or excluded. Organization has few or no advantages.

The third factor limiting the scale of the firm is involvement with art. Scientists and engineers lend themselves well to organization. Although professional vanity celebrates their inspired individual creativity, they function normally in teams and with considerable and costly equipment which also requires management. The artist lends himself much less well to organization. Accordingly, if the product or service involves original and genuine (as distinct from repetitive or banal) artistic expression, the firm will always be small. Frequently, as in the case of personal services, it will be identical with an individual.

Finally, the firm is on occasion kept small by law, professional ethos or trade union restriction which prohibits the technology or organization (e.g., group medical practice) that would allow of the growth of the firm. This has especial application to the professions and the building trades, although in both cases it exists in combination with the geographical dispersion of the activity which also limits the size of the firm.

The chapters following return to the operation of the foregoing restraints on the growth of a firm.

3

The combination of a powerful thrust to the expansion of the firm in some parts of the economy with effective restraints on growth in other parts produces a remarkably skewed pattern of economic development. This is manifest in all nonsocialist industrial countries; the skewness is also evident in the Eastern European states and the Soviet Union. In the United States one may think of one thousand manufacturing, merchandising, transportation, power and financial corporations producing approximately half of all the goods and services not provided by the state. In manufacturing the concentration is greater. The two largest industrial corporations, General Motors and Exxon, have combined revenues far exceeding those of California and New York. With Ford and General Electric they have revenues exceeding those of all farm, forest and fishing enterprises. In the first quarter of 1971, the 111 industrial corporations with assets of a billion dollars or more had more than half of all the assets employed in manufacturing and received substantially more than half of the earnings on more than half of the sales. The 333 industrial corporations with assets of more than $500 million had a full 70 percent of all assets employed in manufacturing.[4] In transportation, communications, power utilities, banking and finance, although the concentration is somewhat less, the tendency is similar; in merchandising the concentration is also high. An assembly of the heads of the firms doing half of all the business in the United States would, except in appearance, be unimpressive in a university auditorium and nearly invisible in the stadium.

Making up the remainder of the economy are around twelve million smaller firms, including about three million farmers whose total sales are less than those of the four largest industrial corporations; just under three million garages, service stations, repair firms, laundries, laundromats, restaurants and other service establishments; two million small retail establishments; around nine hundred thousand construction firms; several hundred thousand small manufacturers;[5] and an unspecified number serving the multivariate interests of an advanced society in what is collectively called vice.

No agreed level of assets or sales divides the millions of small firms which are half the private economy from the handful of giant corporations which are the other half. But there is a sharp conceptual difference between the enterprise that is fully under the command of an individual and owes its success to this circumstance and the firm which, without entirely excluding the influence of individuals, could not exist without organization. This distinction, which may be thought of as separating the twelve million small firms from the one thousand giants, underlies the broad division of the economy here employed.

[4] Testimony of Willard F. Mueller, Hearing before the Select Committee on Small Business, United States Senate, 92d Congress, 1st Session, November 12, 1971, p. 1097. The inclusion of unconsolidated assets would increase the share of these corporations in all industrial assets. Summarizing, Professor Mueller observes in the same testimony, "there exists an extremely asymmetrical industrial structure, with the bulk of economic [i.e., industrial] activity controlled by an elite of a few hundred enormous corporations and the remainder divided among four hundred thousand small and medium-sized [manufacturing] businesses."
[5] Statistical Abstract of the United States, 1972, U.S. Department of Commerce. Figures are for 1969.

It distinguishes what is henceforth called the market system from what is called the planning system.

4

That the planning system does not conform to the neoclassical model — that its firms are not passive in response to the market or the state — will not be difficult to establish. Mainly it is a matter of breaking with accustomed and stereotyped thought. To this part of the economy we will return. The market system, in its admixture of monopoly and competition, does conform in broad outline to the neoclassical model. The latter model is a rough description of half of the economy; it has lost touch with the other and, in many ways decisive, half. Precisely because of its capacity for radical change the nonmarket part has transformed itself into something very different. But the market system also departs from the neoclassical model in two respects: Intervention by the state in this part of the economy is more extensive and altogether more normal than the theory suggests. And the market system must exist alongside the planning system. As might be imagined, its development is powerfully affected by this latter fact.

Subject to the constraints of knowledge, energy and ambition the firm in the market system, competitive or monopolistic, does maximize its profits. For this there is an affirmative incentive; in contrast with the firm in the planning system, where organization has taken power from the owner, the man in charge gets the profit or, at a minimum, can be tested and rewarded in accordance with his ability to produce profits. But the negative motivation may be even more compelling. If profits are good, the tendency of the firm will be to expand. Others will do likewise. In the usual case yet others can enter the business, for the required capital, in keeping with the small size of the firm, is also small. And, in contrast with the firms in the planning system, those already in the field do not have the advantage of a ready-built organization. All of this is to say that a little monopoly is far harder to protect than a big one. So, in the market system, production and prices are not likely to be effectively and reliably under the control of the firm. Nor are they likely to be subject to the collective authority of a few firms. So, if profits are abnormal, they will soon come down. This means that the entrepreneur does not for long have the luxury of preoccupying himself with any goal except that of making money. He must always, where this is concerned, do the best he can. Amateur defenders of the market, enchanted to discover, as did Adam Smith two centuries ago, that good seems to proceed from evil, have often gone on to conclude that avarice is an original virtue. This is to make virtue of what, in fact, is necessity.

It follows also from the absence of control over prices and production that in the market system much of the egalitarian tendency of the neoclassical system survives.

Since in the market system earnings are not likely long to be above the level that compensates the entrepreneur for his effort and capital, there will be no very reliable source of savings from business earnings. Accordingly the firm will be dependent — as the firm in the planning system is not — on outside sources of capital. This is a circumstance of much importance, as we shall see when we come to consider the public regulation of the economy. Should this involve the regulation of borrowing, as it does, the market system will be affected with particular force.

The firm in the market system can, by itself, do little to influence the behavior of its customers. The resources are lacking for the effort. Additionally the farmer who tried as an individual to recruit customers for his wheat, cattle or tomatoes would be charitably shaping consumer preferences for all the producers of these staples since wheat, cattle and tomatoes are largely indistinguishable whatever their source. And all know this to be so, as they may not in the case of gasoline. This homogeneity of product, coupled with the unappealing scale of their operations and income, is why no farmers are seen on Madison Avenue.

As an individual member of the market system cannot typically influence his customers,[6] so he cannot influence the state. The president of General Motors has a prescriptive right, on visiting Washington, to see the President of the United States. The president of General Electric has a right to see the Secretary of Defense and the president of General Dynamics to see any general. The individual farmer has no similar access to the Secretary of Agriculture; the individual retailer has no entrée to the Secretary of Commerce. It would be of little value to them if they did. The public bureaucracy, as we shall later see, can be effectively and durably influenced only by another organization. And between public and private organizations there can be a deeply symbiotic relationship.

[6] Agriculture is the purest case of the firm that is powerless in this regard. In the service industries, as I note presently, the firm does have some relation to its customers.

Innovation in the market system also conforms generally to that depicted by the neoclassical model. That means that it is very limited. Most innovation requires that there be capital to cover the period of development and gestation and to pay for the equipment which is its counterpart.[7] This the firm in the market system lacks; even more significantly it lacks the specialized technical and scientific talent and counterpart organization which modern technical development all but invariably requires. No important technical development of recent times — atomic energy and its applications, modern air transport, modern electronic development, computer development, major agricultural innovation — is the product of the individual inventor in the market system. Individuals still have ideas. But — with rare exceptions — only organizations can bring ideas into use. Innovation in the market system remains important mostly in the minds of those who cannot believe the small entrepreneur ever fails.

5

While the firm in the market system is subject to the market constraints and disciplines of the neoclassical model, it does not accept them with any pleasure. We may lay it down as a firm rule that all participants in the economic system will wish to modify such constraints in their own favor. They will try to influence prices, costs, consumer decisions and the actions of the community and the state. And this will be as true of the market system as the planning system. The difference is not in intent but ability. The market and its disciplines are greatly praised by scholars. They are rarely applauded by those who are subject to them.

Some limited independence of market constraints is inherent in the geographical dispersion of economic activity, the small volume of activity at any particular location and the high serviceability of the incentive system associated with individual entrepreneurship. This dispersion means, very often, that there is room in a particular area for only one or a few entrepreneurs. More neighborhood drugstores, pizza merchants, laundromats, and all would starve. Thus the firm acquires a measure of control over prices and production. And through the charm of his personality or the modest eloquence of his persuasion the proprietor may develop a certain hold on his customers. Instead of

[7] See Edwin Mansfield, "Innovation and Size of Firm," in *Monopoly Power and Economic Performance*, Edwin Mansfield, ed. (New York: Norton, 1964), pp. 57–64.

competition there is differentiation of product or service by its association with the personality of a particular seller.[8] It is, needless to say, a highly circumscribed control — a motorized and mobile population is uniquely able to escape any effort at exploitation by its neighborhood monopolist.

The neoclassical model takes product differentiation and local monopoly more or less in stride. It is less tolerant of collective efforts at market control. These are numerous and frequently invoke the assistance or initiative of the state. The worker rejects the opportunity of selling his services on the market as an individual and unites with others to sell them through the union. The union thus gains power over the common price of such services and, through control of apprenticeship or membership, on occasion over supply. Government support to collective bargaining reinforces this control. The small clothing manufacturer or builder uses the union scale which is common to all plus a conventional markup as the basis for pricing his product. So do others, and all thus win control (sometimes tenuous) over prices. Physicians, chiropractors, osteopaths, optometrists, lawyers and the building trades control or influence supply by control of educational requirements, apprenticeship requirements or state licensing. Farmers persuade the state to fix prices by government purchase and, through acreage or marketing quotas, to limit supply. Small manufacturers seek publicly enforced retail price maintenance, small retailers protection against preferential treatment of large competitors under the Robinson-Patman Act. All of these efforts reflect the tendency of all producing firms, whether in the market or planning system, to control their economic environment and not be subject to it.

In agriculture this effort has gone beyond the control of production and prices to embrace somewhat elementary efforts to influence consumer response. The nutritional and moral benefit from consuming milk and its products is advertised. Similarly fruits, nuts and other agricultural specialties. In recent times the effort of the United States Department of Agriculture in promoting the consumption of tobacco has been in interesting contrast with the effort of the Department of Health, Education and Welfare to portray its lethal effects.

In agriculture there has also been a notably successful effort to exempt technology from the constraints imposed by the market sys-

[8] See Edward H. Chamberlin's *The Theory of Monopolistic Competition* (Cambridge: Harvard University Press, 1933). Market control which depends on such product differentiation was called by Chamberlin "monopolistic competition."

tem. This has been accomplished (as also we shall see in the planning system) by the socialization of technical innovation and its propagation — this being the accomplishment of the federal and state experiment stations and laboratories, the colleges of agriculture and the agricultural extension services. The planning system has also contributed heavily to technical innovation in agriculture through the farm equipment and chemical industries. So, in lesser degree, have corporations which are directly participant in agriculture either through contracts with farmers for feeding poultry or livestock or by direct operations, as in the case of fruit and vegetable growing. Those who cite modern agriculture as an example of the progressive tendencies of small enterprise and the market economy invariably overlook the role of the government and the supplying corporations. No innovation of importance originates with the individual farmer. Were it not for the government and the farm equipment and chemical firms, agriculture would be technologically stagnant.[9]

6

The difference between the planning and the market systems does not lie in the desire to escape from the constraints of the market and to effect control over the economic environment. It is in the instruments by which these are accomplished and the success with which they are attended. Participants in the market system who want stabilization of their prices or control of their supply must act collectively or get the assistance of the government. Such effort is highly visible and often ineffective, unsuccessful or inefficient. Voluntary collective efforts can be destroyed by a few deserters. Legislators do not always respond — even to farmers. If action is taken, it is often taken

[9] As noted earlier in this chapter, the large firm is impelled to control its prices (and other aspects of its environment) in order to protect the investment that technology requires. This is also one of the important services to agriculture of government price-fixing. Such price stabilization makes it possible for farmers to invest in the working capital and equipment that such technology requires in a manner that would never be possible were they subject to the vagaries of unmanaged prices. This does much to explain the great increase in agricultural productivity since farm price support legislation was initiated in 1933. This intervention does not accord with the instruction of the neoclassical model — it puts prices above the equilibrium level and keeps them from clearing markets. In consequence it is deplored as unsound policy and as a source of social inefficiency. This criticism is regularly voiced by scholars who praise the efficiency and technical progressiveness of the American farmer.

apologetically, for it is recognized that the established economics disapproves.

In the planning system, in contrast, the firm wins its control over prices automatically and with no public fanfare merely by being large. Similarly over output. And it can be large because its tasks lend themselves to organization. There are also things for which it needs the support of the state. But its approach is not to the legislature but to the bureaucracy. This is more reticent. And, the bureaucracy being more powerful, it is also likely to be more effective. The consequence, not surprisingly, is that firms in the market system get much attention for accomplishing very little by way of setting aside market constraints or otherwise modifying the economic environment to which they are subject. And the large firms in the planning system get no attention for accomplishing much. This is extensively reflected in economic pedagogy. The political power and depredations of the farm lobby are much celebrated by economists. The far more powerful control by General Motors of prices, costs and consumer responses and its far more influential association with the Department of Transportation, the Department of Defense and the regulatory agencies are much less remarked.

7

The planning system seeks to exercise control over its economic environment, and, as later chapters sufficiently establish, it succeeds. The market system manifests the same desire, is much more visible in its effort and is much less successful. The one system dominates its environment; the other remains generally subordinate to it.

But the planning system is very much a part of the environment to which the market system is subordinate. It supplies power, fuel, machinery, equipment, materials, transportation, communications that the market system uses. It also supplies a large share of the consumers' goods and services that participants in the market system purchase. And it is an important purchaser of the products of the market system — most notably in the case of agriculture. A prime feature of this relationship will already be evident. The market system buys at prices which are extensively subject to the power of the planning system. And an important part of its products and services are sold at prices which it does not control but which may be subject to the market power of the planning system. Given this distribution of power, there is a prima facie case that things will work better for the planning system than for the market system. The terms of trade between the two systems will have an insouciant tendency to favor the system that controls its prices and costs and therewith the prices and costs of the other system as well. A further effect, unless there is unimpeded mobility between the two systems, will be inequality of return — a relatively secure and favorable income for participants in the planning system, a less secure and less favorable return for those in the market system. To these hypotheses I will return, for, alas, they have solid substance. First it is necessary to examine more carefully the central characteristics of the two systems.

THE MARKET SYSTEM AND THE ARTS[10]

AS SERVICES RESIST organization, so also do the arts. This has not been much noticed, and the oversight is not remarkable. Economics has never had a serious view of art. Science and technology are important matters. Painting, sculpture, music, the theater, design are more frivolous. The manufacture of canvas, paint or pigment is a worthy concern of the economist; anything that lowers the cost of these commodities or expands their output contributes to economic goals. But the quality of the painting as distinct from the paint or what causes artists to colonize, multiply and prosper has never been thought a proper concern of the subject. Artistic achievement may, in principle, be part of the claim of an age or place to development. But as compared with the production of goods or technical or scientific accomplishment it has no practical standing. None of this is an accident. The relevant attitudes are firmly grounded in the nature of modern economic society.

2

The artist is, by nature, an independent entrepreneur. He embraces an entire task of creation; unlike the engineer or the production-model scientist he does not contribute specialized knowledge of some part of a task to the work of a team. Because he is sufficient to himself, he does not submit readily to the goals of organization; to do so

[10] Chapter VII, "The Market System and the Arts," *Economics and the Public Purpose*, pp. 61–70.

is to sacrifice his view of what is artistically worthy to the organization view. That is to sacrifice artistic integrity, for the latter, whether the result be good or bad, is always coordinate with the artist's own view of his task.

Not needing the support of organization and not being able or allowed to accept the goals of organization, the artist fits badly into organization. As so often, everyday speech reflects the fact. The excessively independent man is regularly defended in an organization as "something of an artist." The brilliant nuisance or unemployable eccentric is said to be "altogether too much of an artist." The artist, on his side, finds life in any sizable and successful organization cloying, restrictive or even stifling. And he is required, if he is to have the good opinion of his peers, to say so.

In consequence, except in some slight measure where the discipline of organization is itself artistic — that of a symphony orchestra or a ballet company — the artist functions as an independent entrepreneur (a term he is unlikely to employ) or, as in the case of a self-respecting architect, as a member of a very small firm which he can dominate or in which he can preserve the identity of his work. A few industries — the motion picture firms, television networks, the large advertising agencies — must, by their nature, associate artists with rather complex organization. All have a well-reported record of dissonance and conflict between the artists and the rest of the organization. A small literature — Budd Schulberg's *What Makes Sammy Run?*, Evelyn Waugh's short story, "Excursion in Reality," Rod Serling's *Patterns* — celebrates this conflict and the crudities of organization men as viewed by artists. Frequently the problem is solved by removing actors, actresses, script writers, directors, composers, copywriters and creators of advertising commercials from the technostructure of the film studio, television network or advertising agency and reconstituting them in small independent companies. The large firm then confines itself to providing the appropriate facilities for producing and — more importantly — marketing, exhibiting or airing the product. Similarly painters, sculptors, concert pianists and novelists[11] function, in effect, as one-man firms or, as in the case of rock, dance and folk music groups, as small partnerships and turn to larger organizations to market themselves or their product.

[11] When the late Ian Fleming, the manufacturer of James Bond, turned himself into a limited company a short while before his death, it was a matter of worldwide comment.

3

Where manufacturing requires a measure of artistic effort and is judged in part by this, the artistic superiority of the small firm will often allow of its survival in competition with the large organization. Since the good artist cannot or will not be subordinate to organization, the large, relatively immobile enterprise commands not the best talent but the most accommodating. This, more or less by definition, is second-rate. Nor is this purely a matter of poor or perverse taste on the part of the organization. The large firm must have designs that will lend themselves to long and economical production runs. Artistic sense must also yield to the will of those who, on the basis of instinct, experience or market research, are knowledgeable on what the public can be persuaded to buy. Artistic judgment is subject to a supervening view of acceptability, and this, in turn, is powerfully influenced by the common working assumption, sometimes articulated, that no one ever went into receivership underestimating the popular taste. In consequence the large firm gets long runs, technical efficiency, low costs and a considered marketing strategy at the expense of good design. The automobile industry, the mass producers of furniture, the household appliance industry, the container industry and numerous others amply illustrate the point.

In the smaller manufacturing firm in which the artist has a dominant role or in which, at a minimum, the discipline of organization is less severe, there is more scope for individual assertion which is essential. In consequence design can be much better. Further, the artist having a dominant role, the design will not be subordinate to efficiency on the production line. It will reflect the artist's sense of what is good, not the technician's knowledge of what can be efficiently produced or the marketing man's sense of what can be sold. Thus, although technically less proficient, the small firm has, because of its small size, the advantage of superior art. In the manufacture of apparel, jewelry, timepieces, furniture, other household artifacts and in cooking, house construction and publishing this advantage can be considerable. Invariably the small firm serves what is called the upper end of the market, i.e., that providing a more expensive product to more affluent consumers who have superior taste or (perhaps the more common case) superior guidance thereto.

On occasion small firms are kept in being by large firms which need, but cannot themselves employ, the talent the small firms command. The big dress manufacturers buy models from the small designers; the automobile manufacturers seek the help of Italian entrepreneurs; DuPont turns to small firms in Paris and New York for fabric designs. It is easy to hire chemists, a DuPont official observed in conversation a few years ago, and to know what you are getting. But no one knows how to hire good artists, and they won't live in Wilmington, Delaware.

The small firm also derives an advantage from the distinctive nature of the demand curve for the work of the artist. The position of this demand curve — the amount that people will buy at any given price — is a function of time. People, as presently to be emphasized, are persuaded strongly to believe that technical innovation is a *good* thing — that it is coordinate with progress. This being so, the market response to such innovation is generally favorable. Such attitudes, of course, coincide with and reflect the needs of the planning system. Public attitudes toward artistic innovation, by contrast, have been subject to no such conditioning. Accordingly the first impression of artistic innovation is almost invariably unfavorable. What is new is commonly thought offensive or grotesque. So it was with the Impressionists, the Cubists, the Abstract Expressionists, and so it is with the modern exponents of Pop Art. The situation is similar in prose, poetry and much music. It follows that the initial market for innovative work in the arts is almost always small; only as taste develops does demand expand. But some are attracted and some have pleasure in seeming to appreciate what others reject. Thus they are willing to pay. This situation — a small market in which cost is secondary to the quality of the artistic achievement — also lends itself well to the individual or the small firm.[12]

4

In the past one of the most common manifestations of affluence was expenditure on the arts. The quality of the public and ecclesiastical architecture and its embellishment and of the public entertainment was the visible test of community achievement. For the private

---

[12] While the contrast between the popular reaction to technical and to artistic innovation depends on social conditioning, this may not be the whole explanation. It may be that visual reactions are inherently conservative and then, with time, undergo accommodation. For this reason new grotesqueries in dress or automobiles — those for which no one would dream of advancing any artistic claim — become after a time visually tolerable.

household the excellence of the dwelling and its painting, sculpture, furniture, food and conversation provided a similar test. This was especially true of those communities — Venice, Florence, Genoa, Amsterdam, Bruges and Antwerp — where the orientation was strongly to economic achievement. Military and sexual prowess, accomplishment in courtly routines and manners and commitment to gastronomic and alcoholic excess have always been the principal rivals to the arts as manifestations of civilized accomplishment. The commercial cities, as compared with the courts, were generally more resistant to all these forms of display.

In modern times the arts, as a measure of both community and private achievement, have undergone a great relative decline. Scientific and engineering accomplishments have become overwhelmingly more important, and these have also invaded the esteem that was once associated with military prowess. Few now speak of the discipline, parade-ground virtuosity or bravery of soldiers, sailors or aviators. It is the excellence of their tanks, nuclear submarines, aircraft or the guidance systems with which they are equipped that excites comment and measures national accomplishment. Space exploration is an even more dramatic example of the use of scientific and engineering virtuosity as a measure of national achievement. As medieval towns once compared the magnificence of their cathedrals and the munificence of their decoration, modern superpowers parade the number, conception and cost of their expeditions, manned or unmanned, to the moon and the planets or their laboratories in orbit around the earth. The reward, however, continues to be partly metaphysical and spiritual.[13] It is part of the normal argument for scientific or engineering expenditure that there is great ultimate human benefit. In the case of the exploration of the moon it is generally agreed that there was little or none. That we did not ask for such benefit was, in this instance, a measure of our intellectual and spiritual maturity. Again we see the influence of the convenient social virtue.

Scientific and engineering accomplishments are likewise the ac-

---

[13] In his prepared remarks for the return of the first astronauts from the moon Dr. George C. Mueller, space-flight director for NASA, urged Americans not to "substitute temporary material welfare for spiritual welfare and long-term accomplishment." He went on to plead that we "dedicate ourselves to the unfinished work so nobly begun by three of us to resolve that this nation, under God, will join with all men in the pursuit of the destiny of mankind . . ." The power of such spiritual commitment should not, however, be exaggerated. Dr. Mueller subsequently accepted a higher salary as a vice president of General Dynamics. See Richard F. Kaufman, *The War Profiteers* (Indianapolis and New York: Bobbs-Merrill, 1970), p. 80.

cepted measure of achievement in other fields — physics, chemistry, genetics, aviation, computer technology. No one would think of according similar importance to the comparative accomplishments of the Soviet Union and the United States in painting, the theater, the novel or industrial design. At least until recently, in any competitive display of painting, poetry or music, both countries would have been compelled to delete their best or most interesting offering. Americans, selecting art for such display, would have had to avoid what numerous congressional critics would condemn as Communist-inspired work. The Soviets would have had similarly to exclude work that reflected bourgeois decadence. Since engineering and scientific accomplishments are the accepted measures of community achievement, it follows that education and other support for these subjects is not only a proper but a highly desirable employment of public funds. The arts, for obvious reasons, have no similar claim.

No one will be in doubt as to the source of these attitudes. It lies with the technostructure and the planning system and with their ability to impose their values on the society and the state. The technostructure embraces and uses the engineer and the scientist; it cannot embrace the artist. Engineering and science serve its purpose; art, at best, is something which it needs but finds troublesome and puzzling. From these attitudes come those of the community and the government. Engineering and science are socially necessary; art is a luxury.

5

While artistic accomplishment has ceased to be a test of social achievement, the esoteric and pretentious apart, it has a continuing and perhaps increasing importance for the individual and the household. The everyday standards for assessing the reputability and general social position of a family do eschew any artistic element. They center, instead, on the supply of standard goods. The inhabitants of a three-bedroom house are thought "better off" than those of a two-bedroom house; they gain further distinction from having a fully equipped kitchen and being a two- as opposed to a one-car family. The technical character and novelty of goods, not their beauty, is stressed in advertising. To attack the design of a consumer product as banal is often to invite an indignant response. It is what the people want. The critic is an elitist.

However at higher income levels an artistic sense or pretense in domestic architecture, interior decoration, furniture, landscape design and even in food and entertainment tends either to be enjoyed for its own sake or is part of the claim to esteem. This, in turn, sustains a substantial and growing market for the work of artists as well as for individuals who provide guidance to those who, often perceptively, lack confidence in their own taste. As a consequence an appreciable volume of modern economic activity depends not on the technical efficacy of the product or the efficiency with which it is produced but on the quality of the artists associated with the design. Some industries are so based. Danish and Finnish furniture owe their modern distinction not to engineering competence but to artistic worth. The postwar renaissance of Italian industry had a similar basis. Italian products excel not in engineering but in appearance. And there is a similar if less visible development in the United States. It is as yet little recognized — no one would think of encouraging the artist as opposed to the engineer, scientist or business manager as the foundation of future industrial development. But its monopoly of artistic achievement provides an important assurance of the survival of the small firm.

6

Over a longer period of time the arts and products that reflect artistic accomplishment will, for the foregoing reasons, be increasingly central to economic development. There is no reason, a priori, to suppose that scientific and engineering achievements serve the ultimate frontiers in human enjoyment. At some point, as consumption expands, a transcending interest in beauty may be expected. This transition will vastly alter both the character and structure of the economic system.

It will first have to contend, however, with the social conditioning of the technostructure and the planning system which, as just noted, relegate to a minor social role what cannot be embraced or used. The transition will have also to contend with the convenient social virtue of the artist. This requires a word, for it is what causes the artist to accept an inferior economic and social role both for himself and for art in general.

Specifically the artist has been persuaded that the world of economics is one to which, by nature, he has little relation. It is part of his pride that the number who can appreciate the work of the true artist — who have a valid response to its meaning — must always be very small. So his market and the resulting compensation must be meager. This meagerness, in turn, shows his merit. The more deprived his life, the more truly is he an artist. Only the more modest religious offices share the artist's belief that merit is inversely related to compensation.

This view of the artist of himself has two social advantages. It economizes expenditure on the arts, for, if pecuniary reward does not improve and possibly even damages performance, it should obviously be kept to the minimum. And it means that all but a minority of artists are kept safely in that subordinate and anonymous state that is reserved for the indigent or near-indigent. They do not in consequence compete with managers, scientists or engineers for social esteem. Nor do they compete with scientists and engineers for public funds to support the arts.

The claim on public resources is further reduced by the belief, also accepted in varying measure by the artist, that not much can be done about education in the arts. Given only the money, any number of scientists and engineers can be supplied. These can be processed from almost any lumber. The number of artists produced cannot, however, exceed the number of people with intrinsic talent, and the part of the population with such talent is assumed, although on no known evidence, to be small. And it is part of the folk attitude toward the arts that the truly inspired artist will excel, whatever the barriers to be overcome. The convenient social virtue thus minimizes the need for expenditure on education in the arts.

It is worth recalling that until about a hundred and fifty years ago the convenient social virtue held the scientist to be an unworldly and monkish figure whose support was properly the function of a private patron. The public dignity of the artist, being older and better established, was then far greater, and the artist had a strong claim on public resources. The scientist has long since escaped from these monkish origins; personal affluence and public support are no longer imagined to be damaging to his creative instinct. On the contrary they are deemed necessary for it. The artist, by contrast, still depends extensively on private patronage; he has come, along with the rest of the community, to accept the view that public support to the arts could be dangerously repressive of the artistic spirit.[14] It is obvious that the resulting saving in public funds — as compared with a society that sets the same store by the arts as, say, by moon travel — is very great.

[14] Architects, being needed by industry, are emancipated from the belief that artistic achievement is damaged by economic association or personal affluence.

7

Thus the arts. They will continue to be a major stronghold of the individual and the small firm. They will also be an expanding part of economic life. The opportunities for enjoyment from artistic development have no visible limit; they are almost certainly greater than those from technical development.

But this expansion would be much greater were the sources of our present attitudes on art, science and technology better understood. The arts now have an infinitely smaller claim than science and engineering on both private and public resources. This, we have seen, is the result not of public preference but of conditioned belief. People — including artists themselves — are persuaded to accord importance and priority to what is within the competence and serves the needs of the technostructure and the planning system.

The means for emancipating belief — for releasing it from service to the planning system — is a matter to which, obviously, we must return.

THE NEGATIVE STRATEGY OF ECONOMIC REFORM[15]

REFORM IN MODERN economic society proceeds directly from the diagnosis. There would be little need for emphasizing such a notably unsubtle point were it not that the present diagnosis leads to remedies that are at variance, sometimes by 180 degrees, from the standard liberal or social democratic prescription. Yet, on reflection, this will not seem surprising. Were the standard remedies working, the anxieties just examined would not be present.

The invariable liberal or social democratic response to economic power is adverse. It is to dissipate, regulate, civilize or socialize it. In the United States the automatic liberal response on encountering industrial power is to call for vigorous action under the antitrust laws. Or the regulatory agencies — the Federal Trade Commission, Federal Communications Commission, SEC, FDA, Bureau of Standards, Department of Transportation or the Office of Consumer Affairs — are summoned to their duty. In its pricing, procurement, service or product design the corporation must be made to respect the

[15] Chapter XXI, "The Negative Strategy of Economic Reform," *Economics and the Public Purpose*, pp. 215–220.

public interest. Or, a very recent remedy, a campaign is mounted to place people who will speak for the public on boards of directors of offending corporations. Finally, if the complainant is radical, the offense extreme, the power of the offending enterprise great and the expectation of action minimal, there may be call for public ownership. Private enterprise has failed.

2

Mention has already been made of the useful futility of the antitrust laws. The practical experience cannot easily be ignored. The Sherman Act, the basic antitrust law, is only a little under a century old — it was enacted in 1890. The Federal Trade Commission, the principal agency of general industrial regulation, is about to celebrate its diamond jubilee. Were something to have happened, it would surely have happened by now. But we now see that there is more than long experience to induce doubt. The remedy implicit in the antitrust laws — the dissolution of the large corporate enterprise and therewith its power — is dramatic and even Draconian in aspect. Each new generation, as noted, can imagine that lack of past accomplishment was the result of the excessively pusillanimous tendency of their predecessors. All can assert hope, however exiguous, for the future.[16] Both the prosecution and the defense of the antitrust laws sustain among lawyers, in the manner of traditional automobile insurance, a rewarding pecuniary return. But from the standpoint of the techno-structure and the planning system the antitrust laws are admirably innocuous. Were there only a handful of great corporations exercising power over prices, costs, the consumer and over public attitudes, per-haps their dissolution into smaller units and therewith the dissolution of their power might be possible. But a government cannot proclaim half of the economic system illegal; it certainly will not do so if its test of sound public policy is what, in general, serves the goals of this part of the economy. The planning system need fear only peripheral

[16] Not always, though, with great confidence. See Donald F. Turner's interesting essay, "The Scope of Antitrust and Other Economic Regulatory Policies," in *Industrial Organization and Economic Development*, edited by Jesse W. Markham and Gustav F. Papanek (Boston: Houghton Mifflin, 1970). Professor Turner, a firm supporter of the antitrust laws and a former Assistant Attorney General in charge of their prosecution, concedes "the past inadequacies and periodic atrophy of antitrust in the monopoly and oligopoly areas." But he contents himself with suggesting that "as a matter of public policy, there ought to be at least a modest expansion [in enforcement]." P. 76.

harassment by the antitrust laws. This has the principal consequence of persuading the public that something is happening.

But it will now also be evident that the antitrust laws, if they worked as their proponents hope, would only make problems worse. Their purpose is to stimulate competition, lower prices, otherwise unshackle resource use and promote a more vigorous expansion of the particular industry. But the problem of the modern economy is not the inferior performance of the planning system — of the monopolistic or oligopolistic sector, to revive the traditional terminology. The problem is the greater development here as compared with the market system. And the greater the power, the greater the development. Where the power is least — where economic organization conforms most closely to the goals envisaged by the antitrust laws — the development is least. If they fulfilled the hopes of their supporters and those they support, the antitrust laws would make development more unequal by stimulating development further in precisely those parts of the economy where it is now greatest. That would be unfortunate. If the expectations of the present analysis were realized — if the market were genuinely restored — competence would be lowered to the level of the market system. Policy unrelated to reality ends in absurdity.

Once it was argued that the antitrust laws, if vigorously enforced, would reduce the power of the monopolist to exploit his workers. Thus inequality would be reduced. Not even devout supporters of the antitrust laws now so argue, and we also have seen the reasons. The planning system does not exploit its own workers in the classical manner; in comparison with those in the market system, these workers are a privileged group. This is one reason why unions representing these workers do not share the liberal's passion for enforcement of the antitrust laws.

It will be evident that the antitrust laws are more than a blind alley along the path to reform. They are, as previously observed, a cul-de-sac in which reform can safely be contained.

3

The preceding chapters illuminate also the problem of regulation. If the purposes of the firm are believed to be those of the public, there will be a heavy burden of proof on regulation and the regulatory body. Unless there is a contrary showing, it will be assumed that any particular intervention by the state is against the public interest. In the name of the people it can be righteously opposed. This is a severe handicap. And one must expect that the planning system will at least partly capture any regulatory body for its own purposes. Many have noted that regulatory agencies tend to become the instruments, even the puppets, of the industries they are supposed to regulate. This we see to be normal.

Before the state can regulate in the planning system, it must be perceived that public and planning purposes normally diverge and that realignment through regulation is natural, not exceptional. And the state must be broken free from the power of the planning system. To this we will presently return.

It will also be evident from this analysis that, some useful offense to corporate dignity apart, nothing can be accomplished by efforts to influence corporations by way of their stockholders or boards of directors. The initial political task would be attempted only by those who have not taken its measure. Voting in the corporation is weighted pro rata with ownership. Such is the distribution of share ownership that the votes of the few and very rich invariably outweigh those of the many. What is called corporate democracy may be compared, roughly, with an election at large for the New York state legislature in which the votes of the officers of the New York banks and the members of the Rockefeller family as a bloc are weighted equally with and against those of the rest of the citizens of the state. Not many legislators would be elected by the citizens.[17]

In the case of the corporation there is also the unfortunate absence of power in the event that a representative of the public *is* elected. The technostructure, we have seen, has the power which derives from knowledge and active participation in decision-making. With this, in the mature corporation, no board of directors meeting for a few hours monthly or quarterly can contend. A minority on a board of directors on which the majority is devoid of power can have little sense of its omnipotence. Such is the position of the public interest director.

Though innovative in other respects, the technostructure of the modern corporation is rarely adventuresome in political matters. Were it so, every large corporation would have on its board of directors

[17] The recent effort via the stockholders to force modest social reforms on General Motors (Project GM), despite considerable effort and organization, produced minuscule votes — never as much as 3 percent of the total vote on any issue. See Donald E. Schwartz, "Toward New Corporate Goals: Co-existence with Society," *The Georgetown Law Journal*, Vo. 60, No. 1 (October 1971), p. 57 et seq. General Motors did yield to the extent of appointing a distinguished black leader to its board. Professor Schwartz concludes, mainly from this, that "The results, apart from the voting, were very impressive." He is too easily pleased.

a woman, a black, a devout ecologist, a consumer representative and the most ardent available exponent of safety. All known agitators would be so employed. All would meet every month or quarter with the board, ask searching questions, be advised of the value of their observations, be promised the most careful consideration. Nothing would happen. At least until the innocuousness of the arrangement was discovered, the planning system would be at peace.

4

The foregoing chapters also delineate the role of socialism as a remedy. The socialist, like the American liberal, is attracted to the positions of power. His antidote to the private exercise of power is public ownership. As with antitrust enforcement this does not remedy underdevelopment or exploitation of workers in the areas of power, for it is here that these ills are least. And public ownership is not a promising solution for privately exercised power if the state itself is the instrument of such power. As with regulation the emancipation of the state from the control of the planning system must come first. Additionally the problem of power derives not from private organization but from organization. All organization excludes interference from outside or above; its goals are those which serve the interest of its members. This is the behavior of an organization before it is taken over by the state; it will be its behavior after it has been taken over. This will be especially certain if its operations are technical in character and its power is derived from more or less exclusively possessed information.

Goals may differ. A public organization will not need a minimum level of earnings to protect its autonomy. Technological virtuosity for its own sake may be more important than growth. But it will not be less concerned with pursuing goals important to its members than the private organization. Nor will there be any greater certainty that these goals will accord with public purpose. In recent times there has been at least as much complaint about the indifference of the Atomic Energy Commission to public interest as that of General Motors. In any superficial view the nuclear test explosion at Amchitka, even though ultimately harmless, was as impersonally indifferent to public opinion as GM is on automobile safety or exhaust emissions. Few will think the Department of Defense more subject to public pressure and concern than the American Telephone and Telegraph Company. This accords with expectations.

None of this, however, excludes a role for public ownership in the management of power when the latter is rightly perceived. Where public and private organizations react symbiotically with each other, there is power in the symbiosis — in the division of labor that allows of lobbying, deployment of political funds, encouragement of political action by unions and local authorities, access to the legislature, management of intelligence information by whichever organization, public or private, is best equipped for the task. Here, as we shall later see, there is a strong case for full public ownership. And the case for such public ownership becomes stronger as the state is broken free from the influence of the planning system. We shall also see that public ownership is indispensable — and almost certainly inevitable — in important parts of the market system where inability to deploy power and to command resources is the problem.

THE EMANCIPATION OF BELIEF [18]

THE EMANCIPATION of belief is the most formidable of the tasks of reform and the one on which all else depends. It is formidable because power that is based on belief is uniquely authoritarian; when fully effective, it excludes by its nature the thought that would weaken its grasp. It can also be pleasant — a womb in which the individual rests without the pain of mental activity or decision. Or, to change the metaphor, as with Tolstoy's happy soldier all personal responsibility is given over to the regiment. And the drums to which all march are those of others. The present task is to win freedom from the doctrines that, if accepted, put people in the service not of themselves but of the planning system. There is help from circumstances, for, as the previous chapters have shown, the practical consequences of this subordination — in uneven development, in unequal income, in proliferation of dangerous weapons, on the environment and on personality itself — are increasingly painful. Pain or even modest discomfort is better for persuasion than more abstract argument.

The belief to be contested is that the purposes of the planning system are those of the individual. The power of the planning system depends on instilling the belief that any public or private action that serves its purposes serves also the purposes of the public at large. This depends, in turn, on popular acceptance of the proposition that the production and consumption of goods, notably those provided by the planning system, are coordinate with happiness and virtuous

[18] Chapter XXII, "The Emancipation of Belief," *Economics and the Public Purpose,* pp. 223–226.

behavior. Then all else becomes subordinate, more or less, to this end.

The virtue in question is that which is convenient to the purposes of the planning system. The virtuous head of a family works hard for an income that, however, is never quite sufficient for the things the family needs. These, as a practical matter, always increase a little more than income. If the man is on the shop floor, he is reliably on hand and welcomes any opportunity for overtime. He never stops working on the excuse that he has enough money for the moment and would prefer idleness. In recent years workers on the automobile assembly lines have taken to extending their weekends to increase their enjoyment of hunting, fishing, indolence and alcohol. None of these enjoyments is, in itself, thought wicked. But their pursuit in place of income is powerfully condemned.

If the individual is a professional or an executive, the foregoing compulsions are much increased. He is, in addition to all else, an example. So he is peculiarly relentless in his effort. He, of all people, cannot be negligent in his commitment to what is always called a better standard of living and on occasion is accorded the cachet of being called an American standard of living. The genuinely easygoing (as distinguished from the hard-driving) executive is a rarity. The bohemian executive — the corporation man who houses himself simply, dresses shabbily, feeds and entertains himself indifferently — is unthinkable.

The required virtue extends to the family. A wife is good if she devotes her time to procuring and processing the commodities and maintaining the artifacts that comprise the highest possible living standard. Sons are good if, whatever their adolescent oats, they settle down at the appropriate age to study engineering, science, business administration or other of the useful arts and become, with the aid of a like-minded woman, high achievers, the latter being the close synonym for those seeking high income and consumption. Likewise daughters if, after some juvenile experiment with art, indifferent dress or promiscuity, they adapt themselves to their mothers' mode of life. The virtue, it may be added, is heightened if the family accords support to measures — taxation, zoning, a reasonable attitude on air and water pollution — which ensure what is called a good climate for industry in the community, if they have an instinct for policies and politicians which promise a steadily expanding national economy and if they are patriotically sympathetic to the need for a strong national defense.

At all points the virtue of this family serves the purposes of the planning system. Even the process by which its virtue is kept convenient to the changing needs of the dominant economic power is impressively efficient. Once, when all possible income was wanted by the capitalist, it was the frugal workman, the poor but faithful book-keeper, who invited praise and who was known to have a simple but rewarding life. Now, growth being a prime goal of the planning system, admiration is for those who spend and consume expansively and even accept indebtedness in order to maintain a decent standard of living.

It is possible to imagine a family which sets an income target as its goal; which has husband and wife share in the provision of that mini-mum; which makes a considered and deliberate choice between leisure or idleness and consumption; which specifically rejects con-sumption which, by its aggregate complexity, commits the woman to a crypto-servant role; which encourages self-fulfilling as against useful education for the offspring; which emphasizes communal as opposed to individual enjoyments with the result that it resists industrial or other economic encroachment on its living space; which, in its public outlook, sets slight store by increased production of the goods of which it has a sufficient supply; and which is indifferent to argu-ments for expenditures on behalf of national prestige or military power from which it derives no identifiable benefit. This family is not formally condemned as wicked. It is not ostracized by the com-munity. But such esteem as it enjoys is the result, primarily, of its eccentricity.

2

The need, very simply, is recognition that our beliefs and the con-venient social virtue are derived not from ourselves but from the planning system. This seen, we also see that the patterns of a successful life are many and that a successful economy may well be one that enhances the opportunity for exercise of such choice. The maximization of income and consumption is one such option. So is the maximization of leisure — so long, at least, as it can be done without imposing cost on others. So is the setting of a target income and consumption which, when achieved, allows of other and non-remunerative use of time. And there is, of course, an infinite range of choice in such use of time. And there are different patterns of life and leisure in different years or at different times in life.[19]

19 It has long been expected that young people will pursue income only to the extent required for consumption including such artifacts as a bicycle or an automobile or such services as travel. Then these are enjoyed. Only beyond

It goes without saying that any attack on existing belief and the associated virtue will not be welcomed by those who reflect the attitudes and needs of the planning system. Nor will it necessarily be welcomed by those who are chained by existing belief to the purposes of the planning system. All of us rejoice in the vanity that we are the agents of our own will. And, as just noted, the need to think deeply about life and to choose between alternative economic styles will be for many an onerous burden. Better the accepted patterns of life than the terrible costs of thought and choice.

It will also be urged that for many or perhaps most families alternatives to the existing patterns of life do not exist. The pressures of physical or otherwise inescapable need — for the minimally essential food, clothing, shelter, medicine, education — preempt all energy. For many in the market system this must be conceded. But it is the further truth that, as income increases, needs continue to preempt all energy and eliminate all choice. This is the artifice of the planning system. The belief that this is necessary is what is being here resisted. The prime purpose of improving income, and especially of improving distribution of income, should be to increase the number of people who are removed from the pressures of physical need or its equivalent and who are able, in consequence, to exercise choice as to their style of economic life.

FISCAL POLICY, MONETARY POLICY AND CONTROLS[20]

[He] showed remarkable courage in facing up to the problem that this nation, and this Free Enterprise System, and this Free Society faced. He enforced wage and price controls.
—Former Secretary of the Treasury
John B. Connally, speaking of President Nixon

THERE REMAINS THE QUESTION of how the planning and market systems are to be guided so that they yield a reliable flow of income and product at reasonably stable prices. However

---

a certain age does respectability require that the individual settle down, which means that consumption and income should be maximized as the planning system requires.
[20] Chapter XXX, "Fiscal Policy, Monetary Policy and Controls," *Economics and the Public Purpose*, pp. 303–308, 316.

essential the other reforms they do not eliminate the need for competent economic performance. One cannot have a socially excellent economic system without having an economic system. Fortunately equitable performance and effective operation of an economy go together. And failure is all but invariably the result of policies that are in the interest not of the many but of the few, and invariably also with the pretense that it is the many who are being served.

The usual reminder is in order on the problem to be solved. The planning system cannot ensure that demand is sufficient to keep the system operating at capacity. Decisions to save and invest are concentrated in a comparative handful of firms — a few thousand. There is no machinery that ensures that the aggregate of the decisions to invest will be sufficient to offset the aggregate of the decisions to save. If investment is insufficient, the system will be subject to a downward spiral of output and income which — by reducing investment more than saving — may for a substantial time be cumulative and persistent.

Nor has the planning system the power to arrest the counterpart upward spiral in prices. Nothing confines the modern union, in seeking pay increases, to what can be afforded at going prices. And the modern corporation has the power over prices that allows it to pass the resulting increases along to the public. Competition between unions and the need to anticipate increases in living costs from yet unrealized wage increases make the upward spiral also cumulative and persistent. Without action by the state the planning system is prone to depression or inflation.

Past and current action by the state to prevent depression or inflation has had five major shortcomings, to wit:

(1) The heart of the strategy for stabilization is a large publicsector expenditure supported by a progressive and flexible tax system. The public spending which is central to this process has been extensively in the service of the planning system. Its effect in distorting development, on income distribution, in depriving other parts of the economy of needed capital and in the potential for universal destruction has been sufficiently remarked.

(2) The supporting tax system has also come to reflect, increasingly, the preferences of the planning system — and notably the preferences of the higher-salaried members of the technostructure. In consequence it has become steadily less progressive in its incidence, steadily less responsive to increases and decreases in income and steadily less efficient for stabilizing income and expenditure.

(3) Further, in the last decade, when it has been necessary to increase demand, there has been general reliance on tax reduction instead of increased public spending. Economists and legislators, mistaking the planning for the public interest, have approved. Such reduction has extensively favored the higher incomes in the technostructure. Or, as in the case of the suspension of the automobile excise tax in 1971, it has favored the products of the planning system. Or, as in the case of the tax credit for investment in the same year, it has directly subsidized the planning system. These tax reductions have increased the inequality in income distribution. They are also an inefficient method of expanding demand, for income is returned to affluent taxpayers where, in substantial part, it is saved. Savings from increased public expenditures to employ people on needed public tasks are much lower. Finally, when it is necessary again to restrain or contract demand, taxes are not easily increased. Instead exponents of the conventional wisdom call for economy in public outlays, and men of compassion are reduced to wishing they wouldn't. Since expenditures in behalf of the planning system are protected by pleas of high national purpose, it is spending for public purposes that is vulnerable.

(4) Those in charge of the management of the economy have been unable to perceive the decline of the market or — reflecting a natural vested interest in painfully acquired knowledge — have been unwilling to concede it. Accordingly faith in orthodox fiscal and monetary policy has died slowly, and efforts to come to grips with the wage-price spiral have been apologetic, halfhearted and avowedly temporary.

(5) Finally the efforts both to expand and contract demand have invoked monetary policy. This operates with punishing difference in effect as between the market and the planning systems.

2

The remedy begins not with the needs of stabilization but with those of general reform. And reform also requires a large and stable flow of public expenditures — expenditures that are related to public purposes, not those of the planning system. And an equitable distribution of income requires that these be paid for with a strongly progressive tax structure — a tax structure that reflects the public interest in fairness, not the interest of the planning system and the constituent technostructures in their own reward. Both these expenditures and these taxes accord exactly with the needs of stabilization policy.

For supporting the economy, expenditures that reflect the public cognizance are categorically more efficient than those that serve the interests of the planning system. The latter go in large amounts for higher-salaried members of the technostructure or for profits. In both cases the ratio of saving to income is high. Such saving does not add to demand. Spending for public purposes, by contrast, is, in greater part, for ordinary salaries or wages or it is in the form of payments for pensions, unemployment compensation, income maintenance or other assistance to those in need. Saving is much smaller and from some classes of expenditure nonexistent. So, much more of what is spent adds to demand. In the United States, it should be kept in mind, there is no net saving among people in the lower half of the income scale.

Similarly with taxation. Those taxes that serve the goal of greater equality are those that are most efficient for stabilization. The corporation and personal income taxes do most to equalize income. They are also the taxes that increase more than proportionately with increased income and purchasing power and decrease more than proportionately with decreased income and purchasing power. Thus they are the taxes that serve best the goals of stabilization. And the more substantial (within all reasonable limits) the reliance on the corporation income tax and the more progressive the personal income tax, the greater both the stabilization and the equalization effect.

The more comprehensive the tax system — the fewer the loopholes — the better it serves both equality and stabilization. The avowed purpose of special concessions or loopholes is to stimulate particular classes of economic activity. In practice the beneficiaries are far more often firms or individuals in the planning system than those in the market system.[21] The stimulation, so far as there is any, is to the overdeveloped not the underdeveloped part of the economy. The proper rule in the modern economy is to treat all enrichment alike — to apply a common rate of taxation to any enrichment whether it accrues in the form of salary, capital gains, property income, inheritance, gift or, since one must be meticulous, larceny, fraud or embezzlement. The enrichment is the basic fact; given that, the tax follows. This rate, since there would be no untaxed income, could be lower than under the present system of selective taxation of income. It would, of course, be strongly progressive.

[21] The result, in particular, of the preferential taxation of enrichment in the form of corporate capital gains.

In recent years the discussion of taxation has been increasingly along the foregoing lines. A Canadian Royal Commission has proposed such a tax system; Joseph A. Pechman, perhaps the leading American tax authority, has made similar proposals. It is a reform of great and urgent importance both for the more effective operation of the modern economy and for its civilized effect on income distribution.

3

To summarize, the proper fiscal policy begins with the level of public expenditure. This is not given by the needs of fiscal policy itself; it is given by the need for public services as opposed to those supplied by the market and planning systems. The level of public expenditure so established gives, in turn, the amount of taxation required.

There is no assurance that the combination of expenditure and progressive taxation just given will yield the proper level of demand. It may be too great or too small by the tests presently to be mentioned. If demand is excessive, the *generally* appropriate procedure will be to increase taxes. The required level of public outlays has been decided on the basis of need. That the planning system uses its power to win priority for the private consumption of its products has been sufficiently established. This includes priority over public services not important to itself. The effect of tax increases is to cut back on less important private consumption and to protect more important public consumption. To the extent that the tax system is progressive and the tax increase falls more heavily on the affluent, the case for reducing private as opposed to public consumption is that much stronger.

If demand is deficient, the generally proper procedure will be to increase public expenditure. This, as earlier noted, is the most efficient way of adding to demand; it also reflects the generally higher need for public, as opposed to private, consumption.

It will be suggested — and by some trumpeted — that the policy here proposed means, over time, an upward drift in taxation. This is so. But this only means that fiscal policy would correct the general bias of the economic system in favor of the products of the planning system — the products that reflect, among other things, its superior powers of persuasion. And no policy is forever. Conceivably the time may come when public needs — including those of the large cities — are as amply supplied as the present private consumption of those who pay income and corporation taxes. When that day comes, it will be sufficiently noticed and celebrated. Then it will be time to use tax reduction as a corrective for a deficiency in demand.[22]

7

In the administration of price and wage controls, as in lesser measure in the guidance of fiscal policy, there is a dilemma: A major role must be assumed by the Executive, and the specific tasks involved could hardly be more exposed to the resulting influence of the planning system. Yet these are tasks which, in their performance, must reflect the public cognizance.

There is no easy answer. The only hope is a publicly cognizant President and, above all, a publicly cognizant and vigilant legislature. Fortunately the rules that reflect the public interest are rather simple. If public expenditures are increasingly for public purposes, if taxes are increasingly progressive, if monetary policy is passive, if expansion of demand is accomplished by increased public expenditure and contraction of demand by increased taxes, if wage increases are kept in accordance with productivity gains, if increased equality is a major consideration in making wage adjustments and if price increases are allowed only in response to hardship resulting from the evening-up of wages and the absence of productivity gains — then an essentially public management is being achieved. The enforcement of such rules is not beyond the capacity of a publicly cognizant President and legislature. What is suggested also accords with progressive instinct in these matters. But energy and vigilance are certainly required.

[22] There is a case for a type of public expenditure that increases more or less automatically with an increase in unemployment and reduces itself as unemployment diminishes. This is so-called public service employment — the use of the state as a general employer of last resort. Resulting employment would be auxiliary to present sanitation, park, police, custodial, health and primary, secondary and higher education employment. The administrative problems — including the relation of their levels of compensation to those of regularly employed workers — are considerable. So, however, are the advantages to the people who get the work and the community which gets the services.

BOOK
VI

---

*Other Parts
of
the Wood*

PART ONE

COMMUNIST CHINA

SELECTION

15. China Passage

*T*he first entry in China Passage *is for September 4, the* last for September 25.

Galbraith's "passage" took only three weeks. That was in 1972. China Passage *was published in 1973 less than a year later and some months before* Economics and the Public Purpose. *Clearly the Chinese junket could not have affected the thinking in the last volume of the triad. The reverse on the other hand is almost surely true. Galbraith must have found the Chinese economy, as a comparative study, altogether absorbing.*

The trip was sponsored by the Federation of American Scientists who had been arranging for exchanges of views in various fields. As president of the American Economic Association, Galbraith became the leader of a delegation of three, consisting of himself and two of his predecessors in the presidency.

It was an intensive experience—three weeks of steady, unremitting lecturing, discussing, interviewing, sightseeing, banqueting, traveling, and observing without let up through a thousand miles by train and by car from Peking to Hangchow. Only Queen Elizabeth could be expected to survive such an ordeal.

On the first page of the introduction, Galbraith sets important limits on what he expects to gain from a stay so short and so constantly supervised. A footnote quotation from a piece in The New York Review of Books by his friend, colleague at Harvard, and authority on Far Eastern affairs, John K. Fairbank, tells the story:

> The big generalizations are all agreed upon: There has been a tremendous betterment of the material life and morale of the common people. Incredible hard work has produced a credible miracle reshaping both land and people. ... But China is not America. Individualism is not esteemed. Art and letters are at a mass propaganda level. The national political process remains shrouded in mystery. Higher education is slowly reviving after a four-year shutdown.*

Galbraith expected to see what he was shown and nothing else; but circumscribed as that may have been, he saw it for himself and what he saw, however limited, worked. He found a nation, egalitarian, except presumably for the party inner circle, serious-minded, hardworking and brainwashed. Some of these qualities are desirable; some, necessary for survival. All were useful to the Chinese. Here was an economy exactly fitted to time and circumstance.

An understanding of economic forces, like pretty much all knowledge, is a tool like a computer or a telephone. It can be used by societies of many stripes. At a time when the Nixon recession was beginning to take hold, the three American economists found China's economy working well for the Chinese. To observers from a society using an economic tool prescribed by the conventional wisdom and obsolete for its own purposes the spectacle must have been ominous.

Behind the great curtain of masonry, among the ancient tombs and palaces, the modern pictures of Mao, and the sober, hardworking people, lay a confirmation, not of the communist world, but of the thesis of the triad volumes. The Chinese had an economy that worked during a post-revolutionary period in an underdeveloped country. In a highly developed country—during a period of considerable political stability, America suffered from unemployment, depression and inflation. For Galbraith an inference that it was past time for the acceptance of a new view of the American economy, freed from the conventional wisdom, must have been doubly, and triply, confirmed.

* Quoted in A China Passage, p. xi. This quote by Fairbank originally appeared in "To China and Back," The New York Review of Books, October 19, 1972.

Two selections are presented; one consists of a few pages which suggest the pace and confusing variety of the trip; the other consists of Galbraith's summing up of what he saw. It was written while he was still on his way back to America.

China Passage[1]

September 18 — Nanking, Shanghai, Hangchow

After a tranquil night — my first in weeks without additives — we departed the Nanking Hotel at eight. For our journeys yesterday three cars about the size of a Swedish Volvo were produced. After my height had been remarked, a big Red Flag limousine was forthcoming — despite my usual explanations about how collapsible I am. As we were about to leave, a porter came running out of the hotel with a look of extreme urgency on his face. He handed me four Chinese cents — the equivalent of two American pennies — that had fallen out of my pocket in my room.

We drove to the station through the town, out through the wall and across the islands of Xuan wu Lake. I had not noticed before how vast is the city wall. The original one, which mostly still exists, was thirty-five miles around and encircles most of the modern town. A slight mist hung over the lake, islands and gardens. A pagoda rose above the cloud. All was fine. Obviously also the landscape requires attention to keep it so. Gardeners were deploying widely over the islands, and women were sweeping the roads and walks. A huge contingent of schoolchildren — perhaps a hundred in all — were being marshaled along the walks by their teachers. In contrast with their elders — as in Peking — their costume included all the rainbow colors and quite a few that I had not noticed in any recent rainbow.

[1] A *China Passage* (London: André Deutsch, 1973), pp. 84–89, 92, 118–137.

Eventually we came to the railroad station; now we are on the train. Rice terraces, here of lurid green, are on each side, mile after mile. The villages are more frequent and the houses, with tile roofs, more substantial. Occasionally there are patches of cotton, much not good. Just now, by a pond, a large group of workers were filling pails. Others were on their way with their cargo, two pails on a yoke, evidently to moisten fields above the irrigation ditches. We've yet to see the first tracor. We do see many more new industrial plants and much building in the towns. As we get closer to Shanghai, cotton replaces the rice, and the pickers, in groups of twenty or more, are moving across the fields. It is a little like the old South but not much. It's ever so much tidier.

Later — Shanghai station

We pause for a half hour here. The railroad station is still the center of activity in a Chinese city. In an American city no one any longer knows where it is. A prominent feature of the scene, everywhere in China, is the PLA. Members wear a clean, remarkably shapeless uniform of grass green with a soft, peaked cap. Except for red collar tabs and the red star in the cap, it is the garment of a fairly casual motor mechanic. Footwear runs from sneakers to sandals to cloth-top shoes. Both sexes are enrolled, and the uniform — like much though not all work clothing — is the same for both. There are no insignia of rank. The men know their own officers; others need not know and can only judge by age and bearing. One of our three colleagues from the University of Peking who is accompanying us remarks that he can make a close estimate as to who is an officer but he cannot be sure. Any reflection on the number of military men in a community is highly misleading. In China as in numerous other countries they wear uniforms off duty. In other countries, including the United States, they do not. But there are many here.

Jim Tobin[2] has committed the journey to learning Chinese chess and teaching the Western or Fischer version. He has won great respect for both.

Later — Hangchow

We arrived here a bit after five and were given a warm welcome by the Responsible Person of the Foreign Affairs Department of the

[2] Sterling Professor of Economics at Yale and formerly Member of the Council of Economic Advisers. He is the author of numerous books on economics.

Hangchow Revolutionary Committee and the head of the local Scientific and Technical Association. I have a feeling that whoever was in charge before the Cultural Revolution was usually designated head of the Revolutionary Committee — that there has been more continuity than the name implies. Had the revolution come to Harvard, Nahan Pusey would doubtless have gone, but in New Haven Kingman Brewster would still be Chairman of the Yale Revolutionary Committee. A large crowd — several hundred — had gathered to welcome us, attracted less, I fear, by our fame or authority on economic questions than by the huge car with curtains that awaited us outside the station. They returned our waves and cheered Leontief's photographic effort with gusto. Then we went through the city which was full of homewardbound cyclists and pedestrians and out on the wide avenue that borders the Western Lake. The sun, large and very red, was setting behind the distant hills. The water was smooth, utterly serene. Again the haze and distant pavilions and pagodas. I was brought back to reality by my host. He asked if I hadn't been made familiar with the scene by television during Nixon's visit. I had to explain that I had been away from home and negligent.

Item: I've earlier noted the resemblance between South China and Bengal. Approaching Hangchow the similarity is striking. One passes field after field of tall jute — a noble plant — with, of course, much rice and many mulberry trees.

Item: Tobin observes that there are no dogs or cats in China. The reason is presumably economic; if food has been scarce and rationed, affection for a participating pet must diminish. This seems especially probable if the pet is itself edible.

September 19 — Hangchow

Morning in Hangchow. We depart at eight by boat from in front of our hotel for a journey over and around one of the larger sections of the Western Lake. Our vessel is a big motor launch of deliberate pace; we sit aft around a tea table over mugs of tea. Everything favors the journey; the sun is warm with a gentle haze; the distant hills are still mysterious and lovely. Seven hundred years ago this was the most famous resort in all the world; there is still nothing to rival the marvelous sweep of tranquil water, the islands, bridges, causeways and pavilions. Everything has been downhill from 1276 to Miami Beach.

We pass the pavilions, some jutting into the water, with red columns and curving tile roofs. Between are willows in a row without end and flowering peaches. People stroll on the terrace that runs along the water; in the distance we see the steeply pyramidal Bao Shu Pagoda. Some very large, very fat fish jump out of the water in the wake of the boat. Fish abound; the guide tells us that the revenues of the fishing brigade help pay the cost of maintaining this grandeur. We continue by a hotel for overseas Chinese and later see many of the clients; they are easily identified by their bright unorthodox clothes and their much more luxurious bottoms. Our guide says a few come from the United States but most — I suspect nearly all — are from Hong Kong, Singapore and elsewhere in Southeast Asia. Nothing keeps a bona fide resident of Hong Kong from getting a visa and visiting the ancestral scene, and many do.

We have now traveled for half an hour or so, and the lake is dotted with canopied boats — usually one man paddling in front, one behind, a largish passenger list relaxing in between. Earlier we went by Solitary Hill; now we pass the promontory of "Orioles Singing in Willows" and come to an island which encloses a lake in which there is an island. It is called, correctly, "Island within an Island." We disembark and wander along paths and over high-arched bridges below which are pale pink water lilies and strong reddish-pink lotus. Just beyond the island three small stone towers rise from the water. They are "Three Towers Reflecting the Moon." During the autumn festival they are lit and valuably supplement the moon. On the other side of the "Island within an Island" our boat is waiting. We stop before a fairy-tale pavilion to take some pictures. As usual a large crowd is attracted by the Polaroid. We pose with our companions; the picture is snapped; Jim Tobin pulls on the film, and everything disintegrates. The crowd looks disappointed; Edwin H. Land, of all people, has failed. I ask Jim to explain that such failures are part of our system and to mention the C5-A. He declines. The next picture is completely distinct, our technology vindicated. We board the boat and pass on to the "Flower in the Pond" garden featuring huge and voracious goldfish and then on to the Peony Pavilion featuring, not surprisingly, peonies which are gone and flowering trees which are still bright. Fifty or so children of twelve or thereabouts are busy weeding a bank and make an ostentatious point of not being interrupted as we pass. We are taken to view a tree, one of four contributed by President Nixon on his visit. It looks to survive.

It develops that we have passed from the islands to the mainland, and our cars are waiting. The next stop, past some tea gardens, is the

Liu He Pagoda, 1002 years old, with a sweeping view of the Qian tang River and the railroad bridge to Foochow and the south. In the past a tidal bore coming up the river from the East China Sea caused great distress to the city at certain high tidal seasons. The first public works effort, though supplemented strongly by prayer (the problem being deemed beyond human strength) proved inadequate. Then in 910 the Governor, Qian liu, later King of Wu Yue, set about seriously building the definitive wall. He had great trouble, for each tide washed away what had just been accomplished. But he hit upon the plan of stationing arches in a row on the unfinished dike with instructions to shoot at the top of the waves as they rolled in. This worked; the wall was completed and it still stands.

From the pagoda we went to a cluster of pavilions on a hillside. By the highest of the pavilions is Tiger Spring. The spring traces back to a monk who appeared in the vicinity a considerable time ago, rejoiced in the beauty of the location but then discovered there was no water. He appealed to a couple of friendly angels who happened along, and they told him that God would look into the matter. And next morning He did: two tigers appeared, dug industriously into the hillside and found water.

We went into one of the pavilions where we learned about the remarkable quality of this water. A waitress demonstrated. You can fill a tea bowl with it, not full but heaping full. And then you can float coins on the gently upward-curving surface. We had tea made from this talented water, and it was time to come back to the hotel for lunch.

September 24 — Paris

I've now managed to organize my view of the Chinese economy into a reasonably coherent whole. I've drawn primarily on our lectures at the University but also on numerous other discussions.

A description of an economic system turns on the answers — preferably the right ones — to a half-dozen basic questions. They are: What makes people work, which often, employment being unavailable or toil unpopular, they don't? And what things, in consequence, do people produce? And with what organization? And in response to what guidance or in accordance with what plan? And for whose benefit? And with how successful a result? There is the problem in all societies that the answers to these questions usually reflect the approved doctrine, not the reality. Thus the devout free enterpriser in the United States regularly pictures a freedom from government assistance, a level of competitive self-reliance, under which he could never survive. So it is also in a Communist country. The following deletes a certain amount of official doctrine. It is my view, not always that of our Chinese tutors, of the reality.

The first word must be said about the last question — that of the success of the economy. There can now be no serious doubt that China is devising a highly effective economic system. Development is from a very low level of per capita production, and that product is still low. With the liberation, decades of national and civil war, endemic pillage and public anarchy came to an end. Under almost any kind of economic system this would have led to economic gains. Law, order and honest government are very productive. But there is massive evidence of great continued movement — new housing, new industrial plants, new building at old plants, the impressive figures on the increase in local industrial and agricultural production and employment, the supply of basic staples in markets and shops, the people thronging through to buy them and the estimates of relative or percentage increases in production of agricultural and some industrial products. Without question we were taken to see and were told about the best. But in all travel one sees much that one is not shown, and Potemkin, whatever his skill, would have had more difficulty dealing with decently experienced economists.

Against this visual evidence is the nearly total absence of figures on absolute output, either of the economy as a whole or for individual industries or items. The figures are not published; the Chinese economists with whom we talked were forthcoming and helpful but did not appear to have them either. Frank Coe and Sol Adler, as I have mentioned, guess that the rate of expansion in Chinese industrial and agricultural output is now between 10 and 11 percent annually.[3] This does not seem to me implausible though it means a performance (always remembering the low point of departure) rivaling that of Japan. But they do not know for sure, either.

The Chinese economic system would not please most Americans or Europeans but it is not used by them. It does strike me as better adapted to its particular circumstance — more flexible, practical and dynamic and with a strikingly more successful protection of quality —

[3] There is no Chinese figure for Gross National Product, i.e., total output including that of service enterprises and the government. This is considered a bourgeois concept.

than that of the socialist cum Communist states of the West. But let me get back to the questions.

People work for a variety of reasons. With us pecuniary incentives — principally the desire to make money — are greatly celebrated. But we also have people who march, as in the Marines or IBM, to the command of leaders, the desire for the good opinion of comrades or colleagues or in response to pride in the purposes of their outfit or organization. The Chinese have not rejected pecuniary incentives. As earlier noted, some 80 percent of the people are still associated with agriculture. The production team, the basic unit of the People's Commune, gets paid, less cost and taxes, what it earns. And members share in production in accordance with their hours of toil as modified by the point system. This is pecuniary reward in accordance with work performed. Similar incentive systems seem not to exist in larger-scale commerce or industry. But, we have seen, there is a modest graduation in accordance with skill, experience and responsibility.

But clearly the Chinese rely heavily — more heavily even than the other socialist economies — on organization. The economic system is a great battalion in which some lead, in which many march and in which there is much emphasis on the soldiers' sense of purpose. That the Chinese have a genius for organization seems to have been the revelation of an infinity of scholars. This capacity to enlist the energy of many for common purposes is everywhere in use. It involves unremitting exhortation — exhortation to work hard to build the nation, to ensure Chinese independence, to advance the revolution and, of course, to please Chairman Mao. Economic toil, and the resulting product, have been made identical with the highest national purpose. The emphasis on production as an end in itself now rather startles the American visitor. Evidently we have been getting economics into perspective in relation to other aspects of life. But it was not long ago that many Americans identified an increased National Product with all progress, and some still do.

To see the role of organization is to understand the otherwise (to me as to others) puzzling logic of the Great Proletarian Cultural Revolution. Organization is by its nature hierarchical — an organization is a built-in class system in which some command, many comply. The officer class has also a tendency to harden into a privileged and self-perpetuating caste which invites the next revolt. The Cultural Revolution attacked this tendency. Thus its emphasis on a reassociation of leadership with the masses and, at the more practical level, making the managerial, educational and other elites get out and do manual work themselves. There is a hint in the thought of Mao Tse-tung that a periodic churning-up is necessary.

The Cultural Revolution, it may be noted, remains a major point of reference in all Chinese conversation. There was actual conflict in the industrial plants as well as in the universities and elsewhere. (The countryside seems not to have been so much affected.) Industrial production has fully recovered. In factories, universities and even the secondary schools PLA representatives are still present, evidently as a stabilizing force. But in the industrial and commercial establishments, as well as from the economic reporting, one gets the impression of normal operations.

One thing is beyond doubt: The Chinese do work hard, effectively and intelligently for six days a week and without vacations. Vacations, as noted, are reserved for those who are separated by their work from their family. The impression of diligent effort — in town, countryside, construction sites, schools, public works — is overwhelming. Maybe there is a further explanation for this diligence. In the United States and Europe we greatly praise work. All good and honest people are held to rejoice in it. The work ethic and all that. This proposition we then deny by the attention we lavish in our economics and business practice on the means for making people expend energy. Maybe, in addition to all else, the Chinese, like the Japanese, really like to work. A disconcerting thought.

Work has a second dimension which is the opportunity; it doesn't matter how willing people are if there are no jobs available. In a heavily populated, agricultural country such as China or India there are three kinds of unemployment, namely (1) Ricardian unemployment, which means that because of the vast number of people in relation to land and capital there are many who cannot find jobs the product from which yields the equivalent of a living wage; (2) recurrent unemployment, which means that, given the nature of most agricultural operations, there are many dead hours in the day or days in the year when there is nothing to be done; and (3) disguised unemployment, which means that two or more people share tasks which could be done by one. The test of disguised unemployment, to repeat, is that, when the extra workers are withdrawn, production does not fall. A fourth kind of unemployment, the familiar Keynesian kind which plagues the Western economy, is not so serious. This unemployment is the result of a shortage of demand, and that tends to occur only when income and savings (which may not be invested or spent) are high.

The Chinese have tackled all their three kinds of unemployment. Recurrent and disguised unemployment are together the target of the industrial and handicraft enterprises on the commune. These use people who are seasonally idle or who cannot effectively be used or are not needed for crop production. They pay less than the urban industrial wage. But they use people who, otherwise, would be earning nothing. The opportunity cost of the labor is zero. No other country has attacked this problem of recurrent and disguised unemployment — the endemic waste of manpower in the Asian countryside — with the energy and imagination of the Chinese. One senses, also, that their effort still falls well short of solving the problem.

The attack on Ricardian unemployment is by a massive public employment program. The consequence has been sufficiently celebrated in the preceding pages — the meticulous cleaning and repair of streets, an attention to parks and gardens that approaches the English standard, high standards in other public housekeeping, extensive rehabilitation of public monuments, and the planting of the trees that I mentioned and that caused Barbara Tuchman[4] to speak of the greening of China. Chinese economists now speak, perhaps a trifle disingenuously, of a labor shortage. It is, in part, the result of the lavish use of manpower for such work. The latter is doing wonders for both the countryside and the cities. It will be some time yet before a real labor shortage forces the Chinese to forgo street cleaning, park maintenance, flower planting and other practices now considered archaic in the more advanced economy.

Judging from the number of men (and fewer women) wearing the shapeless uniforms of the People's Liberation Army, military activity must also absorb a good deal of manpower. It is not a subject which a sensibly tactful visitor who also seeks information on more mundane matters should raise.

Coming to what the Chinese economy produces, the first choice, as everywhere, is between various things for present use and between such consumption and investment to increase output in the future. Let me begin with the last; it involves a most interesting point.

[4] Historian and author of *Stillwell and the American Experience in China* (London: Bantam, 1973).

In the years following World War II the new Communist regimes of Eastern Europe, influenced more by ambition for the future than by present poverty, concentrated heavily on investment. The consumption of the current generation was sacrificed to the greater affluence of children and grandchildren. Rates of saving for investment were 30, 40, even 50 percent of product. The generation being so sacrificed to the future found the resulting sense of righteousness insufficient compensation for the current privation. Revolts or near revolts in Yugoslavia, East Germany, Poland, Hungary (of which there were also other causes) brought a sharp reversal of policy. What, partly by the accident of association, is called Stalinist economics came to an end. There was everywhere greater emphasis on consumer goods for current consumption.

Stalin (with Marx, Engels and Lenin) still survives in the Chinese Communist pantheon. His picture, deeply avuncular, is in most places of public ceremony. But the policy of planned deprivation associated with his name is strongly rejected. Investment in capital plant is high. Chinese experts assume a substantial military investment but concerning this also we did not ask. There is, however, much emphasis on the need for an immediate improvement in the standard of living. The first rule of Chinese planning (as put by one of the economists who briefed us) is "raising the living standards before accumulation." The priority that is accorded agriculture and light consumer industry as compared with heavy industry is much mentioned. Food, textiles and other elementary consumer products must be available in quantity sufficient for increased consumption before there can be allocation of product to investment. People must be persuaded that they are working for a stronger nation and a better future. But, as a wholly practical matter, they must see the bird in the hand.

Decision as to what consumer goods will be produced (and which will have investment for future expansion) is facilitated in China by the low standard of living. There is an obtrusive quality about physical need. And so, in contrast with luxury products, the demand for goods that satisfy such need is relatively easy to predict. The first requirement, accordingly, is to fill the grain and clothing ration — rice or its cereal equivalent and cotton textiles are the two commodities that are rationed. Rationing, it may be noted, is all but universally regarded as a manifestation of scarcity. The Chinese speak with satisfaction about this or that product having been derationed. But it is also a useful device for securing to everyone an ample supply of an indispensable commodity at a stable price. There has been too much snobbish comment about the uniformity of Chinese clothing. General appearance is better, as noted, than on an American campus. But that is not the point. In a poor country an arrangement by which every person gets two sets of sound basic garments every year at low prices seems to me an exercise in the greatest good sense. The proper comparison of the comfortably clad Chinese is not with Americans or Europeans but with the huddled and half-clothed people of northern or upland India in the winter months.

Housing, health services and medicine are also produced in response to obvious physical requirements. Housing, especially in the cities, falls far short of physical need. The makeshift housing, so-called, is not on display but must be poor. Medicine and medical services, on the other hand, are major achievements. The cost of standard medicines is now about one-fifth the 1950 cost; the basic antibiotics, as I have mentioned, are available at nominal prices without prescription. I am prepared to believe that Greater Shanghai, with a population of around 12 million and its 424 hospitals, 44,000 beds and around 11,500 doctors (including the traditional practitioners), has a better medical service than New York. The average quality of practice is no doubt far higher in New York. But the chance of getting no care is also much higher. For the man who is dead because he cannot get to a doctor or get into a hospital or risk the resulting financial disaster, averages are very misleading. One gathers that health services in rural areas, especially the more remote ones, are much less good but also the object of much effort.

For other goods, production decisions are in response to consumer demand, reflected through a rough approximation to the ordinary price system. Prices of different products reflect different average costs with taxes and profit margins added. A premium (specifically unrelated to costs) in added for higher quality. This last, I judge to be very important in explaining the seemingly high quality of Chinese goods.

Interest is charged on borrowed capital. Currently the rate is 5.04 percent to industrial and commercial establishments, 4.56 percent to communes, 2.16 percent for basic construction and irrigation works. The People's Banks pay 3.24 percent on time deposits.[5] Interest rates,

[5] The exceptional precision is caused by converting monthly rates used by the Chinese — one-twelfth of the above — to a yearly basis.

we were advised, are coming down. The prices once established, what people then buy determines what is produced. The prices of about 300 products come within the purview of the central government. The rest, called "small commodities," are set by state or local planning authorities although "sharp changes" must be reported to the central government. As in the West taxes on cigarettes (differing as between kinds of cigarettes), cosmetics and wines express social disapproval. The yield of the cosmetics tax cannot be large. Cigarette consumption is unapologetically high and, the taxes apart, still unresisted by the government. In consequence, and aided by an encouraging increase in air pollution, lung cancer is keeping pace with the general progress of civilization at least in the larger cities.

In agriculture the instrument of production is the People's Commune with, as in the case of the *kibbutzim*, its industrial sidearm. Elsewhere the basic instrument is the familiar and universal industrial firm. The People's Commune, to summarize, is a large, essentially administrative and policy organization. Membership ranges from 5000 to 6000 up to 10,000, and a few have 30,000 to 40,000. In units of this size obviously there can be no visible relationship between individual effort and result, and the same is true of the production brigade with a membership of around 1000. So, increasingly, the operating unit is the production team of 150 to 200 members. This deploys workers to their tasks; individual compensation is established according to the neo-socialist principle (as put by one of our discussants) of "Each does his best; each according to his work."

The tax on the commune remains fixed in absolute amount and thus declines with increasing output. It now averages about 8 percent. After deduction of a percentage or two of the proceeds for management and 5 to 7 percent for welfare and capital accumulation, and the cost of fertilizer and other cash production expense, the receipts are divided between the teams in accordance with their production and by the teams, as noted, in accordance with the quantity and quality of each member's work.

On form, if there is a weakness in the Chinese economy, it should be here. Agriculture everywhere else in the world has yielded reluctantly and, more often than not, inefficiently to socialism. The production team seems still too large for the individual work to see a close relationship between *his* work and reward. There must also, surely, be serious problems of administration. The mind boggles at the problem of getting good management for tens and hundreds of thousands of communes. But this is only a thought. For a serious judgment, one should see several hundred communes picked at random.

By U.S. or Japanese standards Chinese agriculture is grossly deficient in the use of commercial fertilizer — some Chinese leaders seem to take seriously the old peasant superstition that such fertilizer is damaging to the structure of the soil. Mechanization, even if not needed to conserve manpower, allows of better and more timely cultivation. Mechanization too must be slight. The extent of use of modern high-yielding hybrids is unclear. Progress, notwithstanding, has been substantial — grain production in 1971 was reported (one judges now reliably) at twice the low 1949 level, and cotton was up fourfold. Given fertilizer, mechanization and the new hybrids, output could be very greatly increased. The Indian and Pakistani Punjab, which seems well ahead of China in this regard, has shown what is possible.

Except that there is no sales, merchandising, marketing or advertising staff — cadre is the word in Chinese — not much distinguishes the Chinese from the American or European industrial plant. For producing a given product, industrial plants are everywhere about the same. The terminology is different. Lee Iacocca, in a suitably large plant in Shanghai, would be the Principal Responsible Person; some more ceremonial figure, preferably Henry II, would be Chairman of the Revolutionary Committee. Leonard Woodcock would not at the moment be visible. Unions seem to have been a casualty of the Cultural Revolution. The factory would employ women indifferently along with men although men would still predominate in the executive and supervisory posts. The principal problem would still be getting out the product at low cost.

By the universally offered estimate, about 80 percent of the Chinese labor force is employed in, or in association with, agriculture but around 50 percent of the product, by value, comes from industry. And 90 percent of the revenue of the state is held to come from profits of, or taxes on, industrial and commercial enterprises or products. Incomes in agriculture are well below those in industry as Chinese economists concede — indeed stress. For this reason agricultural taxes are kept low. As a further corrective farm prices are kept relatively high and consumer food prices low, and the difference is made up with a subsidy from industrial profits and taxes. Agricultural income in communes in areas of high population but poor soil must be lower than in the better agricultural areas seen by the visitor. This would be the usual consequence of dividing less product among the same number of people.

As noted the Chinese appear to have developed a plain but remarkably efficient system for the distribution of consumer goods. The industrial establishments that we saw, a minuscule sample, seemed workmanlike, not overmanned and comparatively modern in their equipment. There can be few things, from a strict technological viewpoint, that the Chinese cannot — or do not — make. They may have been isolated in these last years but they have been studying lots of books, journals, models and products.

The flow of revenue from industrial profits and taxes has an admirable effect on Chinese public finance. The government has no external or internal debt — a loan from the Soviets negotiated at the time of the Korean war was paid off ahead of schedule in 1968. There is no income tax. The budget operates with a slight surplus. In our discussions in Peking information on Chinese finances was provided with great precision and competence by a member of the Institute of Economics of the Academy of Sciences.[6, 7] One of the more engaging moments of the visit was when James Tobin, who with Walter Heller was one of the men who made the New Economics legitimate under President Kennedy, undertook to explain in response to a question why it was often good for the United States to have a budget deficit and to increase its debt. He might have had it easier with Andrew Mellon.

In any other country (including the Soviet Union) the difference between urban and rural incomes that exist in China would set in

[6] She noted that "The Chinese currency [is] one of the most stable in the world. In contrast with some capitalist countries, no borrowing, no inflation, no devaluation." Being, like all our hosts, impeccably polite she did not specify the capitalist country.

[7] The Institute of Economics is a sizable and prestigious research organization still suffering, one member indicated, from some disorientation following the Cultural Revolution. As in Eastern Europe and the Soviet Union, work with a research institute appears to bring its members into much closer relationship with practical questions than does a position on a university economics faculty. Faculty members are more inclined, perhaps out of necessity, to substitute theory for fact, a circumstance not unknown with us. It might be added that if there is a dominant figure in Chinese economic planning, he is anonymous. Many will think that such anonymity for economists is a major contribution to culture and, given the high failure rate of economic ideals in all countries in recent times, sound personal strategy.

motion a large movement of people to the cities, and in China it once did. This is not now happening. There is some recruitment of labor force in rural areas but, in the main, factories are staffed from the natural increase of population in the cities. The reason is straightforward: The Chinese are assigned to jobs, and they are required to remain where they are assigned. Though evidently enforced with some flexibility, this is not an arrangement that much appeals to the Western visitor. It does continue an antecedent practice by which people were held firmly in place by debt, poverty, ignorance or the condign punishment visited on deserters from armies of the state or the warlords. This was compulsion without saving security or reward.

Many details of Chinese planning are far from clear. As described it begins with agriculture. A crop is projected which averages the past results of one bumper, two average and one poor harvest. From this come estimates as to the supply of food and industrial raw materials, notably cotton, jute and silk, that may be expected. The possible supply of cotton textiles and some other consumer goods can then be projected. The purchases of a population of modest and highly egalitarian income are predictable and wholly so for the rationed grain and cotton textiles. From the surplus of product over consumption needs comes an estimate as to what can be invested.

The resulting requirements for different commodities are distributed as targets to producers of consumer goods or, in combination with investment needs, to firms that produce capital goods or fill the production requirements of other firms. It seems possible that they are supplemented or filled out by orders directly from one firm to another. On this I am unclear. Aggregate income available for spending, an aspect of the conservative financial policy, is held down in relation to the expected supply of staple products. As a plausible result of this (and the highly egalitarian income distribution) queues, so familiar in front of the Soviet store, seem rare in China. People do not line up to buy what they do not have money to buy.[8]

This elementary planning framework involves a great many more problems than here implied. To ensure that the numerous production needs of one industry — spare parts for textile machinery, tires for trucks — are available in adequate quantity from other industry and that there is balanced development (what the Chinese call, somewhat

[8] My Harvard colleague Professor Dwight Perkins also stresses the firm control of wages including the absence (unlike in the Soviet Union) of competitive bidding for scarce kinds of manpower.

ambiguously, synthetic balance) between various branches of industry and agriculture is no slight task. Extensive calculation is involved; this is a task that, one assumes, would be facilitated notably by computers. Computer use, we were told, had been neglected in the past but it is now being energetically studied.

Some other details were also filled in. Where local products are produced for local markets, planning decisions are now being decentralized to provincial government. This decentralization with accompanying encouragement to local initiative in planning and development is greatly emphasized. Prices are fixed but where — as in the case of fruits and vegetables — supply can easily exceed or fall short of demand at the given price, there appears to be little hesitation in changing prices as needed "in a planned way." Industrial expansion is being encouraged in the cities of the interior, restrained on the coast. One economist said flatly that Shanghai was already "too big." Although the specification of definite production goals is thought important, there must be "leeway" in all planning for accommodation to particular need and circumstance. This flexibility is stressed. There is thought to be a place for industry of varying size; large, medium and small. The small local firm is obviously being thought of as one answer to the bureaucratic tendency of modern large-scale industry. Education, especially in the primary and secondary grades, has a major claim on resources, as do the medical services. Much emphasis is placed on the flow of recommendations up from the plants and workers: "Good plans are not made by a handful of people shut up in [a] room."

Earlier plans following the withdrawal of Soviet assistance and technicians stressed the self-sufficiency of China. The current five-year plan (which began in 1971) contemplates drawing on the best of foreign technology and accords an important role to foreign trade. The latter — now amounting to between 2 and 4 percent of agricultural and industrial output — will, one senses, remain small. Exports last year were divided almost equally as among industrial products, processed agricultural products and raw agricultural products, mainly rice. To the United States the Chinese foresee the export of "traditional" products including tea, silk, hog bristles and some foods. Prospective imports are industrial equipment, machines and aircraft. The communications satellite and the Boeings received particular mention. "Everything depends on the developing political situation."

The scale and character of the official planning establishment —

national and provincial — is something of which we got no impression. One somehow has the feeling of a smaller and more flexible organization than the massive Soviet apparatus. But I would have difficulty adducing any evidence in support of that instinct.

As to whom the production is for, there is a quick and easy answer: It is for everyone in about the same amount. Somewhere in the recesses of the Chinese polity there may be a privileged Party and official hierarchy. Certainly it is the least ostentatious ruling class in history. So far as the visitor can see or is told, there is — for worker, technician, engineer, scientist, plant manager, local official, even, one suspects, table tennis player — a truly astonishing approach to equality of income. Older skilled workers, doctors and professors retain the higher incomes, rising to as much as Y300 or roughly U.S. $150 a month (though in basic purchasing power considerably more), that they had before the Cultural Revolution. But with age and retirement these higher incomes are being phased out. A younger generation from apprentice to plant manager is in the range from Y35 to a maximum of Y100 or Y150 a month, or roughly from $17 to $50 or at the very most $75. In agriculture, as noted, incomes are less. Since food and basic clothing are cheap, housing costs nominal and medical care mostly free, these are not starvation wages. The urban standard of living includes a bicycle, a watch and, in the few houses we saw, a sewing machine. In each excursion group thronging the parks and public monuments there is at least one camera. People reach places of work and recreation by public transportation that is cheap and looks efficient. Clearly there is very little difference between rich and poor.

One or two points seem worth additional emphasis. As compared with the Eastern European economies or that of the Soviet Union, the Chinese economy sustains a far lower standard of living. (There are far fewer automobiles than in India, and the shops are much plainer and less interesting. This, however, must be attributed not to a lower but a much more egalitarian living standard.) But along with the lower living standard goes a seemingly more effortless economy. One has the feeling, very simply, that the economy works better than in Russia or Poland — at least as I saw those countries a few years ago. Things in China give the impression of meshing; slighted workmanship, diminished quality are much less obvious. Something depends on the easy, affable and sensitive manners of the Chinese. One transfers his reaction to this to the society. Dissidents are brought firmly into line in China, but, one suspects, with great politeness. It is a firmly authoritarian society in which those in charge smile and say please. The leadership rebukes what is called "Commandism." And there is also the obvious willingness of the Chinese, given the opportunity, to work. But, for whatever reason, the Chinese economy appears to function very easily and well.

Thus the Chinese economic system. Ever since Lincoln Steffens returned from Russia to proclaim (to Bernard Baruch), "I have been over into the future and it works," travelers to the Communist countries have been reluctant to risk hard conclusions. When things went wrong, the skeptics remembered and rejoiced. One should not be craven. The Chinese economy isn't the American or European future. But it is the Chinese future. And let there be no doubt: For the Chinese it works.

PART TWO

CAPITALIST MONEY

---

*I*n the grand cycle of Galbraith's writing a place for *Money* is not immediately apparent. The author's central thesis has already been fully stated, but an iconoclastic book with the seriousness and impact of *Money* cannot be classed as an appendix, or a footnote. By nature it is not an epilogue or afterword; *Money* is not subordinate to the train of logic hitherto carried consistently forward in all the author's economic writing. *Money* is supportive of its fellows but not dependent on any preceding work. It admirably justifies its subtitle, *Whence It Came, Where It Went. It is a critical, constructive history which stands apart.*

Two paragraphs near the beginning of the book fix its beginning, its direction and its tone:

> The reader should proceed in these pages in the knowledge that money is nothing more or less than what he or she has always thought it was—what is commonly offered or received for the purchase or sale of goods, services or other things. The several forms of money and what determines what they will buy are something else again. But that is the purpose of the pages following to reveal.
>
> . . . There was a chance also that the note would continue

its passage from hand to hand and to yet further hands and never be returned for collection. The loan which led to its emission would earn interest and in due course be repaid. The note meanwhile would continue its rounds. Against the original coin that allowed of the original loan, no claim would ever be entered. In the 1960s, Mr. George W. Ball, an eminently successful lawyer, politician and diplomat, left public office to become a partner of the great Wall Street house of Lehman Brothers. "Why," he was heard to ask a little later, "didn't someone tell me about banking before?"

A paragraph in the next to last chapter, which is used in its entirety for this selection, suggests the later course of the argument and its destination:

But also it is now evident that only in the extremes of in-flation or depression is there a choice. Otherwise, if only the accepted and orthodox remedies are applied, we get both. For this combination no one, liberal or conservative, speaks. And at this combination, after 2500 years, we have at last ar-rived. Few histories could have a less happy ending.

Such are the nose and the tail of that perplexing abstraction, money. The reader may fill the intervening space with the body of whatever chimera appeals to his fancy. That will suffice for his purposes.

The whole monetary structure seems, like the emperor's clothes, to be no better shield to modesty than can be constructed from the vanity and credulity of man. Money is what you think it is, Galbraith seems to say; and the now deeply instructed reader will understand that it is a protean substance, the value and form of which is created by the hand of whoever spends it.

We have classed this book along with The Great Crash, 1929, as a "study" book. In fact the two seem almost as close together as cause and consequence. The Great Crash begins in the thick of the argu-ment; Money's place is before the beginning and after the end of the Galbraith thesis. The line, "Few histories could have a less happy ending," puts a Q.E.D. to the theorem so succinctly stated in the introduction of Economics and the Public Purpose: "Left to them-selves economic forces do not work out for the best except perhaps for the powerful."

As with The Great Crash, Galbraith tells us that he much enjoyed the writing of Money and, as with The Great Crash, it seems certain that the reader will equally enjoy the reading.

Money

WHERE IT WENT[1]

THE CIRCUMSPECT HISTORIAN ends his work well before the present; then he takes his seat with the others for the day's parade. A solemn reason is offered for this: History cannot be written too soon, perspective must be gained. The tactical advantage of this restraint is even greater. Of current happenings people are often informed. They will question the historian's interpretation, even perhaps his facts. His professional advantage is thus lost. Better then to stay safely with the past.

The circumstances of this essay, alas, do not allow of this careful solution. It seeks to tell of the wisdom and folly of the past but it seeks to use these to illuminate the present. Accordingly, there is no decent escape in these last pages from the perplexities of the present and of a world beset, as so often in the two-and-a-half thousand years since the kings of Lydia, with the tendency for its money to become bad or for the management of money to make much else, including production and employment, bad. Still there are mitigating circumstances. Much that has happened in the recent present is not terribly in dispute. And much was foretold by the events of the near and distant past. Much of what must be done is also foretold — but on this there will be more disagreement.

The good years of economic management in the United States came to an end with the Vietnam war. Wartime spending and resulting demand put pressure on prices. The guideposts succumbed. Prices pressed upward.

Spending for the war and the associated deficit are held especially responsible. In fact these were rather quickly neutralized. In the calendar year 1967, the Federal government had a deficit of $12.4 billion in the national income accounts. Income taxes were then

[1] Chapter XX, "Where It Went," *Money: Whence It Came, Where It Went* (London: André Deutsch, 1975), pp. 283–301.

increased by the addition of a surtax; as a principal though not exclusive consequence, the deficit was a modest $6.5 billion the following year. And in 1969, there was a surplus of $8.1 billion.[2] With the ending of the surtax and other tax reduction the deficit then returned.

The sequence of events just mentioned is of importance; in later years the economists of the Nixon Administration attributed the increasingly serious inflation to the fiscal disorder they had inherited. Through repetition the explanation acquired a wide measure of acceptance. There is an obvious convenience in attributing one's shortcomings to one's predecessors in office. Carried to its logical end, it would mean that no administration would have to take responsibility for economic performance until it had been in office for several years. A valuable alibi. But, in fact, the fiscal position inherited by the Nixon Administration was, as such matters are usually described, remarkably sound. This was not so true of the efforts of its economists to make economic causation a branch of archaeology.

Nor, in fact, were the price movements that the new Administration inherited especially alarming. From a base of 100 in 1967, the wholesale index had risen to 102.5 in 1968. It went on up to 106.5 in 1969.[3] In economic matters misfortune is, obviously, a relative thing. However, these price increases seemed sufficiently grave so that the new Administration came to office in January 1969 with a firmly announced determination to bring them to an end. For doing so, the new President boldly announced his intention of extending and making more dangerous all of the flaws, real or potential, in the previous economic management. On January 27, 1969, in his first press conference after taking office, and with the uncertainty of syntax that the Watergate tapes were later to celebrate, Mr. Nixon said: ". . . what we are trying to do without, shall we say, too much managing of the economy — we're going to have some fine tuning of our fiscal and monetary affairs in order to control inflation. One other point I should make in this respect. I do not go along with the suggestion that inflation can be effectively controlled by exhorting labor and management and industry to follow certain guidelines."[4]

All possible damage was here. Management of the economy, though ever more demanding as to need, was to be minimized. The mention of fine tuning, a phrase from his economists, gave currency

[2] *Economic Report of the President, 1974,* p. 328.
[3] *Economic Report of the President, 1974,* p. 305.
[4] The *New York Times,* January 28, 1969.

to a ridiculous cliché. As well fine-tune a Mississippi flood. While the reference was to both fiscal and monetary policy, it had to mean a heavy reliance on monetary policy. By no stretch of the imagination of even a new presidential adviser could Federal expenditures or taxation, both subject to congressional action, be thought susceptible to sensitive adjustment. Present also was the thought that the success of both fiscal and monetary policy depended not on superior wisdom but on superior technique. This, all will know by now, has never been so. Were it the happy case, the economic problem would have been solved long since, for in all fields of endeavor good technicians abound.

And as the hopeless course was emphasized by the President, the important power was rejected. There would be no interference with prices and wages. The previous hope for restraint was replaced by an invitation to corporations and unions to exercise whatever market power they possessed and might find immediately rewarding. In dealing with Mr. Nixon, it is not easy to be unfair. He invites and justifies all available criticism. However, something must be reserved in this case for the most reputable of his subordinates. Testifying a few days later on the guideposts which, if straightforward results be accepted, had helped keep prices stable during the Kennedy years, Secretary of Labor George Shultz held that:

> . . . (1) . . . *they had not been very effective while in force:*
> *(2) they may well have strengthened the forces of inflation in the long run by diverting attention away from the fundamental weapons of monetary and fiscal policy and manpower policy; (3) they may have contributed to more labor unrest and to higher wage settlements after their demise than would otherwise have occurred. Further, (4) they are contrary to the spirit of competition and subvert the forces of the market; and (5) when combined with jawboning they are possibly in defiance of the nation's antitrust law.*[5]

Not much remained to be said in favor of direct restraints on prices and wages. Mr. Shultz was soon to emerge as the dominant voice of the Administration on economic policy.

[5] This summary of the Shultz position is from an essay by Neil de Marchi, "Wage-Price Policy in the First Nixon Administration: Prelude to Controls," which will be included in a volume on the development of wage-price policy in the United States, to be published by the Brookings Institution in 1975.

This policy in the next two years reflected with remarkable precision the President's projection. Fiscal policy was tight in 1969. Then, as noted, with the phasing out of the surtax, other tax relief and increased expenditures, it greatly eased. The Federal deficit in the national income accounts was $11.9 billion in 1970, a large $22.2 billion in 1971.[6] For resisting inflation, reliance was on monetary policy; this was tightened, with sharply increasing interest rates, in 1969, and kept so until the closing months of 1970. So much for the fine tuning.

In mid-1970, the long period of boom and euphoria in the stock market came to an end. There was nothing here for which the Nixon Administration could be much blamed. The causes of any collapse are always imbedded in the previous boom. In 1929, those who were believed to have unlocked the secret of the market were found to have unlocked only the secret of a rising market. Now again. As the great holding-company and investment-trust promotions were before, so the performance funds, hedge funds, growth funds, offshore funds, real estate funds and the gossamer creations of the computer age were now. By making it difficult for bad or weak companies to borrow money, the tight-money policy may well have hastened the end. Conservatives are notable for inflicting such suffering on themselves or their kind. But sooner or later the end would in any case have come.

However, the effect of monetary policy on price increases and unemployment, by now predictable, was to allow the worsening of both. Unemployment, which averaged 3.5 percent of the labor force in 1969, rose to 4.9 percent in 1970 and to 5.9 percent the following year. And wholesale prices, which were 106.5 in 1969 (1967 = 100), went up to 110.4 in 1970, and 113.9 in 1971.[7] Unemployment, as before, was not the alternative to inflation. There could, as before, be both. Monetary policy could suppress activity and increase unemployment, and especially in those industries — housing, and the construction industry generally, being the leading examples — which depend on borrowed money. The market power of corporations and unions meanwhile could keep prices going up as before. The modern capitalist economy could suffer inflation. And it could suffer recession.

[6] *Economic Report of the President, 1974,* p. 328.
[7] *Economic Report of the President, 1974,* pp. 279, 305. Although there was increase in all categories, it was strong in durable consumers' goods and particularly in finished producers' goods. In both those parts of the economy the market power of corporations and unions is strong.

And it could, up to a painful level of unemployment, have both at the same time. However, the economists whom Mr. Nixon had brought to Washington were not men of shallow faith. Concessions might be made to the reality but this could be only out of short-run political necessity.

Such concessions were made. Political courage is a much admired force for public good. The benign impact of political cowardice deserves more praise than it commonly receives. By the summer of 1971, a presidential election was only a year and a few months away. All polls showed that the public reaction to the new combination of inflation and unemployment was, not surprisingly, adverse. The major candidates for the Democratic nomination showed evidence in the polls of swamping Mr. Nixon. Economists can urge suffering for a principle. And they can urge the public to exercise patience while processes, presumed to be ultimately benign, work themselves out. Unfortunately patience cannot be legislated or achieved by Executive Order. And pleas for its voluntary exercise have their primary impact on those making them.

Strong overtures were made to higher economic principle and to patience. On July 28, 1971, Paul W. McCracken, the scholarly head of the Council of Economic Advisers, affirmed stoutly the virtue and efficacy of the current reliance on monetary policy, the unwisdom, even eccentricity, of any direct intereference with prices or wages. He conceded that a contemporary observer, the present author, who had urged that the market power of corporations and unions would defeat monetary policy unless unemployment was very severe, "has the merit of being logical within the limits of his peculiar view of the economic system." But he strongly rejected such peculiarity, dismissed the economics of a freeze of prices as "illusory" and warned solemnly that "General wage and price control would be a serious threat to individual freedom."[8] That corporations and unions already exercise such control and thus, presumably, endanger freedom was not stressed.

In his stand for principle, Dr. McCracken had the initial support of his President. At a press conference in early August, Mr. Nixon, referring again to the same observer, said he was "unalterably opposed" to the "Galbraith scheme which is supported by many of our Democratic Senators," the scheme being modest direct intervention

[8] The *Washington Post*, July 28, 1971.

on wages and prices. The President noted that such policies were favored only by "extremists of the left," adding generously, "I don't say this in a condemning way, it is only an observation."[9] A few days later, on August 15, the extremist specter suddenly ceased to stalk; principle collapsed in face of overriding political need. All wages and prices, farm prices and a few others excepted, were frozen.

Simultaneously with the freeze, the budget was liberalized and tax reductions were requested, these being enacted at the end of the year. And monetary policy was relaxed. The ancient faith was not, however, jettisoned. The action against market power was temporary. The controls were "designed to create conditions in which a more expansive budget policy would be safer and more effective." All would then be well. The controls, by then, would have broken the inflationary thrust; they were "emergency expedients, required in a particular historical context but expected to fade away, leaving no permanent change in the system except the eradication of inflationary expectations."[10]

It is hard not to dwell on the foregoing statement. The combination of wishful thought and sheer recklessness is impressive. The problem addressed by the controls — that created by the market power of corporations and unions — is not new but old. No one suggested that corporations and unions would soon disappear. But the *problem* would disappear. The consequences of such irresponsibility are not small. Some people lose income in consequence; some lose their jobs; international and domestic economic affairs are disoriented; there is social tension and frustration: the reputation of capitalism suffers; so does that of economists. Least damaged, perhaps, are the scholars who make such statements, offer such hopes.

The controls were not seriously administered — more accurately, they were largely unadministered. In contrast with the World War II and Korean war experiences, no serious organization was established for administration. Those responsible, by their own subsequent candid admission, remained strongly opposed to the principle.[11]

---

[9] The *New York Times*, August, 5, 1971.
[10] *Economic Report of the President*, 1972, p. 24.
[11] A point often made in conversation by Herbert Stein, who was soon to succeed McCracken as Chairman of the Council of Economic Advisers. C. Jackson Grayson, Jr., the administrator principally in charge, emerged from his service to mount an energetic attack on the policy. See his "Controls Are Not the Answer," *Challenge* (November/December 1974), p. 9.

Firms had difficulty in getting answers as to what was required of them. Such interpretation as was available was frequently provided by members or former members of the industry affected — a form of self-dealing against which the World War II and Korean war price administrations had established the most careful safeguards. No enforcement arm was established; instead officers whose experience and career prospects were in tax collection were borrowed from the Internal Revenue Service.

Nonetheless, in something between moderate and remarkable measure, the action achieved its purposes. The increase in unemployment was arrested; in 1972, as again in 1973, there were small decreases. Wholesale prices during the freeze in the latter months of 1971 were stable. Phase II, which followed the freeze, limited the controls, broadly speaking, to union contracts and the prices of the large corporations, that is to say to the areas of market power. It reflected not at all badly the logic of control. Through all of 1972, under this regime, industrial prices rose by 3.6 percent. Consumer products (other than foods, which were not controlled) rose over the year by 2.2 percent.[12] Writing of the experience in January 1973, the Administration economists said, not without satisfaction and not without reason, that, since August 1971, there had been "a dramatic deceleration of the rate of inflation."[13] They noted that the action had dealt with causes, not symptoms. The controls were "not merely a suppression of price increases that would burst out if controls were removed."[14]

None of this meant that the old faith was dead. Confidence was simultaneously expressed that the United States did not face any problem of inflation "beyond the capacity of prudent fiscal and monetary policy to control."[15] So the controls would now be jettisoned. On January 8, 1973, Secretary of the Treasury George P. Shultz, now the chief economic policy-maker of the Administration, met with newspapermen to affirm his continued opposition to the policy. He noted that controls had worked well in a slack economy but expressed the conviction that they would work less well now that full employment was being approached and they were more needed. The election had also been won. Steps were taken to dismantle the controls.

[12] *Economic Report of the President,* 1974, p. 309.
[13] *Economic Report of the President,* 1973, p. 30.
[14] *Economic Report of the President,* 1973, p. 68.
[15] *Economic Report of the President,* 1973, p. 54.

[453]

The dismantling proceeded erratically and with some backtracking through 1973. On the whole, fiscal and monetary policy were, in fact, reasonably prudent. Revenues gained in relation to expenditures; a Federal deficit in the national income accounts of $15.9 billion in 1972 became a surplus of $600 million in 1973.[16] Money was kept tight and expensive; by the end of 1973, the rediscount rate was an unprecedented 7.5 percent. The lending rate of the large commercial banks — the prime rate — was above 9 percent.[17] A "prudent fiscal and monetary policy" thus received a remarkably fair trial. During 1973, the cost of living increased by nearly 9 percent, nearly three times as much as during 1972. Wholesale prices in 1973 went up 18 percent. Thus for the prescience of Secretary Shultz and his colleagues. A persuasive claim of success for their promise of what prudent fiscal and monetary policy would accomplish will require ingenuity and some literary skill.

In the autumn of 1973 came the Yom Kippur war, the oil embargo and a very large increase in petroleum prices. These were widely blamed by the Administration economists, among others, for the inflation. Around three-fourths of the price increases of 1973 occurred before the war and before the oil prices went up appreciably.

In 1974, the prudent policies continued. The preliminary estimate of the Federal deficit on national income accounts was $7.6 billion.[18] Monetary policy remained tight until early autumn when, in response to bitter complaint from the allected industries and criticism from economists, it was slightly relaxed. During 1974, the further reward of what was proclaimed to be prudence was an 18.9 percent increase in wholesale prices, an 11.0 percent increase in living costs.[19] At the end of the year farm prices were leveling off. So were prices of raw commodities and evidently also of services. These are the areas of slight market power. Where there was market power, the resistance to constraint was predictably more stalwart. In December 1974, the

---

[16] *Economic Report of the President*, 1974, p. 328.
[17] *Economic Report of the President*, 1974, p. 318. It is argued, rightly, that these rates are not excessive from the standpoint of the one who receives them. The purchasing power of the money he is lending is declining. After offsetting this loss, the lender receives little if anything net from his lending. The argument is, however, less persuasive when interest is viewed as a cost to the borrower. Here it must be related to the income or revenues of the borrower, e.g., the would-be home-owner, which will not ordinarily have increased in proportion to such wide increases in interest costs.
[18] *Economic Report of the President*, 1975, p. 329.
[19] *Economic Report of the President*, 1975, pp. 304, 309.

United States Steel Corporation announced a nearly 5 percent increase in the prices of a wide range of steel products and later retreated fractionally at the request of the President. Large increases were being sought in utility rates, including telephone rates. Prices of most manufactured products were still being marked up, although, as inventories accumulated, with diminishing enthusiasm.

The costs of this approach to price stability were far from slight. Monetary restraint, the principal reliance, had by then produced an unprecedented slump in the housing industry. Once again that devastating discrimination of monetary policy against those who must do business with borrowed money. Economic output as a whole had also declined modestly for the year, and references to a healthy rate of growth had now an antique sound. Unemployment at the end of 1974 was the highest in absolute numbers since the Great Depression and, at 7.1 percent of the labor force, at very nearly the highest rate since those distant days. In Detroit, it was noted, the collection of unemployment relief checks involved a two-and-a-half-hour wait in line. A considerable sprinkling of higher-salaried white-collar workers and minor executives was to be found in the queue. However, the commitment to principle remained strong. In December of 1974, Mr. Alan Greenspan, the Chairman of the Council of Economic Advisers (replacing Dr. McCracken and his successor, Mr. Herbert Stein), summarized his position before a gathering of Washington economists in two notably elegant sentences:

> *Thus once the inflation genie has been let out of the bottle it is a very tricky policy problem to find the particular calibration and timing that would be appropriate to stem the acceleration in risk premiums created by falling incomes without prematurely aborting the decline in the inflation-generated risk premiums. This is clearly not an easy policy path to traverse but it is the path which we must follow.*[20]

Inflation was still a thing that, once exorcised, would be gone forever. Capitalism functioned normally on an even keel. Once man had put it there, God, a good conservative gentleman too, would keep it stable. All that was needed was the will to suffer the requisite pain. Such, in 1974, was the state of economic thought. And again, also, it was on a collision course with political necessity. In

[20] Alan Greenspan, "Economic Policy Problems for 1975," an unpublished speech before the National Economists Club, December 2, 1974.

the closing moments of the year, with the inflation genie still very much out of the bottle, the President's advisers gathered on a snowy landscape in Colorado to concede that the pain was too great. Perhaps it would be better to have less unemployment, more inflation.

An unhappy passage proving, however, the power of faith in economics as opposed to experience.

With the American failure came world failure. In all of the industrial countries from the late '6os on, prices were being pulled upward by demand, pressed upward by wage claims. The two forces were, on closer view, both parts of a larger whole. In the last century and in the earlier decades of this one, incomes in the industrial countries were deeply stratified. So, conveniently, was consumption. It was taken for granted that a white-collar worker would have a higher standard of living than a blue-collar worker, a professional family more than either. Managers were meant to have yet more; property owners most of all. At the bottom, and at best only partial participants in the common product, were the ethnic poor — the blacks in the United States, the Irish in England, the Algerians in France, the Italians in Switzerland.

Increasingly, in all countries, these accepted and prescriptive limits on income and consumption were under strain. Everywhere the less privileged were asserting more strongly their claims to some part of the consumption that previously had been thought the natural right only of the privileged. Nothing, in modern times, has sustained more learned discussion than the prospect for more leisure for the masses, the hope for a more nearly classless society. And nothing has caused more dismayed discussion than the economic consequences of the decline in the work ethic, the ever more vigorous assertion of the income demands of those, the blue-collar workers in particular, who had always been thought content to accept less.

The tendency for the claims of consumers to press ever more insouciantly on the capacity to supply them — and the associated and by no means unnatural reluctance of governments to limit these claims — was one cause of inflation in the industrial countries. The incapacity or ineptitude, both in principle and in practice, of the effort to control inflation in the United States was the other. There is a notable asymmetry in the relation of the United States to the rest of the trading world. The United States is sufficiently self-contained in its economic relations with other countries so it can go far, given the will and wisdom, to stabilize its own prices. But if prices in the United States are rising, there are few other countries that can avoid the resulting impact. They can have more inflation than the United States; they cannot easily have less.

In the nineteenth century Britain and a gold-based sterling were fixed points in international economic policy; other countries adjusted their action to this known. In the '50s and earlier '60s — the good years — the United States and the dollar played a similar role. American prices were stable; dollars were an eminently safe asset that anyone would wish to hold. When dollars were being lost by a country, something was wrong. So, on this signal, governments took steps — tighter fiscal policy, higher interest rates, in the case of some exceptionally tractable countries such as Holland, a curb on wage increases — to put things right. *In extremis* there could be a devaluation. It was by such adjustment to the United States and to the dollar, not by meetings of central bankers and finance ministers, that coordination between the domestic policies of the industrial countries in these years was effected. Such internal coordination, in turn, is the first requisite for international-currency stability. Only if internal prices are relatively stable or moving in harmony with each other can exchange rates be stable and hence predictable.

It was this harmony that instability in the United States and related inflation in the other industrial countries in the late 1960s brought to an end. A further and complicating factor was a fundamental difference in movements in costs and productivity between the industrial countries — a difference dramatized by the contrasting position of Germany and Japan on the one hand and the United States on the other. In these years Germany and Japan, their arms expenditures restricted by the victorious powers after World War II and their enthusiasm for warlike activity usefully diminished by defeat, were using their savings to build new and efficient industrial plant. This, in turn, was producing civilian goods at low cost. The United States, by contrast, had come through World War II with its prewar industrial plant intact and thus, by comparison, obsolescent. And a large share of its savings was going into weapons systems and later into its eccentric misadventure in Vietnam. So, apart from the pull of demand and the press of wage claims, the United States was suffering also in these years from the higher costs of relatively inefficient production. For so long as the dollar was maintained at a fixed rate of exchange with the mark and the yen, there was great advantage in buying in Germany and Japan, selling in the United

States. It was said in the late '6os that the dollar was overvalued. So it was.

In consequence of the foregoing, foreign corporations, beginning in the late '50s, accumulated dollars from their flush sales in the United States. These were not absorbed by the much smaller purchases from the United States. In the hands of the recipient firms or deposited by them in European banks, the dollars became the newest mystery of the monetary *cognoscenti* — the Euro-dollars. And when borrowed or loaned, they became the Euro-dollar market — as always, when examined, a simple thing. Numerous of the dollars so assembled, not surprisingly, were turned into gold. So now in the decade of the '6os the great gold hoard of the United States, with history going back to 1914, began to melt away. Partly this was a penalty of power. From 1914 until after World War II, when men of means thought of sanctuary for their wealth in the event of war, they thought of the United States. Now the United States, a superpower, entangled in Vietnam and one arm of the balance of terror, no longer seemed safe. Better Switzerland, even better Germany. In the late '6os the outward flow of gold from the United States became a flood.

At intervals through the '6os finance ministers, treasury secretaries and central bankers met to consider what might be done about the increasing disarray in international monetary affairs. They were described as emerging grim-faced from these meetings. Reporters questioned them under the handicap usual in monetary matters of having to simulate knowledge of the questions to be asked. After appropriate thought the participants almost invariably declined comment. The tradition of Schacht[21] and Montagu Norman[22] was still strong. Not surprisingly, nothing was accomplished at these meetings, for those attending had no access to the underlying causes of difficulty — to the varying rates of inflation, the varying movements in costs which were ultimately responsible for the disequilibrium.

In the late '6os the United States ceased, in effect, to furnish gold to all comers and confined itself to providing it to other central banks in settlement of their claims. The other central banks, in turn, undertook to restrict their gold sales to their sister central banks.

[21] Schacht (Hjalmar Horace Greeley) was a German banker and financial expert who held positions of authority under the Weimar Republic and Hitler.
[22] Governor of the Bank of England, 1920–1944, a record tenure.

Private individuals wishing to possess gold had to bid for it from other private holders. Gold now had two prices: There was the old or official price for settlement between central banks and the new open-market price established by private traders. This, in the further invention of the *cognoscenti*, was the two-tier market. It was the beginning of the final step away from gold.

The end came in August 1971. As part of the larger package of policy changes announced during that month, the United States ceased to supply gold to other central banks in accordance with the arrangement just described. Not many noticed what would once have been an heroic act. That was at least partly because heroic language was avoided. Men did not speak of the final abandonment of the gold standard. Instead it was said that the gold window had been closed. No one could get much excited about the closing of a window. No one much noticed that the gentle Bretton Woods[23] system had by now succumbed. It was not intended to cope, nor could it, with the larger, divergent movements in prices and in currencies that now were commonplace.

Dollars, as noted, now existed in large accumulations. Better bargains could be obtained by changing these into marks, yen or other currencies and buying goods in Germany, Japan or other lands. Safety also suggested these currencies as the ones to hold. In consequence, the dollar was now a weak currency. Other countries did not necessarily rejoice. A situation in which they could sell easily to the United States and were not unduly pressed by American competition was not without comfort. There was advantage in allowing a currency to go down with the dollar. This could be readily arranged, at least for the short run, by having the central bank sell the local currency freely for dollars. The dollar would thus remain conveniently overvalued.

Negotiations now got under way to arrange the devaluation and restabilization of the dollar. These were held in the late autumn of 1971 in the buildings of the Smithsonian Institution in Washington. Eventually new exchange rates were agreed upon; these reflected varying rates of devaluation of the dollar from approximately 17

[23] The Bretton Woods Conference of the United Nations held July 1944 established the International Monetary Fund to facilitate international monetary cooperation, and an International Bank for Reconstruction and Development. These organizations began operations in 1946 with a combined authorized capital of almost 19 billion dollars.

percent for the yen and 12 percent for the mark down to little or none for the Canadian dollar. The participating governments pledged themselves, through their central banks, to buy and sell currencies so as to hold exchange rates within a range of 2.25 percent of the agreed parities. Congress, in a symbolic act required by the International Monetary Fund, dutifully reduced the gold content of the dollar. The result was described with relative modesty by Richard Nixon as the greatest monetary reform in the history of mankind. Secretary of the Treasury John B. Connally, who received credit for the agreement, basked momentarily in the esteem which people who do not understand what is happening accord to those who presume to knowledge of money. For both the Smithsonian Agreements and Connally the esteem was short-lived. Both were soon casualties of the times.

Early in 1973, coincidentally with the abandonment of the Phase II controls, there was a massive movement out of dollars into other currencies. This was in expectation of further inflation in the United States, a further devaluation of the dollar. Both expectations were soundly justified by events. (There were similar speculative movements in other currencies.) To maintain the Smithsonian parities proved impossible. Currency instability now became the approved policy; this also achieved a benign cognomen. It was called a float. The economists of the Administration graced their surrender with a superlative manifestation of bureaucratic prose:

> In the area of international economic relations, the year 1973 may be characterized as one of continuing adjustment to past disequilibria as well as to new developments that entered the picture during the year. Early in the year the governments of most major countries abandoned attempts to fix exchange rates at negotiated levels. While central banks continued to intervene to some extent, foreign exchange markets played the major role in determining the exchange rates that would clear the market. This process was marked at times by unusually large fluctuations of market exchange rates. Nevertheless, the market performed its intermediating function well. . . .[24]

The reference to "past disequilibria" was meant to shift the blame to predecessors, a tactic somewhat impaired by the fact that the

[24] *Economic Report of the President,* 1974, p. 182.

writers were also the predecessors. The reference to "unusually large fluctuations of market exchange rates" was a euphemism for serious disorder in international business. Of the fact of disorder no one was very much in doubt.

In nearly all business transactions — international even more than domestic — there is an element of futurity. Bargains are made now against later payment. Such bargaining becomes difficult if neither party knows what the payment will be worth. This is the case if the buyer does not know what he will have to pay for the currency in which he makes the later payment. Or if the seller does not know what he will receive in his own money for the currency in which he accepts the payment. Such is the case if exchange rates are unstable.[25] As a matter of urgency, the central banks had in fact to intervene in order to provide a modicum of certainty. A floating currency thus became an imperfectly stabilized one. Floating became, as it was called, dirty floating. In 1974, the International Monetary Fund initiated discussions designed to formulate rules for the conduct of dirty floating by central banks.

The consequences of dirty floating for international trade were not immediately adverse. Aided by exceptionally large transactions in grain and other food products, international trade continued to expand in 1973. Not many, although there were some,[26] could imagine that this disorderly improvisation reflected progress. The hopes of Keynes and White at Bretton Woods were for something better. They were right to hope.

Beginning in 1973, but with full effect in 1974, came the great petroleum price squeeze. In keeping with much else in this history this too was extensively misunderstood. In part it resulted from the

[25] Futures contracts — buying currency for future delivery at prices quoted today — can reduce the risk. It is a device that is available only at considerable cost to sizable traders and not in all currencies.

[26] See Ronald A. Krieger, "The Monetary Governors and the Ghost of Bretton Woods," *Challenge* (January/February 1975). In addition to perceptive comment on the world monetary situation, some in conflict with the present conclusions, Professor Krieger contributes a valuable verse on the reaction of the Governors of the International Monetary Fund, meeting in 1974, to the collapse of the Bretton Woods system:

> Humpty Dumpty sat on a wall.
> Humpty Dumpty had a great fall.
> . All the king's horses and all the king's men
> Formed an ad hoc committee to consider the situation.

discovery of hitherto unused bargaining power by the producing countries; in part it was the product of inflation. The effect of high prices that are derived from strong demands, we have seen, has always been to turn the terms of trade to the favor of producers of food and raw products. The tendency of such producers is to operate at or near capacity, sell for what the market will bring. Strong demand raises such prices in relation to those who are better able to regulate supply. In the case of the oil-producing countries the effect was a slight variant; strong demand in the consuming countries made it possible for producers to raise prices without immediately suffering an excess of unsold oil that would threaten the agreement that sustained the price. To sustain the OPEC prices during a period of noninflationary demand would have been far more difficult. Such commodity agreements do not have a marked record of success. Without inflation this one too could fail.

Everywhere the higher oil price was considered highly inflationary; in the United States it served invaluably as an excuse for official inadequacy in the control of inflation. In fact, it was deflationary. Especially in the Arab countries but also in Iran and elsewhere, the revenues accruing from the higher prices were far greater than could immediately be spent for either consumers or investment goods. So they accumulated in unspent balances. Thus they represented a withdrawal from current purchasing power not different in immediate effect from that of levying a large sales tax on petroleum or its products.[27] The effect, increasingly evident as 1974 passed, was the predictable effect of fiscal astringency. As demand faded, prices in competitive markets — those for food, commodities, services — began to weaken. Prices subject to corporate market power continued to rise. So did unemployment. The oil-producing countries had provided the industrial countries with a surrogate tax increase. Its effect, like any general fiscal or monetary action against inflation, was to increase unemployment well before acting to arrest inflation.

Not much in the history of money supports a linear view of history, one in which the knowledge and experience from one epoch provide the intelligence for improved management in the next. Of those who give guidance on these matters history says even less. Out of the

[27] This effect of the oil-price increases was perceptively identified at one of President Ford's so-called Summit Conferences on Inflation in the autumn of 1974 by Professor Richard N. Cooper. Few, not including the present author, saw the force of his position.

2500 years of experience and 200 years of ardent study have come monetary systems that are as unsatisfactory as any in the peacetime past. In recent times conservatives have reacted adversely to inflation, though not with great enthusiasm to the measures for preventing it. Liberals have thought unemployment the greater affliction. In fact no economy can be successful which has either. Inflation causes discomfort and frustration for many. Unemployment causes acute suffering for a lesser number. There is no certain way of knowing which causes the most in the aggregate of pain. It was the prime lesson of the '30s that deflation and depression destroyed international order, caused each nation to try for its own salvation, indifferent to the damage that its efforts caused to neighbors. It has equally been the lesson of the late '60s and early '70s that inflation too destroys international order. Those who express or imply a preference between inflation and depression are making a fool's choice. Policy must always be against whichever one has.

But also it is now evident that only in the extremes of inflation or depression is there a choice. Otherwise, if only the accepted and orthodox remedies are applied, we get both. For this combination no one, liberal or conservative, speaks. And at this combination, after 2500 years, we have at last arrived. Few histories could have a less happy ending.

BOOK
VII

A Glimpse

of

the Seventh Day

PART ONE

A BEGINNING AND AN END

---

*T*he pleasures of reminiscence are many and mixed. Much of it all is summed up in such phrases out of nineteenth-century romance as "Little did he realize. . . ." or "Had I but known. . . ." *There will be laughter over past naiveties, a shiver for remembered embarrassment, a real sinking of the heart over crises avoided only because unseen, but above all there is self-reappraisal and a search for the future as it is reflected in the past. For most of us a moment of reminiscence is a fortifying interlude.*

Galbraith tells us that he wrote The Scotch as a defense against those frustrations of enforced idleness to which the formalities of diplomacy inevitably render its servants liable. It was a well-chosen recourse. The Indian assignment created a dramatic break in the life of the professor of economics and offered an opportunity for an equally dramatic change of direction in his career. In remembering Iona Station from New Delhi, Galbraith seems to turn back to his boyhood as one of the Scotch to seek advice from the men of standing whom he describes as the chief-counselors of the clans.

The Affluent Society had fixed Galbraith's hold on the attention of the world. Though that book seemed complete in itself the author had long since foreseen the need for an enormous extention of its thesis. The New Industrial State and, as it turned out, Economics and the Public Purpose were still to be written. Galbraith has told us of the difficulties of writing while on the public payroll. A change of direction might well endanger the completion of his statement of the necessities of modern economics. What should be his next step?

In the closing lines of The Scotch there is implied an answer; the passage reads as follows:

> Everyone recognized me for we were the tallest of all the clans. Most asked me whether, in my travels, I had found a place as good as this. I said no for this could have been the truth and, when I faced up to it, I found I did not wish to have people think me irresponsible.

The men of standing had replied. After the success of the Affluent Society and with an audience waiting, to risk the completion of the triad volumes would be the very soul of irresponsibility.

Tender, amused, nostalgic, The Scotch seems the picture of a man looking back at his beginning, regarding the distance in between and finding it all to his liking. Though it may celebrate nothing more serious than a putting in of the last piece of a picture puzzle, all of us know the feeling. It is the mood of Jehovah on the seventh day. So much The Scotch must have been for Galbraith, but for the rest of us it is much more. That reverie in India of a childhood in distant Ontario seems the decisive step toward a new understanding of economics and the delineation of a good economy for our time.

The Scotch[1]

THE McINTYRE HOUSE

THE McINTYRE HOUSE stood nearly in the center of the east side of the single block that comprised Main Street. Unlike the square brick-fronted buildings across and on either side, it was

[1] *Made to Last*, Chapters 11, 12, 13 (London: Hamish Hamilton, 1964), pp. 119–145.

longer, lower and of frame construction. Once it had been white with green trim, and traces of the original paint remained. At the north end was an arch cut through the building which gave access to the livery stables behind and to another blacksmith shop run by Jim Bruce who, on all festival occasions and for a moderate fee, closed his shop, donned the ancient tartan of the Bruce and took up his pipes to provide the only music the Scotch understood and loved. Also in the hotel yard were the privies, a massive bank of cells, undifferentiated as to sex or precision of user, each cell giving on to a single trench which was cleaned out only at infrequent intervals. They gave off an astonishing smell. Immediately adjacent was the kitchen.

However, it was not for its food that the McIntyre House was renowned but its drink. A door within the arch led into the bar; there was another in from the street. In the 1920's this valiant room was already in decline; pool tables had been moved in to retrieve, however ingloriously, some of the revenues that had once accrued exclusively to whisky. But the scars of the greater days could still be seen on the wainscotting, the doors and deep in the bar itself. Before prohibition came to Ontario in 1916, it had been the resort of the drinking Scotch. As the result, it had been the scene of some of the most uproarious violence that alcohol has ever produced.

The effect of alcohol on different races is as remarkable as it is invariable. An Englishman becomes haughty; a Swede sad; an Irishman sentimental; a Russian fraternal; a German melodious. A Scotchman always becomes militant. It was on Saturday night that the Scotch gathered at the McIntyre House to make merry and seek one another's destruction. Whisky bottles were emptied and used as weapons; sometimes the bottom was knocked off to make a better impression on the thick epidermis that so admirably protected the average clansman. Boots and even furniture were also used, although on gala occasions the furniture was removed. On a Sunday after one of these festivals, men would be in poor condition from Port Talbot to Campbellton and from Iona Station nearly to West Lorne.

Even among the nondrinking Scotch, the tales of the McIntyre House were part of the legend. Once a commercial traveler from Toronto had called for a cocktail and gave instructions on how to make it. The patrons were outraged but Johnnie McIntyre quieted them down and went out for ice. This he got from a little iceberg by a tree in the yard. It owed its origins to the dogs who frequented the tree and to the Canadian winter which quickly converted all moisture to ice. Johnnie thought this would return the man to whisky and so did those to whom he quietly confided the stratagem. The man from Toronto praised the flavor and called for another.

There was also the night that my great-uncle Duncan, then the family ambassador to the drinking Scotch, sat next to one of the McPherson boys who had begun to worry lest whisky was getting the better of him. After once again confiding sadly of his fears, he drank a large bottle of carbolic acid. To the surprise of all who had known his capacity, he died a horrible death.

Finally, there was the gala evening — it must have been about 1910 — when one of the Campbells who inhabited the country north and west of town mounted the bar and announced his intention of avenging, once and for all, the insults that had been heaped on the Clan Campbell ever since it had fought on the wrong side at Culloden a hundred and sixty-five years before. He specifically promised to lick any man who lived between Lake Erie and the Michigan Central Railway. A score leaped to the challenge; the Campbells rallied round. It was a glorious struggle. The outcome was indeterminate although it was said that the Campbells acquitted themselves well. Next morning a half-dozen clansmen were still stacked like cordwood in the livery stable back of the hotel. None was seriously hurt.

2

Prohibition was advocated in Ontario partly as a product of the natural desire of better men to impose their virtue on the worse. But partly it was considered an important pacifying influence which would raise markedly the productivity of the farm labor force. The slogan of the prohibitionists, "Abolish the bar," showed the way in which their concern had become associated not with whisky but with the theater of combat. Prohibition came and when it was later repealed in Ontario, the principal concern was not to control the intake of alcohol but to insure that it occurred in surroundings which were inconsistent with physical violence. This the institution of the cocktail lounge accomplished.

Once the bar of the McIntyre House was closed, the Scotch deserted it in droves. The poolroom was taken over by the idlers of the town and no good was thought to come of anyone who frequented the place. In point of fact, none did.

Commercial travelers must have stopped at the McIntyre House. Certainly a horse-drawn bus went down to meet each train at the

MCR station. Occasionally one of the girls of the town who worked there as chambermaid would be seen leaning out an upstairs window exchanging insults with a boy friend in the street. In the main lobby adjoining the bar was a desk and a yellowed and dog-eared guest register. Out back was the dining room. But in its days of glory, the McIntyre House meant the bar. The rest must have been operated as an afterthought.

3

I have memory of only one moment when the McIntyre House was in its glory. It must have been on the first of July of 1914 or 1915 when I was approaching the age of either six or seven. We had gone to Dutton to celebrate Dominion Day, the Canadian Fourth of July, and to attend the Caledonian games. There had been running and broad-jumping, and throwing of weights for distance and height, and a great deal of sword dancing and piping. Some of the dancing we found tedious but the rest was wholly fascinating. My father, one of the officials of the West Elgin Caledonian Society, had looked very grand in a modified kilt of the McDonald tartan — not many of the clansmen owned a complete kilt so they made do with what they had. Then at four o'clock my sister and I were bundled into the family democrat, a large four-wheeled affair with a fringed top, and we started for home because word had come that the fighting had begun. As we passed the McIntyre House, we saw it. Some forty or fifty clansmen, the drinking Scotch at nearly their maximum effective strength, had been reinforced by elements of a Scottish regiment which had come to grace the celebration and provide music. Some of the celebrants were in the bar; others were struggling to approach it or shouting to those inside to pass out the bottles. A number of fights were already in progress in the crowd outside; from within came joyful shrieks and loud crashes indicating that hostilities were much more advanced inside. Pipers around the edge of the struggling mass were offering a competitive combination of pibrochs, marches and laments to inspire the combatants to greater feats of violence. We got by as quickly as the traffic and our alarmed mare would allow.

We drove down Shackleton Street and across Willey's Sideroad, and the memory of that journey on a summer evening by the bare hayfields and through the fields of ripening wheat has never forsaken me. The sound of the pipes did not recede and fade; on the contrary, it grew in volume as the whisky was passed out and the pipers warmed to their work. And at intervals, over the spiel of the pipes came the high demoniac shrieks which for a thousand years on ten thousand battlefields has struck terror to the hearts of the brave. It is the cry of uncontrollable joy of a drunken Highlander as he rushes toward personal immolation.

A year or two later, the McIntyre House was selling nothing more dangerous than Orange Crush.

4

The pavement stopped at the end of the business section by the town hall. A gravel road led on by the tiny office of the veterinary surgeon, in front of which on fine days the good doctor could be seen tipped back in his chair resting. A stout, amiable and only moderately intelligent man, he was much respected in the community for his good humor and his devotion to patriotic causes. On Dominion Day, Armistice Day and the anniversaries of other occasions important in Canadian annals, he willingly chaired committees and gave his energies selflessly to the arrangements. There may have been something compulsive about this, a lurking need to compensate, for he was an American citizen.

At a bend in the road was the Baptist Church; beyond that were the frame houses of the lesser merchants and the clergy and then came the public school, Hollingshead's mill where we sold our wheat and had our oats ground or rolled and beyond that the Dutton High School. The High School played a large role in the important, complex, and wholly fascinating interaction between town and country to which I now turn.

HIGHER EDUCATION

THE DUTTON HIGH SCHOOL in those days was a gaunt two-story building of white brick and hideous aspect. It stood in a small yard in which only ragweed and plantain reliably survived the dense foot traffic. Land in Canada is plentiful and inexpensive and thus not highly regarded. So only a few square yards are provided for a school. In England where it is scarce and costly and much admired several acres of playing fields would have been considered a minimum.

The school had a front door that was reserved for girls and a back door that was available to either sex. No one ever explained the reason for this rule or its contribution to adolescent purity for we led a fully integrated existence once inside. Beyond the back door was a well and pump. There was no baseball diamond, no basketball hoop, no football posts, not even a pond for ice hockey. Our protection from the socialist interdependence inculcated by the team spirit continued to be complete.

The only relief from the barrenness of the yard and the board fences that surrounded it was provided by nice trees which provided some shade and two outdoor toilets. A friend of mine, the son of one of the fishing families by the lake, could stand in the middle of one of these and pee out of a window a good six feet distant and a full five feet up from the floor. It never did him any good in after life, poor fellow, for after graduation he got a job with the local branch of the Royal Bank and was sent to jail shortly thereafter for walking out with several thousand dollars. This was not the crime that it might seem. The big Canadian banks tested their new emloyees by having them work with considerable sums for practically no compensation. An occasional failure was inherent in the system.

2

Autobiography is famous for the odd figures that it parades across the pages of literature. But anthropology also has its accidental specimens. In the interests of science it is now necessary to accord immortality of a kind to the unexpectant memory of Mr. Thomas Elliott, principal of the Dutton High School for several decades in the first half of the twentieth century.

Old Tommy, as he was known unaffectionately by many generations of adolescents, was a man of a little more than medium height and of substantial though not stocky build. He must have been in his early fifties in the middle 1920's and he carefully combed his sparse gray hair, which had something of the appearance of crab grass in a dry autumn, over his bald spot with an increasing absence of plausibility. His face was full and covered by a gray, unhealthy skin and, although he shaved every day, slight gray wisps always survived between the swaths. In the winter he wore a dark gray suit of hard, very shiny, very durable material; in the summer he changed the jacket for one of lighter gray. In many men this predominant gray in hair, complexion and attire would have left one with the impression of a colorless personality. In Old Tommy the impression was countered by the appearance and employment of his eyes and moustache.

Both of these were full and dark and they worked in unison. Before addressing you, Old Tommy partly closed his right eye and brought it down toward the corner of his moustache in what was evidently intended to be a look of infinite guile. At the same time, perhaps more accidentally, the moustache rose up to meet the eye. This remarkable configuration he could hold for an indefinite time while he transfixed you with the full force of his left eye. Then he addressed you. In the young this exercise aroused a quavering fear. It was a mark of maturity when it came only to inspire mistrust.

In any calling Old Tommy would have been counted a man of remarkable ignorance but as an educator he excelled. As one of four teachers, three of whom happily were always better, since they couldn't have been worse, he taught geography, spelling, zoology, physics and chemistry. In all of these, with the possible exception of spelling, he was grossly uninformed.

In matters unrelated to pedagogy Old Tommy was equally uninstructed. The 1920's were years of much excitement in Canada. As noted following the war, the farmers rose in righteous anger over their high costs and falling prices and installed their own government, the United Farmers of Ontario, in Toronto. In Ottawa ministries rose and fell. All the most respectable people had invested their moral and political capital in the war. Now after the expenditure of hundreds of millions of dollars and tens of thousands of lives they seemed as uncertain as everyone else about what had been accomplished. Few escaped blame. General Sir Arthur William Currie, Canada's most famous soldier, was honored on his return with the post of Principal of McGill University and shortly thereafter found himself in court (as result of a libel case) denying that he had contributed unnecessarily to the butchery of Canadian soldiers on the Western Front. (It was as though Ike, having gone to Columbia University as its president, had been forced on to the stand by his detractors on his management of the Battle of the Bulge. He would not have liked it.) Railways were nationalized in these years. The highways were laid out across the Ontario mud. Women got the vote. Old Tommy would often express an opinion on these events but we knew even as youngsters that it was worthless. We never cited it at home for we also knew that it provoked a serious conflict between two strongly held beliefs of the Men of Standing among the Scotch. Nothing should ever be said at home that undermined a schoolmaster's authority. Equally, people should know what they were talking about.

3

On one thing Old Tommy made a certain approach to competence. That was in exploiting the dislike between the people of the village, who more than incidentally controlled the school, and the ordinary citizens among the rural Scotch. This skill had something to do with his survival.

Every community must have some form of social conflict. Harmony is praised in principle and by the clergy but faction is what people really enjoy. It gives a welcome sense of companionship to those on the same side; it arouses no less than organized athletics or aggressive nationalism the competitive ardor of those involved. The important thing is not to avoid such conflict but to guide it on to issues where it does no damage to life and limb or the real income of the community. The conflict between town and country in our community was probably as benign as any that careful planning could have contrived.

The Scotch disliked the townspeople partly for reasons of race. They did not, on the whole, think as well of the English as of themselves and quite a few of the leading citizens of the town were English and even supported — it was thought by some out of sheer snobbishness — a small Anglican church. But this was only a partial cause for the Scotch had established strong outposts in the village: John McCallum was the tailor and operated an informal club for the Men of Standing; Johnny Campbell sold Massey-Harris implements and Ford cars; Johnny McIntyre had been the Delmonico of the drinking Scotch; John Archie McNeil was the undertaker; Douglas Galbraith was the doctor.

Politics played some role. The merchants were Tories in politics; the Scotch with rare exceptions were Liberals. They disliked having their votes cancelled out by people who did not use the franchise intelligently. But there were also numerous Scotch Liberals in town.

Economic determinism had more to do with the struggle. Contemplating the considerable well-being of the elder Hockin, a Scotch farmer could only conclude that it was the result of buying cheap and selling dear. It could not be attributed to harder work; running a store was obviously easier than running a farm. Superior intelligence would not be conceded. Tom, it was evident, had got rich at the expense of the farmers. And the merchants had a reciprocal grievance. The farmers gave a lot of business to the great Toronto mail order houses of Messrs. T. Eaton Co. and Robert Simpson & Co. This showed a callous lack of appreciation for the efforts of the local merchants to supply good merchandise at reasonable prices. It also overlooked the elementary economic truth that a dollar spent at home does ten times as much good as a dollar spent abroad, especially to the man who gets it.

But mostly the conflict resolved itself, as most such conflicts do, into a difference of opinion as to who was superior. The Scotch believed, I have always thought rightly, that they were. They considered agriculture an inherently superior vocation. It placed a man in his fit relation to nature; it abjured the artificialities of urban existence. It gave him peace and independence. It was morally superior for it required manual labor. The finest aphorism of the Scotch was: "A good man isn't afraid of work." Not one of them believed that clerking in a store or weighing in at an elevator was work.

The people of the town, like most urban dwellers through history, regarded the farmers as unkempt rustics to whom, for reasons of commercial expediency, they had to be affable. Veblen's system of social precedence based on exemption from manual toil they would have regarded as sound. To sell drygoods or serve as chief executive of the livery stable was an undoubted mark of superiority or should have been.

An aristocracy that is accepted comprises, without doubt, the most contented of men. But privilege to be completely pleasant must be above dispute. No one is to be less envied than the aristocrat whose position is not conceded. And no one is to be more pitied than the man whose nobility is known only to himself. The Indian princes — Nizam, Maharana, Maharajas, Nabobs, Rajahs — were once very happy men. Their unchallenged distinction was affirmed to them in varied and elaborate ceremony by their far from reluctant subjects a hundred times a day. But democratic India has ceased to be conscious of their grandeur. The princes must explain to the visitor that their house was entitled by the British to a nineteen-gun salute and then what is worse they must explain the system of salutes, for the visitor does not even know about that. This is all very difficult and they are, on the whole, a subdued and saddened caste. Quite a few have abandoned the effort to sustain an aristocratic position and, depending on taste and talent, have taken refuge in either democratic politics or alcohol.

The Dutton merchants were also an unappreciated aristocracy. They could have survived the suspicion and dislike of the average clansman. But the Scotch had their own hierarchy. The men of standing, the clansmen who dominated the Scottish community and ran the township and county, stood for parliament and gave sanction to the views which others applauded and adopted. They ignored the burghers of the town. They did not defer to the political views of Tom Hockin. They did not credit him with any of importance. But here Old Tommy re-enters the picture. He was a townsman to the core. No New Yorker out of O. Henry, Horatio Alger or Damon Runyon was more passionately devoted to the urban way of life and the town party controlled the school. So, singlehandedly he set out to redress the balance in favor of his side by making life hideous for the children of the rural Scotch. Since it was the more prominent clans which principally patronized the school he was able to register his fire on those who, in the opinion of his party, were most in need of being reduced a peg or two.

4

Some years ago I became involved in a controversy with the then congressman from Georgia, Mr. Gene Cox. I was taken to task by another congressman, Mr. Joseph Starnes of Alabama, for becoming involved with his fellow southerner. "You have no business biting at Ole Gene," he said. "He is the nicest mean man in the House of Representatives." Although Old Tommy was not considered nice by anyone, he had invented — or more likely, by the simple empiricism of trial and error had chanced upon — some remarkably effective forms of meanness. What was more remarkable, all could be employed with an outward aspect of reasonableness.

Thus Old Tommy had learned that reasonable and equal laws when applied to individuals in unequal situations can have a highly unequal and wholly indefensible effect which, since the laws are reasonable, will usually go unnoticed. He had also learned that equal laws, unequally applied, can also be quite discriminatory and he did not hesitate to resort to such outright favoritism when that was indicated. He was not legalistic or hidebound in any respect.

As an example of impeccable laws with unequal effect, there was the elementary matter of promptness. It is right to insist on it in the young. Old Tommy did so and this contributed to his reputation as a wise if stern disciplinarian. But promptness presented a radically different and easier problem for town dwellers as compared with the rural Scotch. The youth of the town awoke, dressed, had breakfast and walked a few hundred yards to school. The time required for all of these acts with the possible exception of the awakening was subject to strict control. The offspring of the rural Scotch got out of bed, fed and groomed a horse, breakfasted, harnessed the horse, hitched it to a buggy or cutter, drove from two to seven miles to town, unhitched and stabled the horse somewhere near the school and then made their way to the academy on foot. A remarkable number of mishaps might occur in this sequence: a horse might be lame; traces could break in the mud; cutters could tip in the deep snow; once as the result of a moment's carelessness a mare walked off without us and made her way some four miles to Mrs. Crawford's stable — Mrs. Crawford was the dowager of the Dutton hardware hierarchy — where we rented a stall. To be covered against all such accidents one would have had to start at midnight. Every morning some of the adolescent Scotch were late and, inevitably, a few were prone. Old Tommy cherished these derelictions; he prepared his insults as other pedagogues (but not Old Tommy) prepared their lessons. After this complicated passage, we also arrived smelling a little, or more than a little, of horses, harness and stable. After an articulate analysis of the cultural deficiencies which caused us to be late, Tommy in his greater moments would go on to deal with the smell. The remarkable contortion of eyebrow, eye and moustache could, with only a minor variation, be made into a violent reaction to an offensive odor. Occasionally some especially serious offender would be sent to the pump to purify himself. He would return unimproved, as Tommy could foretell and would point out, for nothing less than total immersion would have made any difference.

Tommy's most ingenious assault on the children of the rural Scotch concerned, curiously enough, the matter of military preparedness. At the time of World War I, in one of those aberrations to which the military mind in all countries is recurrently subject, corps of cadets were organized in the Canadian high schools. A subsidy was paid for every teen-ager so trained. However, training is not the word; in many of the schools, including that of Dutton, there was no one with the slightest military experience to give instruction. So the latter was provided by the principal, or even by an older student, after reading and placing his own very original construction on the manual of infantry drill.

It seems possible that even Old Tommy realized that these exercises were without any practical consequence. But the subsidy slightly reduced the school tax and besides being a stern disciplinarian, he was well regarded by the school trustees for his extreme penuriousness. Accordingly, twice a week, on Tuesday and Thursday mornings, the male students had close-order drill. At twenty minutes before ten we made our way upstairs and equipped ourselves with a leather army belt and a Ross rifle or its more important remnants. The Ross rifle was the weapon with which the earliest Canadian participants in World War I had been equipped. Under conditions of practical combat it was discovered, not without cost to the individuals most immediately concerned, that it did not work. It was replaced, along with nearly all of the men who had carried it, and the pieces still available were used for training. With time many of these had lost their bolts and the sights had been brushed off. So armed and formed in a ragged line with the big seventeen-year-olds at one end and the infinitesimal twelve-year-olds at the other we marched back and forth across the front yard while Old Tommy shouted the cadence.

At least the boys from the town and a few of the more adaptable of the Scotch marched back and forth.

The rest of us had trouble. A farm boy early learns to accommodate his step to that of animals — to cows coming up the lane or to horses pulling a harrow. This is not a stride but an effortless saunter which one can sustain, if necessary, all day. To convert from this to marching tempo, or rather to Old Tommy's particular interpretation of the military choreography, was for many of us impossible. After two or three paces we would be out of step; thereafter we would be back in step only as our unique cycle brought us into momentary harmony with our neighbors. That one kept in step was, perhaps, the only thing that Old Tommy really understood about military drill.

Our difficulties gave him his finest hour. Our inability to keep step he identified with acute and irremediable inferiority. And our easily suspected dislike of drill he denounced as not only seditious but damaging to the financial well-being of the community. The hopeless cases (of which I was invariably one) were put into a special formation that was formally and not inaccurately designated the Awkward Squad. Old Tommy would then turn the more tractable soldiers over to one of the fifth formers and concentrate on us. We would straggle across the yard for four or five minutes and then halt for ten while Tommy told us of our deficiencies. Believing, correctly, that an inability to concentrate our minds on our extremities had something to do with our handicaps, he would send us home night after night with the requirement that we write out five hundred times the simple declamatory sentence: *My left foot is not my right!*

For one brief moment each spring Old Tommy would forego aggression. For then we would be visited by a resplendent colonel from a regiment in London, Ontario, whose task it was to see if the school had earned the subsidy and how much. The amount depended on the number marching for the inspection and it would become evident to Old Tommy that pleasant as it all had been we still could not march. So the utterly hopeless cases, of which I was still one, would be seated on a bench, complete with leather belt, and told to explain if asked that we had been sick or lame. When enlisting us in this conspiracy against the public treasury, Old Tommy would be almost kind — his eye and moustache would come together not in their usual alarming manner but in what was evidently meant to be a knowing wink.

In practice we were never asked. Old Tommy's explanation of our incapacity was, of course, accepted. All military organizations are alert to malingering. But suspicion runs to the malingerer himself. Malingering by order of a commanding officer is something for which the average British-trained colonel would not have been prepared.

Once the subsidy had been earned, Old Tommy went back to normal.

5

Needless to say Old Tommy used the same tactics that gave him so much satisfaction in combating tardiness and promoting military preparedness in compelling attention to academic duty. Here they were not entirely without merit.

Terror is no longer well regarded as an instrument of statecraft. It is, of course, hard on the people principally affected. But as a practical matter it is a difficult technique to administer over any period of time. A terrorist is, more or less by definition, lacking in popular appeal. And he must delegate to a rather sanguinary and unscrupulous class of subordinates. He faces in consequence the ever-

glistening blue of the lakes both north and south. The country was green and golden; when we landed there was a slight smoky haze. The fair seemed much as before except for some little tykes who were racing tiny homemade automobiles. Everyone recognized me for we were the tallest of all the clans. Most asked me whether, in my travels, I had found a place as good as this. I said no for this could have been the truth and, when I faced up to it, I found I did not wish to have people think me irresponsible.

Index

A & P: and countervailing power, 123, 125, 128, and anti-trust laws, 140

acceptability: of ideas, 219–220; and conventional wisdom, 221

Acheson, Dean, 270

adaptation, 303–305

Adenauer, Konrad, 334

Adler, Sol, 430

advanced development: general theory of, 387–399

The Affluent Society, 6, 7, 112, 152, 153, 155, 156, 205, 217, 277, 278, 279, 280, 383, 384, 467, 468

agriculture: and Scotch Canadians, 31–37, 476; and countervailing power, 120, 129; and original power, 138–139; and market control, 396–397; in China, 436–437, 439

Airey, Colonel Richard, 14–15

Albert, Prince, 272

alcohol: and Scotch Canadians, 40–41

Allen, Frederick Lewis, 167, 174

Alsop, Joseph, 270

Ambassador's Journal, 277, 311

American Capitalism, 6, 7, 97, 112, 113, 114, 151, 155, 156, 383

American Economic Association, 423

American Telephone and Telegraph Co., 411

America's Needs and Resources, 103

animals, 44

anti-trust laws, 84–85; and countervailing power, 137–142; and reform, 407–409

architects, 406

arts, the: and organization, 391; and market system, 399–407; and the technostructure, 404; and social achievement, 404–405; education in, 406

Ascoli, Max, 270

Associated Farmers of California, 50

Aswan Dam, 342

The Atlantic Monthly, 330

Atomic Energy Commission, 411

Ayres, Colonel, 170

Ayub, Prime Minister, 354, 358

Babson, Roger W., 184

Backe, food minister (Germany), 68

Backer, George, 367

Bagehot, Walter, 187

[487]